INDIAN
RAILWAYS

INDIAN RAILWAYS

Senior Editor Rupa Rao
Project Editor Hina Jain
Editor Ayushi Thapliyal
Consulting Editor and Researcher Vatsal Verma
Proofreader Dipali Singh
Project Art Editors Devika Awasthi,
Bhavika Mathur
Additional Design Support Tanvi Sahu
Jacket Designer Bhavika Mathur
Senior Picture Researcher Sumedha Chopra
DTP Designers Nand Kishor Acharya,
Vikram Singh
Pre-Production Manager Narender Kumar
Production Manager Pankaj Sharma
Picture Research Manager Taiyaba Khatoon
Managing Editor Chitra Subramanyam
Managing Art Editor Neha Ahuja Chowdhry
Managing Director, India Aparna Sharma

Writers Vatsal Verma, Chitra Subramanyam

Consultants Sanjoy Mookerjee,
Manoj Pande, JL Singh

Contributors Ramarao Annavarapu,
Warren Miller, PK Mishra,
GK Mohanty, JK Saha

First published in India in 2020 by
Dorling Kindersley Publishing Private Limited,
208, Ansal's Laxmi Deep
Laxmi Nagar District Centre
New Delhi 110092, India

Copyright © 2020 Dorling Kindersley Limited
A Penguin Random House Company
10 9 8 7 6 5 4 3 2 1
001−316568−July/2020

A CIP catalogue record for this book is available
from The British Library.

ISBN: 978-0-2414-1484-2

Printed and bound in India

For the curious
www.dk.com

CONTENTS

1830–1870
The Beginning

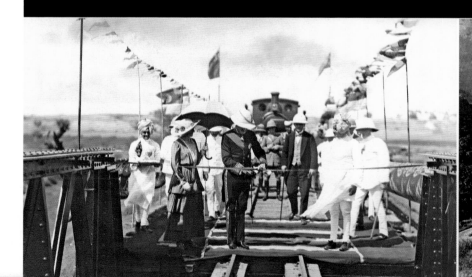

1871–1920
Development and Expansion

1981–1999
A Time of Transition

2000 Onwards
The New Millennium

FOREWORD

There is a section of the Indian Railway system known as the hill section. This is one of India's mountain railways, though certainly not as famous as Darjeeling Himalayan, Kalka Shimla, or Nilgiri Mountain. This hill section is the Lumding–Halflong–Badarpur stretch and used to be a metre-gauge line, built in the 1890s by what was then Assam Bengal Railway. As the train zigged and zagged, those steam engines had a system of catching, which meant another engine at the rear for pushing. As a child, because my father worked in that part of the world, I recall travelling quite a bit along the hill section. You watched out for tunnels, dark and forbidding. You leant out of the window, heard the gibbons, smelt the smoke, and got coal dust and soot in your hair. On one occasion, the train stopped somewhere and the engine driver, a handkerchief tied around his head and his face covered with soot, came to say hello to my father. My father went up in my esteem. To the children of that generation, an engine driver was a hero. I dare say many boys wanted to become engine drivers then, extremely unlikely today. Have you stood by the side of a railway line at night and seen a train with a steam locomotive thunder past, the red tinge lighting up the driver's face as he shovels coal into the fire? Have you laid a coin on the track, waiting for the train to pass over it and flatten it out?

Those are the bygone pages of history, whiffs of nostalgia for the past and one's childhood. Steam locomotives gave way to diesel and diesel to electric. Every once in a while, a steam engine needed to stop, to top up water and coal, say every 100 miles or 160 km. A stop meant passengers could get down, stretch their legs, and purchase food. Cleaners could get onto the train and clean coaches and toilets. As one switched from steam to diesel/electric traction, these water stops became unnecessary. In the US, there is documentation of ghost towns, created because water stops became redundant. While growing up, those water stops were part of train travel, an opportunity to explore new stations. Once air-conditioning was introduced in trains, you could no longer raise or lower the windows. Somehow, you no longer felt that you were travelling. The journey was more comfortable, but surely less fun. I remember travelling on the Howrah Rajdhani in 1971, soon after it was introduced. There was a library and the food was completely different from what used to be the norm on trains earlier. Back then, civil aviation wasn't that easily accessible and was relatively much more expensive. Trains were the most popular form of travelling long distance, but the Rajdhani and Shatabdi changed our perceptions of trains and train travel. A part of the romance vanished.

There was plenty of romance associated with trains. Trains were introduced in India soon after they were introduced in Britain and elsewhere (1853 is the official year of birth). Therefore, quite a bit of experimentation took place with, and in, Indian Railways. There were so many novel solutions, proposed and often not implemented. For example, Colonel Grant of the Bombay Engineers, who authored a monograph in 1850, thought that permanent railway tracks along the surface of the ground were not practical, because of high mountains, impassable rivers, thick forests and jungles, and herds of cattle and other animals. He proposed that railway tracks should be suspended through the entire length using suspension chains, at a minimum height that was eight feet above the ground, high enough to avoid animals and to allow for a fairly uniform alignment. Extraordinary though the idea was, models of this plan were prepared and exhibited. The Court of Directors of the East India Company posed some questions to the Governor General, Lord Dalhousie.

What about periodic rains and inundations, continued action of violent winds, the influence of a vertical sun, the ravages of insects and vermin, the destructive growth of spontaneous vegetation of underwood upon earth and brickwork, the unenclosed and unprotected tracts of country through which the railroad would pass, and the difficulty and expense of securing the services of competent and trustworthy engineers? How would railways in India handle these problems? But the railways were eventually introduced as they were regarded as a marvel.

In 1880, Durgarcharan Ray published a longish story, a bit like a travelogue, in Bengali. This was titled "Debganer Martye Agaman" (The gods come to earth). The gods, that is, Brahma, Indra, and Varuna, visit earth. More specifically, they visit Calcutta, then the capital. The purpose is to take stock of the effects of British rule in India. This involved the railways as well, as they took a train to Calcutta and were barred from entering the waiting room at the railway station, because the definition of "gentlemen" who were entitled to use the waiting room did not include the non-British, gods or otherwise. But the gods were so impressed that they resolved to replicate many of these marvels, including the railways, in heaven.

The younger generation doesn't identify with railways. With civil aviation expanding and more airports being built, combined with better roads and more comfortable cars, who travels on trains? Who identifies with trains? The ones that do are the older generation, who identify with strange objects such as steam locomotives. On rare occasions, the young may visit the National Railway Museum, or the Rewari Heritage Steam Locomotive Museum, or the other railway museums and heritage galleries or parks. There are 34 of these and three more are being developed. But those will be rare occasions.

Until bullet trains and better stations start to wean people back towards train travel, even multi-modal travel, who will tell them about this heritage and legacy? Even when they are drawn back towards train travel, this will be a different kind of train travel, different from the history. Yes, there are books on the history of railways in India, several of them in fact. However, those are generally academic and unattractive, somewhat boring to read. I am delighted this present volume is being brought out, delightful in pictures and content. Across seven chapters, it takes us from the beginnings (those beginnings were in the 1830s, much before 1853) to the present and the future. As this book is being published, a series of reforms have been introduced for the Indian Railways by the government. The Indian Railways will never be the same. The future looks different. But this volume is a wonderful way to take stock of the past.

B. Debroy

Bibek Debroy

An economist by profession, Bibek Debroy is currently Chairman of the Economic Advisory Council to the Prime Minister of India. He has written and edited several books, including *Indian Railways: The Weaving of a National Tapestry* (2017) and *The Railway Chronicles* (2019).

RAILWAYS IN THE WORLD

As the first train chugged along two parallel lines of steel, one thing was inevitable – the world was going to change. Men and material would move, as if compressing time and swallowing space. The invention of railways has been one of the most extraordinary human endeavours in the world. It is one of the few systems that have been able to keep up with changing times and not crumbled under the weight of rapid-paced development.

"The introduction of so powerful an agent as steam will make a great change in the situation of man," predicted US President Thomas Jefferson (1801–09) in a letter in 1802. Two years later in 1804, on a different continent in South Wales, Britain, a steam locomotive trundled across about 16 km hauling wagons packed with iron and 70 men. Mechanical engineer and inventor Richard Trevithick's invention, the locomotive, though slow, impractical, and clumsy, marked the beginning of the steam age, changing the world, and revolutionizing the concept of distance and speed. Today, there is barely any region in the world that has not witnessed the magic and romance of the railways, as it has evolved from a mere vehicle of transportation into a symbol of modernity and progress. For the traveller, it is much more than an iron horse; it provides an invaluable space where communities meet and stories unfold.

Dawn of steam locomotion

Trevithick did not give up on his machine. By 1808, he created *Catch-Me-Who-Can*, another steam locomotive, which pulled people around a circular track in London. Brittle rails unable to bear the weight of his machines, however, meant that he discarded the project, moving on to other things.

◀ **A coloured engraving** showing a steam locomotive being hauled beneath Rainhill's skew arch bridge. The bridge was opened 1830, one year after the famous Rainhill Trials.

Built by Foster, Rastrick & Company in 1829, *Stourbridge Lion* was the first locomotive to be exported to the US. Owing to its weight, the locomotive wasn't very successful.

It was British inventor William Hedley who managed to build a steam locomotive that proved to be more useful than Trevithick's. His *Puffing Billy* began pulling coal trucks at the Wylam Colliery in northeast England in 1813. The true revolution, however, came about in 1814 after British engineer and inventor George Stephenson built *Blücher*, a locomotive for Killingworth Colliery in Newcastle-upon-Tyne, which hauled eight wagons carrying 30 tons of coal at 6 km/h.

Locomotives, however, would not become synonymous with passenger railways until September 1825 when the world's first passenger line to be paid for by public subscription opened between Stockton and Darlington in northeast England. The father-son duo George and Robert Stephenson created their locomotive, titled rather unimaginatively, the *Locomotion No. 1*.

The technology went global, adapted, rather quickly, in France in 1828, when engineer Marc Séguin built his own locomotive. The British-built *Stourbridge Lion* brought the steam age to the American shores in 1829, on the Delaware and Hudson line. Around this time, Stephenson was appointed as engineer to oversee the construction of a 64-km railway line connecting Liverpool and Manchester. The famous Rainhill Trials were held to decide which locomotives would run on the line. There were several competitors, but George and Robert Stephenson's *Rocket* took home the glory, running at 58 km/h. The machine went on to become almost a blueprint for future locomotives until the end of the steam era. *Rocket*'s success led to a flurry of construction as lines were laid and locomotives built, on both sides of the Atlantic. The *Tom Thumb*, an American-built machine, built by American philanthropist Peter Cooper, made its debut on the Baltimore and Ohio Railroad, marking the beginning of the railway revolution that would change not just the US, but the world as well.

Around the world

The mid-19th century was of particular significance in the history of the railways. The construction of railway lines, a crucial

▼ **A silver medal** depicting steam locomotive *De Hoop* (Hope) of Netherlands.

hallmark of development, began at a furious pace across Europe as tracks connected cities across the continent providing access to even the most inaccessible of places. The first line connecting Dublin and Kingstown opened in Ireland in 1834. Germany was close behind as Leipzig and Dresden were linked, making it the country's first long-distance line in 1839. Netherlands' first railways connected the cities of Amsterdam and Haarlem that same year. In Britain, Queen Victoria took her first train journey, travelling on the Great Western Railway on her way to Windsor in 1842. The railways reached Basel in Switzerland, via

▼ **Shimbashi station** served as Tokyo's terminal from 1872 until 1914, when it was made a freight terminal and renamed Shiodome.

France in 1844 and Switzerland's first domestic line opened in 1847. India, too, marked its presence on the world railway map, with the inauguration of the first passenger train to run from Bombay to Thana in 1853 (see pp.32–33).

In the US, the most significant moment took place on 10 May 1869 after a ceremonial golden spike was hammered into a dusty part of Utah at Promontory. As the locomotives *Jupiter* and UP No. 119 were pulled up towards each other, it marked the completion of the first transcontinental railway and a key moment in the development of the US. The railways era had truly begun.

A period of experimentation
The entrepreneurial spirit emerged during this time, gradually changing the definition of travel. Most significant among them was Thomas Cook, a cabinet maker, who later founded the famous British travel company under his name and is considered to have redefined tourism in the modern age. Cook organized a special "charter" train for temperance supporters that ran from Leicester to Loughborough, UK in 1841. These soon became a regular feature, until 1845, when Cook organized a trip to Liverpool marking the beginning of what would become an international travel agency. Comfort became a byword for train travel in 1865 when George Mortimer Pullman launched the lavish and ostentatious Pullman Car.

▲ **Eagle Pass** was one of the last stretches to be completed for the Canadian Pacific Railways. Sir Donald Smith drove the last spike at Craigellachie on 7 November 1885.

This was also the period of the infamous "gauge war" in Britain. Engineering genius Isambard Kingdom Brunel decided to experiment with gauges when he built the Great Western Railway (GWR) in Britain not to the normal 4 ft 8.5 in track gauge but the much wider 7 ft 0.25 in, which allowed for high speeds and more spacious trains. However, much of the track in place was of the narrower width and so the UK Parliament decided against Brunel's idea. Stephenson's 4 ft 8.5 in gauge line became the accepted standard across the world. In India, however, the broader 5 ft 6 in was preferred with narrower gauges for the mountain railways (see pp.84–85). In 1869, George Westinghouse developed the fail-safe air brakes, a version of which continues to be used around the world even today.

The most significant development was the emergence of the concept of mass city transit meant to cater for a growing population of commuters, with the opening of London's first underground line in 1863.

Human genius
The period from 1870 onwards saw railways engulfing the entire globe reaching as far as Japan, with the first line between Tokyo and Yokohama, in

1872. In 1885, the Canadian Pacific Railway's transcontinental route was completed, creating a second route that spanned an entire continent.

There was no line too difficult or impossible to construct as trains climbed mountains, tore through tunnels, weaved their way through treacherous landscape, and crossed expansive rivers. For instance, the construction of Switzerland's Gotthard Tunnel pushed a main line through 15 km of mountain rock. The landmark Forth Bridge in Scotland opened in 1890, crossing the Firth of Forth for more than 2.5 km. A UNESCO World Heritage Site today, it remains one of the longest, multispan cantilever bridges. In India, work began on

opening up the mountains as the Darjeeling Himalayan Railway (see pp.86–87) and then the Kalka Shimla Railway (see pp.90–91) connected the hills with the rest of the railway network in the country. Later, 1905 saw the opening of the legendary Victoria Falls Bridge across the Zambezi River in Africa and the Simplon Tunnel in 1906, which stretched more than 20 km under the Alps to connect Italy and Switzerland, becoming the world's longest tunnel.

This was also the period that saw the emergence of the Orient Express, the epitome of glamour and luxury travel, which by 1891 connected Paris and Constantinople (Istanbul) via some of Europe's most

important cities. That same year, work started on one of the most ambitious engineering projects: Russia's Trans-Siberian Railway. The Moscow–Vladivostok line spanned 9,289 km and continues to be a vital link in the country's transport system.

Trials for electric tramway began in St Petersburg a little earlier, following Werner von Siemen's demonstration of an electric locomotive in Berlin in 1879, paving the way for a future different from the steam age.

Electric beginnings
Cities emerged, grew, and expanded, bringing with them the need for better connectivity. Metro services were almost inevitable. In 1900, the

▼ **This illustration** from the Italian newspaper *LIllustrazione Italiana* of 4 April 1880 shows the opening of the Gotthard Tunnel.

▲ **Union Pacific Challenger No. 3999** and Union Pacific Big Boy no. 4011 double-heading a train on Sherman Hill, US, in 1946.

iconic Metro system in Paris opened its first section followed by the Subway in New York a few years later in 1904. Rapid advancement, however, did not mean the end of steam locomotives, yet. They still had plenty of life left in them and it would be a while before they would truly be replaced. Until then, work continued on making them efficient. Perhaps one of the key innovations during this time was in Britain when GWR's George Jackson Churchward developed the innovative 4-6-0 shaping the future of steam traction.

Yet the beginnings of the electric era were laid in the US when, in 1895, the Baltimore and Ohio Railroad began running an electrified route through its Howard Street Tunnel in response to issues with locomotive fumes. By 1903, an experimental electric railcar running on a military line in Germany set a new world speed record. The early 20th century also saw the appearance of the compression ignition, oil-fuelled

locomotive – a precursor of the mass move to diesel traction that followed later.

World goes to war

The railways proved to be invaluable during the American Civil War (1861–65) and played a crucial role once again, during the Great War as World War I (1914–18) came to be called. During the course of the four years, trains moved men, supplies, and munitions across great distances. Railway-mounted artillery was a common feature especially along the frontlines with France becoming the first country to use rail-mounted howitzers adapted from naval guns. Special locomotives were built in some countries and narrow-gauge railways were laid specifically, often close to frontlines, to serve the war effort.

The end of the war saw the creation of many new countries, which inherited these rail systems, adapting and reorganizing them to suit their nation's needs. Germany brought all

its railways together under the Deutsche Reichsbahn or the national railway, in 1920. In Britain, the government merged all the private rail companies into the "Big Four", which included the GWR, London. Midland and Scottish Railway (LMS), London and North Eastern Railway (LNER), and the Southern Railway (SR). In 1938, France brought all its railways together under the state-owned Société Nationale des Chemins de fer Français (SNCF).

Steam and speed

As cars and aeroplanes shortened time and distance, the competition increased, the railways dived into the age of speed with the emergence of futuristic trains. Speed and comfort became the catchwords. In 1931, Germany's petrol-powered Schienenzeppelin set the speed record of 230 km/h. Steam wasn't far behind as Sir Nigel Gresley's Flying Scotsman, set a record of 161 km/h in 1934. Gresley, one of Britain's most famous steam locomotive engineers went on to build the streamlined Mallard in 1938, which clocked 203 km/h, a steam speed record that has officially never been beaten. Known as the Golden Age for steam, the 1930s also saw lightweight diesel trains making their presence felt in North America and Europe. However, soon, the shadow of war loomed over the world once again.

And the world went to war again

The railways had an integral role during the course of World War II (1939–45) for the Allied and Axis forces. Cheaply constructed yet powerful freight locomotives were used extensively. The German wartime locomotive Class 52 Kriegslok was an epitome of the machines built for war, and proved so reliable and durable that it played an important part in post-war reconstruction as well. The trains transported troops, military equipment, ammunition, and food. In Germany, however, they took on a more horrific role, transporting millions of people to concentration camps. The end of the war brought with it a time for rebuilding as the austere, powerful locomotives built for battle were now used to help with reconstruction.

Fare thee well, steam

Diesel and electric power rapidly replaced steam during the post-war period as the latter was fast considered outmoded and dirty. Europe started seeing the last of the steam locomotives by the 1950s and the No. 23.105 rolled off the West German production line in 1959 as the last to be built for the Deutsche Bundesbahn. Electric locomotives had proved their usefulness in the Swiss and Austrian Alps in the early 20th century and after the war, the transition to electric trains in most

▲ **During its time**, the English Electric prototype *Deltic*, first tested in 1955, was the most powerful diesel locomotive in the world.

European countries picked up speed. Significantly, in 1955, the French electric BB 9004 and CC 7107 set a new world record after reaching 331 km/h. The UK with its newly nationalized British Railways decided to continue using steam until after the publication of the Modernization Plan in the mid-1950s.

However, towards the late 1950s, neither the US nor Europe were making ground-breaking strides in rail transport. That honour went to Japan.

Staying modern

On 1 October 1964, as the two inaugural Hikari Super Express Shinkansen, or bullet trains as they popularly came to be called, pulled into Tokyo and Osaka in Japan, they revolutionized the way the world looked at speed and train travel. Japan's innovation came on the heels of the French Le Capitole, which was introduced in 1960 and became the world's first 200 km/h passenger service. Railways tried to keep up by focusing on modernizing their

▶ **The opening** of the Tōkaidō Shinkansen line was accompanied by an official ceremony at Japan National Railway's Tokyo station on 1 October 1964.

services from using diesel and electric locomotives and focussing on comfort to bidding farewell to steam.

However, it seemed like the railways were fighting a difficult battle. Car sales were increasing and airplane travel was fast becoming the preferred means of transport. The 1963 Beeching Report in Britain's recommendation involved closing 30 per cent of the railway network. The US took drastic measures consolidating 20 passenger railway lines under Amtrak, which began services in 1971 and focussed on making long distance train travel profitable.

Faster and faster

The mid-1970s kicked off what would become a continuing quest for speed as countries followed in Japan's footsteps. British Rail began its High Speed Train trials in 1973, which continue to hold the diesel speed record of 238 km/h. In 1981, France launched its Train à Grande Vitesse (TGV) with a line running from Paris to Lyon, followed by Germany in 1991 with its InterCity Express. New tram systems opened in some places, such as the tram-train services in Karlsruhe, Germany in 1992. These innovative vehicles had the capacity to run on local rail and tramways.

The change in the world order with the end of the Cold War and unification of Germany, meant the building of new lines even as the East and West Germany railway systems merged to become the Deutsche Bahn. Britain witnessed a sea

change as its Parliament voted for privatization in 1993, following which new companies took over and developed. The year 1994 proved to be iconic with the opening of the Channel Tunnel connecting France and Britain for the first time.

The future beckons
With crucial advancements in speed, the emergence of energy-efficient locomotives, and growing emphasis on comfort and luxury travel, the railways have succeeded in reinventing themselves to become important in the travel industry once again. Metros have become a viable alternative in city travel as operators focus on automation, such as in Dubai, which launched the world's longest fully automated metro at 75 km, in 2010.

The quest for higher speeds continues to drive operators. The Maglev or magnetic levitation train made its presence felt in 2003 after an experimental train reached a speed of 581 km/h. A year later, the world's first commercial high-speed Maglev began operations in Shanghai, China. In 2007, France tested an experimental TGV which set a new world record for conventional-wheeled trains at 575 km/h.

Connections continued to be made as in 2006 when train services started to Lhasa, Tibet. The line, which passes the Kunlun mountains, reaches an altitude of more than 5000 m, and is the highest railway service in the world. The railways are here to stay.

▼ **In 2006,** services started on the world's highest conventional railway between Qinghai and Tibet. The route in Tibet reaches up to 5,072 m above sea level. Seen here is a train running through Kunlun Mountains.

1830–1870
THE **BEGINNING**

1830–1870

The invention of the railways changed the world and how it moved. As with the beginning of any technology, there was a great deal of learning from trial and error. In India, these were the pioneering decades, of establishing the presence of the railways, while negotiating and building the physical, social, and institutional environment crucial to its operation.

1830 The first modern railway, the Liverpool and Manchester Railway, comes into operation, marking the dawn of steam-powered rail travel.

1833 The East India Company (EIC) becomes a purely administrative body through the Charter Act of 1833.

1845 The Madras Railway Company (MRC) and East Indian Railway (EIR) Company are formed.

1844 Rowland MacDonald Stephenson's "Report upon the Practicability and Advantages of the Introduction of Railways into British India" is published. This report lays the foundation for railways in India.

17 August 1949 The "Old Guarantee" System, providing free land and guaranteed rates of return to the private English railway companies is finalized.

1830–37

1838–45

1846

1837 The Red Hill Railway near Madras, considered India's first railway, comes into being.

1832 The first proposal for railways in India is made in Madras.

1845 Incorporation of the Great Western Bengal Railway Company, the first Indian company to attempt developing railways in India.

1 August 1949 The Great Indian Peninsula Railway (GIPR) Company is incorporated in Britain by an Act of Parliament.

Opening of the Liverpool and Manchester Railway

Opening of the Madras Railway

Lord Dalhousie

> **Everywhere**, in every direction, **the wanderer** comes up against **rail-road track,** meandering about like a **colossal centipede.** Yet there is **romance and legend,** too, amidst the dust and smoke.

JOHN W MITCHELL, ASSISTANT TRAFFIC SUPERINTENDENT OF THE BENGAL–NAGPUR RAILWAY, IN HIS MEMOIR *THE WHEELS OF IND* (1934)

20 April 1853 Lord Dalhousie issues his famous Railway Minute.

1855 The Panama Railway is completed, linking the Atlantic and Pacific Oceans.

2 August 1858 The Government of India Act of 1858 transfers powers over India from the East India Company to the Crown.

1870 Lord Mayo introduces metre gauge as a compromise amidst proposals for narrow gauge and broad gauge.

August 1855 EIR 21 (*Express*) and EIR 22 (*Fairy Queen*) begin operations.

1859 The Calcutta and South Eastern Railway (CSER) Company is formed.

September 1859 The agrarian indigo revolt begins in Bengal.

March 1857 The Revolt of 1857 begins.

1862 India's first narrow-gauge line between Dabhoi and Miyagam in Gujarat opens.

10 January 1863 World's first subway, Metropolitan Underground Railway, opens in London.

1866 Completion of the Yamuna bridge in Delhi links Delhi and Calcutta by rail.

1862 The Bhore Ghat incline is constructed.

53

1854–61

1862–70

16 April 1853 The first train in India makes its maiden journey from Bombay to Thana.

1856 The Bessemer process, to mass-produce steel, is developed.

12 April 1861 The American Civil War begins.

1863 First luxury carriage in India is built.

1869 More than 6,000 km of railway lines are laid across the country so far.

3 March 1859 First train in the north, between Allahabad and Kanpur, begins.

February 1862 India's first full-fledged railway workshop at Jamalpur is set up by the EIR.

15 August 1854 The first passenger train in eastern India, from Howrah to Hooghly, is operated.

June 1855 The Bombay, Baroda and Central India (BB&CI) Railway Company is incorporated.

1858 The Eastern Bengal Railway (EBR) and Great Southern of India Railway (GSIR) companies are formed.

7 March 1870 The GIPR line reaches Jubbulpore from Itarsi, linking up with the EIR track and connecting Bombay with Calcutta.

Bombay, Baroda and Central India Railway office

Construction at Bhore Ghat

SETTING THE STAGE

There is little doubt that railways had a huge impact on the Indian landscape. The reasons for its introduction in the subcontinent were a combination of vested British interests in their colony as well as the perceived role of railways in driving a country on the route to modernization. Whatever the intentions might have been, the preliminary context for the introduction of railways in India can be explored in the state of transportation and communication after the end of the Mughal Empire.

▲ **Sculpture of Lord William Bentinck,** who was the Governor-General of India from 1828 to 1835

From trunk roads, trade routes, *kos minars* (milestones), and *sarais* (inns), to waterways and irrigation canals, the Mughal Empire (1526–1761) witnessed considerable development in the transportation system for trade and administrative purposes. Even then, harsh weather conditions, especially during summers and the monsoons, posed great difficulties in movement, with the rivers often becoming unnavigable. Moreover, the chief means of transport remained rudimentary, comprising palanquins, country boats, bullock carts, and animals, such as horses, elephants, and cattle, due to which journeys were long, slow, and dangerous.

With the subsequent British occupation of the Indian subcontinent, most of the administration's attention was diverted towards political and military undertakings for territorial expansion. While no concerted effort was made towards new public works, even the erstwhile road network was neglected and reached a deplorable state. The breakdown of the transit system further fragmented the country into small towns, far from each other. Consequently, transportation of goods became expensive and impractical, trade collapsed, and prices and policies varied across

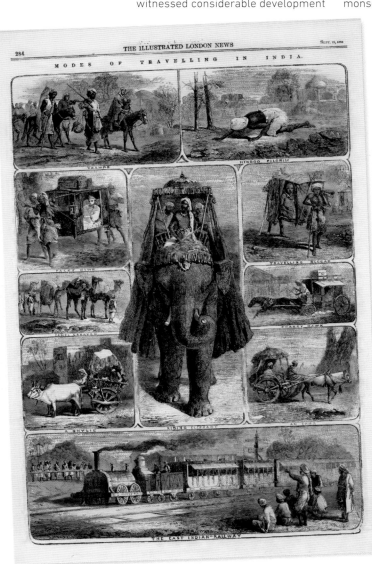

◀ **This lithograph** from *The Illustrated London News*, 19 September 1863, depicts various modes of transportation in India.

THE EAST INDIA COMPANY

During the Mughal rule, a joint-stock company, called the East India Company (EIC), was formed in Britain in 1600 with a monopoly over trade in the East. Over the course of years, it expanded its trading activities and subsequently gained political control over India. In the second half of the 18th century, the British Parliament started closely monitoring and regulating the EIC's activities. It established the Government of India under the governor general in council, who reported to the Court of Directors of the EIC. The Court was placed under the Board of Control, whose chairman was a member of the Cabinet. The territorial units included "provinces", some of which were "presidencies", administered by governors. After the Revolt of 1857, the Crown took complete control of India.

different regions. In effect, goods could be moved through animals only to nearby places, eroding the demand–supply across the country.

Efforts towards road construction
As the British rose to power in India, the administration realized the need to reform the transportation system. Even though Warren Hastings, the first Governor-General of India (1774–85), undertook some road construction projects towards the end of his term in 1785, it was really during Lord William Bentinck's term

(1828–35) that the administration spared serious thought over transportation and communication systems. Up to 48,280 km of roads were constructed but they failed to provide a sufficient network for the country. Even as late as 1856, when the railway had just sprung up on Indian soil, journeys remained long and tiresome.

Bengali philosopher, Debendranath Tagore, in his autobiography *Atmajivani* (1898) writes about his arduous travel from Calcutta in the east to Simla in the north in the same year. He travelled via boat from Calcutta for more than a month to reach Benaras, from where he proceeded on a coach to Allahabad. It took him 14 days to reach Agra and another month in a boat to get to Delhi. From Delhi, he travelled by coach till Ambala and then finally in a *jhampan*, a kind of palanquin, to reach Simla. Moreover, the roads were marred with thugs and murderers. British soldier and administrator William Henry Sleeman wrote, "the *thugs* reigned the highways and under the guise of friendship, win the confidence of unsuspecting travellers and merchants and after accompanying them for a stage or two, on reaching the first selected and retired spot, murder them and plunder their property". However, it was not the problems of the common travellers that precipitated the introduction of railways in the country.

Colonialism and its web

The birth of the railways in India was primarily centred around the social and political system of colonialism, which operated primarily on two grounds: military – for expansion and consolidation, and economic – for accruing financial gains. German philosopher Karl Marx spoke about the annihilation of the Old Asiatic Society and laying the material foundation of Western society in Asia, including railways, in "The Future Results of British Rule in India" (1853). The military importance of

> ❝ The day is not far distant when, by a combination of **railways and steam-vessels,** … when that once fabulous country will thus be actually **annexed to the Western world.** ❞
>
> KARL MARX, "THE FUTURE RESULTS OF BRITISH RULE IN INDIA" (1853)

railways can be ascertained when Marx said, "Railways will afford the means of diminishing the amount and the cost of the military establishments."

The British administration saw railways as a practical means of receiving intelligence inputs from and sending instructions to even the most remote parts of the country. It would bring immediate, immeasurable advantages while repelling hostile attacks by stationing troops in far-off regions. A firm system of internal communications was even more imperative, considering that it was only a few British men, who were trying to control a vast geographical territory, outnumbered by a huge native population.

The Industrial Revolution (1750–1830) changed the economic policy Britain adopted towards India.

Till then, India had remained a colony primarily as a source of land revenue and luxury goods. However, with industrialization and the loss of Britain's American colonies, it became a source of raw materials and a market for finished products as well. For instance, cotton, which grew in abundance in India, appeared lucrative for supporting the textile mills in Lancashire and Manchester. With railways, cotton could be transported easily from plains to ports. Similarly, factory-produced goods from Britain could find new markets in distant locales. At the same time, the British administration also felt that railways would bring social changes in the country and unify it as a political whole, even though scepticism about its acceptance by the native population lingered in the background.

▼ **With the Industrial Revolution,** India was recognized as an important source of raw materials and a market for British goods.

THE EARLY PROPOSALS

The genesis of railways in the Indian subcontinent is hard to pinpoint as it began long before the tracks for the first line were laid. Though proposals and schemes did not materialize immediately, they did set the stage for the introduction of rail technology. The first train that ran – in 1853 – was a result of more than two decades of discussions, deliberations, and proposals.

▲ **A scene from the Liverpool and Manchester Railway** depicting one of the early trains. The success of the railways in Britain drove private investors to invest in railways in India.

The East India Company's (EIC) trade monopoly in India came to an end with the Charter Act of 1833. This opened the doors for British capitalists to seek investment opportunities in the Indian subcontinent. It was a timely move as profit-making industries would help curb the revolting labour forces in England. Also, the export of cotton and coal from India was imperative for the running of the mills in Lancashire and in the industrial markets in Birmingham. Moving the cotton, coal, and other raw materials to ports before being shipped to England needed an efficient transportation system.

The British were motivated to invest in railways in India because of the success and profitability of the British railways. Around the time when Lord William Bentinck, Governor-General of India (1828–35), undertook road construction projects,

the idea of introducing railways and constructing canals was considered for the first time in the Madras Presidency in the south where there was a growing demand for cotton for its textile industries.

It was estimated that the costs of construction and maintenance of canals vis-à-vis railways were nearly the same. However, the latter were preferred. To this effect, a rail line, with animal-drawn vehicles in southern India – from Cauvery-Pattam to Caroor – was proposed to a committee overseeing EIC affairs in Britain. The committee did not pay any attention to this proposal and it never materialized. Instead, Bentinck's administration undertook road construction and made substantial headway during 1839–49. However, roads alone could not have provided an efficient communication system and transport conditions remained poor in many parts of the country.

Deluge of proposals

Soon, the question of railways began attracting individuals with vested interests in the enterprise. In light of communication problems due to poor roads in the Madras Presidency, Sir Arthur Thomas Cotton (see p.26), a civil engineer, wrote to the Inspector General of Civil Estimates in 1836 for a railway connecting Madras in the south to Bombay in the west. A member of the Board of Revenue at Madras later put forth the matter to the Madras government, stating that the railway would aid transporting salt from the southern coast. In 1837, the Court of Directors sanctioned surveys and estimates for the recommended line.

The Bengal Renaissance

In the eastern region of Bengal, the first railway proposal came from the Calcutta and Saugor Railway and Harbour Company in 1836 to construct a line from George's Point to Calcutta. However, with high construction costs and no support from the Government in Britain beyond a land grant, the project could not be executed.

In the 1830s, Dwarkanath Tagore, a businessman from Calcutta, bought collieries in Raneegunge. To facilitate transportation of coal, his company Carr, Tagore, and Co undertook a survey for a rail line between

Raneegunge and Salkea Ghat. One of the first of its kind, the survey was backed by prominent individuals, including British railway engineer Rowland Macdonald Stephenson. These advocates of the railways observed the potential of a line in the east for coal that was currently being transported through canals. In 1841, Stephenson thought of connecting Calcutta via a railway line with the North-West Frontier. He focussed on this, not for the coal but, because the railway line would cross the Indo-Gangetic plains, which were densely populated. Stephenson was one of the most prominent advocates of a rail system in India.

Historian Dipesh Chakrabarty argues that it was Stephenson's strategy to publish articles and reports about railways to bring "railway consciousness" to Bengal. He writes that it was a time when political awareness had started to hit the region. While the attitude of the locals towards the railways has not been explored in detail, Chakrabarty provides some correspondence between Stephenson and Indian men to suggest that they were in favour of the enterprise. He states that this group of individuals were a part of the Bengali elite and while they may not have promoted colonialism, they were entrenched in it through economic pursuits. This might have been why, Chakrabarty theorizes, they backed the railways in India.

A detailed proposal

Soon after the first proposal in Bengal, some members of the EIC looked at the possibility of a rail route connecting ports across the Indian peninsula as a shorter route to China. Railway engineer Charles Blacker Vignoles was called upon for an assessment in 1842. He presented a detailed report on how the construction of railways in India was perfectly feasible. He referred to the availability of good-quality labour and raw materials in India which, in his opinion, was better than in England. He also drew attention to the potential role of railways in military as well as in commercial matters, primarily for cheap distribution of manufactured goods from Britain, developing local markets, and attractive returns. He proposed an elaborate plan for a rail line connecting Bombay and Calcutta, which would pass through highly fertile and populated regions as well as districts rich in coal and iron.

The trend continues

Many other reports were submitted to the Court of Directors advocating the construction of railways in India. Captain JR Western of the Bengal Engineers proposed a railway line from Calcutta to the Upper Provinces. These preliminary discussions planted the seed of introducing the railways in India and the railway mania finally began to touch the Indian shores.

▼ **This lithograph shows bales of cotton** in Bombay ready to be exported to Lancashire cotton mills. These were to supplement shortages caused by the blocking of southern ports of the US during the American Civil War (1861–65).

EXPERIMENTAL RAIL LINES

Even as official attempts for the introduction of railways were being made, some experimental rail lines, primarily for the carriage of construction material, came up in the middle of the 19th century. This was in response to the huge expenditure usually incurred for road construction and the search for an economical and efficient haulage system. Although these rail systems were only of local importance, the dawn of railways on the Indian horizon can be effectively traced to these precursors.

It has been suggested that perhaps one of the earliest railway networks in the world, connected end-to-end, came up for the construction of the Taj Mahal in the 17th century. Indian author and railwayman MA Rao says that for easy transportation of marble from Makrana in Rajasthan to Agra in Uttar Pradesh, stone slabs were fixed in the ground, creating a path so that the wheels of bullock carts carrying the marble could easily roll over them. Another similar route was constructed in parallel for the return journey. Along the way, depots were built at regular intervals for the animals and drivers to rest. Although the existence of this network is not certain, it is evident that the origin of railways in India lies in the knowledge that movement of vehicles on a set path reduces the amount of human effort that may be required otherwise.

Little labour, huge gains
The first rail line was laid as an experiment near the Chintadripet Bridge in the Madras Presidency in 1836. The experiment included moving a cart loaded with stones up an inclined plane by hand to show how, with little labour, it rolled down to its source by its own weight. This line was later merged with the permanent line of the Red Hill Railway. A British General and engineer, Sir AT Cotton (see box), who was appointed to inspect the areas near Madras, noted that the construction of rails to the Red Hills and to the stone quarries at Little Mount would save nearly half of the annual expenditure on carrying material along the roads. It would also bring in profits through the line's use by private traders. His recommendations were approved, and thus began the work of laying down possibly the first rail line in the Indian subcontinent.

Connecting Red Hill
The construction of a short rail line southwest of Madras connected the Red Hills with Cochrane's Canal, and came to be known as the Red Hill

SIR ARTHUR THOMAS COTTON (1803–99)

A British general and an eminent civil engineer of Madras, Sir Arthur Thomas Cotton was born in Cheshire, England, on 15 May 1803. He was a part of the Madras Engineers from the 1820s and was instrumental in the construction of many irrigation and navigation canals from 1828. His well-known projects include canals on the Rivers Cauvery, Coleroon, and Godavari. Apart from irrigation, Cotton was also a significant figure in the development of railways in India. In 1832, he proposed a line connecting Madras and Bombay. In a document dated 4 May 1836 to the Inspector General of Civil Estimates, he argued for the advantages of railways over canals. Cotton retired in 1860 and was knighted in 1861 for the development work he undertook in India. There is a museum built in his honour in Rajahmundry, Andhra Pradesh, and barrages constructed across River Godavari are named after him.

▼ **The 1845 irrigation project** on the Ganges River included the construction of an aqueduct to cross the Solani River.

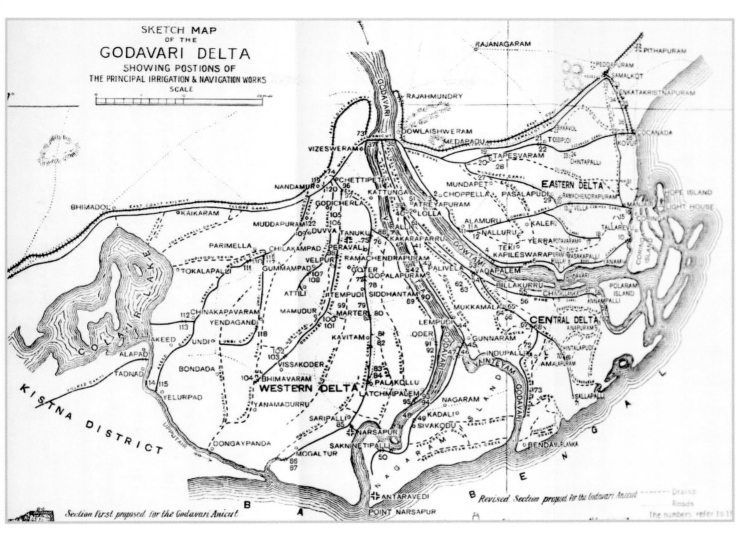

SKETCH MAP
OF THE
GODAVARI DELTA
SHOWING POSTIONS OF
THE PRINCIPAL IRRIGATION & NAVIGATION WORKS
SCALE

Railway. The construction might have begun in 1836 but the line was certainly in operation by the middle of the 19th century. There is evidence from newspaper articles suggesting that the iron works industries in Cuddalore district in Tamil Nadu were fully operational for the construction of this railway. Reports also suggest that the line cost the Government Rs 50,000 and parts of it had wooden structures. The exact type of locomotive used on this line remains unknown. Author Simon Darvill suggests it could have been a wind-powered or animal-hauled carriage, or even a William Avery's rotary steam engine, or a version of it. Still, the project was short-lived and certainly non-functional by 1845.

In 1844, Sir AT Cotton continued his work on the Red Hill Railway while also supervising the construction of an irrigation dam on the Godavari Delta, and also built a railway line from the Quarry Hill to the Godavari bank to transport material. Tracks were made of broken and cut stone as well as teak tree battens fixed with iron bars. Wagons, pulled by ponies and men, rolled on these tracks, except on the slope at the end where they could roll down by themselves. With the opening of this line, stone could be easily transported to the river bank from where it was taken on boats. Even though the line was supposed to be permanent, it ceased to exist post the completion of the dam project in 1852.

The first locomotive

In 1845, work began on an irrigation project on the Ganges Canal. It included the construction of an aqueduct to flow the canal across the Solani River in Roorkee (in modern-day Uttarakhand). Ballast trucks and wagons, hauled by humans and animals, rolled across the extent of this railway. It is also, perhaps, the first instance of the use of a steam locomotive, named *Thomason*, which was a 4 ft 8.5 in gauge tank engine, an EB Wilson 2-2-2WT, imported from England. Reports suggest that the locomotive was used only for a short time before meeting with an accident. It did, however, usher in a new era in the history of transportation in India.

▲ **The fertile Godavari** delta had many irrigation and navigation works. The first railway lines came up to support the construction of dams near it.

TAKING SHAPE

When the second promotional phase for the railways in India began, the commercial ports of Bombay in the west and Calcutta in the east became the natural choices to be the first railway hubs. Soon, two primary groups of promoters emerged; one made concerted efforts in the west, even as the other led the discussions in the east. After receiving Government support, the two groups organized themselves into private companies.

Edward Davidson in *The Railways of India: With an Account of Their Rise, Progress, and Construction* (1868) noted: "the first great point to which a railway naturally tends is a commercial port, and of them, for its extent of coast-line, India has very few". There was, thus, no doubt that the port cities of Bombay and Calcutta would be the first to be linked by rail. In Bombay, even though there were multiple interested groups, it was John Chapman, whose company, the Great Indian Peninsula Railway (GIPR) pressed the Government to back the project. In Calcutta, English engineer Rowland Macdonald Stephenson piloted the project through his company, the East Indian Railway (EIR).

On the western shores

By the mid-1840s, railway mania had sufficiently captured western India. The first local attempts were made in 1844 by British officials of the Bombay government and local merchants whose company, the Bombay Great Eastern Railway, found favour with Sir George Arthur, the Governor-in-Council of Bombay. However, official examinations showed that their proposals lacked concrete surveys. The company was ultimately dissolved, as, despite Arthur's backing, it drew criticism from some government

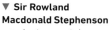

▼ **Sir Rowland Macdonald Stephenson** was instrumental in the establishment of the EIR.

▶ **In the west, John Chapman** (1801–54), along with other railway enthusiasts, set up the Great Indian Peninsula Railway.

officials, who were against, not only the introduction of railways in the country, but also the idea of any company based in India (as opposed to London) to engage in a venture with capital from Britain.

In 1844, Chapman, who wrote extensively on commerce and trade, proposed a railway line from Bombay to Coringa in the south, under the name Great Indian Railway. Like many proposals before this, it failed to gather support from the East India Company (EIC). However, Chapman's effort found support in politician John Stuart Wortley, who became the Chairman of the Great Indian Railway. It was renamed the Great Indian Peninsula Railway, and was backed and managed by a group of highly motivated and connected individuals.

In the east

Meanwhile, recognizing the demographic importance of the Indo-Gangetic plains, Stephenson, proposed a railway link between Calcutta and the North-West Frontier in 1841. This plan did not find favour with the EIC either. Stephenson was

determined to stand by his railway project, however, and in 1843, he reached out to the local population in Calcutta where he acquainted them with the potential benefits the railway connections would provide. He also collected and compiled data to support this mammoth project.

Having garnered enough support, Stephenson wrote about the proposal in the *Englishman* in 1844. In it, he discussed the ambitious railway link that criss-crossed the land – from Calcutta to Mirzapur and Delhi, with links to Ferozepur, and a line from Bombay to Hyderabad and Coringa, to be continued to Calcutta. Both these lines would also be connected at Mirzapur. From Hyderabad, a line would branch off south to Madras,

from where one line would go to Calicut and the other would link Tirunelvelly. In July of the same year, he put forth his idea to the Bengal government, which assured him a thorough consideration of his proposal. At his insistence, the first survey was prepared by the Bengal government for a 675-km line from Calcutta to Mirzapur in the United Provinces.

Against all odds

By early 1845, provisional committees had been formed for the EIR and GIPR. When the question of investment arose, Stephenson, with support from the Bengal government, managed to get the backing of mercantile houses for his company, East India Railway Company, later called EIR. In his document, *Report Upon the Practicability and Advantages of the Introduction of Railways Into*

> ## " ... the **Bombayans** ... write, speak, think about **nothing but railways** ... "
>
> *THE LEADER,* 20 SEPTEMBER 1845

British India, he spoke extensively about the advantages of rail communication, including those in trade, the details of routes that would be adopted, and the backing of the Government. He presented his dealings and correspondence with the Government of Bengal and other documents he believed would help convince the public to invest in the venture. In January 1845, the EIR finally submitted its prospectus to the Court of Directors. Seeing the growing popularity of railways among the masses, in May 1845, the EIC announced that it would lend its support to the well-considered proposals.

With this encouragement, the same month, the EIR's provisional committee established EIR into a joint-stock company. This energized the GIPR's provisional committee,

which soon released its own prospectus. The objective was to connect the interiors of the country with Bombay on one end and with the port on the eastern coast.

Scepticism and solution

The Court of Directors, however, were still not convinced about the feasibility of railways in India. It saw the country's climate, vegetation, and unskilled population as impediments to the enterprise.

A group of engineers, including FW Simms as civil engineer and J Fraser as assistant engineer were deputed to examine the railway question. They proposed some alterations to the lines, but concluded that the problems the Court feared had practical solutions and that the railways in India could be seamlessly constructed and operated.

▼ **This sketch from the** *Illustrated London News* depicts the EIR workforce at a camping site in the United Provinces in 1857.

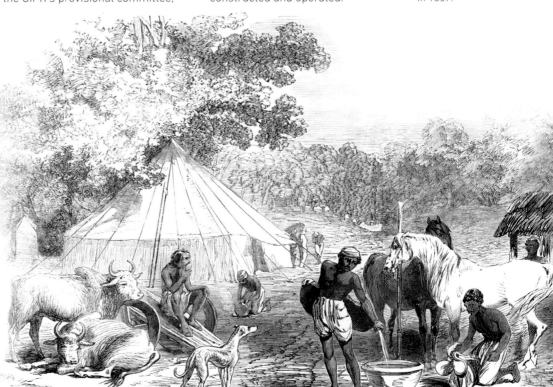

FINANCING THE RAILWAYS

By the time Dalhousie became the Governor-General in 1847, India was crying for progress. It was Dalhousie's vision that unfolded a master plan for public works, irrigation, communications, agriculture, transportation, including the railways. The Government's financial inadequacies, however, seemed to pose a roadblock.

Insignia of the Bombay, Baroda & Central India Railway, 1855

To attract much-needed private capital for projects, newly formed railway committees agreed that a guarantee of high returns from the Government might help with their financial woes. The Government, however, believed that free grants of land would be sufficient incentive to attract private capital, and was unwilling to guarantee dividends to railway entrepreneurs. It, however, wished to retain the powers of supervision, inspection, and regulation of profits of the developers.

Many of these conditions were not acceptable to the investors as they found it extremely difficult to raise funds without Government guarantees. These disagreements led to prolonged discussions, delaying the projects.

Discussions and resolutions

In 1846, British railway engineer Sir Rowland Macdonald Stephenson presented definite proposals for the East Indian Railway (EIR) Company to the Government. The Court of Directors of the East India Company (EIC), however, were not prepared to agree to the terms, which included more than a 4 per cent return on invested capital up to £5 million to EIR, at an average cost of £15,000 per mile, with equal profit-sharing with the developer. The investors did not find this acceptable and the proposal fell through.

American cotton supplies for British mills had substantially dwindled and the Chambers of Commerce at Manchester and Glasgow, pressed for early construction of railways in India to facilitate the export of cotton from Bombay. This coincided with an aggravation of a financial crisis in England. The situation added pressure on the EIC's stance on the railways as, finally, its directors reluctantly agreed to raise the rate on the guaranteed percentage to a 5 per cent without a time limit. By 1849, the EIR and the Great Indian Peninsula Railway (GIPR) were already incorporated by an Act of the Parliament. Soon, the first contracts for building railways in India were signed by the Government.

The "Guarantee System"

The first two experimental lines constructed in the Bengal and Bombay Presidencies were undertaken under a "Guarantee System". This system had some important provisions: The contract was drawn for 99 years, with guaranteed interest varying from 4.5 to 5 per cent; the finances advanced for the guarantee were to be repaid from the profits of the line and the Government had the right to purchase the railway after 25 or 30 years; the company could surrender their lines to the Government at any time during the contract; land would be provided free of cost with the Government approving the route, gauge, and technical construction details. The Government retained the power of control and supervision, including the approval of tariffs.

In 1849, the clamour for a joint-stock company to construct railways in the Madras Presidency increased and a short, experimental line was approved in accordance with the Guarantee System and the Madras Railway Company was incorporated in July 1852. The next railway contract was awarded to the Bombay, Baroda, & Central India (BB&CI) Railway Company in 1859 to develop a coastal line in the west, initially from Surat to Ahmedabad, to be extended later till Bombay.

During the first two decades of railways in India, many other contracts were drawn under the Guarantee System, including the Scinde, Punjab, and Delhi, Eastern Bengal, Great Southern of India, Calcutta and South Eastern, Oudh, and Carnatic Railway Companies.

Disadvantages of the system

Soon, however, the drawbacks of the Guarantee System became visible and criticism followed. Since the Government relieved the shareholders of all risk, it killed the latter's urge to economize, promoting recklessness that engulfed India in liabilities much beyond its means.

In the two decades since the inception of the railways in India, the country had a mere 6,464 km of railway lines opened, with another 3,284 km of tracks under construction. The Revolt of 1857 (see pp.42–43) halted the process till 1859, but the average annual addition for two decades was only 431 km, which was far below the Government's expectations. Moreover, the revenue of the country during the mid-1800s was barely sufficient to meet the current investments. The Revolt had unhinged the financial equilibrium of British India entirely. In 1857, the public debt of the country stood at about £60 million. By 1863, this had risen to £110 million. The original cost of construction was estimated to be £15,000 per mile for a double line and £9,000 for a single line. But, it was discovered that, at the construction stage, the trunk line cost worked out to more than £20,000 per mile. The rise in the exchange rate of the Indian Rupee vis-à-vis Sterling during this period, added further challenges for the Government. The Guarantee System in India using British capital, was, at best, a moderate success.

While, as connectivity improved, the revenues of the railways grew remarkably, except, during the 1857 Revolt, they never exceeded 3 per cent of the capital expenditure. Yet the Government was required to pay larger and larger amounts annually as guaranteed interest.

Solution to the financial crisis

By the time Lord Lawrence assumed office as the Viceroy (1864–69), the financial crisis had peaked. By 1885, inclusive of the capital invested in the Guaranteed railways, the public debt of India had skyrocketed to £250 million.

▶ **Viceroy Lord Lawrence** urged on the importance of Government construction of railways in India.

Various modifications to the Old Guarantee schemes were proposed to the secretary of state for India in Britain. The secretary, however, suggested that railway projects should be classified into "Commercial" and "Political", the former being built through the Guaranteed System, while for the latter, direct Government agency was preferred. In March 1869, Lord Lawrence pressed for Government construction of railways. The secretary of state finally agreed to this suggestion and in the financial statement to the British Parliament, mentioned the policy change in the construction and operation of railways.

▼ **An early 20th-century artwork** of the office of the Bombay, Baroda, & Central India Railway.

▲ **One of the early GIPR trains**
running on Harris Bridge, which
was constructed around 1858
near Dapodi, Pune.

THE CURIOUS CASE
OF THE FIRST TRAIN

On 31 October 1850, the Chief Justice of Bombay, JP Wilson, laid the foundation stone
for the Great Indian Peninsula Railways (GIPR) line in Sion, Bombay. This auspicious
inauguration or *bhoomipujan* was the first of its kind for railways in India. Three years
later, the first passenger train made its run to Thana, forever changing India's landscape.

THE CURIOUS CASE OF THE FIRST TRAIN

The construction for this line was entrusted to English contractors William Frederick Faviell and Henry Fowler. The two employed nearly 10,000 local workers, battling several problems, including working in harsh terrain, communication issues with native workers, and culture clashes. By the end of 1852, the line from Thana to the Masjid Bunder area of South Bombay was complete. At this time, the GIPR undertook trial train runs with the locomotive, *Lord Falkland*, named after the then Bombay Governor.

A sight to behold

The locals found the steam locomotive, stationed in a grove of toddy trees. fascinating. The *Bombay Telegraph* of 17 February 1852 reported: "The native population appears to evince great interest in the 'Fire Chariot' as they name her, and crowd round to have a look. The weight and massive character of the whole is quite at variance with their notion of speed; and after observing the slow progress she made when being dragged along the public road by 200 coolies their incredulous look of astonishment is not to be wondered at when told, that in a few days she will be able to pass the race course swifter than their fleetest Arabs."

In action

The first trial run on 18 February 1852 was from the Byculla to Parel stations. The second run occurred eight months later on 18 November from start to finish. The locals saw the train as a giant monster, whistling and throwing steam, generating many emotions. Some called it *lokhandi rakshash*, or iron demon in Marathi, an evil entity that drew its power from young people who had been buried under its tracks. Others saw it as a means employed by the British to flee after taking their lands and money. The rest were just confused about this miracle.

History in the making

A year later, on 16 April 1853, the first passenger train finally made its maiden run from Bori Bunder station to Thana, a distance of 33 km. The day, according to *Bombay Times*, "was observed as a public holiday".

The train comprised 14 railway carriages hauled by three locomotives named *Sahib*, *Sindh*, and *Sultan*. Although their presence has been recorded, there is photographic evidence of only one locomotive as taken by Jamsetjee Jeejeebhoy, an Indian merchant and philanthropist. There are theories that suggest that the other two were back-ups. Nevertheless, the train carrying more than 400 passengers, left Bori Bunder, with a 21-gun salute, at 3.30pm and reached Thana at 4.45pm. According to *The Illustrated London News*, there was a massive crowd waiting to witness the arrival of the train. The trip back was scheduled for 5.45pm on 17 April and the train reached Bori Bunder at 7.00pm.

This glorious event was snubbed by the Governor of Bombay, Lord Falkland, who chose to retreat to his hill station home, though his wife was present on the day. After the event, *Overland Telegraph and Courier* wrote: "the opening of the Great Indian Peninsula Railway will be remembered by the natives of India when the battle fields of Plassey, Assaye, Meanee, and Goojerat have become the landmarks of history." The *Illustrated Weekly of London* reported: "the long line of carriages conveying nearly 500 passengers glided smoothly and easily away amidst the shouts of assembled thousands."

The excitement was palpable among the locals. So much so that, the very next day, Jeejeebhoy booked the entire train to travel to Thana and back with his family and friends.

A series of delays

Even though the GIPR rolled out its train first, the East Indian Railway (EIR) was the frontrunner in terms of construction. By the end of 1853, it had completed 61 km of track. The inaugural run in the east was, however, delayed due to several factors. The line went through French-occupied Chandernagore and it took a while to settle disputes with the French and ultimately acquire permissions. To make matters worse, the ship HMS *Goodwin*, carrying the carriages for the EIR sank at Sandheads near Diamond Harbour off the Bay of Bengal. John Hodgson, EIR locomotive chief engineer remained unfazed and built the carriages locally with the help of coach-building firms Messrs Steward and Company and Seton and Company.

Although, the problem of the carriages was solved, the ship bringing the locomotive lost its way towards Australia and reached Calcutta in 1854, aboard the HMS *Dekagree*. Had it not been for these events, the story of the first train in India would have arguably been completely different.

▲ **A crowd waiting** at the Byculla station, which was also the starting point for trials of the first passenger steam locomotive.

▼ **An illustration of the ship** carrying the carriages sinking at Sandheads.

FAIRY QUEEN
2-2-2 MAIL LOCOMOTIVE
5'-6" GAUGE

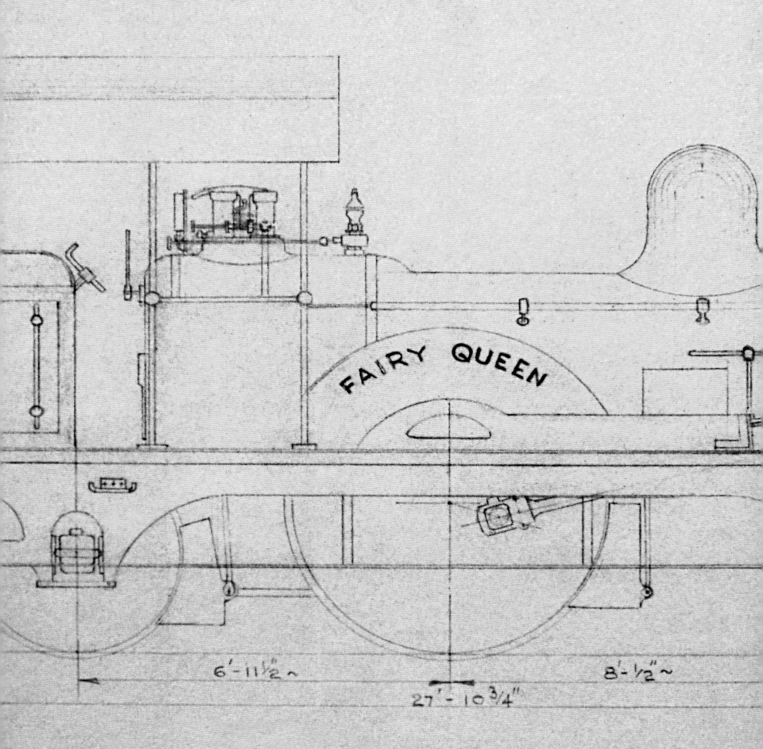

FAIRY QUEEN

6'-11½"~   8'-½"~

27'-10¾"

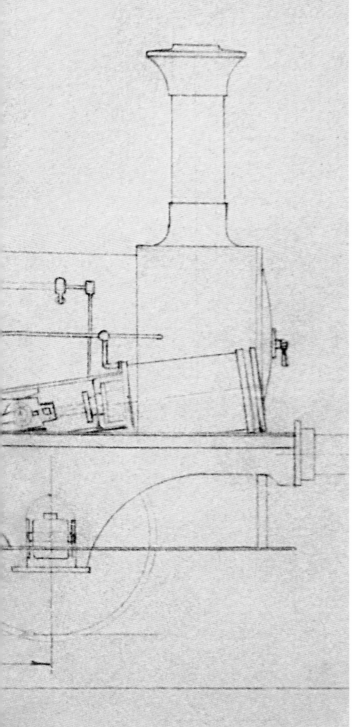

This drawing of the *Fairy Queen* is a part of the collection in the National Rail Museum in New Delhi, India. The specifics of the engine can be seen mentioned here.

FAIRY QUEEN

Regarded as the world's oldest working steam locomotive, the *Fairy Queen* was built in January 1855 by Kitson, Thompson and Hewitson, a British locomotive manufacturing company in Leeds, UK. Supplied to the East Indian Railway (EIR), this 2-2-2 Well Tank BG Locomotive began work in August 1885 as Loco No. 22. It later came to be known as the EIR 22 before finally being named *Fairy Queen* in 1895.

The 1.7-m-long locomotive initially hauled mail trains in West Bengal on the 195-km-long Howrah–Raneegunge line. There are also records of it being used to haul trains of troops, from Howrah to Raneegunge, deployed to quell the uprisings during the Revolt of 1857. The locomotive was later dispatched to line construction duty in Bihar. After 1909, it was withdrawn from service and taken back to Calcutta and plinthed in Howrah till 1943.

It was exhibited at the National Rail Museum (NRM), New Delhi, in 1977. The 26-tonne veteran was revived and completely overhauled in 1996 in the Perambur Workshop of the Southern Railway. Several modifications were made to bring it back to life. Its driving wheels were reaxled, small compressors were put in, to make it an independently working air-braked unit, and a majority of its brass tubes were replaced with more modern fixtures. In July 1997, the *Fairy Queen* re-entered service as a part of a semi-regular heritage train – the Fairy Express – between Delhi and Alwar in Rajasthan. In July 2004, while parked at NRM, vandals stole a few of its parts – two brass handles and four copper pipes.

This "queen" was withdrawn from service in 2011 because of the need for specially made parts to keep the engine operational. In 2017, it was reintroduced into service as a part of the "steam express" programme of tourist trains.

The *Fairy Queen* was listed in the Guinness Book of Records as the world's oldest working locomotive in 1998.

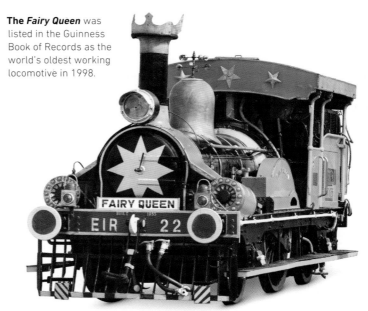

EIR 21

The EIR 21, better known as the *Express*, was one of the first steam locomotives of the East Indian Railway (EIR). It is widely believed to be a sister locomotive of the *Fairy Queen* (see pp.34–35), both of which were manufactured by Kitson, Thompson and Hewitson around the same time. However, there are conflicting sources that suggest that the EIR 21 was built by Stothert, Slaughter and Company of Bristol. This almost 8-m-long locomotive began its operations in August 1855. It is said to have been the locomotive that ran on the Howrah–Hooghly line and, during the Revolt of 1857, transported British troops from Howrah to Raneegunge.

Initially, locomotives were not given names, and were distinguished merely by their manufacturing serial number. Known by its number 21, this engine was called EIR 21. After almost 40 years of service in 1895, EIR 21 was rechristened the *Express*. It was withdrawn from service and preserved in front of the Jamalpur Locomotive Works office in Bihar in 1901. It would be decades before it was seen again by the public, now as an exhibit at the Railway Museum in Howrah, West Bengal. While at the museum, the locomotive suffered corrosion, some of its parts went missing, and it was even permanently damaged. Unlike its sister locomotive, the *Fairy Queen*, which was restored in 1996, the *Express* was declared unfit for restoration.

More than a decade later, in 2010, this steam locomotive was finally resurrected by Perambur Loco Works of the Southern Railway. It was fitted with a new injector and air brakes and readied to run the Heritage Special Service. Its first heritage run was on 15 August 2010 – Independence Day – from Chennai Central to Avadi in Tamil Nadu with two coaches, as part of the day's celebrations.

The *Express* now boasts of various technological advancements, including a GPS-based speedometer. Today, it operates once a week as a tourists' special, carrying sightseers to and fro. The engine's restoration posed a challenge to the *Fairy Queen's* record of being the world's oldest working steam locomotive. Interestingly, the *Express's* fleet number 21 makes it older than the *Fairy Queen*, which is also known by its locomotive number, EIR 22.

The *Express* seems to have a knack for being mired in controversies. In 1953, the Indian Railways issued a stamp to celebrate the enterprise's centennial year. The postage stamp is supposed to be a representation of the first train journey from Bori Bunder to Thana, hauled by the three steam locomotives: *Sindh*, *Sultan*, and, *Sahib*. No known photograph of that maiden train journey exists, and any pictorial representation of that trip should have three engines. Instead, the stamp showed a single locomotive on it, which is incorrect, and is, in fact, the EIR 21.

◄ **The refurbished EIR 21** getting ready to run the Heritage Special Service to commemorate India's Independence.

EXPANDING THE WEB

With the successful run of the train from Bori Bunder to Thana, a working
blueprint was put in place. It was now time for the pioneers of railways in
India to look inwards and lay the lines that would connect the rest of the country.

Engineers were to soon find out
that Indian terrains were not easy to
subdue. If the west had the plateaus
with their impenetrable nooks and
crannies and craggy mountains, the
east had intricate river systems,
some of which turned into untameable
torrents during the monsoons.

In the north and the North-West
Frontier lay ravines, canyons, and the
Himalayas, while Sind and Rajputana
offered vast expanses of desert.
Nevertheless, the trailblazers took up
the challenge to cast a web of railway
lines across the country.

They surveyed terrains and adapted
their technological know-how to meet
the demands of the location and
inhospitable weather, often at
great human cost, such as in the
construction of the high-inclined
Bhore Ghat (see pp.50–51) where
about 25,000 people died due to
accidents as well as diseases.

Birth of a blueprint
It helped that there was a plan in
place, penned by one of the most
influential proponents of the railways
in India, Governor-General Lord

Dalhousie (see box). Written between
1850 and 1853, his Minutes proved
to be invaluable. The first document,
notes author Roopa Srinivasan in
the introduction to *Our Indian Railway*
"developed a vision of railways as
a single national 'works' or project."

The second, a 216-page handwritten
Minute, is what can perhaps be called
the blueprint for the railways in India.
It drove home the importance of
laying lines across the country for
commercial advancements and
political and military purposes. There
were "immeasurable advantages,"

▼ **This antique print
from 1856** shows
the opening of the
Madras Railway at
the Royapuram station,
easily recognized by
its Corinthian pillars.
A bishop can be seen
(on the left) offering
his blessings.

Dalhousie notes, while emphasizing the need for trunk routes. He proposed three in particular, which were favourable for engineering and ideal for future subordinate lines. The first was from Calcutta to Delhi and the North-West Frontier, the second from Bombay to Delhi, and the third from Madras towards the west coast. The railways would mushroom from these three hubs, encompassing the entire country.

He sent this Minute to the Court of Directors hoping that they would "resolve at once to engage in the introduction of a system of railways into this Indian Empire, upon a scale commensurate with the magnitude of the interests involved, and with the vast and various benefits, political, commercial, and social, which that great measure of public importance would unquestionably produce." The Court finally agreed in August 1853.

Standardizing the widths

All the lines, Dalhousie insisted, had to have a single, standard gauge. He was drawing from his experience of the British Railways and its challenges. Consulting engineer of the Indian administration, FW Simms, supported him. While the East India Company (EIC) wanted to go with a 4 ft 8½ in gauge, they were not too picky. Dalhousie, who preferred 6 ft, was open to suggestions, as long as there was a single gauge used across the country. Simms recommended a broad gauge measuring 5 ft 6 in as he felt that it was most suited to India. The severe storms and winds, he noted, could topple a narrow-gauge train, but not the more stable broad gauge. It helped that the latter was more economical. Work began in earnest and it seemed that gauges were no longer a matter of concern.

Connecting the dots

Construction began in the Bengal and Bombay Presidencies and, by 1856, the first lines opened for the public. The returns were quite profitable, with many Indians taking

to train travel quickly, reaffirming Dalhousie's stance that the railways did have some use in India. Meanwhile, the British, who had made inroads into Burma, felt an urgent need to build a connection between Calcutta and Dacca (now Dhaka, Bangladesh), and Dacca and Akyab (now Sittwe, Myanmar). The Revolt of 1857 (see pp.42–43) further emphasized the urgency of building lines that would allow for quick movement of troops. By 1858, political control shifted to the Crown and construction efforts accelerated.

Between 1853 and 1862, several guaranteed companies established themselves. Of these, the Great Indian Peninsula Railway (GIPR) and East Indian Railway (EIR) had already started work on the Bombay and Bengal lines, respectively. The third, Madras Railway, received the contract to build the entire system of Madras trunk lines, towards the west coast, where it would meet the Bombay line, and the north-west. The first train service in the south, a journey of about 100 km, finally started in 1856, between Royapuram in Madras and Wallajah Road in Arcot. The Great Southern India Railway, registered in 1858, built lines from Nagapattinam to Tiruchirappalli.

The Bombay, Baroda and Central India (BB&CI) Railway – connecting Bombay to Baroda with lines to Surat and Ahmedabad – opened to the public by 1865. They faced several challenges, including heavy flooding of the River Narmada, which washed away the construction twice and forced the engineers to go back to the drawing board and come up with a new plan.

Construction in north India to connect Sind with Delhi began under four separate undertakings. While

LORD DALHOUSIE (1812–60)

The Governor-General from 1847 to 1856, Lord Dalhousie was the youngest man to be appointed to the post. During his tenure, he focussed on boosting the transportation and communication systems in India. His Minutes on the railways are crucial in understanding the development of the network. He also instituted telegraph lines, promoted the completion of the Grand Trunk Road between Calcutta and Delhi, and began a central postal system.

the Scinde Railway built the 173-km Karachi–Kotri line in 1861, the Punjab Railway constructed the 408-km Multan–Amritsar line that opened in 1861. The Indus Steam Flotilla company connected the two lines via a steamer that operated between Kotri and Multan, until it was brought together under the Scinde, Punjab and Delhi Railway (SPDR) in 1869.

The Eastern Bengal Railway, formed in 1858, built two lines – from Calcutta to Kushtia via Barrackpore, and another that branched off to Dacca via a junction near Calcutta. In 1862, subsidies were also granted to the Indian Branch Railway Company and the Indian Tramway Company. The former was to build feeder branches in north India, while the latter focused on areas around Madras.

By the end of 1868, 6,400 km of track were in operation, and another 3,200 km were under survey or construction. It was only a matter of time before the entire country was connected, and, eventually, unified.

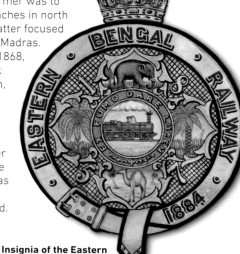

Insignia of the Eastern Bengal Railway, 1884

This sketch immortalizes the reception of the esteemed guests who travelled in the inaugural train to a lavish banquet at the Burdwan station.

ALL ABOARD: THE FIRST TRAIN JOURNEY TO RANEEGUNGE

The line which extended to Raneegunge, famous for its coal mines, opened for commercial use in February 1855. Its inauguration was an extravagant affair as both fine gentry and bewildered natives witnessed the majestic locomotive puff away.

THE FIRST TRAIN JOURNEY TO RANEEGUNGE

An immense crowd of spectators, including leading members of Calcutta society, gathered on both sides of the Hooghly river, on Saturday, 3 February 1855. They were there to watch as the first train to Raneegunge made its inaugural run from the Howrah station. A select group of guests were guided past a decorated arcade, festooned with flowers and evergreens, to the river bank, where they boarded two steam ferries hired specially by the railway company for the occasion. The ferries took the guests to the other side of the bank, from where they made their way to the railway station.

At precisely 9am, Governor-General Lord Dalhousie and his staff arrived. He was, however, unwell and so inspected only the arrangements and flagged off the train after a 19-gun salute. He did not board the special train, with 15 carriages, which left Howrah at 9.40am after the reading of prayers by the Lord Bishop of Calcutta.

The fire chariot

The train crossed a distance of 193 km, weaving its way through brightly decorated stations and curious villagers waiting to get a glimpse of the majestic fire-belching leviathan.

The following day, a newspaper described the excitement created by the event: "To ignorant natives who understand nothing of the means by which the *Aag ka Gahrie*, or fire chariot, is moved, few things could have been more astounding or more convincing of the miraculous power possessed by the English. One curious explanation was that the locomotive was made to go simply by the '*Hookum* or order of Lord Dalhousie'!"

The festivities continued after the train reached Burdwan at 12.30pm, where it stopped for three hours for some much-needed breakfast. "The entire party, without the slightest delay, all evidently in the best possible appetite, partook of the repast, scarcely waiting till the Bishop, had breathed a prayer over it," a correspondent for the *Calcutta Papers* reported. Toasts followed,

▶ **An 1862 map of Bengal** showing the East Indian Railway (EIR) route (in purple) from Calcutta to Raneegunge.

including one by EIR agent, Rowland McDonald Stephenson, the engineer who had pushed for the development of the railway line system in Bengal.

The train left at 3.30pm, reaching Howrah by 4.42pm. It is important to note that the special train was not taken to Raneegunge as the guests would have been unable to reach Calcutta that same evening, and the EIR did not run steamer services at night for safety reasons. A second, commercial train would later carry on towards Raneegunge.

A civil servant and, later, Commissioner of Patna, William Tayler noted the inaugural train run from Burdwan to Raneegunge with a "rather amusing anecdote". It involved a carriage jam-packed with youth, huddled together, even as more were pushed in and the door closed. That's when cries of protests went up with pleas to be allowed out. Apparently, a joyful bulldog somehow entered the carriage and merrily bit the exposed ankles of all passengers. "The scene was supremely ludicrous, the stifling crowd squeezed together as with a vice, the weak melancholy tone and expression of the victims, complacent grin of the guard and the evident enjoyment of the spectators, formed such an absurd scene that shouts of laughter greeted the sufferers instead of sympathy," Tayler wrote in his autobiography *Thirty-eight Years in India: From Juganath to the Himalaya Mountains*.

The road to profit

This "fire chariot" had the desired impact as in the 15 weeks after the line opened, the number of passengers it carried was 179,404, with an average of up to 12,000 a week. Earnings rose to £900 a week. There was no doubt that this was going to be a profitable venture and an enterprise that would be impactful for centuries. The railways in Bengal turned out to be invaluable, not only as an efficient mode of communication and transportation, but also as the ace up the East India Company's (EIC's) sleeve during the Santhal Rebellion and later, the Revolt of 1857 (see pp.42–43).

REVOLTS AND THE RAILWAYS

Apart from commerce and transport, one of the primary objectives of introducing railways in India was easy troop movements. The rail infrastructure, however, was so vast that it was not easy to protect it from vandalism during the uprisings and rebellions that plagued the British in its colony.

▲ **An artwork** depicting an attack by the Santhals on the soldiers of the 40th Regiment Native Infantry.

On 11 May 1857, a group of soldiers, after killing European officers in Meerut the day before, marched to the Red Fort in Delhi. They proclaimed Bahadur Shah Zafar, the "nominal" last Mughal Emperor, to be the Emperor of India, and set off what has retrospectively been called either the First War of Indian Independence or the Sepoy Mutiny, depending on the narrator. The movement spread quickly, engulfing most of northern and some parts of central and western India. The south remained more or less unaffected. Railway construction came to a screeching halt as it became a popular target for the rebels. While uprisings and rebellions were not new, the earlier ones had remained contained. The Revolt of 1857, however, left an impact on the British as it resulted in a change in how the colony was governed, with India coming under direct British rule in 1858. Before this, however, came the massive Santhal Rebellion, known for its strong connection to the railways.

> " The **ghosts of 1857 haunted** the British … the colonial residents viewed the **railways** as their **only reliable escape route** in the event of another major uprising. "
>
> DAVID CAMPION, "RAILWAY POLICING AND SECURITY IN COLONIAL INDIA, c.1860–1930"

The rise of the Santhals

In 1855–56, the Santhals in the east took up arms because of increasing oppression by local landlords, European indigo planters, and railway builders. With charges of builders bullying labourers and humiliating women, the rebels, armed with bows and arrows, destroyed rail lines,

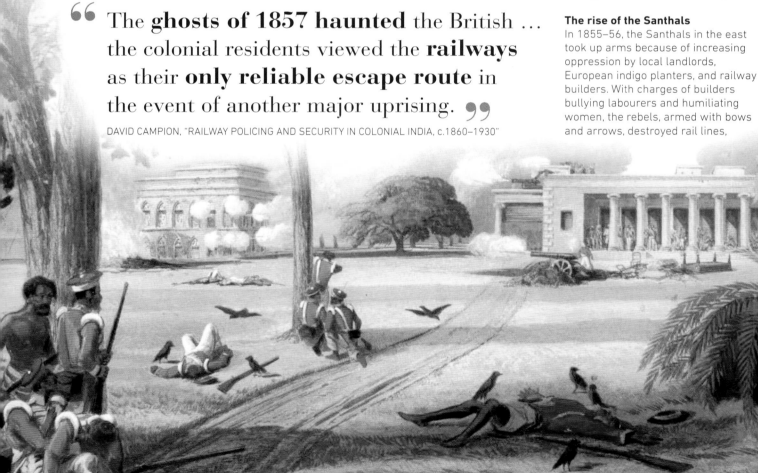

stations, and bridge works. British retaliation was swift, and troops wielding firearms were brought in on trains to quell the rebellion. About 20,000 Santhals were killed.

Rebel soldiers

By 1857, about 440 km of lines were already in operation. The British used them to move troops and supplies. The "revolt" had a greater effect on the railways. The rebels saw them as a soft target, and destroyed lines. Railway engineers working in remote areas volunteered to fight against the rebels, helped to fortify defences, or found themselves hiding.

The Illustrated London News reported one such incident that occurred in Barwarie near Allahabad in June 1857, when a group of railway engineers and contractors took refuge in a water tank at a railway station. They held off a mob of 3,000 people who threw brickbats and stones at them after looting and burning a bungalow that belonged to contractors Messrs Morris and Company. Soldiers from the 35 Irregular Cavalry, dispatched from Allahabad Fort, finally rescued them after an ordeal of 32 hours.

"Little House at Arrah"

One of the most famous stand-offs during this period was between railway engineers and the armed rebels at Arrah in Bihar. Railway work was still on between Dinapore and Arrah, as was the construction of a bridge over the River Sone. The resident engineer Richard Vicars Boyle took the reports of unrest quite seriously. He fortified a building in his garden (originally meant to be a billiards room), bricked up the verandah, and stocked it with provisions and arms.

In July 1857, the Dinapore regiments mutinied and marched towards Arrah, plundering and destroying everything along the way. Chief engineer Edward Davidson wrote in *The Railways of India, with an Account of Their Rise, Progress, and Construction* that the resident engineers, inspectors, overseers, and their families managed to escape in iron boats belonging to the railway company.

In Arrah, the mutineers released all the prisoners in the jail and laid siege to Boyle's house that sheltered 16 Europeans and 45 Sikh policemen, who defended themselves for a week against constant musket fire. The mutineers even mounted a gun on the roof of a house and fired at the fortified building in an attempt to destroy it. They managed to ambush and drive away the relief force as well. Finally, the siege came to an end after a second force of the 160 Fusiliers and volunteers from the railway force defeated the mutineers.

Davidson noted that property worth £42,000 was destroyed at the Sone bridge, but that the total loss over the whole line amounted to an equivalent of three million sterling.

◀ **An illustration of** Richard Vicars Boyle's house at Arrah being defended from mutineers by British sepoys.

Fortified stations

Many, including Lord Dalhousie, had often discussed the railway's military potential. The Revolt served to drive home the point, emphasizing the importance of having key lines in strategic areas. Historian Ritika Prasad, while quoting public statements made after the Revolt, wrote, "The urgent need for more railways was emphasized in public statements about the 'all-important' ability to transport 'compact and highly trained bodies of European troops from one point of India,' and the dangers of allowing a colonized population to believe that 'on any point, whether 10 miles or at 1,000 miles away, the authority of England can be overthrown for a day by Asiatics of any race or creed'."

It was no surprise, therefore, that once the rebellion was completely quelled, work on expanding railway lines restarted at an almost feverish pace. Focus was also on ways to safeguard railway infrastructure and rolling stock. Anthropologist Laura Bear noted that there was an emphasis on developing railway stations into safe havens for British citizens in case of any future civil unrest. So much so that stations constructed after the Revolt were near cantonments. The architecture, too, started resembling forts. The terminal at Charbagh in Lucknow had an armoury and barracks, the Delhi Junction resembled a castle with turrets, and the Lahore station had bomb-proof towers and loopholes.

▲ **The Lahore station** was one of the first railway stations built immediately after the Revolt. It was designed to provide a safe haven for the railway staff in the event of another attack.

EARLY STATIONS

Small and often dreary, the first stations were designed and built for efficient British rule and easy mobility of resources. With these two principal concerns in mind, the stations favoured functional designs and simplicity over excessive ornamentation. Over the next few decades, however, these stations would transform into elaborate edifices, a visible testament to colonial power.

▲ **The original Byculla station** in Bombay was one of the stops on the Bori Bunder–Thana line. It was initially a simple wooden structure with a bridge. By 1891, it was rebuilt and moved to its present-day location.

Around 1910, a dissatisfied European traveller passing through Wadi Junction in Hyderabad commented: "of all the dreary stations in this land, Wadi is the dreariest." Perhaps, for his sake, it is fortunate that he had not witnessed earlier Indian stations, which were built for practical use.

Smaller stations of the time could usually be described as shanties surrounded by small huts for railways staff. Larger stations boasted of added benefits of separate rooms for men and women, space for bedding on the floor, and washrooms. Waiting rooms, when provided, were used by engineers and railway officials who required overnight lodging while on duty and did not offer much comfort to passengers. In fact, "dreary" Wadi was slightly grander as it had a refreshment room, built mainly because of its location on the junction of the key Madras–Bombay line.

The original Byculla and Howrah stations are examples of such spartan structures. Today's grand Howrah station building was little more than a singular booking window with a small line for dock platforms that were used for freight when the first train began its journey from the station in 1854. It was rebuilt in 1905 and is today, one of the biggest stations in India.

New requirements

Throughout India, stations were located according to population distribution, industrial centres, and terrain. The general opinion was that there was no need for elaborate structures, as it was an unnecessary expense. This attitude changed in 1854 after Madras approved the classification of stations into four categories. While those used by Europeans fell into the first and second class, towns with larger traveller populations were placed under the third-class category. Smaller stations with a low passenger footfall qualified as fourth class.

These mostly had provisions for shelter from the weather. Third-class stations were scarcely better with booking offices made slightly larger for any passing European travellers, and an inadequate number of ticket offices. Significant stations such as Jamalpur and Cawnpore (present-day Kanpur) often saw large crowds fighting to purchase tickets from one clerk as there were not enough third-class ticket windows. By 1864, a Government of India circular acknowledged the need for better facilities, such as lavatories and refreshment rooms.

Defensive forts

The Revolt of 1857 changed the way the British viewed the railways. Stations were now incorporated into the colonial defence strategy (see p.43). They also became potential shelters for the British if the need arose. The architecture of these stations began reflecting this change in ideology. Lahore is perhaps the best example. Built shortly after the Revolt, the station was, described author Rudyard Kipling, "the work of devils", which was designed like a medieval European castle. It was an imposing structure with giant, sliding iron doors, tall walls with loopholes for muskets, and bomb-proof turreted towers. British anthropologist Laura Bear in her book, *Lines of the Nation* wrote about the post-1857 railway stations as changing from "places of commerce" to arenas "for the expression and protection of state authority and the hierarchical relationships of command." The architecture and location, she wrote, "reflected a tension between a desire to materialize a neutral public sphere of commerce and a fear that Indian populations were hostile."

◄ **European-styled** Sealdah station also served as a tram terminus till 1978. Today, one of the busiest, this railway station has three terminals: Sealdah North, Sealdah Main, and Sealdah South.

From simplicity to grandness
Plans for prominent stations in busy cities veered away from functionality to include decorative elements. Architectural styles incorporated in the designs of these stations echoed European trends. The original 1862 Sealdah station in Calcutta was constructed in the Italianate style, nostalgically placing a little slice of England in Bengal. Sealdah's low-pointed roof mirrored those of

the stations found along England's Great Western Railway. This expansive terminus would later become a temporary home for Hindu-Bengali refugees fleeing East Pakistan after Partition in 1947. The Royapuram station in the Madras Presidency displayed characteristically Greek-style neoclassical features. Inaugurated in 1856, this station was the first in Madras and functioned as the region's

premier terminus until 1907, after which further routes were extended, making Madras Central more prominent. Railway stations from this period onwards were no longer utilitarian buildings.

▼ **The old Churchgate station** in Bombay was built in 1860 and named after a church gate, which was demolished for an expansion programme. The station pictured here does not exist anymore, as it was torn down and moved to another location.

A train pulls into an unidentified station in this photograph from 1867. Earlier stations were mostly functional structures with basic facilities for travellers. Over time, these evolved into elaborate buildings with English, Italian, or Greek architectural influences.

CONSTRUCTION AND OPERATION

One of the most overlooked challenges in the tale of the railways in India is its construction. Behind the building of every rail line is the story of hundreds of Indians – women, men, and children – labouring over tracks that wound across punishing mountains, treacherous jungles, and raging rivers. It is also the story of stoic and resolute British engineers and contractors who led the mammoth operations.

▲ **Thomas Brassey,** a prominent British railway engineer and contractor, was the brains behind the construction of many railways across the world.

During the "pioneering phase", construction relied on the expertise of engineers – civil and military. Before 1870, many icons of the British Railways were brought in as consultants. Isambard Kingdom Brunel, a prolific engineer of his time, consulted for the Eastern Bengal Railway, and outlined proposals for the Sealdah Terminus station in Calcutta. British contractors, such as Victorian railway builder Thomas Brassey, executed the building of lines, employing vast numbers of Indian labourers. There were some British Indian contractors and the Indian Jamsetjee Dorabjee, who secured four contracts.

Skilled and experienced workers came to India for construction. In 1861, according to Canadian historian Ian J Kerr, there were about 500 Britishers overseeing the building of the railway lines across India, sharing their knowledge with local workers. Technology transfer, wrote Kerr, was a core element of construction and operation.

Material matters
All know-how was British, whether it was rulebooks, procedures, or equipment. All signalling equipment, machinery, wheel units for carriages, and rails were imported from Britain. By the end of 1863, noted Kerr, 3,571 ships carrying nearly three million tonnes of railway materials had made

their way to India. By the end of 1869, some 1,045 British locomotives were in operation. This was also the time when workshops were set up – not to construct locomotives, but for minor repairs. The first workshop was set up in 1854 in Bombay followed by one in Calcutta. The iconic Jamalpur Workshop (see pp.54–55) was constructed in 1862.

Back-breaking work
One of the least technical, yet most labour-intensive processes was building rail beds. This included extensive earthwork and building embankments to create ground levels and set rails. There were several instances where masonry and brickwork were involved in order to protect the tracks against floods, as in Bengal. Most of the workers were unskilled and hired from nearby villages. For heavy construction in remote areas, labourers were even hired from far-flung places.

Often there was a need for skilled workers, such as masons, carpenters, or blacksmiths, and if there was no skill available, engineers ensured that they taught labourers what was required. It was just a matter of time before knowledge was transferred between workers who would often travel between sites as and when their expertise was required, wrote Kerr.

Cultural differences
British engineers and contractors often faced resistance when they tried to change the technologies and

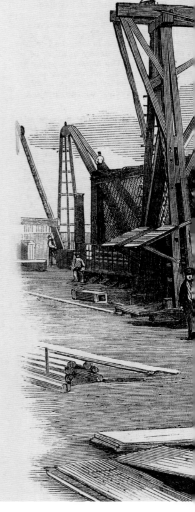

practices that were already in use. Henry Fowler, contracted to build the first part of the Great Indian Peninsula Railway (GIPR) line, was recorded complaining of labourers who refused to begin work at 6am, instead preferring the usual 8am. Workers also often refused to take on jobs alongside those of a different caste.

Then there is the story as told by engineer Thomas Going, which, wrote Kerr, "is so evocative as to suggest some embellishment": "It has been often attempted to introduce the wheelbarrow mode of work, but with little success. The basket of antiquity – probably antediluvian – still holds its own. I have heard of an instance of an enthusiast in wheelbarrows who, having exhausted his morning energy in the fond endeavour to restrain a gang of coolies from using the objectionable basket, had the mortification, on making his evening tour of inspection, to find them carrying the wheelbarrows on

their heads, in the belief that it was only a convenient modification of the principle."

Building bridges

One of the greatest challenges for the early engineers and the workers were bridging the rivers, from the Indus and Ganges, to the Narmada, Jamuna, Sutlej, Beas, Godavari, and Hooghly. While Britain had seen significant development in bridge-building for the railways, the technology seemed nearly inapplicable in India.

These almost-gentle rivers with low water levels would become raging torrents during the monsoon, as would the Himalayan-fed rivers, when the ice melted. They would erode rock and weaken bridge supports. Engineers found themselves adapting existing technologies, merging them, on occasion, with traditional Indian practices, moulding them to suit each terrain and area.

Tunnelling through

Building tunnels was not new in India, but the ones constructed to accommodate trains were very different from those made for irrigation or military purposes. Unlike Europe, scholar Ian Derbyshire noted, tunnels were only required in a few places across India. These included the Western Ghats, the North-West Frontier Province, and the Himalayas. During 1850–70, tunnels were mainly built in the Western Ghats, on the Bhore and Thul Ghat inclines. There were 38 such tunnels of around 5,700 m aggregate length. Of these, two tunnels were the longest at about 490 m each.

The human cost

All of this came at a terrible cost. There was always the danger of severe injury or death, with cases of workers falling from heights while building bridges, drowning, accidents while cutting rock in the Ghats, or from blasting tunnels and cave-ins.

However, disease killed the most, cholera being the worst. The number of Indians that succumbed to this were far higher because of their terrible working and living conditions. One of the worst outbreaks was in 1860 in the Ghats where almost 25 per cent of Europeans died, with a far larger, undocumented number of deaths among the Indian labourers. "Jungle fever" or malaria also took its toll, often disabling workers.

Gradually, towards the end of the 19th century, worksites got better as did living conditions with sanitation and housing facilities, which helped in controlling mass outbreaks. Today, India has the fourth-largest railway network in the world, and a total track length of 121,407 km – a feat unimaginable without the human endeavour that started nearly 200 years ago.

▲ **Instead of being constructed from scratch,** railway bridges were assembled using superstructures imported from England.

Reversing inclines were an ingenious
answer to the problem of trains having to
move up extremely steep gradients. The idea
was later used during the construction of
similar railway lines in the Andes Mountains
in South America. This image shows the
reversing incline at Bhore Ghat in 1880.

CONQUERING THE GHATS

Connecting the port of Bombay with railways to boost trade may have been an easy decision, but the actual
endeavour required laying rail lines through the treacherous crevasses of a series of stepped hills – the
Western Ghats – in the Deccan Plateau. The resulting construction is an engineering marvel, no doubt, a
story of human tragedies, perseverance against all odds, and eventual triumph.

British colonial and commercial interests clearly lay in connecting Bombay to other administrative and commercial centres across the country. On Lord Dalhousie's behest, John James Berkley, the chief resident engineer for the Great Indian Peninsula Railway (GIPR), conducted a series of surveys in the Western Ghats region that lay between Bombay and Poona. After years of study, he zeroed in on Bhore Ghat in the south-east and Thul Ghat in the north-east to lay the lines towards Poona and Nashik, respectively.

By 1856, GIPR's line had extended from Bombay to Khopoli, beyond which extended the hills of Bhore Ghat. Two years later in 1858, another line had connected Poona to the hill town of Khandala from the other side. What remained now was a link between Khopoli and Khandala with the mighty Ghats in between.

Challenges and innovations
Constructing a direct line seemed impossible even with such a short route because of the steep incline – the railway line would have to ascend up to 600 m in 24 km. Then Berkley hit upon an innovative solution. Instead of a continuous track that would plod uphill, Berkley proposed a reversing station at the top of the hill.

The track would be laid in a Z-shaped formation. The train would go upwards in reverse on to tracks laid out on an elevation and then move forward to climb further up. This would keep the gradient within the hauling power of the locomotives that would be pulling the trains.

Triumphs and losses
Even with rudimentary technology, around 25 tunnels and eight viaducts were built in the area from cutting about 1.5 million cubic metres of rock and embanking 1.8 million cubic metres of material. The enterprise, however, came at a terrible human price. Constructing bridges and tunnels in the mountains required

▲ **Native labourers** were at constant risk due to unsafe work conditions. They often worked on temporary wooden structures with basic tools and no protective gear.

rocks to be drilled and blasted. For this, workers were often suspended by ropes. Many lost their grip only to fall to instantaneous death in the ravines below. Work often came to a halt due to extreme weather – from heavy rainfall and strong winds to arid, dry heat. Those who managed to brave the weather and escape accidents were lost to diseases such as typhoid, smallpox, and malaria, to name a few. A massive cholera outbreak in 1860 killed around 25 per cent of the Europeans and innumerable Indian workers. Construction was further delayed because of severed labour relations due to discrimination and terrible working conditions.

The Bhore Ghat line finally opened to traffic in 1863 and Thul Ghat in 1865. It is estimated that about 25,000 Indian workers died during the eight years it took to construct the line, which is still in use today. The reversing station was retired in 1929 when the Bombay–Poona line was electrified and a straight line was laid from the Monkey Hill station in Bhore Ghat to Khandala.

JJ BERKLEY (1819–62)
Born in 1819, JJ Berkley studied at King's College, London, and trained under the English railways engineer Robert Stephenson who recommended him to be chief resident engineer of the Churnet Valley Railway in Staffordshire, England. His peers appointed him as the chief resident engineer of the GIPR in 1849. Immediately after his arrival in India in 1850, Berkley entrenched himself in surveys to link Bombay with Thana and then Kalyan and subsequently in the construction of this first stretch of railway on Indian soil. Connecting the Ghats was his brainchild. Unfortunately, he did not live to see the train whistle past the lush green Ghats as his health failed and he died in 1862 at the relatively young age of 42. In the image below, he can be seen seated on the extreme right with his colleagues Geo L Clowser (left), and Swainston Adamson (centre), as an unidentified Indian man looks on.

JAMALPUR LOCOMOTIVE WORKSHOP

The first locomotive, carriage, and wagon workshop facility for the East Indian Railway (EIR) was set up in Howrah, Calcutta, in 1854. This was done in a hurry to manufacture replacement coaches when the ships carrying imported coaches to India sank. However, as the railways grew, the workshop ran into problems related to skilled labour and space, necessitating a move to another site.

On 8 February 1862, the EIR established a larger workshop in Jamalpur, 10 km south of Monghyr (now Munger), in Bihar. The site was strategically selected, as in those days, Monghyr had traditional communities of mechanics and manufacturers of ironware and firearms, and other skilled artisans, so much so that the town was called "Birmingham of the East". Initially, the workshop was meant for minor repairs and periodic overhauling. It gradually progressed towards self-sufficiency with various manufacturing facilities, including a steam-operated rolling mill (1870), Iron (1893) and Steel (1898) Foundry, a signal equipment shop (1894), the Jamalpur Technical Institute with a chemical and metallurgical laboratory (1897), and a steam power plant (1901).

By the turn of the century, the workshop had started manufacturing locomotives, beginning with CA 764 *"Lady Curzon"* in 1899. It was the first facility to produce indigenously conceptualized rail cranes, tower cars (Mark II and Mark III), and breakdown cranes. It also pioneered the manufacturing of high-capacity electrical lifting jacks, electrical arc furnaces, wheel sets, fireboxes, permanent-way fixtures, steel castings, bolts and nuts, and various machines for ticketing. The workshop was heavily damaged in an earthquake in 1934 and was remodelled from 1935 to 1937. The layout was changed to increase the workload capacity and during World War II, it also produced shells, mortars, and bombs.

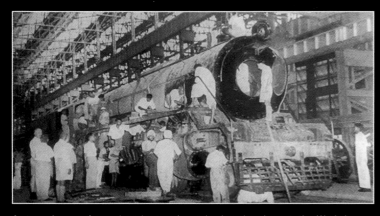

A steam locomotive undergoing repairs at the Jamalpur Locomotive Workshop.

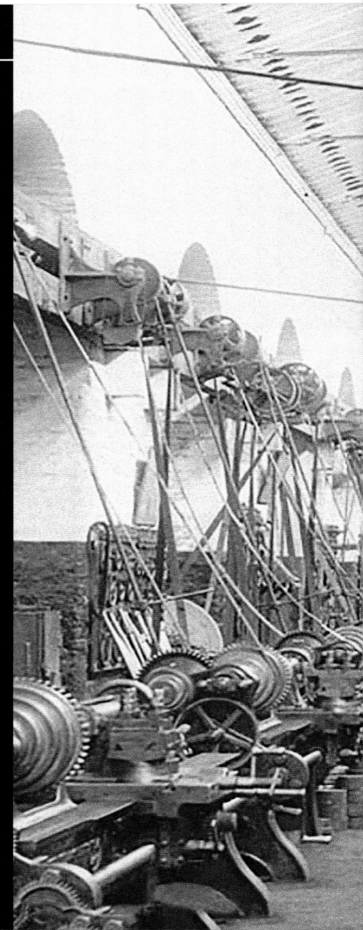

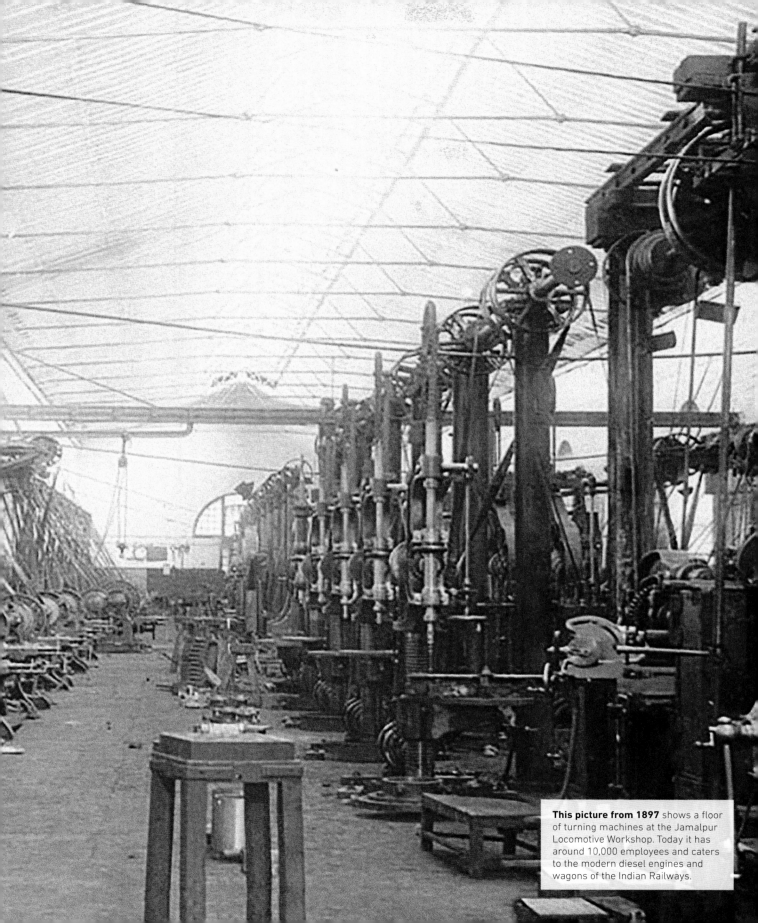

This picture from 1897 shows a floor of turning machines at the Jamalpur Locomotive Workshop. Today it has around 10,000 employees and caters to the modern diesel engines and wagons of the Indian Railways.

EARLY ORGANIZATIONAL PAINS

The initial years of the railways in India saw very little or no particular administrative or legislative structure. Perhaps the institution was too new and the challenges too unpredictable to afford any foresight towards organization. Whatever small measures undertaken at the time, were developed haphazardly or implemented as and when new problems arose. The result was a mishmash of regulations with no coherent design.

Lord Dalhousie, India's Governor-General (1848–56), had always believed that the railways were a national enterprise and advocated that the industry's control and supervision be with the Government via a "regulated authority declared and defined by law". Consequently, the contracts that were drawn with the railways companies carried the provision for State regulation. It held control over the fundamental working of railways: determination and approval of routes, construction, fares, tolls, and finance.

Central Public Works
During the initial years of colonial administration in India, all public works were undertaken by the army's Engineering Department, which was placed under a Military Board. As a result, the railways in India, since its inception, was looked at as works of the military. In 1854, Lord Dalhousie abolished Military Boards in the three Presidencies – Bombay, Madras, and

Bengal. Instead, he brought in a Central Public Works Secretariat, headquartered at Calcutta, then the capital of British India. With this, every local government had a chief engineer to attend to public works of all nature in their territory. Like many other sectors post the Revolt of 1857, all crucial industry matters, especially those relating to finance, were dealt by the secretary of state for India.

Specific to railways, the secretary of state now had the power to make an appointment to the Board of Directors of the railway companies. Actual control over the industry, however, was exerted through a director inducted in the London Board of Directors of all railway companies. Along with the right to veto in all proceedings (except those related to communication with the legal advisers), that Director also held the right to approval of hiring of railway personnel and sanction of orders for materials, among others.

Initial adjustments
The railway companies did not have a well-considered administrative plan when they were formed. Their earliest measures in this regard were temporary in nature, and subject to change and replacement at will. The Great Indian Peninsula Railway (GIPR) appointed a committee of five directors in Bombay to represent its London Board of Directors. Its role was to implement instructions supplied from Directors in London and oversee the company's business, especially its salaried officers. At the same time, its activities were subject to approval and control of the Bombay government.

However, in 1862, the Secretary of State for India proposed that the GIPR replace the Bombay committee with a general manager. Although initially reluctant, in 1864, GIPR agreed. In another instance, as the workload mounted, in 1867, another committee, formed by the chairman and a director, was appointed to deal

> ❝ **I trust they** (the East India Company and Government of India) will ever avoid the **error of viewing railways** merely as **private** undertakings and **will regard** them as **national works over** which the **Government may** justly exercise and is called upon to **exercise a stringent** and salutary control. ❞

LORD DALHOUSIE'S MINUTE TO THE COURT
OF DIRECTORS ON 4 JULY 1850

with invoices, bills, and cheques. The traffic manager's department was earlier supervised jointly by the traffic manager and the locomotive superintendent to take care of the working of trains, traffic, locomotives, other rolling stock, as well as stations, and tickets. It was now separated into the Traffic Department under the general manager and the Locomotive Department under the locomotive superintendent.

Governmental restructuring

Meanwhile, with the growth of the railways and other development projects in India, the Central Public Works Department was undergoing changes as well. A separate railway branch under a special deputy secretary was created in 1866. A consulting engineer for guaranteed companies was also appointed. Even when the railway lines of a company passed through multiple provinces, these were managed by one consulting engineer. Over the course of time, with rigorous construction and expansion, regional consulting engineers, with expert knowledge specific to

provinces, were appointed to work with the local government. Routine work was to be taken care of by the provincial consulting engineers while matters of strategic importance were to be handled by the Government.

Random policies

There was hardly any legislation pertaining to railways passed during this time. The first provision came about in 1854, one year after the first passenger train ran in India, and its scope was limited to regulations, including fares, tickets, illegal activities, fencing, and the liability of railways with regard to traffic. Overall, the Act lacked substance and failed to provide any real legal safety and provisions to the public, especially with regard to working conditions and discrimination. Following this, an Act passed in 1865 primarily dealt with the liabilities of railways and tramways

in case of any loss or injury, and not just those brought on by negligence or misconduct of their workers. Two more acts were passed in 1870 and 1871 to deal with accidents and cattle trespasses.

This motley collection of legislation failed to provide a solid railway policy and was ineffective in the long run. It would not be until the formation of a Railways Board in 1901 (see p.113) that a formal structure was applied to the railway industry in India.

▼ **The 1865 Act codified liabilities** for tramways along with the railways. Pictured here is a tram outside Colaba Causeway in Bombay in the 1900s.

The Kalka railway station is an interchange station on the Delhi–Shimla route. It has two sets of platforms, one for broad gauge trains coming from Delhi and the other for the narrow gauge trains going to Shimla.

1 UP / 2 DN

In its long and varied career, the train 1 Up / 2 Dn has been known by many names. It used to be the East Indian Railway Mail when it was run by the East Indian Railway (EIR) and began operations in 1866, connecting the capital Calcutta with Delhi via Benaras, Lucknow, Cawnpore, and Agra. Most importantly, though, it was the chosen mode of transportation for British officials to make their way to and from Simla (now Shimla), the summer capital.

While once this rail route ended in Delhi, the Scinde, Punjab and Delhi Railway (SPDR) extended the line towards Umballa (present-day Ambala, Haryana) in 1870, making the journey to Simla easier. Realizing the interests of private companies in the region, the Government of India passed a resolution in 1887 that allowed private companies to construct a line from Umballa to Kalka in the Himalayan foothills, and later to Simla in 1903. Construction started in 1889 and two years later, the Delhi–Umballa–Kalka Railway (DUK) Company opened a line to Kalka. The train now came to be known as the "Howrah–Kalka Mail" as it carried not just people, but also postal mail. The line was instantly popular as officials, administrators, army officers, and even tourists, could travel all the way to Kalka where the line terminated. They would then take *tongas* (horse-drawn carriages) up to Simla – a 93-km-journey that would take another eight hours.

Colloquially called the Kalka Mail today, it is the oldest mail train in India and was considered the fastest until the introduction of the Rajdhani Express (see pp.222–23) in 1969. This iconic train even made an appearance in writer and film-maker Satyajit Ray's short story, "Incident on the Kalka Mail". The train also contributed to a memorable moment in the history of independent India when, in 1948, it was rushed from Howrah to Delhi to carry Mahatma Gandhi's ashes to Prayag to be immersed in the River Ganges.

Mail bags are segregated according to the city by the Railway Mail Service (RMS). These are unloaded at specific stations from where they are dispatched to various locations.

This archival image of the Jubbulpore station shows the EIR emblem above the station's name. A major junction in the Indian Railways system today, modern-day Jabalpur station is a sprawling structure with lines to almost all major hubs in the country.

WHEN BOMBAY MET CALCUTTA

Calcutta and Bombay, port towns of no commercial importance prior to the coming of the East India Company (EIC), became cities and, subsequently, hubs from where the railway network spread into mainland India. It was inevitable then that railway lines would connect these two cities someday. The Howrah–Allahabad–Bombay line, as it was called, opened for operations in 1870 when the line from the east met the line from the west at the town of Jubbulpore, right in the centre of India.

Jubbulpore (modern-day Jabalpur) is about 50 km from the point considered to be the geographical centre of India. Before its annexation by the British in 1817, Jubbulpore had long been ruled by the indigenous Gond kings of the land, and later by the Bhonsles, the Maratha clan from Nagpur. The traditional trade route from Nagpur (in modern-day Maharashtra), to Mirzapore (Mirzapur, in modern-day Uttar Pradesh), passed through Jubbulpore. That it would be a major junction in the route connecting east to west was quickly understood by both the Great Indian Peninsula Railway (GIPR) and East Indian Railway (EIR).

Meeting in the middle
Work had already begun by the mid-1860s to connect the EIR line from Calcutta to the GIPR line from Bombay. The 1,180-km distance from Calcutta to Jubbulpore went via Allahabad and the railway route from Howrah (Calcutta) to Naini Junction (Allahabad) had already been completed. Work on the Allahabad–Jubbulpore section – a distance of about 360 km – was completed in 1867. The line opened for general traffic on 1 August 1867, and the route closely followed the Mirzapore road. The route to the west was designed to go from Jubbulpore to Itarsi (in modern-day Madhya Pradesh), another major junction in central India.

One of the most daunting construction works done on this line was building the rail bridge over the Narmada River. *The Imperial Gazetteer of India*, quoting the report of the administration of the Central Provinces, mentions that large quantities of building material came from exhuming the remains of temple edifices and ancient cities found in shapeless masses covered with earth that had accumulated over the centuries.

Epidemics and other woes
Engineers involved in the construction of the line faced numerous problems, including difficulties in the supply of girders and good-quality sleepers, not to mention the inhospitable, hilly terrain, and thick, mosquito-infested jungles. Outbreaks of epidemics, such as cholera and smallpox, were common and caused a large number of deaths among the construction labourers. Mr Smith, the executive officer-in-charge, died of cholera even as the inspector of works, Mr Boast, succumbed to smallpox.

In a letter dated 14 August 1869, the chief engineer Robert Maitland Brereton wrote to the GIPR agent that the severity of cholera and smallpox had kept a large number of the usual hands from upper India away from work. As a consequence, labour was imported from Poona and the Deccan districts. He records, "I am satisfied

◄ **The fourth Viceroy and Governor-General of India** was Lord Mayo. A lot of infrastructure development in railways and expansion of roads took place during this tenure. He was assassinated in 1872 while visiting a penal colony in Port Blair in the Andaman islands.

that but for the extraordinary exertions of the engineers and the contractors, it would not have been possible to have had the through line to Jubbulpore before the cold season of 1870–71." The line from Bombay finally reached Jubbulpore on 8 March 1870.

A link is established
Among the galaxy of eminent persons present at Jubbulpore on 8 March, 1870 was Alfred, the Duke of Edinburgh, who was on a visit to India. Lord Mayo, the Viceroy and Governor-General of India (1869–72), travelled by train from Bombay with the Governor of Bombay, Sir Seymour Fitzgerald. Other dignitaries present included the Commander-in-Chief of India, the British Resident at Hyderabad, and the Indian kings of Rewa, Holkar, Panna, and Maihar, among others.

Immediately upon reaching the station, there was a general rush to reach the point where the GIPR and EIR lines met. The Viceroy received a silver-plated hammer, which he used to strike the silver key that connected the two rails. He then handed over the hammer to the Duke of Edinburgh, who also gave the key a tap and the link between Bombay and Calcutta was officially opened.

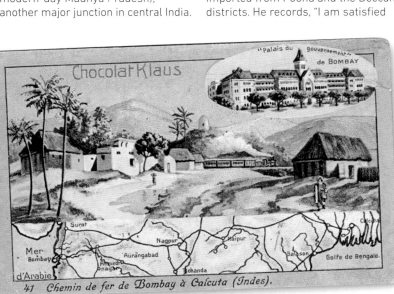

◄ **This Swiss chocolate company's collector's card** depicts an artist's impression of the railway line connecting Bombay to Calcutta.

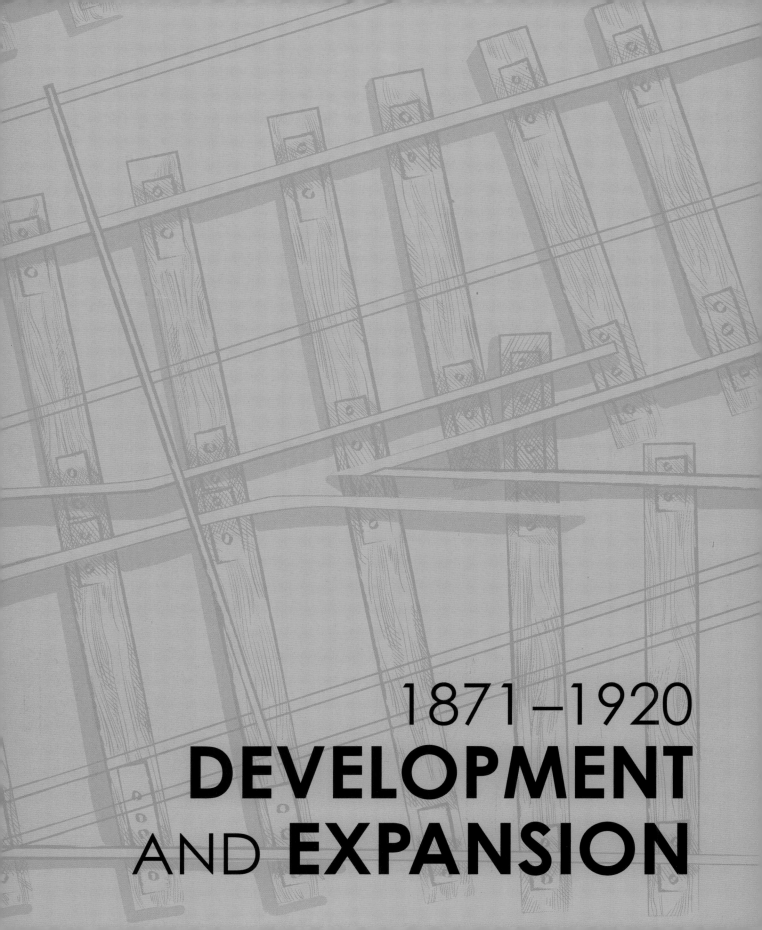

1871–1920
DEVELOPMENT
AND EXPANSION

1871–1920

Development, expansion, and ramifications were the key themes in this period. Processes and institutions associated with the railways became routine. The institution of the Railway Board in 1905 ushered in a centrally directed administration. This was also a time of great, almost monumental, construction. The railways were leaving their mark across the Indian countryside.

1873 The Great Indian Peninsula Railway (GIPR) introduces the Saunders air-cooling system in the first-class coaches.

1 January 1882 The Victoria Terminus, still under construction, is opened to the public. It is completed by May 1888.

1891 Toilet facilities are introduced in first-class carriages.

1874 Wadi–Secunderabad railway line financed by the Nizam of Hyderabad is built.

1893 The Jamalpur Locomotive Workshop set up the first railway foundry in India.

28 December 1885 The Indian National Congress is founded.

1875 A special train is built for the Prince of Wales' visit to India.

1871–80

1881–90

189

1880 The Darjeeling Steam Tramway starts services on the Siliguri–Darjeeling line.

1890 The Indian Railways Act defining the framework for railway construction and operation comes into being.

1895 India's first indigenous locomotive F1-734 is built in Ajmer.

1874–1880 Due to widespread famine, several railway lines are built to provide relief across India.

14 February 1873 The world's first commercial metre-gauge service runs from Delhi to Rewari.

1882 The Modified Guarantee Scheme is adopted.

1892 The diesel engine is patented in Germany. In India, the Assam Bengal Railway Company is incorporated.

Darjeeling Hill Railway (DHR)

Victoria Terminus station, circa 1910s

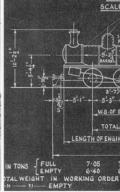

F1-734 blueprint

> " The **railway engineers** approached their task with a sense of high significance. **These were great works**, symbols of an Age, **tokens of an Empire**, even symptoms of a **Faith**, and their style was **deliberately** magnificent. "

JAN MORRIS, *STONES OF EMPIRE: THE BUILDINGS OF THE RAJ* (1983)

1899 Jamalpur produces its first steam locomotive, *Lady Curzon*.

1901 The Robertson Report leads to the formation of the first Railway Board in India.

1906 The largest railway station in India, the Howrah Terminus, is rebuilt and inaugurated.

1912 The world's first diesel-powered locomotive is operated on the Winterthur–Romanshorn railway in Switzerland.

1916 The Trans-Siberian Railway is completed.

1905 The Swadeshi movement begins in Calcutta and Bengal is partitioned.

1909 The Mysore Gold Fields bring India's first electric locomotives.

January 1915 Mohandas Karamchand Gandhi returns to India from South Africa.

10 January 1920 The League of Nations is formed.

13 April 1919 The Jallianwala Bagh Massacre takes place in Amritsar.

900   1901–10   1911–20

28 June 1914 Archduke of Austria, Franz Ferdinand, is assassinated, setting off World War I.

11 November 1918 Allies win the Battle of Mons, ending WW I.

1906 The Muslim League is founded in Dacca.

28 June 1919 The Treaty of Versailles is signed.

1911 Capital of India is shifted from Calcutta to Delhi.

1920 The Non-cooperation movement begins across India.

1900 The Upper Sone bridge, the longest in India at 3.06km, is built.

1902 The Jodhpur Railway introduces electric lights.

1907 The Railway Mail Service is established.

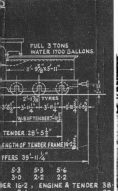

Howrah railway station

Assassination of Archduke Franz Ferdinand of Austria

ECONOMIC EXPERIMENTS

The railway network in India witnessed significant expansion through Government construction during the 1870s. Initially, the Government had to incur heavy expenditure by borrowing capital for the projects directly from British markets. In time, however, the reduction in the interest obligation on the "guaranteed" system was expected to partly offset this liability.

▼ **Up to 5.5 million people** are said to have died in the Great Famine of 1876–78. This illustration from *The Graphic* magazine, dated 26 May 1877, shows victims of the famine being served boiled rice at a relief camp.

In the decade spanning 1868–78, the Home government unfolded several policies of checks and balances and legislated norms of expenditure by the Government of India. A Select Committee of the British Parliament on Indian Finance laid down some restrictions to restrain the Government from exercising unbridled financial powers. It strongly recommended raising all loans in India, in order to cushion the impact on the rupee-pound sterling exchange rate.

Unforeseen liabilities

Around this time, a disquieting factor that hampered the financing of the railway infrastructure in India was the recurrence of scarcity and famines, a circumstance the establishment had not anticipated. In 1877, the Government scrambled to shore up its resources to 1.5 million pounds sterling, partly through fresh taxation, and the rest by exercising austerity measures. This resulted in the creation of the "Famine Insurance Fund", expressly

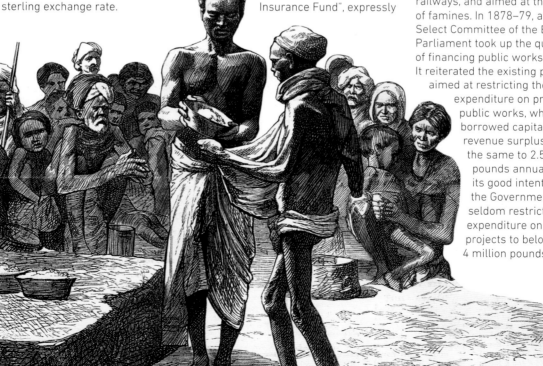

> **GOVERNANCE SYSTEM**
>
> After the Revolt of 1857, the control over India shifted from the mercantile East India Company (EIC) to the British Crown. An act, called the Government of India Act of 1858, was passed by the Parliament to bring this into effect. The restructuring that followed included breaking up of some parts of the "Presidencies" to form "provinces". Thereafter, the system of governance that came about entailed "British India", which included Presidencies and provinces directly administered by the British, and the "Princely States", which were governed by local rulers. The latter enjoyed some autonomy in exchange for recognition of British rule.

formed for catering to famine relief activities and the building of "productive" public works, including railways, and aimed at the prevention of famines. In 1878–79, a second Select Committee of the British Parliament took up the question of financing public works in India. It reiterated the existing policy aimed at restricting the annual expenditure on productive public works, whether from borrowed capital or of a revenue surplus, by limiting the same to 2.5 million pounds annually. Despite its good intentions, the Government could seldom restrict the annual expenditure on railway projects to below 3.5 to 4 million pounds.

Local investors

One of the heartening features of these new guidelines was the progressive interest and participation of Indian landowners, capitalists, and local governments in developing and managing the railway lines within their territories.

The Government on its part enabled this positive mood of Indian investors further by delegating to the provinces the power to raise debenture loans in the name of the secretary of state. The debenture holders were entitled to a share of the net profit of the enterprise. With the purchase of the East Indian Railway (EIR) by the Government in 1879, more and more local Governments came forward to participate in this great Indian railway "adventure". By the end of 1881, up to 1,390 km of railways were taken over by them. This pushed the use of cheaper Indian capital, reducing construction costs to a large extent.

Simultaneously, the Princely States started investing in the Government's railways. To begin with, many of the "political" lines were constructed either with the funding of or with direct participation of the Princes, namely the Nizam of Hyderabad, Gaekwad of Baroda, Holkar of Indore, and Scindia of Gwalior. Soon enough the States of Mysore, Bhavnagar, Gondal, and Bhopal joined in. Even the French and Portuguese territories of Pondicherry and Goa linked their railways with British India through reciprocal arrangements.

Economies of the gauges

The selection of the correct gauge for building railways in India had been the focus of deliberations right from the 1830s. Initially, the wider gauge of 5ft 6in was considered appropriate for the trunk routes due to its ability to carry larger volumes in this vast country. For the feeder lines, however, a plethora of unregulated gauges sprung up during the first two decades of railway construction. By 1870, the debate (see pp.70–71) intensified due to the rapid expansion

of the network all over the subcontinent. With the Government being the promoter, the issue of "cost" versus "carrying capacity" became the potent point of discussion. By this time, the Government had already defined financing policies for the "Commercial" or profitable lines and the "Political" lines, created for political or strategic reasons.

The balance sheet

In order to settle the issue, an expert committee was appointed during 1870–71. This committee delved into the masterplan of the railways, specially keeping in mind the views of the military establishment for the strategic north-western sector. Other factors to be borne were proposed interlinkages in various States, the cost implications for the creation of fixed stock (immovable structures such as train stations) and rolling stock (railway vehicles such as locomotives), including transhipment requirements across gauges as compared to the cost of creating a seamless, broad-gauge railway system all over India.

Based upon the cost-benefit analyses of proposed railways other than those created for strategic reasons, such as military needs (to give one example), the Government decided to accept the reality of multiple gauges, with two major networks, one on a broad gauge of 5 ft 6 in width and the other with a gauge of 3 ft 3⅜ in or 1 m, called the metre gauge. The subsidiary or feeder lines would be developed on narrow gauges as necessary. This era of Government construction ensured rapid expansion of the railway network in India.

By 1881, the Government railway system accounted for 3,862 km, the provincial railways covered 1,371 km, and the Princely States boasted of 692 km of network. The new policy regarding the gauges proved to be more economical vis-à-vis the average costs of construction and vindicated the Government's decision

to accept the multiple gauge formula. Freight and passenger tariffs were also reduced at this time.

Fiscal discipline

When a famine in Bengal and the North-Western Provinces led to an acute shortage of food grains, the EIR carried more food grains at a reduced tariff to the stricken areas. The results were remarkable as large profits ensued, and for the first time the railways added to the Government's coffers. Between 1879 to 1881, the Madras Railway and the EIR lowered their third-class passenger fares, reaping immediate benefits. The railways now began encashing upon volumes by increasing revenues through reduced tariffs and economy in expenditure also began to show a reduction in the cost of running trains.

Revenue generation and a prudent project financing policy had indeed proved beneficial to the railways. These measures, however, were hardly adequate to render the railway system profitable just yet.

▲ **Insignia of various Princely State railways** operated either as part of the Government railways or as separate administrations.

THE MODIFIED GUARANTEE SYSTEM

Connecting the country through railways enhanced the general financial health of the Government of India through improved revenue streams and an increase in trade. However, the enterprise was still making losses. By 1880, the Government was convinced that developing railways in the country required deeper pockets, and it began looking at a revised management policy based on its previous learnings.

▲ **This M 4-6-0 steam locomotive** ran on the metre-gauge Jodhpur–Bikaner railway line that began operations in 1882.

Insignia of the EIR

Within three decades of the launch of railways in India, and many financial experiments later, the Government of India once more begun to feel that the enterprise's fiscal responsibility needed to be shared by all its stakeholders and beneficiaries. It began encouraging provincial governments to build light, economical railway networks.

Fresh experiments
By the end of the year, the Darjeeling Steam Tramway Company opened its first section. State assistance was limited to free land and a guarantee from provincial revenues. Meanwhile, in 1879, the Government bought back the East Indian Railway (EIR) after 25 years, according to the contract

provision. This opened up a new financial arrangement of allowing the company to utilize its experience to manage and work the lines, while retaining State ownership. This became a successful template for many such future cases. In the years between 1880–84, a modified version of the Old Guarantee System (see p.30-31) evolved to attract private enterprise for railway construction.

In order to limit the escalation of interest pay-outs on sterling loans, the modifications, in most cases, entailed linking the "guarantees" with the value as well as the assured duration of the completion of railway projects. During this period, four contract templates were developed to suit the needs of prospective railway

companies. These also became the basis of the Government's efforts to work towards a policy framework of railway construction in the decades that followed.

Legislative confusions
In 1884, the Parliamentary Select Committee made recommendations on the railway construction policy in India, which resulted in a complicated variety of railway workings and owning agencies. Often, the Government made contradictory arrangements based on competition among various administrations within the Government, the restrictions on sterling pay-outs, and the politically strategic importance of the railway lines, to name a few. The *laissez-faire*

unleashed by such guidelines led to severe financial stress on the Government, which it had wanted to avoid all along. By 1886, the sky-rocketing guarantee liabilities led to the serious possibility of imposing fresh taxation. Instead, as a last resort, the Government halted assistance to all private enterprises that were using off-shore finance.

Local investors

The State found a way out of this financial dilemma in 1889 when it incorporated a non-sterling Indian company, namely the Delhi–Umballa–Kalka Railway Company. It was given land free of cost, and certain revenue-sharing deals and a percentage of assured dividend returns were struck. Its operations would be taken over by the EIR. The necessity of attracting Indian capital for investing in railway enterprise

prompted the Government to embark on a branch line policy. After a few experiments, the final policy was rolled out in 1896, for the construction of branch lines of less than 160 km in length, with Government support. Broadly, the terms were a modified form of the old Guarantee System.

In this case, apart from the free land, some of the points agreed upon were that the main line administration would have the first right to build branch lines. The Government guarantee, not exceeding 3 per cent, would be provided with a negotiated share of net profit. The capital account would be kept in rupees and the Government would retain the right to purchase the line after 21 years, the price for which would be based on a percentage of the line's earnings in the last three years.

Royal guarantees

The Modified Guarantee templates allowed for many financing options, which encouraged interested parties, such as the Princely States, to confidently invest in the railways' expansion within their territories. Various combinations of the deals ranged from agreements where these States would undertake the construction themselves or advance

money to the Government at a specific rate and profit sharing. These financial options, beneficial to both parties, relieved the British Indian exchequer of substantial up-front costs.

Moreover, the railways improved the economic welfare of the Princely States. However, as most of them opted for cheap, light lines, this decision loaded the railway network with added transhipment costs, affected speed, and led to capacity constraints.

In order to strengthen the "last mile" connectivity, the Government encouraged the establishment of both unassisted, industry-oriented, and District Board railways funded by stakeholders or through local revenues. The first such railway was built from Ledo to Margherita in Assam, northeast India, in 1883. It was used by the Assam Railways and Trading Company for extracting and transporting coal.

In 1901, Great Indian Peninsula Railway (GIPR) became a Government-owned company. An early Railway Board (see p.113) was constituted, but the powers were formally invested under the Viceroy. For the first time in its history, the railways in India began to make a profit.

▼ **The Bombay Port Railway** began operations in 1915 to facilitate the movement of cargo to and from the Bombay port.

BATTLE OF THE GAUGES

Viceroy Lord Dalhousie had always been adamant about India having a uniform, standard gauge. As soon as he left India, however, different viewpoints emerged, leading to a tussle between gauges, which continued to plague the country even after Independence.

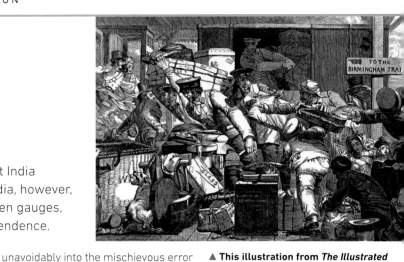

It did not matter to Dalhousie which gauge was approved – 6 ft (his preference), 4 ft 8½ in (that the East India Company [EIC] wanted), or 5 ft 6 in, the one that was finally chosen. All he wanted was a standard gauge.

This determination stemmed from Dalhousie's experience as the president of the Board of Trade, the British Government's commerce and industry department, where he had witnessed first-hand the negative impact of the British Railways using different types of gauges. In 1850, he wrote: "The British legislature fell unconsciously and perhaps unavoidably into the mischievous error of permitting the introduction of two gauges into the United Kingdom. The numerous and grievous evils which arose from that permission are well known and will long be felt throughout all England. The Government of India has in its power, and no doubt will carefully provide that, however widely the railway system may be extended in this Empire in the time to come, these great evils should be averted."

Little did he know that these "great evils" would make a comeback nearly two decades after he had left India, turning the country's railways lines

▲ **This illustration from *The Illustrated London News*** of 6 June 1846 depicts the commotion that would ensue as the carriage shifted gauges. Dalhousie tried to avoid this situation in India, but failed.

into a hotch-potch of gauges. The challenging process of standardizing the gauges would only begin in the 1990s with Project Unigauge (see box).

A case for different gauges

Dalhousie left India in 1856 and by the 1860s, strong advocates for narrower gauge lines emerged.

▼ **The Rajputana–Malwa Railway,** a metre-gauge line, connected Delhi with Ajmer, Indore, and Ahmedabad. It was known as the Rajputana State Railway until 1882.

They refuted earlier safety concerns and instead extolled the advantages of the narrow gauge, including the low cost of construction and maintenance. They also noted the advantages of building these lines in areas that could not profit from the more expensive broad-gauge lines.

The Indian Branch Railway Company was one of the first to build a line on a smaller gauge. Built at a cheaper cost, this special 4ft-gauge ran from the East Indian Railway's (EIR) Nalhati station to Azimgunj (in present-day West Bengal), and opened to traffic in December 1863. The EIR took over the line in 1872 and altered it to broad gauge. In 1865, the Indian Tramway Company opened a line from Arakkonam to Little Conjeevaram in Madras on a 3ft 6in gauge, which was converted to a metre gauge in 1878.

The British Government in India agreed to allow for a break in the gauge, as long as it was provisional, and would not compete with the standard broad gauge. In 1869, Lord Lawrence, the Viceroy of India (1864–69), initiated a serious

discussion with the British administration in London on gauge change in a detailed minute. The railways were in a terrible financial condition. Building the lines had been expensive as had been their maintenance, and the profits were small. While acknowledging the importance of the expansion of lines, he wrote that it was important to at least consider adopting narrower gauges in some areas, instead of ruling them out completely. He also advocated for Government-constructed and Government-run railways. His successor, Lord Mayo (1869–72), reiterated the economic viability of narrower gauge lines until finally the administration agreed, and in early 1871 fixed it at 3ft 3⅜in.

Breaking the gauge

The debate did not end here and even found its way to Britain and the House of Commons. Assurances had to be given to the Members of Parliament that the introduction of different gauges would be carefully considered.

This happened as the construction on the highly strategic frontier lines of the Indus Valley and Lahore to Peshawar (in present-day Pakistan) began, using the metre gauge. Following a huge hue and cry in England, the secretary of state had to reconsider using the metre gauge for places of military importance. After four years of debate, the frontier lines were built using the standard broad gauge (5ft 6in) rails.

The Government's plan now was to use two gauges. The trunk lines would be broad gauge to serve key stations, which were of economic and military or strategic importance. They alone would have access to the ports. The narrower metre gauge would be used as secondary lines for areas that were not profitable.

The rise of the metre gauge

Between the late 1800s and early 1900s, metre-gauge lines had started making a real impact. They expanded from the north and east of the River

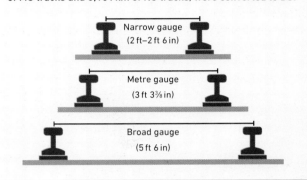

Ganges into the states of Rajasthan and Gujarat (the Rajputana–Malwa line was on a metre gauge) and also towards the south and west of Bombay and Madras. Canadian historian Ian J Kerr noted that some metre-gauge lines were no longer "subservient" to the broad gauge, but had become "competitors".

Metre-gauge lines had become more efficient with improved rolling stock and soon connected other lines, giving them access to the economic hubs previously reserved for the broad gauge. "The prospect of two competing national rail networks operating on different gauges emerged and regional competition became an actuality where lines of different gauges crossed or paralleled one another," wrote Kerr.

He noted that independent India, in 1947, had three different types of gauges criss-crossing the countryside. There were 24,029 km of broad-gauge and 15,752 km of metre-gauge lines. The two connected at 53 trans-shipment points including the crucial Mokameh Ghat in Bihar. The third type included 2,290 km of narrow-gauge lines.

ROYAL RAILS

There was a major shift in the ownership and management of the railways by the late 19th century. Private British companies were no longer the sole beneficiaries. Instead there were 33 separate administrations ranging from State-owned lines that were worked by private companies, State-owned and State-worked lines, lines owned and worked by private companies under new and old contracts, and District Board lines.

▲ **This sun-shaped insignia** belongs to the Jaipur State Railway, which was owned by the Princely State of Jaipur.

▲ **Opened in 1906,** the Gwalior Light Railway (GLR) was a narrow-gauge railway built by Maharaja Scindia of Gwalior. Its lines were changed to broad gauge in 2010.

The Princely States of India also jumped into the fray to build and own railways across their realms. In 1902, for instance, the railways were worked by five such States. Some were a part of the Government railway system and others, such as the Nizam of Hyderabad's State Railway, had their own separate administration.

This was a far cry from the early years when the British Government in India did not invite Indian States to take part in railway construction. It may have been a political decision then but the cash-strapped Government soon accepted the advantages of including the Princely States in developing the railways. It was not just monetary support, but also served distinct military and trade purposes. It was no surprise then that by 1950, in independent India, the lines had expanded considerably to about 11,265 km of which 1,609 km, noted British historian JN Westwood, were "worked by adjacent main-line railways". Of them, the Nizam's railway was the longest at 2,212 km.

Providing financial aid
As the Indian States started vying for railway lines, three systems fell into place. There were Princely States that funded, constructed, and managed the lines themselves or handed the work to the main companies. Some such as Morvi, Bhavnagar, Jodhpur, Bikaner, Gwalior, and Baroda fell into this category with lines opening up between 1873–1900. Then there were those who provided money to the

Government of India in exchange for interest, a share of profits, or certain privileges, as did Maharaja Holkar of Indore or the Scindia Railways. The Government was in charge of construction and management.

The Nizam's and the Mysore State Railways followed the third system wherein they signed a contract with guaranteed companies who managed the lines as well as the construction and working of the extension. It was partly funded by the Princely States.

The Princely pioneers
In the early 1850s, the Government of India obtained concessions from the royal Gaekwad (the ruling family's name) of Baroda so that the Bombay Baroda and Central India (BB&CI) Railway could build a line between Bombay and Gujarat. By the early 1860s, the Gaekwad had decided to build a narrow-gauge line of his own between Miyagam, a village in Gujarat on the BB&CI line and Dabhoi, a key trade centre about 32 km away.

It was initially supposed to be a light tramway drawn by bullocks, but the line was repaired the following year. Bridges were strengthened, the stations built and staffed, and the line opened for use in April 1873. Through the 1880s, the Gaekwad paid the Government of India to build a series of light railway lines across his state connecting the towns with BB&CI railway stations. A workshop was built as well near Pratapnagar,

► **Shah Jahan Begum** who was also known as the Begum of Bhopal, jointly built the Bhopal–Itarsi Railway with the Government of India. The Begum provided the land free of cost and the Government offered capital for construction.

Gujarat, to repair locomotives. The Nizam of Hyderabad and Maharaja Holkar of Indore, rulers of their respective States, followed suit with the former providing 1 million pounds sterling to build a line from Wadi on the Great Indian Peninsula Railway (GIPR) line to Hyderabad. This opened for traffic in October 1874.

Connecting the heartland
Similarly, the British wanted to develop Central India, which had no railways at that time – GIPR and the East Indian Railway (EIR) ended at Khandwa (in present-day Madhya Pradesh) and Agra respectively.

Lord Mayo, Viceroy of India (1869–72), was keen to connect the GIPR line to Indore and then Neemuch and Ajmer (in present-day Rajasthan), for strategic and trading purposes. After long negotiations that lasted five to six months, Holkar of Indore gave the Government of India 1 million pound sterling to construct the Khandwa–Indore line.

In exchange, he would receive an interest of 4.5 per cent per annum and half the surplus net profits. By 1878, lines were open across the region, including Sanawad, Mortakka, Choral, Indore, and the important Mhow, because of its military base. Lines on the Holkar State Railway handled most of Malwa's export and import.

Maharaja Scindia of Gwalior followed suit. He offered the Government of India a loan of 750,000 pounds sterling to construct the Gwalior–Agra line followed by another payment of the same amount to build the Indore–Neemuch line. Following the success of Holkar and Scindia, the British hoped that the royal family of Bhopal would join too, which they did, and the Bhopal–Itarsi Railway was built with the Government paying for sections in its territory as well as half the cost of the bridge over the Nerbudda (Narmada). The Itarsi–Hoshangabad section opened in June 1882 and

the Hoshangabad–Bhopal section opened in November 1884. The royal state of Rajpipla (in present-day Gujarat) got its first stretch of a 30 km line in 1897. It connected to the BB&CI railway line at Ankleshwar and was extended to Nandod in 1917 with the construction of the Karjan River bridge.

▲ **Lord Willingdon,** Governor of Bombay (1913–19), cutting a ribbon on a railway bridge over River Karjan to inaugurate the Rajpipla Railway in Gujarat in 1917.

THE ROBERTSON REPORT
Concerned over the multiple lines and administrations that had come about, the Government of India requested the British Government to send an expert to advise on the situation. Of these, the Robertson Report is revealing for its time period. Sir Thomas Robertson, the expert, spent months travelling across the country on an all-expenses-paid visit and submitted, what historian JN Westwood calls, was an "ill-written string of platitudes". Lord Curzon, the Viceroy of India (1899–1905), cancelled his passage home and made him rework the report. The results are quite astonishing. In 1902, there were about 41,000 km in operation. Of this, the Government was financially responsible for around 32,000 km, but controlled about 9,600 km. His recommendations led to the formation of an early version of the Railway Board in 1901.

NIZAM'S STATE RAILWAY

Plans to connect the Princely State of Hyderabad by rail can be traced back to 1845. For the British, Hyderabad, the Nizam's territory, was not just a valuable market but also a strategic location to station troops in case of threats by neighbouring Princely States.

Arrangements for the construction of the railways were made by a British administrator, Sir Richard Temple, during the reign of Nizam Afzal-ud-Daulah (1857–69). The Nizam was not too keen at first, however discussions continued between his prime minister, Salar Jung I, and the British.

Finally, in 1870, Lord Minto, the Viceroy of India (1869–72) signed an agreement with Salar Jung to establish lines across the State on behalf of the new Nizam, Asaf Jah (1869–1911). They were to build a railway line from close to Gulbarga (present-day Kalaburagi) to Hyderabad. This came to be called the Nizam's State Railway and it was the exclusive property of the Nizam's Government, receiving all the profits.

Soon, funds were a concern, which led to the formation of the Nizam State Railway Company in 1873. The line for Hyderabad took off from Wadi (in present-day Karnataka), instead of Gulbarga, which was a bigger city in comparison and was far more beneficial for trade. However, the purpose of the railway line was, after all, military. The almost 320-km Wadi–Secunderabad section opened on 8 October 1874.

In the following years, new lines were added, connecting towns and cities across the State. However, financial difficulties continued to dog the company with construction costs bleeding Hyderabad's coffers.

Then, the Nizam's Guaranteed State Railway (NGSR) Company, which was a British company, came into being. It was to extend the railways in the Nizam's dominions, including profitable regions where iron, coal, and copper were available in plenty. In December 1883, this new British company signed an agreement. According to it, the Nizam's Government would deliver the existing railway lines freed from all encumbrances and claims to the company. The Nizam's Government was to also pay an annuity for 20 years. Thus, ending the story of the Nizam's State Railway.

Interestingly, when the NGSR was integrated in November 1951 into the Central Railway, it was the largest railway system run by any Indian Princely State. It was 2,351 km in length, of which 1,107 km was broad gauge and 1,244 km was metre gauge.

▶ **Mir Osman Ali Khan, Asaf Jah VII,** the last Nizam of Hyderabad, is seen here with his staff awaiting the arrival of Lord Willingdon, the 22nd Viceroy and Governor-General of India, in 1933 at the platform of the Nampally station. The station was commissioned by the Nizam in 1907 and is today known as the Hyderabad Deccan station.

SALOONS AND COACHES

In the early days of the railways, many high-ranking British officials and royals were interested in utilizing this new mode of travel. By the 1880s, many of them had begun commissioning personal railway saloons, which were lavishly decorated and reflected the status of their owners. Some of these were used for field checks and inspections by railway officers. As there was limited standardization, numerous styles of passenger coaches came into being.

▶ Prince of Wales Saloon

Year Introduced	1875–76
Gauge	Metre
Type	Saloon
Built by	Agra Workshops, Rajputana Malwa Railway
Number of Wheels	4

This saloon was specially designed for Albert Edward, Prince of Wales at the time, and later for King Edward VII, during his visit to India for the Royal Durbar of 1875–76. It had seats for four armed guards and windows fitted with sunshades. The wooden outer shell was decorated with emblems signifying the British Crown.

▲ Viceregal Dining Car

Year Introduced	1889
Gauge	Metre
Type	Saloon
Built by	Ajmer Workshops of Bombay Baroda and Central India Railway
Number of Wheels	8

This was part of the five-coached Viceregal train built for the Viceroy. Coloured white on the outside, this wooden dining car had a water filter, crockery cupboard, space for four armed guards, and vacuum brakes. The inside was decorated with wooden carvings. The original plain bearings were later replaced with roller bearings.

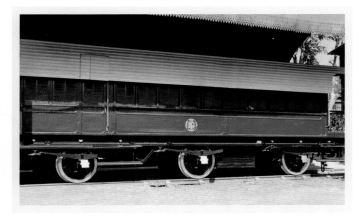

▲ Gaekwad Baroda Saloon

Year Introduced	1886
Gauge	Broad
Type	Saloon
Built by	Parel Workshops, Bombay Baroda and Central India Railway
Number of Wheels	6

This royal saloon was made for the royal family of the Gaekwads of Baroda (in present-day Gujarat). The inner ceiling was decorated with gold enamel. The saloon was also uniquely fitted with two outer axles controlled by a central spring system that would move to accommodate any curves of the railway tracks. The outer axles had vacuum and hand brakes.

▶ ERC 4910

Year Introduced	1890
Gauge	Broad
Type	Saloon
Built by	Central Workshop, Alambagh, Lucknow
Number of Wheels	4

This saloon was made for eminent personalities travelling along the Oudh and Rohilkhand Railway. It had a kitchen, a lavatory, and sunshades to keep the carriage cool. This wooden coach was also fitted with a steel underframe.

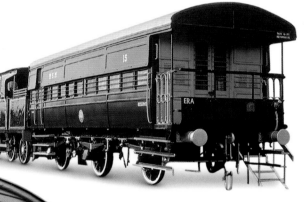

◀ **MSM 15**

Year Introduced	1914
Gauge	Broad
Type	Saloon
Built by	Southern Railway Workshops, Perambur
Number of Wheels	6

Originally numbered ERA-024, this saloon was built for railway officers travelling for inspections. It had a veranda, a kitchen, and a servant's compartment. It ran on the Madras and Southern Mahratta Railway and was later used on the South Central Railway.

▼ **ART Van 404 KSR**

Year Introduced	1903
Gauge	Narrow
Type	Coach
Built by	GR Turner Ltd, Langley Hill, UK
Number of Wheels	4

This coach was part of the Kalka–Shimla line's Accident Relief Train, a crucial safety measure on the hazardous hill railway. Functioning as an accident tool van, the coach carried necessary material for the gang working on track maintenance.

◀ **Nilgiri Coach**

Year Introduced	1919
Gauge	Metre
Type	Coach
Built by	Southern Railway Workshops, Perambur
Number of Wheels	8

This meter-gauge wooden coach was used on the steep Nilgiri Mountain Railway. It accommodated eight passengers in the first class and 44 in the third class. It had canvas curtains that helped to block out the harsh sun and hot winds encountered during summers.

MYSORE MAHARAJA SALOON

Mysore was one of the more developed Princely States in British India. The rulers were great patrons of art and culture and readily embraced the railways in the late 1870s. The Mysore Maharaja Saloon combines the two aspects beautifully. While representing a different side of railways, it also makes evident that railways had permeated all sections in Indian society.

THE ROYAL CARRIAGE

Stationed at the National Rail Museum in New Delhi, this saloon was used by Maharaja Krishnaraja Wadiyar (1884–1940), the 24th ruler of Mysore. It was built in 1899 at the Bangalore Workshop of the Mysore State Railway. Originally, it was part of a three-carriage train that also included the Maharani's coach (CR-7342) and a dining-cum-kitchen car (CR-7345), both of which are preserved at the Mysore Rail Museum. By a simple change of the undercarriage, the saloon could be used on both broad-gauge and meter-gauge tracks.

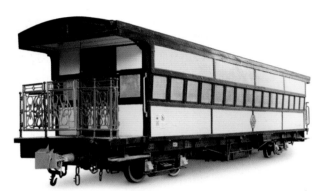

FULL VIEW OF THE SALOON

SIDE SHOWING THE VESTIBULE SYSTEM

Coat of arms
The official emblem of Mysore incorporated the two-headed bird, referred to as *Gandaberunda* in Hindu mythology. The bird is flanked by a lion on each side. The emblem affixed on the saloon's exterior establishes its royal identity.

SPECIFICATIONS			
Number of wheels	8	Gauge	Broad and meter gauge convertible
Manufactured	Bangalore Workshop	Restored by	Hubli Workshop

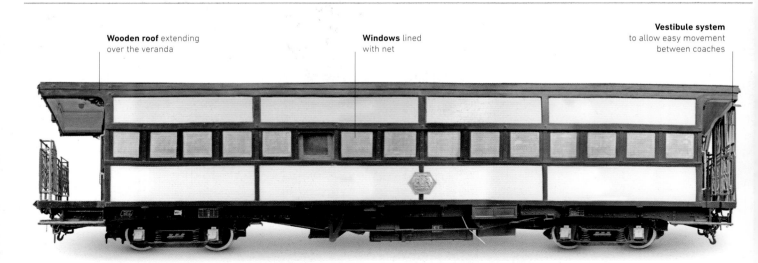

Wooden roof extending over the veranda

Windows lined with net

Vestibule system to allow easy movement between coaches

The royal carriage
The luxurious saloon boasted a comfortable bedroom, fit for its royal occupants. Each element was tastefully decorated and has been restored to its former glory, including original furnishings, upholstery, and electrical fittings.

EXTERIOR PARTS

The saloon has a wooden body and a steel underframe. At both ends, it has small verandas covered by an extended roof, and surrounded by intricately designed brass railings. One of the verandas has a provision for a vestibule system. It is one of the earliest coaches to have this system.

1. Fenced veranda **2.** Metal plate
3. Undercarriage **4.** Metal wheel
5. Shocker **6.** Doorknob painted bright gold **7.** Vestibule system

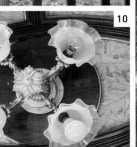

SALOON INTERIOR

The spacious saloon has a living room and a bedroom, interconnected by a passageway. It also has a bathroom with a foldable sink. With wooden panels, a leafy pattern on the ceiling, meticulously carved designs, fancy electrical fittings, furniture, and regal upholstery, its interiors embody the luxurious taste of Indian royalty.

8. View of the bedroom from the entrance **9.** Fan regulator or switch **10.** Brass chandelier **11.** Bathroom with a bathtub, pot, and a foldable sink **12.** Overhead storage space **13.** Emergency chain **14.** Four-bladed ceiling fan fitted within a circular design **15.** Passageway connecting the two rooms **16.** Framed portrait of Maharaja Krishnaraja Wadiyar **17.** Wooden door with glasswork **18.** View of the sitting room **19.** Sleeping berth

THE EXPANSION BOOM

The beginning of the 20th century saw large-scale expansion of rail lines across the country. Railway tracks reached everywhere; development soon followed.

> " ... no engineer who has seen the place can **withhold** his tribute of **admiration** to the patient skill that has daily faced disaster. "

FROM THE *PIONEER*, 3 MAY 1893, ON THE CONSTRUCTION AT MUD GORGE ON THE HARNAI–BOSTAN LINE IN THE NORTH-WESTERN FRONTIER

► **Building railway bridges** in remote regions of the country in the 19th century meant transporting heavy raw materials as well as labour to hard-to-reach places.

The dawn of the 1870s brought with it a vision of a complex network of lines, which would connect every part of the country. By the 1920s, this was on its way to completion as lines managed by various administrations, mushroomed across states.

Between 1869 and 1881, railway lines laid down went from 6,800 km to 15,900 km, with around 1,500 km laid just in 1878–79. By March 1922, 59,973 km had opened for use. India now had one of the longest railway systems in the world. The key focus areas included the North-West Frontier Province, Burma (see pp.174–75), and Rajputana, some significant for military and strategic reasons, others as a solution to the famines that had afflicted many parts of the country in 1860–70.

Expanding into the interiors

If 1870 marked the meeting of the Calcutta and Bombay lines in Jubbulpore (see pp.60–61), the following year saw the Madras and Bombay tracks converge at Raipur in Central India. This was significant as it connected all three seats of power, Calcutta, Madras, and Bombay.

The Bombay, Baroda and Central India (BB&CI) Railway made significant inroads at this time with the help of lines run or financed by the Princely States. The Rajputana–Malwa Railway line introduced a shorter connection between Bombay, Agra, and Delhi, and reached Ajmer, Ahmedabad, Indore, and Neemuch in the west.

The crucial Assam connection (see pp.94–95) came up at this time, as did the iconic hill railway system in the north. The south too, saw extensive growth after 1873 with the opening of more than 900 km of lines, which played a huge role during the famines. In the late 1870s, a line between Pondicherry and Villupuram emerged after a British–French agreement.

Famine relief

From 1872 to 1890, India faced a series of famines, which resulted in more than four million deaths. The 160-km-line connecting Patna to Tirhut in Bihar was a relief to the famine-hit region in 1874 as was the 88.5-km-long line from the left bank of the River Ganges to Darbhanga (in Bihar), built in 65 days to provide support to famine-stricken areas.

In 1880, a Famine Commission was set up, which noted the urgency of the situation and suggested extending lines further to help facilitate relief work.

Guarding the frontier

Craggy, isolated, and inhospitable, the North-West Frontier lines had always been on the British agenda as the line of defence against the hostile Afghans. After three Anglo-Afghan Wars and a looming threat from Russia, ensuring reliable, all-weather access to the Frontier was of utmost importance.

By 1865, Karachi and Amritsar were connected by the Scinde, Punjab and Delhi Railway (SP&DR). Around 917 km of this were via the Indus Steam Flotilla, an unreliable service susceptible to the vagaries of the Indus River. The Punjab Northern State Railway running from Lahore to Rawalpindi also sought to connect Gujarat, crossing three rivers – Ravi, Chenab, and Jhelum.

The Kandahar State Railway's purpose was to connect Quetta in Balochistan (in present-day Pakistan) with the rest of India. It is important to note that the name was somewhat of a misnomer. The line never reached Kandahar, but stopped at Chaman, close to the Afghanistan border.

The first link to Quetta was through the Bolan Pass and opened in 1886. The start of its construction met with a massive obstacle. The proposed Sukkur–Sibi line was 215 km, which crossed a flat, uninhabited desert. For work to commence, labourers, rolling stock, and food were transported to this region. Lines were laid at record speed – the fastest being the day when 1.6 km was completed in two hours.

The final stretch was built in over 101 days and made ready by January 1880, as the Second Anglo-Afghan war was raging in the region.

The bigger challenge was cutting through mountains to get to Quetta. The line crossed the grand Nari Gorge six times. It then passed through the towns of Harnai, Kost, and Bostan, all in present-day Pakistan. Workers and engineers had to deal with tribal attacks as well as disease – one cholera outbreak led to the death of 2,000 out of 10,000 workers. The bridge across Chappar Rift (see p.97) and a nearly 8-km mud gorge of gypsum clay, which turned thick and murky when wet, were significant challenges. Much of the line was destroyed in a flash flood in 1942 and the line was never rebuilt. This line is no longer in operation.

The present Mushkaf–Bolan line via the Bolan Pass was completed in 1895 and was the most successful in ensuring an all-weather connection to Quetta. It had magnificent bridges and castle-like tunnels. British author PSA Berridge in his book *Couplings to the Khyber* said: "there is a rugged grandeur about this sinister place" as though the engineers were "bent on maintaining a standard of construction in keeping with nature's handiwork".

In 1886, all the lines in this region, including several smaller companies, merged to become the State-managed North Western Railway. These connected Delhi with Amritsar, Lahore, Karachi, Quetta, and the Khyber Pass till Partition in 1947.

▲ **Cutting through mountains** to build the tunnel and bridge in Quetta was a massive obstacle while building the Kandahar State Railway.

THE HILL RAILWAYS

Cooler climes reminiscent of Britain made the hills a popular escape for the British. With the Revolt of 1857 came the realization that these towns could also be strategically vital for the military. A flurry of rail construction followed, seeking to link them to the plains. Today, mountain railway systems are unique not only for the connectivity they provide, but also for the views they offer.

A traveller in the 1880s had this observation to make on the laying down of railway lines in the hills of West Bengal: "Men said it was a small thing, the *butcha* (child) of the larger evil that came to Siliguri. It did not burst the bellies of men, but its shriek brought on sickness and many of those working on the line were down with malaria. The line crept forward and one day when the engine came to Darjeeling all were filled with fear, men heard the distant rumble of wheels from behind trees and watched the monster creep into the station."

The "great fire-eater" was now conquering the "hills" as the British called places such as Darjeeling and Simla in the north and Ootacamund in the south. These towns had mushroomed and flourished as popular escapes for the British during the hot Indian summers or as sanatoriums for invalids.

A touch of home
British author and editor of *Railway Times* in 1845–47, Hyde Clarke noted the growing importance of "English towns" in the Himalayas and the Nilgiris, especially after the Revolt of 1857, in his work *Colonization, Defence, and Railways in Our Indian Empire*. Darjeeling, Ootacamund (Ooty), Simla, Soobathoo (Subathu), Dalhousie, and Almorah, he wrote, were almost like capitals competing with cities such as Agra, Calcutta, Madras, and Bombay, for importance. With the climate more suited to the English, these hill towns had become seasonal residences of the Viceroys of India and other senior government officials. Clarke recommended "colonization" of these hill stations as it would "give us a hold which can never be shaken off. In those settlements will be maintained a larger force than is now kept up, and it will be maintained at English pay in English health and efficiency."

However, the arduous and expensive journeys to these places excluded everyone but the rich. Building railway lines to the hill capitals was, therefore, imperative, not just for the British morale, but also to retain their hold over India.

Entering the hills
Initially, building railways in the hills was viewed by the British as an unprofitable venture that required high investment. However, this changed when five remarkable hill railway systems were built across the country. The Darjeeling Himalayan Railway (DHR) opened in 1881 and was the first of its kind (see pp.86–87), famous for its complicated loops and reversing stations. Its highest point, at around 2,300 m, is Ghoom (or Ghum), also one of the highest railway stations in the world. The Kalka Shimla Railway (KSR), one of the most surveyed lines at the time, opened for use in 1903. Its bridges and tunnels, including the 1.14-km-long Barog Tunnel (see p.101), set it apart from the others. On the outskirts of Bombay, the Matheran Light Railway (MLR) with its steep curves opened in 1907. The Nilgiri

◄ **The Neral–Matheran toy train** covers 21 km to the Matheran hill station in Maharashtra. The train was relaunched in January 2018 with upgraded brakes and a modified engine.

Mountain Railway (NMR) followed in 1908, as unusual as its counterpart in the east, except that its uniqueness lay in the rack system and X Class steam locomotives. The Kangra Valley Railway (KVR), a late entrant in 1927, provided services to Dalhousie, Dharamshala, and Palampur, and is known for its breathtaking scenery.

Today, the Darjeeling, Kalka Shimla, and Nilgiri railways have been designated UNESCO World Heritage Sites under the Mountain Railways of India as "they applied bold and ingenious engineering solutions to the problem of establishing an effective rail link across a mountainous terrain of great beauty. They are still fully operational as living examples of the engineering enterprise of the late 19th and early 20th centuries."

Train from the west
Unlike the other hill railways, the one connecting Neral to Matheran, in present-day Maharashtra, stands out as a line conceived, funded, and built by an Indian. A mountain tabletop in the Western Ghats, Matheran was a popular resort for

the British and wealthy Indians, such as Abdul Hussain Peerbhoy, the son of Bombay-based business magnate Sir Adamjee Peerbhoy. Keen to build a narrow-gauge line to his favourite getaway, Abdul Hussain formed the Matheran Steam Light Tramway Company with a capital of Rs 10 lakh. He obtained the authorization for construction in July 1904 and the line began service in 1907. The fleet included four articulated, 0-6-0T locomotives that he bought from Orenstein and Koppel in Germany and a Darjeeling Class "A", 0-4-0 ST engine, which was later withdrawn. About 19 km long, with an average gradient of 1 in 25, the line has 221 curves, the sharpest with a radius of around 18 m, and one tunnel.

The Kangra connection
Inspired by the success of the other hill railways, work on the connection from Pathankot in Punjab to Joginder Nagar in Kangra, in present-day Himachal Pradesh, began in 1925. Built initially to assist with freight for the Uhl hydroelectric project in 1928, the line opened for passengers in April 1929. While there are only two tunnels across the distance of about 195 km, the line has 993 bridges, 484 curves, and ascends at a gradient of 1 in 25. During World War II, portions of its track were removed to assist with the war effort and reconstructed in 1954.

▼ **The Kangra Valley Railway** passes through Joginder Nagar, a hill station near Palampur in Himachal Pradesh. This narrow-gauge line once carried heavy machinery shipped from Britain to the Shanan Power House, almost 2 km away from Joginder Nagar.

THE TOY TRAIN

The Darjeeling Himalayan Railway (DHR) is known for much more than its spectacular views. A UNESCO World Heritage Site today, its sharp curves, tortuous loops, and zigzag traverses represent an era of innovation and groundbreaking engineering.

▲ **The narrow-gauge** trains of the Darjeeling Himalayan Railway run on an elevation that varies from 100 m to 2,200 m, and cross through semi-tropical valleys, tea plantations, lush forests, and villages.

"It seems almost sacrilegious to desecrate those lofty crags with man's petty contrivances," commented writer DT Timins in the 1897 October edition of *The Railway Magazine*, as he gazed at the mountains on his maiden train journey to Darjeeling. Yet, with the passing of each steep curve and formidable loop, through tea gardens, dense forests, and deep ravines, he could not help but wax eloquent on "one of the most marvellous triumphs of modern engineering skill." The 88-km, 2-ft line connecting Siliguri to Darjeeling in West Bengal quickly became a favourite among travellers and rail enthusiasts. Its beginnings can be attributed to the vision of Franklin Prestage, an Eastern Bengal Railway agent, who first proposed the idea of a train connecting Darjeeling with the plains in 1878.

Darjeeling railway station signboard

Beginnings
Prestage believed that building the line was a good way of reducing costs for bullock cart transport for freight, such as rice, which cost "Rs 238 a ton in Darjeeling" compared to "Rs 98 in Siliguri". The scheme was approved in April 1879 and construction began at the end of that year. Built to closely follow Hill Cart Road that connected Darjeeling to Siliguri, the DHR was constructed in three phases and opened in 1881. Initially privately held, the Indian Government bought DHR in October 1948, one year after Independence, to assist with building a line to Assam (see pp.192–93).

Curves, reverses, and loops
The challenges of building the line to Darjeeling were apparent right from the start. It was not just the terrain, soil erosion, or the seemingly insurmountable task of cutting through the mountains. This was

the first time anyone had undertaken such an endeavour – of building a narrow-gauge line over 80 km of unknown terrain. The solution lay in innovative engineering.

The story goes that the engineer assigned to the task faced an unsolvable problem at the town of Tindharia, which happened to be the steepest portion on the line. Erosion on the hills did not allow for building a permissible gradient. Frustrated, he threw up his hands in despair when his wife said, "Darling if you can't go ahead, why don't you come back?" And so six "z-shaped reversing stations", similar to the one built by the Great Indian Peninsula Railway (GIPR) in Bhore Ghat (see pp.50–51), were used on this line. These had the steepest gradient of 1 in 18 and UNESCO noted that the combination of narrow gauge and "zigzag reverses" was the first of its kind in the world.

The line is equally significant for its loops that seem to take the train to the absolute edge of the mountain. Of the five loops, three are still operational and the sharpest, with a radius of about 18 m, is aptly named Agony Point. The famous Batasia Loop, with its view of the

snow-capped Kanchenjunga mountain, is the last as the line approaches Ghoom, which at 2,258 m is one of the highest railway station in the world.

The engines
If any locomotive defines a railway line, it is the DHR B Class. For many years these small, yet powerful, engines have hauled trains up the mountain. The first four were built in 1889 by UK-based Sharp, Stewart and Company. By 1927, the North British Locomotive Company of Glasgow, the Baldwin Locomotive Works of Philadelphia in the US, and the Tindharia Works in Bengal built a further 25. Nowadays, some B Class engines continue to run on the DHR, while several serve as retired exhibits in museums around India.

▼ **This DHR train passes** through the stretch between Ghoom to Sonada. The gradient here is the easiest.

> 66 The **royal Bengal tiger** is in great force there, and is very **bold and unconventional.** From this **lonely little station** a message once went to the **railway manager in Calcutta:** 'Tiger eating **station-master** on front porch; telegraph instructions'. 99
>
> MARK TWAIN ON THE DARJEELING HILL RAILWAY,
> *FOLLOWING THE EQUATOR: A JOURNEY AROUND THE WORLD* (1897)

The Batasia Loop on the Darjeeling Himalayan Railway (DHR) is considered one of the most remarkable engineering feats of its time. Also called a double spiral, this gravity-defying loop was commissioned in 1919. The entire DHR track is 82 km with an open view of more than 12 peaks, including Kanchenjunga, the third highest mountain in the world.

KALKA SHIMLA RAILWAY

n the beginning of the 19th century, Shimla (earlier known as Simla) had become a favourite with British officers seeking to escape the heat of the plains. By 1827, it became the summer capital of the Government of India.

The journey to Shimla was arduous. Coolies or mules hauled luggage as officers and their families traversed the route by horseback, sedan chairs, and doolies or stretchers. Travel became easier with the construction of a road and the beginning of the Kalka–Shimla Tonga Service. An easier route, however, had become imperative. The Delhi–Kalka line via Umballa (now Ambala) opened in March 1891 and talks began to extend it to Shimla. There were lengthy discussions on the type of line most suited to the terrain before the adhesion line made the final cut.

Finally, in June 1898, the secretary of state and the Delhi–Umballa–Kalka Railway Company signed a contract to construct a 2-ft-gauge line. The Government provided the land for free. Work began in earnest until the military recommended a change in the gauge for hilly areas. The contract was revised in 1901 and a part of the already-built line had to be changed accordingly.

The 95.66-km-line opened to traffic on 9 November 1903. The beginnings were not the best. In December 1903, snowfall damaged the track. Despite high fares, Kalka Shimla Railway (KSR) faced financial difficulties until the Government acquired the line in January 1905.

Immense engineering skill was required to build the line. The KSR has 988 bridges and viaducts, some with unique multi-arch masonry galleries, similar to Roman aqueducts. Of the 107 tunnels built between 1900 to 1903, 102 are still in operation. Each proved challenging and had to be lined during construction, as they passed through shale and soft rocks. Of these, Tunnel 33, popularly known as the Barog Tunnel, is the longest at 1.14 km. UNESCO designated the KSR a World Heritage Site in 2008 for its unique construction, significance, and role in "disenclaving" the hill communities.

The terminus station of Shimla, at an altitude of 2,075 m, was constructed in 1903 and rebuilt in 1921.

A train on the Kalka Shimla line passing through Kanoh Bridge, the highest arch gallery bridge of the Indian Railways, which was built in 1898.

Labourers from the Nilgiri Mountain Railway pause to take a picture with their supervisors next to the railway line. The rack system can be clearly seen in the centre.

NILGIRI MOUNTAIN RAILWAY

When Shah Rukh Khan, one of the most famous film stars of all time, gyrated to the Bollywood song "Chaiyya Chaiyya" atop a moving train as it crawled through the Nilgiri mountains, it is doubtful if the film-makers anticipated just how much the location and the railway line would become embedded in the hearts and minds of the audience.

The Nilgiri Mountain Railway (NMR) is a metre-gauge line that starts from Mettupalayam, a suburb in the city of Coimbatore in Tamil Nadu, and snakes its way through 13 tunnels, weaving past plantations and dense forests, crossing the River Bhawani, to reach the town of Udagamandalam (also known as Ooty), which is its final destination some 50 km away. The enormity of the challenge of building such a line sinks in with the passing of each curve, leaving no doubt that the NMR system is the perfect embodiment of the technology of its time.

Before the 1800s, the formidable terrain of the Nilgiris was inhabited by local tribes who kept most outsiders away. However, the first permanent house on the range was built in 1820 by John Sullivan, the British Collector of Coimbatore, and by 1827, a sanatorium had been established in Ooty. This was followed by the appointment of a military commandant in 1830. By 1870, the town had become the summer seat of the Madras governor and his secretariat. The Nilgiri range had now become significant to the British.

The first proposals to build a track were made as early as 1854 but the construction of the hill railway only began in 1891. The engineers were keen to avoid the reversing stations of Bhore Ghat (see pp.50–51) and the Darjeeling Himalayan Railway (DHR). Instead they decided on the latest innovation – the special rack railway system – modelled on the Abt rack and pinion system introduced in Germany's Harz Mountains in 1885. With this technology, the locomotive pulling the train is equipped with toothed pinions, or cogwheels, which engage the rack and provide the necessary traction to scale steep inclines.

Compared to the DHR, the NRM climbs at a higher speed and on steeper grades. From Mettupalayam to Kallar, the railway uses a metre-gauge line to cross the plains. The rack system begins at Kallar on the way to Coonoor; this route has a steep section with 208 curves, 13 tunnels, and a staggering 27 viaducts, including the stunning Burliar Bridge and the Adderley Viaduct. The line was completed in 1908 and run by various companies till it was incorporated into the Southern Railway in 1951. The NMR is a UNESCO World Heritage Site and a part of the Mountain Railways of India.

A postal stamp from 1993 showing the Nilgiri Mountain Railway

ASSAM CONNECTED

At a time when the railways connected key commercial, political, and military centres across British India, Assam in the northeast remained isolated. It had been a part of Bengal until its separation in 1874 and was commercially crucial to the British for its timber, coal, petroleum, as well as production and export of tea. With a steady increase in plantations across the region, there were up to 160 tea plantations by 1862. Quick and effortless connectivity with ports become imperative.

Insignia of the Assam Bengal Railway

An amalgam of the present-day Indian states of Arunachal Pradesh, Meghalaya, Mizoram, and Nagaland, Assam boasted of merciless, swampy terrains full of criss-crossing rivers and thick, unmanageable forests. In the 1830s, travellers to the port of Calcutta had to cross the Rivers Brahmaputra (20 km at its widest), Ganges, and its distributary Hooghly, an estuary that flows into the Bay of Bengal. This trip typically took four months and a rail link seemed the most obvious choice, given that Assam's neighbours – Bengal in the west and Burma in the east – were already so well-connected.

The first connection
Tired of spoilt tea, poor communication, and bad road conditions that often led to little or no food supply, tea plantation owner and surgeon, Dr John Berry White, proposed a metre-gauge line between the town of Dibrugarh and Sadiya – the most northeastern British frontier. The Government of

India agreed and White formed the Assam Railways and Trading Company in 1881. When he could not raise the required money, well-known British railway engineer Benjamin Piercy stepped in. However, the focus was no longer connecting the plantations; it now included rights for coal, oil mining, and timber.

Work began in full swing and the lines were laid from Dibrugarh to the River Dehring with a branch line from the coalfield town of Makum to the River Talap. Workers came from all over the country while all the equipment – from screws and nails to locomotives and rails – came from England. Within a few months, the isolated plantations buzzed with activity; the railway company brought in 5,872 workers and 100 European overseers. Housing colonies sprouted to accommodate all, and soon, in August 1882, Mohonamukh Ghat near Dibrugarh was connected to Dinjan near the town of Tinsukia. By 1883, all 124 km of the Dibrugarh–Sadiya Railway (DSR) in Lakhimpur were connected and open for business.

Coupling-uncoupling
The success of the DSR emboldened other parts of Assam, resulting in the laying of three other lines, including the 48-km-long Jorhat–Kokilamukh line. Constructed by the Government and officially inaugurated in 1884, the first passenger train ran on this line in February 1886. The snail-paced, 2-ft gauge Jorhat Provincial Railway, which is

the only line in India whose gauge was converted twice, from narrow gauge to metre gauge, and then finally to broad gauge, may have had many faults, but it was crucial to the people of the region. Among other things, it was famous for leaving its passengers stranded, because the couplings between its wagons and carriages, which had to be connected manually, often came accidentally undone. The railway would go on to find its way into the reminisces of authors Amiya Kumar Das and Liladhar Barua who wrote in *Asomat Mahatma* of one such incident in 1921 involving Mohandas Karamchand Gandhi.

Translating the text, author Arup Kumar Dutta wrote: "We learnt that … the coach carrying the Mahatma had been left behind! When the train stopped we all got down for a look. True, that coach had been left way behind! We were terrified – the soul of the nation was in that coach and we were responsible for him. And we had left him behind in the dead of the night in an unfamiliar spot with none to ensure his safety!" Gandhi, had a good laugh and told his companions that "he had despaired that the train would ever come back for him."

A part of the network
Despite the several lines within Assam, the network remained detached from the rest of British India. The Government knew that the advantages of linking Assam were not just commercial, but also strategic. Engineer-in-Chief JW Buyers, based on his surveys, recommended that two separate lines be built – for the Surma Valley in south-eastern Bengal

▼ **Dibrugarh's modest beginnings** as a small hub for railways in Assam ended with it being a major link for railway lines in the region. In this picture taken of Dibrugarh's railway yard in 1943, a network of lines can already be seen.

and the Brahmaputra Valley – which would connect at the North Cachar Hills (in the present-day district of Dima Hasao). Chittagong (in modern-day Bangladesh) was chosen as the preferred port for the line that would end in Gauhati (Guwahati).

The Assam Bengal Railway was incorporated in March 1892 and construction started along the three main sections of the 1,190-km-long line. The Chittagong to Badarpur (and the Badarpur–Silchar) section, completed in 1899, ran about 487 km. The third section from Lumding to Makum, which also joined Tinsukia, up to Gauhati, wrapped up work by 1903. For the first time, a part of the northeast was inextricably linked to the rest of India by the rail network.

The notorious hill section

Work on the third section, Lumding–Badarpur, began after fresh surveys in 1896 and Haflong, sitting at an elevation of 730 m, became the headquarters for the operations. It took almost 11 years for the workers and engineers to build a line through the North Cachar Hills as not all their previous learnings from building hill railways could be used here. The 1908 *Imperial Gazetteer* noted that the terrain proved most challenging as it ran through "shale of the worst description, often intermixed with bands of kaolinite, which swells when exposed and causes heavy slips, or exerts immense pressure on the sides of tunnels."

The earthwork involved was massive and tunnelling, which required the expertise of Cornish miners, was no mean feat. The 181-km section had 24 tunnels, seven covered ways, and 74 major bridges, the longest being 198 m and the highest, 34 m above the river bed. The line opened in 1903 and Lord Curzon, Viceroy of India (1899–1905), inaugurated the entire system in 1904 calling it "one of the costliest and most difficult railway enterprises that have ever been undertaken in India." The trials and tribulations notwithstanding, Assam was now connected to the rest of India.

> " The **corpse of a man** lies buried under every sleeper of the **hill section**. "
>
> ARUP KUMAR DUTTA, *INDIAN RAILWAYS, THE FINAL FRONTIER* (2002)

▼ **The varied topography of Assam** was hard to tame for the railways project. This image from 1925 shows an Assam Bengal Railway line being carved through hills.

STRONGER, WIDER, GRANDER

It was only after a few decades of trial and error, some of which proved disastrous for labourers and the trains crossing the bridges, that engineers perfected bridge-building techniques in India to create long-standing structures. Many of these have become examples of exemplary construction.

The period between the 1870s and the early half of the 1900s saw a flurry of new construction. The pioneering phase had passed and the bridge-builders were gradually coming to terms with India's formidable terrain, fickle rivers, and changing seasons. They perfected their techniques drawing from hard-learned, sometimes tragic, lessons. Traditional and British techniques found a happy middle ground and innovation remained key. The bridges became grander, even ostentatious. Some formed key links over mighty Indian rivers, such as the Ganges, Sutlej, and Indus, while others unlocked formerly inaccessible regions, such as Darjeeling, Simla, the North-West Frontier, and Assam.

Learning from the old

The bridge over the Sutlej near Phillaur, Punjab, opened with much pomp in October 1870. Labelled a "work of great magnitude", it was an important bridge on the Ghaziabad–Amritsar line. However, floods in 1871–72 caused severe damage, so much so that the Administrative Report for the Railways in India for 1882–83 called the original design "defective" and a "source of much anxiety and heavy expense". A new bridge with single- and double-lines opened for use by 1915. This one, unlike its predecessor, had some crucial improvements. The foundations of its piers were 20–26 m below the low watermark, unlike the previous one, which ranged from 8.5 to 13 m.

Laying deeper foundations for piers was one of the most significant changes in construction methods during this period. Workers could reach greater depths with the help of new mechanical devices, such as dredgers for up to 18 m, operated by groups of bullocks and men, or steam hoists for deeper levels. Pneumatic caissons, a watertight enclosed structure used for construction in water, were used in places with challenging terrain, such as the Damodar Bridge on the Bengal–Nagpur Railway. It was built over a sandstone and hard shaley rock river bed, and opened for use in 1903. Technology later allowed workers to sink the piers even deeper, as with the Dufferin Bridge. Built over the River Ganges at Benaras, it opened in 1887 with piers that had been sunk to up to 49 m in some instances and was designed to accommodate both rail and road traffic.

Scouring of piers was a big problem for bridges built across rivers, so engineers used protective curtains or "aprons" made of piles of loose stones and cement ballast. They also started spacing out the

piers. This became easier during the 1880s after iron, used for making girder spans, made way for steel.

Applying new learnings

In some places, especially where there were deep channels, engineers opted for the more complicated cantilever design, such as the Jubilee Bridge (now-decommissioned) that opened in 1885 over the River Hooghly in Calcutta. It was built using rivets and without nuts or bolts. The Lansdowne Bridge, which opened in 1889 and crossed the River Indus between Sukkur and Rohri (in present-day Pakistan) was a railway connection between Calcutta and Karachi. Designed by the British civil engineer Sir Alexander Rendel, the bridge had two anchored 52-m-high cantilever structures, with a suspended span of 61 m in the middle, making it an engineering marvel of its time.

Another significant development in construction was the practice of guiding rivers. This started during the 1870s with the building of groynes (low walls) for the Alexandra Bridge over the River Chenab (in present-day Pakistan). By the 1880s, bunds or Bell's bunds – named after British engineer James Bell who devised the method – became popular. These involved building embankments with pitching stones, brought from quarries via rail or water. They protected against scouring and stopped the river from shifting its course. The technique was used successfully for the Curzon Bridge, which opened in 1905, over the River Ganges in Allahabad.

Marvellous structures

One of the most awe-inspiring bridges of the period was the Attock Bridge over the Indus in present-day Pakistan. It opened in 1883 and continues to be used even today. Designed by English civil engineer Guilford Molesworth, it was a crucial connection between Punjab and Peshawar. It was built as a double-track bridge, a speciality of the period, the railway crossing was on the top deck of the bridge and the Grand Trunk Road ran below. The approach from both sides was via imposing iron gates and gun posts.

Not all bridges of this period were built over rivers. Some connected hills, such as the Gallery Bridge inspired by Roman aqueducts on the Kalka Shimla line (see pp.90–91) and the 13 Arch Bridge that stands on granite pillars on the Kollam–Sengottai line in Kerala.

The Chappar Rift, created by a split in the mountains after an earthquake, on the line to Quetta (in present-day Pakistan) in the North-West Frontier Province is another example. It was linked using sequential tunnels, a seven-span viaduct, and a bridge. The 76-m-high Louise Margaret Bridge over the Rift had a single 46 m and seven 12 m girder spans, which crossed over a mud gorge. It was taken down in 1944 after a flash flood destroyed the line in 1942 and an alternative Bolan Pass line to Quetta was developed.

▼ **This image from a vintage postcard** shows a train chugging on the 1883 Attock Bridge over the River Indus.

PAMBAN BRIDGE

By the early 20th century, the British had consolidated their power in India. They were now looking to further cement their hold on the colony by facilitating easy troop movements, streamlining the commutes, and providing connectivity to major sea ports for commercial gains.

As the country was linked through the rail network, the southernmost town of India, Rameswaram on the Pamban island, separated from the mainland by the Palk Strait and accessible only by boats, waited to be connected too. It was decided that the South Indian Railway Company's Mandapam–Dhanushkodi line would be extended.

Architects and engineers came up with an "open-close" mechanism with a drawbridge design across almost 2 km. The final designs were made by the Scherzer Rolling Lift Bridge Company (US) and it was built under Head Wrightson, a British construction company. The bridge was made with 145 spans (that bridged the distance between two intermediate support pillars) and a "rolling lift span" that could move upwards and downwards to enable ships to pass.

Construction began in 1911 but was halted in May 1912 because of a storm, which washed away temporary timber works. In the same year, an outbreak of cholera scared away a lot of the labour. A workforce was imported from other states and Ceylon (present-day Sri Lanka). Finally, in February 1914, it opened to the public. At the time it was the country's longest sea bridge and remained so till the opening of the Bandra–Worli Sea Link in Mumbai in 2010.

Every bridge, big or small, is vulnerable to the ravages of nature and Pamban has been no different. The 1964 Rameswaram cyclone, one of the most powerful cyclones to have ever hit the Indian shores, washed away all its girders and caused a lot of structural damage. It took nine weeks for the bridge to be up and running again. Maintenance work was an ordeal over the years as exposure to the open sea made it highly corrosive and required frequent checks, painting, and reinforcement. Over the years, this architectural marvel has been closed and reopened many times, but has stood the test of time and is still operational.

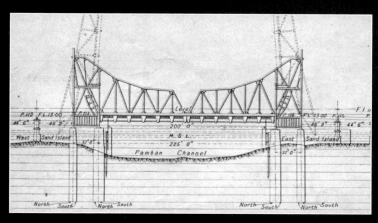

This sketch of the Pambam Bridge illustrates the girder bridge design. This type of structure uses girders or beams to support the main deck.

Using a bascule bridge design concept, the Pamban is a movable bridge that uses an "open-close" mechanism to allow boats to pass under it. Here, it can be seen open, for the movement of water-borne traffic.

TUNNELS

Most railway tunnels in India were built after 1870, when railway tracks were laid along mountainous regions and it became apparent that cutting into steep hills could not be avoided entirely to ensure that the route remained relatively straight. These tunnels, dug through tough rock and steep hills, with a scientific precision that rail technology demanded, were a far cry from the earlier royal escape tunnels built under forts in the Princely States. Many railway tunnels built in the late 19th and early 20th centuries are still in use today.

Tunnels allowed for straight routes through impediments and greatly reduced travel times of train journeys. The length of railway lines also became smaller as laying a track through a hill eliminated the need for a long, spiralling route. The first tunnels were constructed on the Great Indian Peninsula Railway (GIPR) line from Bombay to Poona and Nashik while crossing the Bhore and Thul Ghats (see pp.50–51), respectively in the pioneering phase of railway construction in India.

Lines of defence

The possibility of a faster route proved useful for frontier lines and for occasions that required immediate deployment of troops. One such line was in the city of Chaman, Balochistan (in modern-day Pakistan) where railway materials were stored to build a line to Kandahar in Afghanistan in the event of an emergency (see p.83).

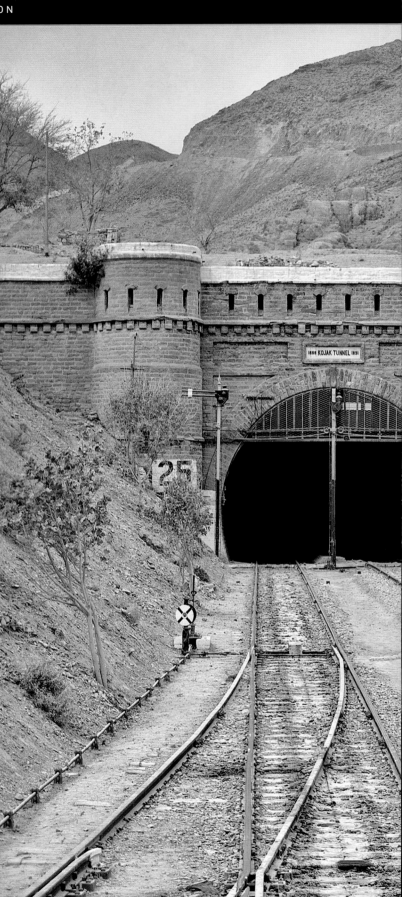

FLIGHTS OF WHIMSY

Along the Matheran Light Railway lies a tunnel curiously named "One Kiss". It was christened thus by a British officer as he pronounced it just short and dark enough for a couple to steal a single, romantic kiss. Tunnel No. 5 of the Nilgiri Mountain Railway, which is cut directly into the side of a solid rock cliff face, also boasts the nickname of "half-tunnel" due to its precarious rock overhang.

◀ **The gateway to Afghanistan,** Khojak's construction began from both ends. The construction met in the centre with exceptional accuracy, making Khojak a remarkably straight tunnel.

This 109-km-long line goes through the Khojak Tunnel, which was built in 1891 under the Khojak mountain pass. This tunnel's construction meant digging through water-bearing rock, and as Indian miners had yet to master tunnelling skills, 65 Welsh miners were hired to do the job – a common practice in those days. At 3.9 km, Khojak was the longest tunnel in India at the time of its completion. Castle-like, with gigantic turrets that loom against the bleak Khwaja Amran Mountains, it is an impressive structure that was featured on Pakistan's five-rupee note from 1976 to 2005.

The only other tunnel as iconic was the 1.3-km-long Parsik Tunnel in Maharashtra, which was built between 1913 to 1916 on the Mumbai line.

Tunnelling was a time- and labour-intensive process and the living conditions at worksites were notoriously difficult. For instance, during the construction of the Khojak Tunnel, water was limited and up to 80 tonnes had to be supplied by rail for thousands of workers daily. The brutal winters also resulted in many deaths due to pneumonia. In the winter of 1890–91, a four-month-long typhoid outbreak proved fatal to around 800 labourers. Workers faced similar challenges in 1892 while building the oldest tunnel in the South Eastern Railway network – the Saranda Tunnel in present-day Jharkhand. The tracks went through dense forests and maintaining a permanent workforce in the jungles of Saranda was near impossible.

On some occasions, Indian workers were driven away by local superstitions and religious beliefs. One such situation involved Tunnel No. 91 on the Kalka Shimla Railway (see pp.90–91). The tunnel was designed to cut through the Taradevi

Hill, on top of which stood a temple dedicated to the "Goddess of Stars". A local superstition stated that the goddess had forbidden the railway construction, and work stopped briefly when labourers panicked after mistaking a long iron pipe in the tunnel for a huge serpent.

Tragic consequences

Another prominent tunnel on this line, the Barog Tunnel is the longest along the Kalka–Shimla rail route at 1.1 km. Also known as No. 33, this tunnel was initially designed by Colonel Barog, a British engineer who began by digging from both ends, a common method at the time. When it was discovered that the two ends of the tunnel would never align, Barog was fined Re 1 by the Government for wasting resources. Humiliated and distraught, he committed suicide. The tunnel was eventually completed by Chief Engineer HS Harrington with the help of Bhalku, a local resident of Chail, whose contributions resulted in the straightest tunnel on the route, and earned him a medal and turban from the then Viceroy, and saint-like status among the locals. This tunnel is still lit using large mirrors, a popular practice for the earlier tunnels as it directed sunlight into the dark passageways.

▼ **The longest tunnel** in the country, before the 1990s, the Parsik Tunnel allowed for the Mumbai–Thana line to be extended up to Kalyan and beyond.

MUGHALSARAI

Railways in India were first and foremost meant to facilitate trade. It was imperative then for the establishment to set up centrally located hubs, or marshalling yards, to disperse freight across the country. Essentially, these yards helped in collecting wagons in specific lines meant for despatch in each direction.

Large goods sheds were maintained for the receipt and despatch of freight, where the commodities were booked and loaded in individual wagons. These loaded wagons were then drawn into a marshalling yard adjacent to the goods shed, assembled into train loads, and sent off to other yards. Then, the train would be broken up, and the loads combined with wagons from other trains coming in from elsewhere. A new train would then be formed with all merchandise to be despatched to a particular part of the country. The process would be repeated at various marshalling yards, which were developed at important junctions.

Mughalsarai in modern-day Uttar Pradesh was identified as an ideal location for a marshalling yard due to its central location. In the early years, the East Indian Railway (EIR) line from Calcutta to Delhi had a branch line from Naini, near Allahabad, extending to Jubblepore. Subsequently, a new line was built connecting Mughalsarai with other towns, such as Moradabad via Lucknow. With burgeoning production of coal in Jharia (in modern-day Jharkhand) and central India, an alternate route called the Grand Chord was constructed in 1906. It connected Sitarampur in eastern India to Mughalsarai in northern India. This line established Mughalsarai as the point where the EIR forked into the important Allahabad and Lucknow trade routes.

The volume of traffic through Mughalsarai increased as coal production increased, and with this, coal from coalfields served by the EIR found markets in remote parts of India. The reach of wagons marshalled in Mughalsarai yard widened as new lines were constructed in these areas. Post-Independence, Mughalsarai, already the largest marshalling yard in the country, became the first one to be mechanized. In 2018, the railway junction as well as the yard were renamed after the Indian thinker Pandit Deendayal Upadhyaya, who was found dead near the Mughalsarai railway station in 1968.

► **With the abolition of four-wheelers** and introduction of through running, the Mughalsarai yard no longer "deals" with the wagons. Nevertheless, the scale of operations for freight trains interchanged with adjacent railways continues to be high. This image shows the yard before it was electrified.

PROTECTIONISM AND PROGRESS

The railways brought with it the promise of technological advancement and progress, but reality was quite different. The import and trade of British goods left India with a rudimentary industry. Some Indian entrepreneurs, however, managed to hold their own.

Work plates from the Hubli Workshop (top) and the Parel Workshop (bottom)

▲ **The Bombay, Baroda and Central India (BB&CI) Railway** built many locomotives at its Ajmer Workshop. One of its steam locomotives, No. 213, can be seen at the Workshop in this 1925 photograph.

In August 1853, the *New York Daily Tribune* published an essay by German philosopher Karl Marx in which he suggested that it was not possible to maintain a network of railways over an immense country without introducing industrial processes necessary to meet the immediate and current needs for railway locomotion.

He also believed that further applications of machinery, not always connected to the railways, would grow out of these industrial processes. Marx then wrote that, "the railway system will, therefore, become, in India, truly the forerunner of modern industry." The last statement seemed to be somewhat optimistic, as India's great industrial evolution was late in coming, bogged down as it was by the demands of a colonial power that sought to promote its own economic interests. Workshops and machine shops set up to effect repairs were well-equipped to build locomotives, yet railway companies almost always "bought British". Railway employers preferred Europeans instead of natives in senior positions.

The iron and steel industry grew, but in fits and starts, until World War I when, in the middle of extreme shortages, the Government turned to Indian steel in order to meet demand. Technological development and modern industry were mere by-products of the railways in India.

Hubs of technology transfer

With railway lines came workshops; some provided basic support ideal for minor repairs, while others were massive units employing thousands of people that contributed to local economies and often resembled small colonies. Lahore had some of the largest workshops after Jamalpur (see pp.54–55), employing about 4,000 workers around Naulakha city (in present-day Pakistan) in the early

1890s. With the expansion of the North Western Railway, the Mughalpura Workshop opened at the edge of Lahore. Sprawled across a 4 sq km-area, it had carriage and wagon shops as well as locomotive shops.

Centres of learning

Innovative machinery and equipment were produced, but were all made by European engineers. Canadian historian Ian J Kerr, in his book *Engines of Change*, noted that workshops were "early centres of the heavy engineering industry in India" and "crucibles of technology transfer."

While certain railway companies such as East Indian Railway (EIR) ran apprenticeship programmes especially for Europeans, Eurasians, and some Indians, the native population, which made up most of the workforce, were generally confined to lower-ranking jobs. Skilled, managerial, and technical positions were mostly reserved for Europeans and Eurasians. The demand to Indianize the railways went up during the Independence movement but was fulfilled only after 1947.

Buy British

Showing a marked indifference towards industrial development in the country, the Government imported everything from Britain – financial capital to build the railways, rails and fishplates for the lines, and machinery for shops to locomotives,

skilled labour, and even complete bridges. An apt example of this was seen in the Government's policy towards the purchase of locomotives.

Nearly 80 per cent of the 14,420 imported locomotives came from Britain. In fact, Vulcan Foundry (which supplied India its first locomotive), along with Beyer, Peacock and Company and North British Locomotive Company– all British companies – looked at India as their primary market. This, despite railway workshops building locomotives from as early as 1865, beginning with Byculla in Bombay. The BB&CI would later go on to build 444 locomotives at its Ajmer Workshop, with Jamalpur producing 217.

The Government's policy was unabashedly aimed at helping British manufacturers, especially towards the end of the 19th century. American historian Daniel R Headrick wrote of manufacturers requesting George Hamilton, the Secretary of State for India (1895–1903), to intervene when there was an increase in the import of American and Canadian locomotives. The development of the British Engineering Standards Association (BESA), which "enshrined the British locomotive designs" and picked five models as the standard for India to follow, quashed all competition.

Of iron and steel

While there had been half-hearted efforts to develop an iron and steel industry in India, it was thought best to avoid creating competition for their British counterparts. Most endeavours, such as the Bengal Iron and Steel Company set up in 1905, failed. So India imported about 96 per cent of its railway supplies from Britain and Belgium.

▲ **Regarded the "Father of Indian Industry"**, Jamsetji Tata is seen with his cousin RD Tata, and sons Ratan and Dorab. Today, this family portrait sits in the office of the managing director of Tata Steel in Jamshedpur, in modern-day Jharkhand.

When rails switched from iron to steel, railway companies continued to import them, until Indian industrialist Jamsetji Nusserwanji Tata, and later his son Dorabji, appeared on the scene. Despite the lack of Government support, the Tatas conducted extensive research and by 1907, had issued a prospectus for the all-Indian Tata Iron and Steel Company (TISCO). Production of steel ingots began in 1912 and the following year, TISCO began manufacturing steel rails. By 1916, production had gone up to 9,072 tonnes of steel rails and sections.

With World War I (1914–18), steel imports dropped, leaving the Government no option but to rely on TISCO to meet the demand. By 1938–39, the company produced 99 per cent of the rails bought in India.

◀ **A Pakistan Railways** locomotive is seen getting overhauled at the Mughulpura Workshop in Lahore.

INDIAN IRON AND STEEL COMPANY

Iron production in India became a reality after the Bengal Iron Works Company set up an open-top blast furnace in Kulti near Hirapur (modern-day Jharkhand) in 1870. Founded by James Erskine, the company produced cast iron. By 1889, it was taken over by the Bengal Iron and Steel Company and provisions were made to produce steel. The Indian Iron and Steel Company (IISCO) was established as an industrial enterprise in 1918, absorbing BIS in 1936 and steel production began on a regular basis. The Steel Corporation of Bengal became a part of IISCO in 1937, bringing with it the Napuria and Hirapur Works. Together, they came to be known as the Burnpur Works. Post-Independence, the Indian Government took over IISCO in 1972, which became a subsidiary of the Steel Authority of India in 1979.

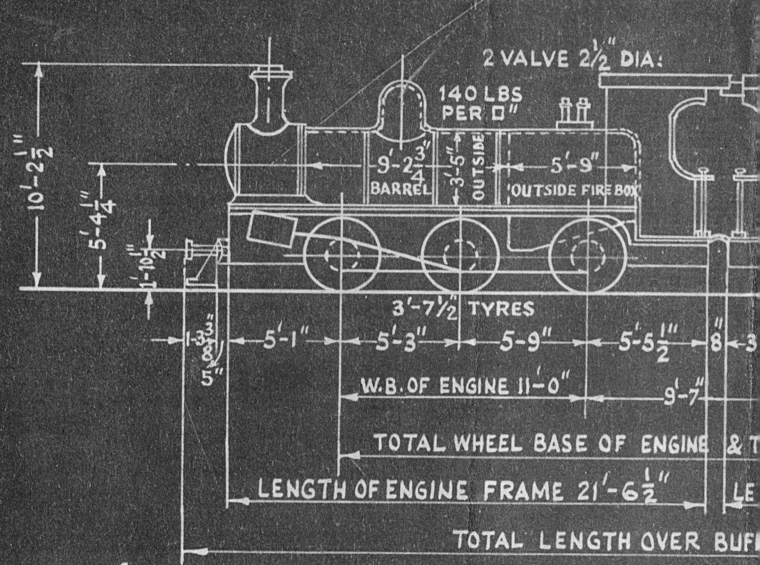

WESTERN RLY: METRE
CLASS F¹ 0-6-0
SCALE ⅛ INCH = ONE FOOT

2 VALVE 2½" DIA:

140 LBS PER ☐"

10'-2½"

5'-4¼"

1'-10½"

9'-2¾" BARREL

3'-5" OUTSIDE

5'-9" OUTSIDE FIRE BOX

3'-7½" TYRES

1-3⅜"

5"

5'-1"

5'-3"

5-9"

5'-5½"

8

W.B. OF ENGINE 11'-0"

9'-7"

TOTAL WHEEL BASE OF ENGINE & T

LENGTH OF ENGINE FRAME 21'-6½"

LE

TOTAL LENGTH OVER BUF

| N TONS | FULL | 7·05 | 7·50 | 7·50 |
| | EMPTY | 6·40 | 6·75 | 6·75 |

TAL WEIGHT IN WORKING ORDER; ENGINE 22·05, TENDE

" — " — 19·90 — "

This blueprint of the F1-734, with detailed specifics of the locomotive, is archived at the National Rail Museum in New Delhi, India.

| PRESSURE | WEIGHT O |

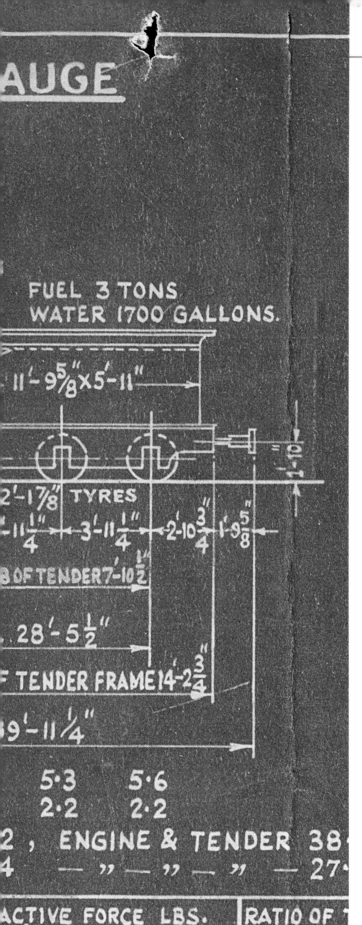

FUEL 3 TONS
WATER 1700 GALLONS.

11'-9⅝"×5'-11"

2'-1⅞" TYRES

11¼" — 3'-11¼" — 2'-10¾" 1'-9⅝"

OF TENDER 7'-10½"

28'-5½"

F TENDER FRAME 14'-2¾"

9'-11¼"

5·3   5·6
2·2   2·2

2 , ENGINE & TENDER 38

" — " — " — 27

ACTIVE FORCE LBS. | RATIO OF

F1-734

India's first indigenous locomotive, the F1-734, an F class 0-6-0 metre-gauge locomotive, is a milestone in the history of railways in India. Prior to this, locomotives were only assembled in the country, and not made.

Built by the Ajmer Workshop (now part of the North Western Railway) for the Rajputana Malwa Railway in 1895, F1-734 cost Rs 15,869 to put together. The F1-734 is a derivative of the F class locomotives, built by Dubbs and Company, Glasgow, UK, which were the most successful of their time.

The metre gauge, a more economical and, therefore, a more feasible alternative to the broad gauge, was decided for railway expansion in India by January 1871. Most of the initial fleet of metre-gauge locomotives were imported and were primarily of British origin with a smattering of a few German versions. In fact, within six years of the metre gauge being adopted, 400 locomotives were imported to India.

Weighing 38.25 tonnes, the F1-734 came equipped with a Stephenson valve gear, which was used to control the inlet of steam into its cylinders. The locomotive had connecting rods inside the frame while the side rods were placed outside. The leaf springs and the sandbox were located on top of the frame, above the wheels of the locomotive. The F1-734 also had a cow-catcher, which was a metal frame mounted at the front to remove blockages from the rail track.

The F1-734 ran from Delhi to Indore and up to Ahmedabad and was also used on the Bombay Baroda & Central India (BB&CI) Railway. The locomotive was retired in 1958 after 63 years of service and arrived at the National Rail Museum, New Delhi in utter disrepair; its iron exteriors corroded and crumbling. It was restored to its former glory over a period of two months by the Museum.

The F1-734 steam locomotive is currently preserved as an exhibit in the National Rail Museum, New Delhi, where it was restored.

STEAM LOCOMOTIVES

Locomotive designs were not standardized in the early years of railways in India. Each company followed its own norms and as a result, there was a variety of steam engines chugging away across the country. It was not till 1903–06 that the British Engineering Standards Association (BESA) established eight broad-gauge and four metre-gauge locomotive classes for the subcontinent.

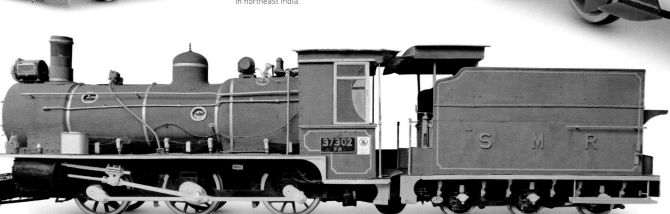

◀ A 885

Year built	1897
Manufacturer	WG Bagnall Ltd, Stafford, UK
Gauge	Narrow (2')
Wheel configuration	0-4-0

Named *Hasang*, this locomotive was considered the smallest steam engine ever used in the Indian subcontinent. It was originally manufactured with a 0-4-2 wheel arrangement. The saddle-shaped compartment over its boiler was used to store water. *Hasang* spent most of its working life shunting wagons in the Ledo coal mines in Assam in northeast India.

▲ FMA 37302

Year built	1888
Manufacturer	M/s Dubs & Co, Glasgow Locomotive Works, Glasgow, UK
Gauge	Metre
Wheel configuration	0-6-0

Originally known as the FM 118, this locomotive's classification changed to FMA 37302 after its coal capacity was increased. It was supplied to the Southern Mahratta Railway where it served both passenger and goods trains. Due to this, it was created with more boiler capacity and was designed to withstand higher pressure.

▶ *Tweed*

Year built	1873
Manufacturer	Sharp, Stewart & Co, Manchester, UK
Gauge	Metre
Wheel configuration	0-4-0

This D class locomotive is one of the oldest working metre-gauge locomotives in the world. It was built to be used on the Oudh and Tirhut Railway. In 1925, it was sold to Saraya Sugar Mills System, a factory in Gorakhpur, Uttar Pradesh, where it was used as a shunting engine.

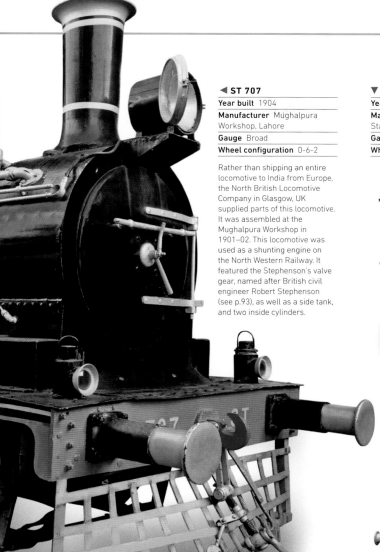

◄ ST 707

Year built 1904

Manufacturer Mughalpura Workshop, Lahore

Gauge Broad

Wheel configuration 0-6-2

Rather than shipping an entire locomotive to India from Europe, the North British Locomotive Company in Glasgow, UK supplied parts of this locomotive. It was assembled at the Mughalpura Workshop in 1901–02. This locomotive was used as a shunting engine on the North Western Railway. It featured the Stephenson's valve gear, named after British civil engineer Robert Stephenson (see p.93), as well as a side tank, and two inside cylinders.

▼ *Decauville*

Year built 1902

Manufacturer WG Bagnall Ltd, Stafford, UK

Gauge Narrow (2'6")

Wheel configuration 2-4-2

This locomotive was built for the Decauville Portable Railway System along the North-West Frontier Province, bordering Afghanistan. It was supplied to the military reserve as one locomotive in a batch of 20, with an inside plate frame, "Bagnall's link" motion valve gear, two cylinders, and a saddle tank. *Decauville* was later employed by the Madras Engineer Group in Bangalore.

▲ MSM 15

Year built 1907

Manufacturer Nasmyth, Wilson & Co Ltd, Patricroft, UK

Gauge Broad

Wheel configuration 0-4-0

Named *Phoenix*, this locomotive was used as a rail motor car for a branch line service on the East Indian Railway (EIR). It was built with an inside plate frame, two inside cylinders, "Salter balance" safety valves, and two vertical combination injectors. It had its coach portion removed and was made into a shunting locomotive in 1927.

▲ X 37385

Year built 1920

Manufacturer Swiss Locomotive & Machine Works, Switzerland

Gauge Metre Gauge

Wheel configuration 0-8-2

This compound locomotive with four cylinders, instead of the usual two, was employed on the Nilgiri Mountain Railway and the South Indian Railway. Of the four cylinders, two used high-pressure steam to directly influence the wheels. Placed above these were the other two smaller ones that let out steam at a lower pressure to drive the rack system (see p.93).

► MTR 2

Year built 1910

Manufacturer Dick, Kerr & Co, London, UK

Gauge Narrow (2'6")

Wheel configuration 0-4-2

This saddle tank steam engine with an oversized chimney was built for use as a shunting and freight engine for the Karachi Port Trust. In 1917–22 it worked at the Marala Timber Depot in modern-day Pakistan. After this it was transferred to a creosoting plant in Dhilwan, present-day Punjab.

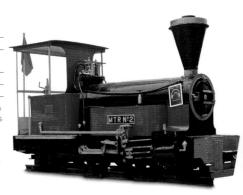

This iconic locomotive of the Patiala State Monorail Tramway (PSMT) was brought to the National Rail Museum, New Delhi, in 1977, where it was restored to full working condition. The PSMT was one of the very few steam-run monorail systems in the world.

PATIALA STATE MONORAIL

Around the year 1900, British civil and mechanical engineer Colonel Charles William Bowles was involved in the construction of the Bengal-Nagpur Railway's (BNR) Workshop in Kharagpur, West Bengal. In order to solve the problems with the narrow-gauge line that was laid for the transportation of concrete to the construction site, he experimented with a monorail system developed by British inventor WJ Ewing in 1894–95.

Bowles, who went on to become the state engineer for the Princely State of Patiala (in present-day Indian Punjab), used the same technology to develop a monorail system in the state. It was built and operated by Marsland, Price & Company, a Bombay-based firm. Under the Ewing System, the main load of the train is borne by a single rail, and the rest by a balancing wheel that runs on the ground.

Patiala had two monorail lines – the main line was from the North West Railway's (NWR) goods yard near the Patiala station to Bhawanigarh, intended to be extended till Sunam, which never materialized. The other line ran from the NWR's Sirhind station to Morinda. There is some ambiguity regarding the specific power used on this system. Author Simon Darvill notes that the Sirhind–Morinda line was solely operated by animal power but there were at least four locomotives, imported from the German engineering company Orenstein and Koppel, that worked the Patiala–Sunam line. There is some evidence of other imported locomotives, two steam and one petrol, perhaps both built by the British shipbuilding firm Thornycroft, as well as a home-built locomotive, but their history remains shrouded in mystery.

Problems, such as termite attacks on wooden sleepers, conflicts with adjoining territories as a section of the line passed through them, and the option of horse-driven carriages and wagonettes, led to the closure of the main line by 1914. The secondary line too, lost its purpose and ceased to operate in 1927 when the NWR built a broad-gauge line from Sirhind to Rupar.

One of the objectives for the construction of this monorail system was to employ the large number of animals, such as bullocks and mules, maintained by the State. Bullocks can be seen hauling a train on the route in this picture.

INSTITUTIONAL REFORMS

In the period from 1870 to 1901, administrative and legislative measures were aimed at establishing a centralized government control over the railways in India. There was a move towards a focussed railway policy instead of scattered Acts. All administrative changes in these decades led up to the formation of a Railway Board.

▲ **Guilford Lindsey Molesworth**, the first consulting engineer for the State railways (1871–89), played a crucial role in shaping them.

The British Government in India stayed away from changes in the railway legislation when it introduced the policy of State construction for railways. All urgent matters had already been dealt with in the short Acts passed in 1870 and 1871.

Moreover, the contracts with the guaranteed companies had provisions for Government control and supervision. It was thought best to observe the working of State railways before introducing a new Act.

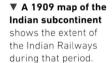

▼ **A 1909 map of the Indian subcontinent** shows the extent of the Indian Railways during that period.

Organizational trials

With the expansion of the railway network, a State Railway Directorate, with a director and a chief consulting engineer, was established in 1874. This separated the railway administration from the Public Works Department (PWD) Secretariat.

All matters regarding policy, however, were still decided by the Railway Branch of the PWD Secretariat, where a special deputy secretary was appointed for correspondence between the Government of India and the officers of the State Railway Directorate. The exceptions to this rule were the Northern Bengal State lines and the Nizam's State Railways (see pp.74–75), which were administered by the Princely States themselves.

In 1877, a decision was taken to divide the State railways into three territorial divisions (Central, Western, and North-Eastern), each under a director of its own. Provincial railways in Burma, the Central Provinces, and the North-West were left under the administration of the local authorities. This system of management, however, led to conflicting orders in the administration of open lines. Therefore, offices of directors of the Central and Western divisions were discontinued in 1879.

In a reorganized set-up, a director-general for railways was appointed and was also entrusted with the responsibilities of the deputy-secretary in the railway branch. He was assisted by a consulting engineer in technical matters, a director of stores for materials and rolling stock, a director of traffic for traffic problems, and an accountant general.

The local consulting engineers, under the direct control of the Government, continued to supervise the guaranteed railways. The same principle applied to the lines developed by the Indian States for local interest.

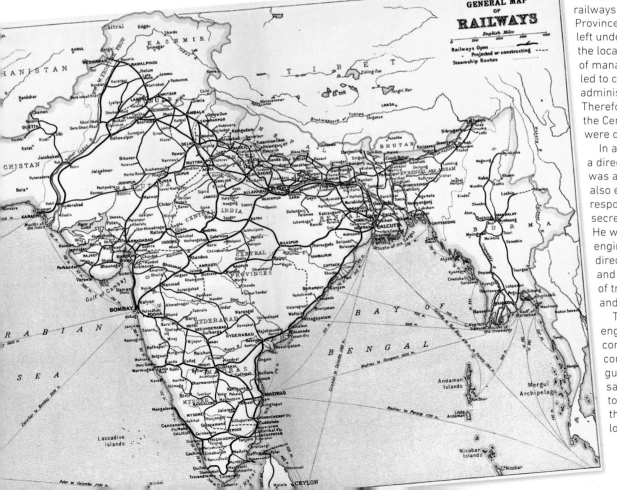

India 1909
GENERAL MAP
OF
RAILWAYS
English Miles
Railways Open
Projected or constructing ----
Steamship Routes

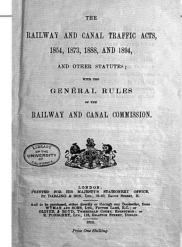
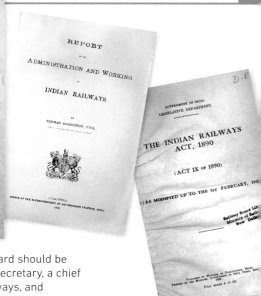

New legislation

Following on from the Act of 1854, railway administrations were given freedom to formulate basic rules for operation of their lines, provided these were sanctioned by the Governor-General in Council, who could also extend the Act or its part to tramways run by steam locomotives. Learning from the accident that occurred in 1875, the Act gave a clearance for the use of locomotives, after it has been sanctioned by the Governor-General in Council. With regard to safety, rules were laid down that no passenger railways were to open without prior notice of such intentions and thorough inspection. Besides, the Act gave classification for accidents and rules for their reporting. To mitigate the one-sidedness of this act, within a few years the Act IV of 1883 was passed. The main focus of this Act was protection of the public.

Revised laws

It provided for periodic inspection of all railways by officers appointed for this purpose. The Government of India could now frame rules for the inspection of all railways prior to their opening. With rapid construction and expansion, differences relating to the interchange of traffic arose and the Government was pressed for arbitration. Consequently, the Bill of 1879 was modified to prepare a new draft Bill. Clauses were added to it for settlement of disputes by arbitration. In the modified draft Bill, the Governor-General in Council was vested with the power to appoint a temporary commission, if he felt the need to do so.

The Bill failed to find favour with the guaranteed railway companies. They perceived it to be a violation of their rights under the contracts with the secretary of state. They were particularly against the temporary commission and, on the grounds that the government had ownership and co-ownership of most railways, feared partiality, especially in cases where the interest of the State was at stake. A Select Committee was appointed to advise on the objections. The Committee opined against introducing any clause relating to the rights of the companies under the contracts. It felt that such a clause might lead to a different interpretation of the Act by every company and this would disturb the consistency in the enforcement of the Act. The Bill was passed as Act IX of 1890.

Four railway companies objected to the provision for traffic facilities and temporary commissions. "The Railway and Canal Traffic Act" of 1888 from where this provision was adapted, was upheld to be appropriate for the British railway situation but the Act of 1890 "was an ill-advised attempt to transplant into India legislation not adapted to its conditions". The Government of India did not yield and remained convinced that the Act was for the betterment of both companies and public. The period of 1890–97 also saw a lot of restructuring of the PWD in the railway branch, with offices and new commands created, even as old ones were discontinued.

An independent observer

In 1901, Sir Thomas Robertson (see p.73) was appointed as state special commissioner for the Indian Railways by the secretary of state to report on railway administration and organization. In his report of 1903, he advocated for a three-member board for control over railway matters in India. He proposed that the board should comprise a president or chief commissioner who should be a member of the Viceroy's Council, and two other commissioners, all of whom should have an extensive knowledge of railway matters. Moreover, the board should be provided with a secretary, a chief inspector of railways, and Government inspectors.

The Railway Board

Following his recommendations, a provisional railway board was formed in 1901, which was then formalized with a resolution issued in 1905 for the dissolution of the railway branch of the PWD. The control over railways was given to a railway board, which was to report to the department of commerce and industry of the Government of India.

The Board had a secretary, examiner of accounts, under-secretaries for construction and Traffic, a registrar, and a director of railway construction. However, the Board soon faced financial problems and in 1907, a Finance Committee was appointed to look into the matter and some substantial changes were undertaken with respect to the Board's autonomy. The office now had direct access to the Viceroy. The Board was separated from the Department of Commerce and Industry and the Railway Department was formed.

Between 1908 and 1920, in a concerted effort to organize the enterprise, many other changes were brought about, including appointments of Government inspectors, a chief engineer, and a financial adviser to the Railway Board. The Indian Railways was slowly on its way to becoming an organized industry.

▲ **The Railway and Canal Traffic Act,** Thomas Robertson's Report on the Administration and Working of Indian Railways, and the Indian Railways Act, 1890, together shaped the foundation of the Indian Railway Board.

THE THIRD-CLASS TRAVELLER

The classification of passengers into three, and later four, classes was a manifestation of social relations between master and subject in colonial India. The basis for these was, on the surface, the provision of comfort for a price. Yet railway travel for Indians was the story of imperialism and segregation, factors that eventually provided ample fodder for nationalists fighting for independence.

▲ An early 20th-century lithograph by Scottish artist William Ralston (1841–1911) titled "Memories of an Indian Tour, Leaves from a Traveller's Diary" shows the deplorable condition of natives in a third-class coach.

In 1845, when confronted with the question of the economic viability of the railways in India, the Court of Directors noted in a despatch to the Viceroy of India that as "the people of India are poor ... remuneration for railroads in India must, for the present, be drawn chiefly from the conveyance of merchandise, and not from passengers." The Court's scepticism, as it turned out, was unfounded. Indians took to rail travel quite enthusiastically despite its unaffordability. As early as 1870, around 18.22 million passengers used trains, a number that shot up to 520 million in 1919–20. Up to 90 per cent of these, noted Indian historian Ritika Prasad in her book *Tracks of Change*, travelled by third class; most were Indians with a marginal number of Eurasians, and some domiciled European military orphans.

A matter of class

While there was no written law against Indians travelling in the first and second class, the numbers were negligible.

It turns out that even those Indians who could afford to travel thus were often coerced or harassed into making other plans by their British or Eurasian co-passengers who were uncomfortable about sharing the space with natives. Indian travellers then were packed in huge numbers into third-class compartments. Within this subsection too, people were steeped in the notions of segregation and discrimination on the basis of caste, class, gender, social rank, or religion among themselves. There were continuous demands by Indians for separate accommodation within third class on the basis of religion or caste hierarchies. So much so that the introduction of females-only compartments met with strong disapproval from the "higher" castes, who considered it beneath their social standing that "their women" would travel with those of lower classes.

Inhumane conditions

A typical third-class carriage on a broad-gauge railway had space for about 120 people. Newspapers from the period, however, report how these carriages were often without seats. The *Rohilkhand Akhbar* dated 14 June 1876, noted

> ❝ ... [passengers were] **huddled and crowded** like **cattle into carriages** often **unprovided** even with seats. ❞

CALCUTTA REVIEW, 1867

that there was "no limit to the number of persons thrust into a carriage so that sometimes they hardly find room to stand and breathe freely". Overcrowding was an issue and it often led to large number of deaths in high summers.

Passengers were often locked inside carriages when the train stopped at stations, thus restricting their access to water, food, or the lavatory. Some railway companies also seated passengers, especially pilgrims holding third-class tickets, in goods wagons.

Extreme discomfort

The problem was compounded by the lack of toilets, an issue that came to the fore during the 1882 Railway Conference. A variety of "reasons" were cited for not providing the facilities. Some argued that excreta would be "perpetually falling from the closets in such volumes as to befoul the line and frighten off the gang men." Others spoke of how this could be a source of danger to health, lead to an increase in labour to clean the permanent way, and even "considerable expenditure". The change began after 1902 when these facilities were finally added to third-class carriages.

Comparative luxury

European and Eurasian passengers able to pay for first- and second-class tickets seemingly travelled in the lap of luxury. British educationalist Oscar Browning in his book *Impressions of Indian Travel* (1903) noted

the first-class experience: "Soda water is offered to you just as you are conceiving the wish for it. Tea comes to you punctually at 6am ... No sooner have you passed your hand over your stubby beard than a barber appears to shave you in the carriage. You get a 'little breakfast' of eggs and bacon, with bananas and oranges at eight, a delightful tiffin in the heat of noon, and a good dinner at sunset."

The spacious compartments had lower and foldable upper berths, an attached lavatory, a shower or sometimes a bath, and a small servant room. Continuous attempts were made to upgrade these facilities. During the 1870s, oil lamps were replaced by gas lamps, followed by electric lights in the early 1900s. Special attention was paid to cooling systems, given the long summers in India.

Sometimes, a large block of ice was placed in the compartment and replenished at stations or scented jute mats, frequently splashed with water, were attached to windows to cool the carriages. Electric fans were introduced in 1905.

The Government did put in place some rules to improve third-class travel. As early as 1854, railway companies had been prohibited from selling more tickets than the space available in its rolling stock. In 1864, instructions were given to paint the permissible number of passengers outside the carriages. Besides low fares suggested to popularize railway travel among the masses, companies were also asked to allow third-class passengers to disembark at stations. Mohandas Karamchand Gandhi's journeys across India in third-class compartments brought the problems front and centre when he wrote about them, but progress was slow. It wasn't until post-Independence that the plight of 97 per cent of the total train travellers in India was given more thought.

▼ **The dining car** of this Great Indian Peninsula Railway (GIPR) first-class coach shows the luxuries available to European and Eurasian passengers who could pay for them. This photograph was taken sometime in the 1930s.

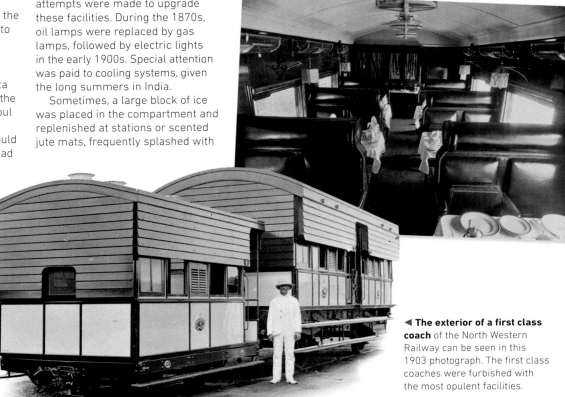

◄ **The exterior of a first class coach** of the North Western Railway can be seen in this 1903 photograph. The first class coaches were furbished with the most opulent facilities.

Pani Pandey **or watermen** collected water from hand pumps and stored them in cans. They would offer passengers water, especially during long, hot summer days. Seen here are the watermen of the Kharagpur Junction railway station, a part of the Bengal–Nagpur Railway, carrying containers of drinking water meant for passengers, on wheel barrows.

A MATTER OF DESIGN

The architectural style of railway stations in India during the late 19th and early 20th centuries began straying from the initial functional designs and gave way to ornamentation. Some of these buildings were built to represent the splendour of the British Empire in India, while others were constructed keeping security in mind. As such, this period marked the creation of some of the greatest railway stations in the country, most of which have outlived the Empire that built them.

▲ **This 1906 photograph** of the Howrah station shows the grand building amidst the city bustling with everyday activity.

Stations built in this period heavily incorporated European styles into their designs. The architects were British themselves, so it was only natural that they would draw upon familiar inspirations, such as the popular medieval Romanesque style.

The Madras Central station (now known as Chennai Central) is an apt example. The instructions were to keep ornamentation to a minimum, an order lost on the Victorian architects who began work in 1868. The result was a grand Romanesque Revival building with round arches, an elaborate central tower accompanied with four corner towers, iron-worked roof ridges, and coloured stone – a design that took five years to complete. Significant increases in passenger traffic over the years meant that the station's facilities were under constant strain. To meet this demand, three more

platforms were added in 1938, taking the number up to seven. Several more were added after 1947 to accommodate the traffic.

The Howrah station in Calcutta, a rickety tin shed with a single booking window in 1854, transformed into its present avatar after its renovation between 1900 and 1908. The red brick structure combines wide Moorish eaves with eight Romanesque towers and has 22 platforms. The stations at Agra Fort, and Bellary (modern-day Ballari) in Karnataka, display similar Romanesque features.

Another prominent European style at the time was Victorian Gothic, which was adopted in a variety of

stations in Bombay, including Victoria Terminus (see pp.120–21), and the Colaba station before it was remodelled in 1931. The original Colaba station was defined by a high tower and a carriage porch, along with unique steel columns made of rails.

For troubled times

In some parts of the country, particularly those affected by the Revolt of 1857 (see pp.42–43), stations were important

▶ **An 1880 photograph** of the Madras Central station as taken by photography firm, Nicholas and Company.

◀ **The Victorian Gothic architecture** of the Delhi Junction has slender octagonal towers as its crowning feature.

in the towers while the station building doubled as a shelter for the railway staff.

Merging ideas

The Indo-Saracenic style, a blend of Mughal, Hindu, and Gothic influences, began dominating the design of public buildings by the early 20th century. The Chennai Egmore station, which was built in 1908, incorporated pillar brackets, eaves, and square cupolas. Hyderabad's Kacheguda station built in 1916 as a part of the Godavari Light Railway, falls into this category as well with ornate brackets as seen in old Indian temple architecture, and dome-shaped pavilions decorated with lotus motifs. It also had a ladies' area sectioned off from the main platform with a purdah wall, which allowed women to privately disembark from the train. In some cases, regional elements were incorporated

facets of the defence network, and resembled fortified medieval castles. Delhi Junction, which opened in 1903, was designed as one such station. It had mosque-like features – somewhat similar to the iconic Jama Masjid mosque nearby – and six octagonal watchtowers. In case of an emergency, water could be stored

THE AH WHEELER STORY

French businessman Emile Edouard Moreau and his friend AH Wheeler, both book lovers, were the men behind the popular AH Wheeler book stalls that dot stations across India. The first stall came up in Allahabad in 1874 or 1877 – the exact year is a matter of some debate – when Wheeler realized he had too many books to carry back with him to London. Ever resourceful, Moreau decided to cash in on the new trend of upper-class passengers reading books to keep themselves occupied on train journeys. He offered to sell Wheeler's books from a wooden almirah at the station. Till 2004, the company had exclusive rights to sell books on railway stations in many parts of the country.

An AH Wheeler Bookstall at Victoria Terminus, Bombay

into stations through the use of local materials for construction, as it lowered transportation costs. This is clearly visible in the Porbandar station in Gujarat, which was constructed in yellow Porbandar stone in 1889.

VICTORIA TERMINUS

Upon British architect Fredrick William Stevens' death in 1900, his obituary in the magazine *The Engineer* called his creation, Victoria Terminus, "a fine example of his creative skill". These sedate words are not enough to express the sheer grandeur of the building that stands in the heart of the metropolis of Mumbai (formerly Bombay).

Victoria Terminus (VT) was a terminal train station inaugurated in 1887 for the Golden Jubilee of Queen Victoria's accession to the British throne. Its name was changed in 1996 to Chhatrapati Shivaji Maharaj Terminus (CSMT), Mumbai, after the 17th-century king and founder of the Maratha Empire, Shivaji Bhonsale I. Today, it is the head office of India's Central Railway besides catering to millions of daily commuters.

Initially, VT accommodated the main station and offices. However, as Bombay grew from a prominent trade city to a bustling metropolis, the station adapted to a growing demand for transportation. The original building has a C-shaped plan made out of two wings that are held together by a central, eight-ribbed dome. This dome is, in turn, topped by a 4m-statue of the Lady of Progress with stone statues of a lion and tiger on the entrance gate piers. The north wing provides passenger facilities and the south houses administrative offices. At the head of the north wing lies the station's main booking hall, which has a wooden, neo-Gothic vaulted roof decorated with golden stars, pointed arches, and stained glass.

As the station expanded, new buildings were added at adjoining sites. In 1929, the station's functions underwent a dramatic bifurcation when a new building opened to specifically deal with main line traffic even as the original building continued to cater to the suburban commuters.

Besides being an active train station, CSMT has been a Heritage Grade I structure since 1997. This, coupled with its status as a UNESCO World Heritage Site since 2004, has ensured that adequate measures are taken to prolong the historic building's life.

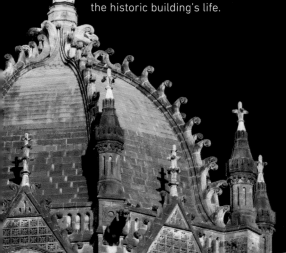

The marble statue of the Lady of Progress holds a wheel in her left hand to signify movement, speed, and change. In her right hand, she holds a torch to light the way towards progress.

Supposedly inspired by St Pancras railway station in London, Victoria Terminus's architecture is an amalgamation of Victorian Gothic styles and traditional Indian motifs. Indian decorative elements, such as peacocks, tigers, reptiles, and tropical plants, painted by English artist John Lockwood Kipling and his students, can be seen throughout the terminus.

For their visit to India for the Delhi Durbar of 1911, His Royal Highness King George V and his queen consort Mary arrived in Bombay and travelled to Delhi, and later, Calcutta via train. This picture shows the royal couple at the Calcutta railway station during their visit.

IN THE TIME OF WAR

The world went to war in the summer of 1914. World War I or the Great War, as it was known at that time, lasted until 1918. India, still a colony of the British Empire, found itself embroiled in the global conflict, which left its railways in a state of complete disrepair. This was also a time when there was a renewed push for an independent India.

On 28 June 1914, a Bosnian Serb, Gavrilo Princip, assassinated Austrian Archduke Franz Ferdinand and his wife Sophie in Sarajevo, Serbia. A month later, Austria-Hungary declared war on Serbia, shaking up Europe and splitting it into warring factions. World War I pitted the Central Powers, which included Germany, Austria-Hungary, Turkey, and Bulgaria against Britain, France, Russia, Italy, Serbia, and later the United States of America, who together formed the Allies.

This "war to end all wars" saw the British mobilize India's resources in service to the Empire in an unprecedented manner. The colony served as a vast reservoir from which large and sustained unilateral transfers of men, money, and material were made. In a telegram sent in April 1918 to Lord Chelmsford, the Viceroy of India (1916–21), British Prime Minister David Lloyd George (1916–22), wrote: "The future course of the war ... depends on our ability to refit our armies as fast as we can ... you should take this opportunity to do everything in your power to increase Indian establishment for war, not only in troops, but in railway materials and military equipments of all kinds ... "

Increased involvement

No other department found itself more closely connected to making contributions to the war than the railways. Increased workload in both civil and military affairs meant the reorganization of the railways administration. The nature and degree of the involvement of the railways in the war effort was so immense that the Railway Board

▲ **The murder** of Archduke Franz Ferdinand while in a carriage as depicted in this magazine illustration, steadily impelled countries to take sides with either the Axis or Allied powers.

coordinated the war effort, collecting ordnance and wartime rations, ranging from hide and clothing to overseeing steel production at the Tata Iron and Steel Works in Jamshedpur (in modern-day Jharkhand).

Several offices were created to deal with the increased workload. The war branch of the Board, formed in September 1916, was later absorbed into the Indian Munitions Board and the adjutant general's branch. Scarcity of wagon supplies to the collieries saw the introduction of a special coal indent system with a coal controller. The management of limited transport fell under the purview of the controller of traffic, a post created in 1917. By 1918, a special member of the Railway Board for the war period was instituted and Priority Certificates were issued to control rail traffic.

Operations of several branches and railway lines were temporarily dismantled to meet the demand for rails and rolling stock in the regions of Mesopotamia, Eastern Africa, and Palestine. India also supplied men

EFFECT ON THE FREEDOM MOVEMENT

World War I gave the nationalist movement a second wind and Home Rule, or self-government, became a popular demand. Indian nationalist Bal Gangadhar Tilak formed the All India Home Rule League in 1916 and campaigned for independence along with British social reformer, Annie Besant. However, most nationalists advocated India's support and service during the war. Mohandas Karamchand Gandhi, who had arrived in Bombay in January 1915, echoed this sentiment. Tilak and Gandhi toured villages, collecting recruits for the war, which became a common cause. Contributing to Britain's war efforts would allow India to cull greater freedoms for itself. This support did yield conciliatory political posturing from Edwin Montague, the Secretary of State for India who, on his 1917–18 visit to India, recommended some Indian control within the provincial government. The nationalists could now work towards a clear and defined goal.

▲ **The English translation** of the book, *Hind Swaraj*, or *Indian Home Rule* by Gandhi, which was banned by the British Government.

► **The Indian Sappers** who were a part of the British Indian Army of the Raj were sent to the Mesopotamian front. Here the Sappers constructed broad-gauge tracks across the desert to help facilitate the British campaign against the Ottoman Empire.

and material for railways in African countries, such as Kenya and Uganda. Locally manufactured railway material sufficient to construct almost 2,800 km of railway track, 229 locomotives, and 5,989 vehicles were sent from India. To meet its wartime debts, the British Government levied a surcharge on railway goods traffic. Expansion came to a screeching halt as well. For instance, the South Indian Railway dropped its plans to construct a 19-km-long bridge between Dhanushkodi and Sri Lanka.

Several trains were discontinued and those that continued to run were severely overflowing with travellers. Passenger comfort, always a problem in third-class carriages worsened as did overcrowding since these were now deployed for troops. Brand-new carriages and locomotives were hard to come by and, as a result, the Railway Board asked Indian members of the Legislative Council to instruct their constituents to avoid unnecessary travel.

Raising questions

Growing discontent with the railways among the masses, set against this backdrop of the war, almost mirrored the general dissatisfaction with British rule. National leaders, such as GK Gokhale, managed to pull the railways solidly into the sphere of Indian politics, which is best illustrated by his speeches and interactions as a member of the Imperial Legislative Council. Gokhale said: " ... if the Japanese ... are managing their Railways, I do not see why we should not be able to do so."

The leaders collectively critiqued the benefits of having the railways in India, and focused on the importance of transferring its management to the State and the exclusion of Indians from senior management roles.

The general disrepair that the railways had fallen into during and after the war, and the resulting deteriorating passenger services only fanned public discontent and anger. This lent force to the demand for an overhaul of railway policy and management and later led to the appointment of the Acworth Committee in 1920 (see pp.132–33).

> 66 Are **railways everything** and **mass education nothing**? Is improved **sanitation nothing**? 99

GK GOKHALE, NATIONALIST LEADER AND MEMBER OF THE IMPERIAL LEGISLATIVE COUNCIL, IN HIS 1906 BUDGET SPEECH

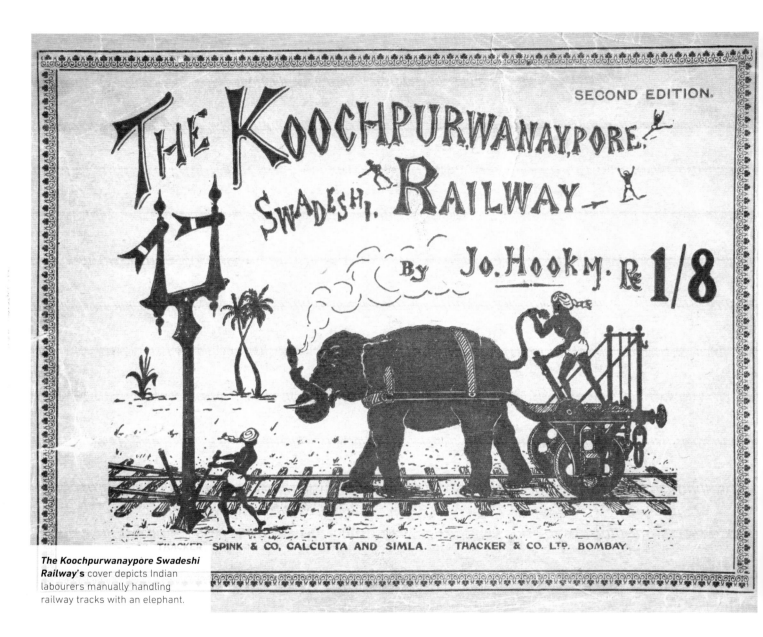

The Koochpurwanaypore Swadeshi Railway's cover depicts Indian labourers manually handling railway tracks with an elephant.

THE LAND OF NO WORRIES

In the early 1900s, a collection of satirical sketches on the railways in India was published anonymously by Calcutta's then leading publishing firm Thacker, Spink & Co. Seemingly a dig at the anti-imperialist sentiment that had sprung up with the Swadeshi movement, the satire's premise was that the people – so keen to run their own country – were not capable of running the vast railway network that had been set up by the British. The sketches first appeared in the Great Indian Peninsula Railway (GIPR) magazine and were reprinted in a book format "to amuse the railwaymen of India and the general public".

Titled the *Koochpurwanaypore Swadeshi Railway*, the sketches depict natives in the make-believe state of Koochpurwanaypore, a name derived from the Hindustani words *kuch parwah nahin*, translated by the author as "it doesn't matter"; a place the artist believes to be a representation of India and its "tribe", a personification of Indians. The interplay between language and satire is reflected in the author's pseudonym as well – *Jo Hookm* – loosely translated to be "as you command". Since the identity of the author and illustrator was kept anonymous – some library sources identified him as a William Henry Deakin – in the absence of any other information on the subject, "his" nationality and other credentials can only be speculated.

A retaliation

The sketches may have been published as a reaction to the Swadeshi movement of 1905, an economic strategy adopted by Indians seeking independence, to boost the local economy. It asked for Indians to boycott British goods and only buy products made in India. The sketches were meant to be a satirical take on the railways, if they were to be "truly Swadeshi in conception, equipment, and management".

The cleverly drawn 53-page booklet was sold at Re ⅛ and depicted scenes on the fictitious Koochpurwanaypore Railway (KPR), punctuated with anglicized versions of local Hindustani phrases. Koochpurwanay was meant to convey the artist's sentiment that Indians, by themselves, were unable to handle a complex and vast enterprise such as the railways.

Colonial chauvinism

The author wrote in his foreword to the book, "The tribe of the Koochpurwanay, as everyone knows, has its home in the heart of India, some of its better known family names are *Pichi*, *kal*, *abbi nay*, and *hazr hi*", which are translated to mean behind (in schedule), tomorrow, not now, and present (in attendance), respectively. The sketches mocked the technological know-how and managerial skills of the natives.

The artist seemed to advance the argument that there was no hint of an understanding of modern technology in the minds of the Indian population. Instead, they seemed to gravitate towards the idea of heavy dependence on manual labour. While the Indian workforce was shown as absurdly ignorant, those in positions of power were portrayed as careless and irresponsible. The shambolic portrayal of the living conditions conveyed the idea of a society so primitive, it would turn into *Mutwalabad* – the land of the inebriated – as soon as the British left.

Representation at last?

With a positive outlook, and the clarity of hindsight, it could be argued that *Koochpurwanaypore* accidentally brought some representation to the natives in the context of the British Indian railways. Even though the book's central focus is railways, the artist slips in, deliberately or otherwise, some insights into the sociocultural set up, or at least the British perception of it. These are reflected in some recurring motifs, such as those of Ganesha (the elephant god), men wearing loincloths, and structures with domes, among others.

The work can also be seen as a part of the larger discourse that projects railways as a colonial endeavour to the British and Indian audience. In this context of representation, the choice of railways as a subject of study has its own foundations. Since railways is often equated with progress and development, and has a huge material presence, it served as the most registered and obvious symbol for British advancement in the colonies.

The booklet carried a glossary with translations of Hindustani to English words. It is likely that the author anticipated a British audience. If he was writing only for English-speaking Indians, he wouldn't have felt the need to provide English translations of anglicized local terms at the end of his work. Moreover, Thacker, Spink & Co had a distribution channel in London and it is likely that the work would have reached the shores of Great Britain.

▼ **Titled "New Shunting Power",** the giant turtle pictured here is what the author perceived to be a "substitute" for shunting engines.

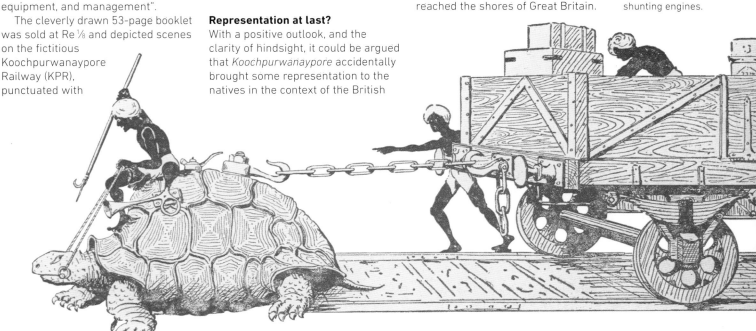

1921–1938

STATE WITHIN

A **STATE**

1921–1938

The railways had found their rhythm with the Government focus on consolidation and refining policies. Yet, this period was marked by upheaval, as the cries for freedom became more strident and nationalists sought to incorporate the railways into their struggle for Independence. Amid all this was the Depression and the rumblings of another World War, one that promised to be far worse than the first.

1920 The Acworth Committee, appointed by the secretary of state for India, makes a series of crucial recommendations that change the face of railways in India.

1921 Railway tracks now criss-cross British India, stretching to 61,220 km.

1922 Mohandas Karamchand Gandhi is tried for sedition for his articles in *Young India*.

1925 The East Indian Railway (EIR) and the Great Indian Peninsula Railway (GIPR) are taken over by the British Government in India.

1925 First Railway Budget is presented.

1926 Final section of the Khyber Pass railway opens for operation.

1 September 1928 The Frontier Mail begins operations from Bombay with Peshawar as its destination.

1928 Electrification picks up pace in Bombay and work begins on the Madras suburban line.

1921–23

1924–26

192⁷

5 February 1922 Clash between an angry mob and the local police in Chauri Chaura leads to Gandhi withdrawing the Non-cooperation movement.

1921 A chief commissioner with overriding powers on technical matters is appointed during the reorganizaton of the Railway Board.

1924 The railways gets its own financial budget and a financial commissioner is appointed to the Railway Board.

3 February 1925 The first electric train runs from Victoria Terminus (VT) to Kurla on the GIPR's Harbour branch.

9 August 1925 The infamous Kakori train robbery takes place.

1927 Simon Commission comes to India.

1928 Automatic colour-light signals are first used on the GIPR's lines in Bombay between VT and Byculla.

The Bombay Chronicle reports Gandhi's arrest dated 11 March 1922

Train emerging from a tunnel on the Khyber Railway

Frontier Mail

> ❝ At every station ... **large crowds surrounded our compartment. They flooded us with flowers** and food and tried to show ... that they appreciated the **sacrifices** that the **leaders were making** to **win Swaraj for** the people. ❞

KRISHNA NEHRU HUTHEESING, *WITH NO REGRETS: AN AUTOBIOGRAPHY* (1943)

1929 Reorganization of the Railway Board leads to separate members for traffic and labour.

12 March 1930 Gandhi sets out on his famous Salt March, kicking off the Civil Disobedience movement.

1931 More than 69,000 km of railway tracks cross the length and breadth of the country.

1931–1932 The Railway Board is reorganized as an economic measure and now consists of the chief commissioner, the financial commissioner, and a member assisted by directors.

1936–37 Indian provincial elections are held across 11 provinces with the Indian National Congress winning in eight.

1936 Some passenger coaches become air conditioned. The Matunga Workshop becomes the first to manufacture five such coaches.

1937 The office of minister for transport and communications is created.

0   1931–33   1934–38

1 June 1930 The Deccan Queen begins operations as a weekend train from Bombay to Poona.

1929 The Indian National Congress resolves to fight for Purna Swaraj or complete independence.

24 October 1929 The Wall Street crash sets the Great Depression in motion.

1931 Hudswell, Clarke and Company Limited construct the first locomotive equipped with a fluid coupling.

30 January 1933 Adolf Hitler becomes the Chancellor of Germany.

29 October 1936 The Wedgewood Committee suggests ways to improve railway finances.

1 May 1937 The Flying Queen (the predecessor of the Flying Ranee) begins its run between Bombay and Surat, reducing travel time to four hours.

Adolf Hitler (centre left)

The EMU railway workshop in Matunga, Mumbai

CHANGE OF POWER

By the end of 1920, even though the British Government in India owned a major part of the railways in the country, it managed and operated but a small share. A majority were run by private companies, the practices of which were fast becoming a subject of widespread public criticism. A strong public debate pushed for direct management of the railways by the government, and a committee was set up to oversee the matter and recommend changes as necessary.

▼ **VS Srinivasa Sastri** was a political leader and India's delegate to the League of Nations in 1921. As a liberal, he championed the cause of equal rights in India.

Within the Indian subcontinent, the North Western, Eastern Bengal, Oudh and Rohilkhand, and Jorhat railways were under the direct control of the British Indian Government. The rest – more than a 100 – were managed by private companies. Lack of investment and operational fatigue during World War I had taken a serious toll on the railway system and, as immediate government attention was drawn to the forthcoming expiration of the contract with the East Indian Railway (EIR) in 1919, the debate regarding State versus corporate management of the rail networks began to take centre stage. The Government, however, was unclear about the future railway policy in India and the company's contract was temporarily extended up to 1924 even as the case was referred to a representative committee for further examination.

The committee
On 1 November, 1920, railway economist and barrister-at-law Sir William Acworth was appointed chairman of a 10-member railway committee. Of the 10, three were British with no prior knowledge about India, three others had substantial experience with the railways in the country, and three were Indians to represent the native population's commercial interests.

VS Srinivasa Sastri was a member of the Council of State from 1920 to 1925, Sir Rajendra Nath Mookerjee was a Calcutta-based industrialist, and Sir Purshotamdas Thakurdas was a Bombay-based cotton trader. Sir Henry Ledgard of Cawnpore (modern-day Kanpur) was appointed to represent the European business community in India.

Creating guidelines
Apart from direct State management, other options on the table were direct management; management through a company domiciled in Europe, with a Board in London; management through a company domiciled in India, with a Board in India; and management through a combination of the last two. The committee was asked to examine the relative advantages of the various systems of management. It was also asked to assess the role and composition of the Railway Board and the system of government control over administration, rates and fares, and the machinery for settling disputes between railways and traders. It had to examine the financial policy, "and in particular the feasibility of the greater utilization of private enterprise and capital in construction of new lines."

Over the course of its operations, the Acworth Committee asked the opinions of 142 witnesses, including 48 railwaymen and 19 government officials. The members also visited Madras, Bombay, Delhi, Lucknow, Kanpur, and Lahore to collect evidence. They reconvened in London to undertake further discussions and after due deliberations with all sections of society, professionals, the government, and railwaymen in India and in Britain, the committee's report was submitted in mid-1921.

The recommendations
On the subject of management, the members unanimously advocated that it should be based in India and not London. To this effect, the committee recommended that the contracts with the companies be terminated at their respective expiry dates. It, however, was divided about the specific system of management in India. While some of its members preferred direct State management, others recommended that some management be given to companies domiciled in India. With respect to finance, all members agreed that it was intertwined with the decision on management. They also unanimously supported a complete overhaul of the financial system, including separation of the

◄ **Passengers travelling in the third-class** compartments faced hardships due to overcrowding and unsanitary conditions. The committee resolved to make a change.

Railway Budget from the General Budget of the State, and agreed on the methods for raising new capital. Members who advocated some degree of private participation in management also provided additional methods for raising capital. On the rest of the matters, the committee was united in its decisions.

The Railway Board
The committee recommended major restructuring in the Railway Board's composition and suggested that it be renamed the Railway Commission. It provided further suggestions related to administration and control, such as appointing a Member of Council at the head of the Railway Department and the creation of a Department of Communications, which would include railways, with an exclusive member of the Viceroy's Council looking after it.

Other suggestions included relieving the Railway Department from the control of the India Office and the Government, except while dealing with finance and general policy, delegation of routine management to local railway administration, and the establishment of Central and Local Railway Advisory Councils for greater participation of the Indian public in railway management.

Forming a budget
For the railways' financial aspects, the committee proposed that the Finance Department of the Government should cease to control the internal finances of the railways and that the latter should have a separate budget. It suggested that the railway accounts should be subject to an independent audit by the Government and that its accounting and statistical systems be remodelled in accordance with best practices followed in other countries.

General railway reforms
The committee also suggested the establishment of a Rates Tribunal for jurisdiction over rates and facilities. It noted that steps should be taken for quick settlement of claims for damage and loss, to improve conditions of the third class, and to provide adequate training and employment opportunities to Indians for higher positions in the railway service. It recommended the construction of branch lines, which were managed by their main lines, with separate branch line companies to be formed only if the Government was unable or disinclined to provide funds for these. The members also urged for a commission to examine the gauge question.

The Acworth Committee channelized much of the public sentiments in its report. It also brought together and gave direction to railway matters that had hitherto remained scattered and dealt with in isolation. A direct result of these recommendations was a centralized railway system in India by the end of the second decade of the 20th century.

▼ **Sir William Acworth** was the chairman of the Acworth Committee in 1921. The recommendation to separate railway finances was followed by the Indian Government till 2017, when the Budgets were merged.

 The **evidence given before us** … on behalf **of all** sections of the **community** was overwhelmingly **strong as** to the urgent need of … reform and **reconstruction** of the entire railway machine. "

ACWORTH REPORT (1921)

REFORMING AND RESTRUCTURING

Once the Acworth Committee had submitted its report in 1921, the Government began its campaign of major railway reforms in administration, management, and finance. Changes were aimed to consolidate railway policy for smoother operations and regulation, and mostly to bring the railway policy under a single rubric.

The British Government in India accepted most of the proposals put forth by the Acworth Committee Report (see pp.132–133) and appointed two committees in 1922 for the sole purpose of executing those suggestions. The Railway Finance Committee, under the governor of Punjab (1924–28), Sir Malcolm Hailey, and Indian Legislative Assembly members, focused on the rules, quantum, and method of capital expenditure allocation, and on separating the Railway Budget from general finances.

Separating the finances

The second committee chaired by Sir James Mackay or Lord Inchcape, a colonial administrator, examined efficient ways to increase revenue and reduce railway expenditure. The sweeping changes that followed the formation of these committees served to revitalize railway finances over the next few years. Following the Railway Finance Committee's approval in 1922, Legislative Assembly members allocated Rs 150 crores, to be spent over five years, for the rehabilitation of overaged and stressed railway assets. They passed the resolution to separate railway finances from the General Budget in September 1924 in what is now known as the Separation Convention. As the sole shareholder of the railways, the Government became entitled to a fixed contribution from the profits of the railways as a dividend, in return for the capital employed.

▶ **Sir Malcolm Hailey,** became the governor of the United Provinces (1928–34) after serving as the governor of Punjab. He was awarded the Order of Companion of the Indian Empire (CIE) by the Crown for his services to the British Raj.

Other financial reforms

The Acworth Committee Report's recommendations also led to the formation of a separate Government audit wing, headed by the auditor general. The wing examined and reported on the finances maintained by the railway's Accounts Department. The new professionally organized Indian Railway Accounts Service (IRAS) managed the finances.

Simultaneously, a series of reforms were introduced to incorporate commercial principles into railway finance. These included the creation of a Railway Reserve Fund and a Depreciation Fund, and the formation of revised rules for capital and revenue expenditure. It also covered the establishment of a clearing house to facilitate interrailway financial transactions and the revamping of the railway statistical system. These structural changes within the financial set-up provided a fresh lease of life. The railways soon started reaping the benefits of both functional and financial autonomy.

Over time, the rules of allocation of expenditure and earnings evolved and enabled seamless recognition and interpretation of the railways' financial statements by the Government and the commercial stakeholders. These protocols also helped the railways to seek active participation from private enterprise in its development.

Managerial reforms

The state or company management debate proved to be a divisive subject after the Acworth Committee failed to provide a unanimous recommendation. This led to a tussle between the Government and members of the legislative assembly. It soon became clear that the management of the

East Indian Railway (EIR) and the Great Indian Peninsula Railway (GIPR), the contracts of which were due to expire soon, would go to the Government.

The Government, anticipating inefficient and expensive management at their end, was reluctant to forgo the role of the companies. The debate reached its peak during the separation proceedings until a clause in the resolution on the Separation of Railway Finance in India (1924) settled the matter. This gave the Government the freedom to enter into negotiations for company management subject to an adequate discussion with the Legislative Assembly, failing which the latter would have the power to terminate all arrangements. The EIR and GIPR were nationalized in 1925. The branch line policy (see p.69), which was terminated at around the same time ensured that District Board

railways and other lines for local benefits could be constructed with the approval of local Governments and on the basis of a minimum guarantee by local bodies.

Administrative reforms
The changes to the Railway Board, which was reconstituted in 1922, came into effect in 1924. They aimed at securing some degree of autonomy for the Board. Its members were also required to engage with local bodies and take into account public opinion. The Government was limited to critical questions of policy and finance.

The Board now comprised a chief commissioner, who was also the ex-officio secretary to the Government of India in the Railway Department, the financial commissioner, four directors for civil engineering, mechanical engineering, traffic, and

establishment, and two members, one for technical matters and the other for general administration. The financial commissioner embraced his dual role as a Railway Board member and the representative of the Government's Finance Department, which supported the capital expenses of the State railways from the public exchequer. A chief mechanical engineer was also appointed in 1922. Deputy directors and assistant directors were assigned as and when the need arose.

The Government implemented other recommendations as well, such as the establishment of the Central Advisory Council in 1922 followed by Local Advisory Councils and a Rates Advisory Committee in 1926. The enterprise was now as organized as it could be and the reforms brought about a major turn in the course of railway development in India.

▲ **GIPR officers** pose for a photograph on the eve of the departure of E Fraser, the chief mechanical engineer of the company at the GIPR headquarters in Bombay in 1930. The nationalization of the GIPR and EIR in 1925 saw a dawn of expansion under a more consolidated Railway Board.

NATIONALIZATION

By 1920, the Government had started taking over India's company-run railways, entering a new phase, in which its manner of functioning was more accommodating of public opinion. This period of prosperity was a welcoming change from the havoc of World War I, although stability was still a far-off dream. Then the Great Depression began in October 1929, shaking up the Indian economy and its behemoth, the railways.

In 1879, the British Government in India acquired the East Indian Railway (EIR). It was the beginning of the State taking control of the railways, in a move that was popularly called nationalization. However, it promptly handed over the operations to the private EIR company, scaling back any impact the purchase may have had on its operations. By April 1905, of the 43,380 km of railways, the State owned and administered 8,964 km, while another 21,293 km were State-owned, but operated by private companies. The rest were run by private companies or Princely States, so much so that in 1921 there were at least 175 such players owning or operating the railways.

It is because of this, that the push towards consolidating the railway network became more concentrated, especially with the appointment of the Acworth Committee (see pp.132–33) by the secretary of state for India in 1921. Its recommendations that the Government take over the direct management of the railways served as a tipping point in the history of the railways in India. It also lent strength to the public and Indian nationalists' demand for central management.

Mergers and acquisitions
The recommendations of the Acworth Committee saw a sea change in Government policies. It stopped renewing its contracts with private railway companies. As these started lapsing, the rail lines gradually came directly under the Government. The vast networks of the EIR and the Great Indian Peninsula Railway (GIPR) were the first to be brought in. The EIR's management was taken over by the Government on 1 January 1925 and the GIPR followed within six months. This continued over the course of several decades with the nationalization of the Assam–Bengal Railway and the Bombay, Baroda and Central India (BB&CI) Railway in 1942 and the Bengal–Nagpur Railway in 1944.

Prosperity and boom
The 1920s was a period of expansion, one driven by the fact that, at the end of 1924, the total coverage was a mere 61,218 km, which was 99,717 km short of the number proposed by the 1908 Mackay Committee (see pp.134–35). To address this shortfall, the member in charge of the railways in the Executive Council, Sir Charles Innes, announced an ambitious five-year programme. It aimed at annually constructing at least 1,609 km of new tracks along with the complete rehabilitation and overhaul of railway equipment.

By the end of March 1926, projects of about 9,656–11,265 km were sanctioned or were being investigated. No expense was spared. By 1928–29, 2,063 km of tracks were added, exceeding the target of a 1,609 km. Through 1924–32, about 8,626 route km was added to the Indian railways at a cost of Rs 441.90 million.

Between 1924 and 1932, the expenditure incurred on open lines work was about Rs 1.22 billion, which amounted to 73 per cent of the total capital expenditure on the railways. This was of two types, stationary equipment and mobile equipment.

The expenditure on stationary equipment, such as road beds, stations, signals, and projects stood at 70 per cent of the capital expenditure, which amounted to Rs 856.7 million. About Rs 372.2 million was spent on mobile equipment, such as locomotives, wagons, and coaching vehicles.

The Railway Board came up with a system of overallotment to drive greater expenditure and rapid expansion. Under this system, though the estimates submitted by the railway administration were cut, they were given the assurance that they could spend up to the amounts mentioned in the allocated Annual Budget. Railway agents were given additional powers to roll out new schemes and, in some cases, all prudence was abandoned and money was sanctioned without estimates or even a blueprint.

The railways in India were so capital-rich during this period that Sir Charles Innes in his 1926–27 Budget speech said, "the principal difficulty with which we are now confronted is that of spending the money, that is, of executing rapidly, sanctioned projects". One of the reasons could have been agents overestimating their expenditure.

▶ **The Bengal–Nagpur Railway, formed in 1887,** was brought under the Government's control in 1944.

The Great Depression

The October 1929 Wall Street crash and subsequent economic downturn, the Great Depression, which extended across the world, put paid to the railway's prosperity and it experienced a period of austerity. The 1937 Indian Railway Enquiry Committee chaired by Sir Ralph E Wedgewood investigated the position of Government-owned railways and recommended ways to increase earnings and help the enterprise become stable.

The committee undertook an exhaustive survey of the financial and operational developments since World War I (1914–18) and gave recommendations. These led to greater operational efficiency, including institutionalized publicity, public relations machinery, and development of the Commercial Departments to increase railway earnings. The committee provided a rational basis for the assessment of the railways' depreciation fund. It also made recommendations regarding the Federal Railway Authority, to be formed under the Government of India Act of 1935. The federal section of the Act never came into operation, neither did the proposals. In the end, the Government accepted most of the committee's recommendations.

Calcutta - Bombay via Nagpur

SUPER SERVICE

By BENGAL NAGPUR RAILWAY

More than 500 trains operate on the Harbour Line daily, the first line to be electrified in India. This picture shows the beginning of the line at Chhatrapati Shivaji Maharaj Terminus (CSMT).

EARLY ELECTRIFICATION

By the early 20th century in India, as city populations increased and cityscapes embraced hinterlands, the limitations of steam traction through coal-powered locomotives become obvious to the railway management. Rising passenger traffic in newborn suburbs created a huge demand for cost-effective commute options. Electrification seemed to be the most logical route to escape any strain on rolling stock as well as congestion, and isolated attempts were made at railway electrification.

The railways had brought on a substantial expansion of Bombay's cotton textile industry, facilitating easy transportation of raw material to the mills and finished products to other parts of India. The opening of the Port Trust Railways and the development of the Great Indian Peninsula Railway (GIPR) and Bombay, Baroda and Central India (BB&CI) Railway lines connected the port of Bombay to the interiors, and consolidated the commercial transportation system in the city.

Rise of the suburbs

As a knock-on effect, employment opportunities mushroomed in the port and the textile mills, and the railways provided an easy travel solution for daily commuters to and from work. Attracted by the possibilities of employment, a large number of people had moved to Bombay. Consequently, the railway passenger traffic was particularly high in certain sections, such as between Victoria Terminus (VT) (see pp.120–21) and the suburbs.

There was a pressing need for alternative spaces to accommodate this growing population. By providing travel services beyond central Bombay, the railways facilitated the suburbanization of the northern area of the island. Every day, a large number of the suburban population flocked via trains to their workplaces in the main city and gradually suburban railways emerged as an intrinsic component of everyday life in Bombay. However, traffic continued to grow and there were limitations, posed by what Canadian historian Ian J Kerr calls "Bombay's insular-peninsular site", to the introduction of more lines. Electrification of suburban train services was sought as an improved means for managing huge volumes of suburban traffic.

Towards electrification

The first electric train ran in India in 1925 but conversations around electrification started much earlier. In 1904, the chief engineer of the

Bombay Presidency, WH White, proposed the electrification of certain suburban sections of the GIPR and BB&CI lines. The Government of Bombay asked the two companies to explore the proposal and although both favoured electrification, they failed to reach an agreement on a joint terminus, as proposed by White. The outbreak of World War I further delayed the project as all resources were now diverted towards the war effort. By 1919, passenger traffic in Bombay had risen to numbers beyond the capacity of steam locomotives. Finally, the Bombay Municipal Corporation (BMC) issued a resolution for the GIPR to electrify its line till the suburb of Kalyan.

The Government drew up schemes for electrification not only in Bombay, but also in the Madras Presidency. All electric railway systems at this time operated on a 1,500-volts direct current electric traction. While the suburban services used Electric Multiple Units (EMUs), the main line was worked by electric locomotives.

Of suburbs ...

A section of the Harbour Line was the first to be electrified when an electric train ran from VT to Kurla on 3 February 1925. The part between Kurla and the Reay Road station had opened in 1910. Further extension of the line could only be on an elevated track due to shortage of land. The hauling power of steam

locomotives was insufficient for a steep climb and so the line was chosen to be electrified. In 1926, electrification was carried out on the line from Kurla to Thane and the Mahim Chord on the Harbour Line. By 1936, all lines till the extreme suburb of Virar were electrified.

... and ghats

Traction in hilly sections also resulted in extreme wear and tear for steam locomotives. By 1930, therefore, electrification was introduced on the main line from Kalyan to Igatpuri on the Thul Ghat and Kalyan to Poona (Pune) on the Bhore Ghat (see pp.50–51). According to Indian author JN Sahni in his book *Indian Railways: One Hundred Years 1853–1953*, passenger trains were worked by special Ghats engines. Goods trains were broken into two parts before they could be transported over the Ghats. Electrification along this route helped in removing the "bottlenecks" on the Ghats.

By 1931, in order to cater to the ever-increasing traffic in Madras City and its southern suburbs, electric power was introduced on a suburban section from Madras Beach to Tambaram. Electrification of this section entailed building double tracks as its single line was ill-equipped to handle increasing traffic. The travel was affordable and temporarily fixed both the cities' congestion problems.

Dabbawalas use the "locals" for tiffin delivery.

THE MUMBAI "LOCAL"

The bustling city of Mumbai is synonymous with its suburban railway network. Over the years, a unique culture has evolved in these trains. From chopping vegetables and knitting to playing cards and singing *bhajans* (devotional songs), people have found a new way of life while commuting within the city. The amusing stories from these trains, fondly called "locals", have been recreated in many films and books. Even the world-renowned *dabbawala* (tiffin porter) service relies heavily on local trains to get food to their customers on time.

DECCAN QUEEN

The 191-km distance between Bombay and Poona (Pune) used to take four days before the railways connected the two cities and reduced the travel time to six hours. The trains negotiated the steep and rapid 600-m ascent to Bhore Ghat (see pp.50–51), before descending into the plains towards Poona. When the Great Indian Peninsula Railway's (GIPR) Deccan Queen debuted on 1 June 1930, this journey further whittled down to two hours and 45 minutes.

Named after Poona's sobriquet, Queen of the Deccan, this intercity train originally ran only on weekends. It was not till 1943 that it became a daily connection. Legend has it that in its heyday, the Deccan Queen ferried Europeans to the races in Poona during the weekends.

The train was introduced with two rakes of seven coaches. While the underframes of the original coaches were imported from England, the bodies were made in the GIPR's Matunga Workshop in Bombay. A rarity for the time, the Deccan Queen was not hauled by using steam traction, but an electric locomotive – the first Indian train to be pulled by one.

It had many other firsts attached to its name – from being the first Indian train to have a vestibule (an enclosed space between coaches to allow easy passage), to having a "Ladies Only" compartment. Its crowning feature, however, was its dining car – half kitchen, half restaurant – which served hot meals to its passengers. The menu included fried fish and chips, baked beans on toast, cheese toast, and chicken cutlets.

One of the most iconic trains run by the Indian Railways, this express train today is the fastest from Mumbai (Bombay) to Pune, a lifeline for those who travel from one city to the other every day for work. The Deccan Queen entered its 90th glorious year of service in 2019.

भोजन यान
DINING CAR

Deccan Queen was the country's first superfast train. Its dining car remains popular with railway commuters even today.

The Bombay–Poona railway route was electrified in 1929. This picture from the 1930s shows an electric engine pulling the Deccan Queen as it passes through the Western Ghats. The engine's number – 4004 – can be seen written in the front.

THE MAKING OF A NATIONAL CONSCIOUSNESS

The railways may have started out as a symbol of British colonialism in the Indian subcontinent, but by the early 20th century, the enterprise had far surpassed its original loftiness. No one had anticipated the railway's role in bringing together a people hitherto so divided through differences in language, creed, and culture.

As part of the Civil Disobedience movement, protesters can be seen blockading rail traffic in this photograph from 1945.

The British Government in India had always advocated the positive economic impact of the railways in the country, promoting its role in India's march towards progress. Indian leaders, including Dadabhai Naoroji, however, took a more considered view. They recognized that the system served British interests first. Yet, it had become intrinsic to the country's social fabric. Historian Bipan Chandra wrote that these leaders were "champions of modern industry" and so were not against the railways. They merely realized that in order for the railways to become a truly "Indian" system, it had to play a bigger role in people's lives. It could no longer be a mere mode of transport, but a system that fostered Indian interests and industry and was also conscious of the needs of Indian travellers.

There was also an awareness, which came about as early as the 1870s, of the role the railways played in the depletion of the country's resources and diminished benefits. It was no wonder then that it became a key part of the nationalists' agenda.

For the people

The condition of the third-class traveller was uppermost on every Indian leader's mind. Mohandas Karamchand Gandhi's essay "Third-Class Travelling" condemned the appalling accommodation they were given and how they were treated. Just as important, and keenly debated at the Imperial Legislative Council of India in March 1911, was the need to

THE FREEDOM STRUGGLE

The Indian freedom movement picked up momentum after the 1919 Rowlatt Acts, followed by the massacre at Jallianwala Bagh in Amritsar, Punjab. With Gandhi's call for Satyagraha, or peaceful resistance, people from different religions and backgrounds came together to protest. The Non-cooperation (1920–22) and Civil Disobedience (1930) movements saw great success. With the Quit India movement (1942), there was a demand for the immediate withdrawal of the British from the country, followed by India's Independence in August 1947.

> The sight of an **Indian arrested merely for travelling** by **rail** in his **own country** provided a ready example of why **colonial rule** was morally **unacceptable**.

DAVID CAMPION, "RAILWAY POLICING AND SECURITY IN COLONIAL INDIA, c. 1860–1930"

employ more Indians in the upper ranks of the railways. Political leader GK Gokhale discussed this at great length in his landmark speech at the Council. By the 1920s, more and more communities joined this call for Indian diversity. With each passing year, leaders also got involved in the workings of the railways. They concerned themselves with a variety of matters, from the dismissal of a machineman at an Eastern Bengal Railway workshop to whether the Government was taking the right steps to address the demands of railway employees. In 1925, Jawaharlal Nehru, as chairman of the Allahabad Municipal Board, imposed taxes on the railways to support the debt-ridden civic body. This audacious step proved beneficial as the money was also used to provide facilities, such as water to passengers.

Ticketless travel
One of the easiest ways to cause disruption was to encourage ticketless travel and this was recorded in the Non-cooperation and later, the Civil Disobedience movements. Gandhi disapproved of this tactic, but it did not stop people. There were multiple incidents of crowds boarding trains without tickets and entering whichever

compartment they chose. "The ultimate goal was to wrest control of India's railways from the state and return it to the people who paid for its operation and to whom it belonged," American historian David Campion wrote. The Railway Board took stringent action to control the mobs by giving their personnel authority to evict people who were not passengers or who did not possess tickets.

A tool for resistance
A key feat of the railways lay in its ability to bring the country together. This was, as Indian historian Tara Chand put it, an "important stage in the evolution and development of national consciousness." It was almost inevitable that it would also play an equally important role in the freedom movement.

The rail system helped in the dissemination of information, and the stations, wrote Indian historian Ritika Prasad, "became vital spaces for anti-imperial mass agitations." For this was where people could gather in massive numbers to catch a glimpse of their beloved leaders. Despite his earlier denunciation of the railways, Gandhi learned to use the trains as a method of reaching out to the people.

Trains also served as an ideal propaganda machine. Everyone, from Congress leaders to the revolutionaries, used them to travel and connect with the people.

For nationalists, these spaces became ideal venues where they could mobilize crowds or even ask for money to fund movements. The Criminal Investigation Department (CID) and railway police would often wait for leaders travelling to a location for a demonstration and arrest them as soon as they got off the train. The national leaders, however, were well aware that an enthusiastic crowd could easily become an unruly mob and often implored people to follow station etiquette, be mindful of other passengers, and avoid shouting slogans until the train had actually arrived at the station.

At the height of the Quit India movement (1942), students used the railways as a way to communicate. In Bihar, trains were covered with the National Flag and carriages inscribed with slogans. Nationalists encouraged third-class travellers to use first-class compartments and there were even reports that those wearing Western clothes were not allowed to board trains.

As the country inched towards Independence, the people and their national leaders had appropriated the railways making it a key part of the freedom movement.

▼ **Dadabhai Naoroji,** was one of the country's first leaders to challenge the colonizer's view of the railways and point out that it seemed to only favour the British.

Gandhi saw railway stations as the perfect platform to address the thousands of followers that came to get a glimpse of their leader. This November 1946 photograph shows Gandhi speaking to a large crowd at a railway station in modern-day Bangladesh.

GANDHI AND THE RAILWAYS

Mohandas Karamchand Gandhi boarded a train for the first time in January 1888 when he travelled from Rajkot to Bhavnagar in Gujarat. Over the course of the freedom movement, his relationship with the railways in India swung from one end of the spectrum to the other – from critiquing the railways as the colonizers' means of spreading social disparity to using the trains as a tool for reaching the masses to spread his message.

◄ **This diorama** or miniature clay model exhibited at the Gandhi Smriti and Darshan Samiti Museum in New Delhi depicts the incident at the Pietermaritzburg railway station in South Africa. This incident influenced him to take up his fight against discrimination.

On a cold night in 1893, as young Gandhi walked to the waiting room of the Pietermaritzburg station in South Africa, he felt the weight of disempowerment looming large around him. He, a Britain-trained barrister, had just suffered the indignity of being forcibly thrown out of his first-class carriage because his fellow traveller – a Caucasian – refused to share the space with a coloured man. Gandhi would later recognize this incident as a pivotal one. The racial prejudice he faced that night not only informed his activism in South Africa, but set into motion the making of the man who would become the "Father of the Nation".

Condemning the railways

The launch of the railways in the Indian subcontinent and the making of the Mahatma (great soul) were both epoch-making events in the 19th century. While Gandhi lived and worked in South Africa from 1893 to 1914, his interaction with the railways was one of withstanding racial prejudice and discrimination. A lot of his writings on the discrimination faced by Indians in South Africa addressed the ban on travelling in trams and first-class carriages. In *The Grievances of the British Indians in South Africa: An Appeal to the Indian Public (The Green Pamphlet)*, he wrote several sections on the indignity of travelling on trams and trains for a "coolie". This was reported in *The Natal Mercury* issue of 18 January 1897.

In 1909, Gandhi wrote *Hind Swaraj*, or *Indian Home Rule*, which went on to be labelled as seditious and was banned. It was a critique of industrialization and the civilizational impulse of the West. Deeply critical of the railways, Gandhi viewed it as symptomatic of a larger denigration of the Indian way of life. A colonial tool, to him it was "beyond dispute that they propagate evil".

By 1915, when Gandhi made his final move to India, the railways had become a part of the physical and social fabric of the country. His mentor GK Gokhale had advised him to travel across the country before launching into active politics.

The Mahatma travels

Gandhi chose the third-class compartment of the railways as his mode of travel. The conditions of travel in the third-class were bleak – a callous bureaucracy, overcrowding, lack of sanitation facilities and hygiene, the practice of social prejudices, and problems concerning railway workers. His unbroken third-class tours during 1915–19 fostered an understanding in his mind of the relationship shared by the institution with the bulk of the Indian population, and gave him insights on his countrymen as well. It was a live metaphor of how the colonial administration treated the natives. He documented the trials of third-class travel in the "Woes of Third Class Passengers", recalling its inconveniences. By 1918–19, Gandhi had fallen ill and had to stop travelling third class. By the time he could finally resume, he had become the "Mahatma". Scores of people would flock to every stop of the train in which he was travelling for a glimpse of him.

Gandhi's views on the railways had softened considerably by the 1920s. The means of building and expansion of the railways may have been exploitative, but the character of the enterprise itself underwent a dramatic change as the Indian freedom movement increased in scale. The railways were now the means to quickly connect with like-minded compatriots and to spread the word of self-rule among all. His incessant political activity, necessitated the use of the railways. During the Non-cooperation movement (1920–22), when Gandhi was on a nationwide tour, he would persuade the mobs that thronged the station for a *darshan* (glimpse), to discard their headgear and *dupattas* (scarf-like garment) on the spot and light a bonfire to boycott foreign cloth.

Gandhi's relationship with the railways would follow him beyond his temporal body. Upon his death in 1948, when the man and the myth of the Mahatma had become inseparable, an urn filled with his ashes was placed in a train made up of five third-class carriages. The Asthi Special wove its way from city to city in north India, till it reached Allahabad, where the Mahatma's mortal remains were immersed into the River Ganges.

> ❝ It must be **manifest** to you that, but for **the railways,** the English could not have such a **hold on India** as they have. ❞
>
> MK GANDHI, *HIND SWARAJ* (1909)

During the freedom movement, railway stations became key instruments in the symbiotic relationship between the freedom fighters and the masses. Apart from being political spaces for mass mobilization, stations witnessed huge crowds of people, who would wait tirelessly in the hope of catching a glimpse of their heroes. Seen here is Mohandas Karamchand Gandhi looking out from his compartment at the crowd at a railway station in 1940.

REVOLUTIONARIES AND THE RAILWAYS

Railways were introduced in India for British commercial gains and later used to consolidate colonial power. By the early 20th century, however, the freedom movement had completely appropriated the railways. Revolutionaries targeted the enterprise as a way of attacking British rule even as they relied on it.

▲ **Sir Andrew Fraser,** lieutenant governor of the Bengal Presidency (1903–06), was the target of many assassination attempts, the most famous one being the attempted derailing of his train in 1907.

The Viceregal Special train passed Purana Qila in New Delhi at 7.40am, as scheduled, on 23 December 1929. Onboard were Lord Irwin, Viceroy of India (1926–31), and his wife Lady Dorothy Onslow, returning from a tour of south India. As the train passed mile marker 952/6, a bomb exploded, blowing out a piece of rail. It left behind a hole in the floor of the fourth carriage, shattered a few windows, and caused minor damage to a few carriages. The train's speed, momentum of coaches, and the pull of the engine saved the day, for the aim had been to derail the train, causing it to plunge down an embankment. Lord and Lady Irwin had had a lucky escape.

The bombing of the Viceregal Special, or the Delhi Conspiracy Case as it was called, caused a furore and was widely condemned by nationalist leaders such as Mohandas Karamchand Gandhi. Railway sabotage and bombings were outside the purview of Civil Disobedience. This, however, was not the first time that the revolutionaries had attacked the railways as an expression of dissent. Over the decades, the railways in India had gained a large visual presence and became an easy target.

Colonial symbol of power

The railway network and the trains themselves were the ultimate symbol of colonialism. "Train-wrecking" was often employed as a form of protest. One of the earliest instances was in 1866 when the people of Bhagalpur (in present-day Bihar) attempted to derail a train as a protest against increasing food prices.

The nature of these protests changed with the partition of the Bengal Presidency in 1905. Radicalized groups demonstrated their dissent by attacking the railways with strategically placed bombs on tracks, or throwing bombs at the rail carriages. In 1907, members of the revolutionary outfit "Anushilan Samiti" conducted a series of attacks on the special trains used by Sir Andrew Fraser, Bengal's lieutenant governor (1903–06). During the first attempt, on the Calcutta–Ranchi route, the dynamite exploded but did not do any damage. The second attempt failed as well. The third involved a mine with almost 3 kg of dynamite near Kharagpur, West Bengal. While the explosion did not derail the train, it did significant damage to the railway line as it blew a hole in the permanent

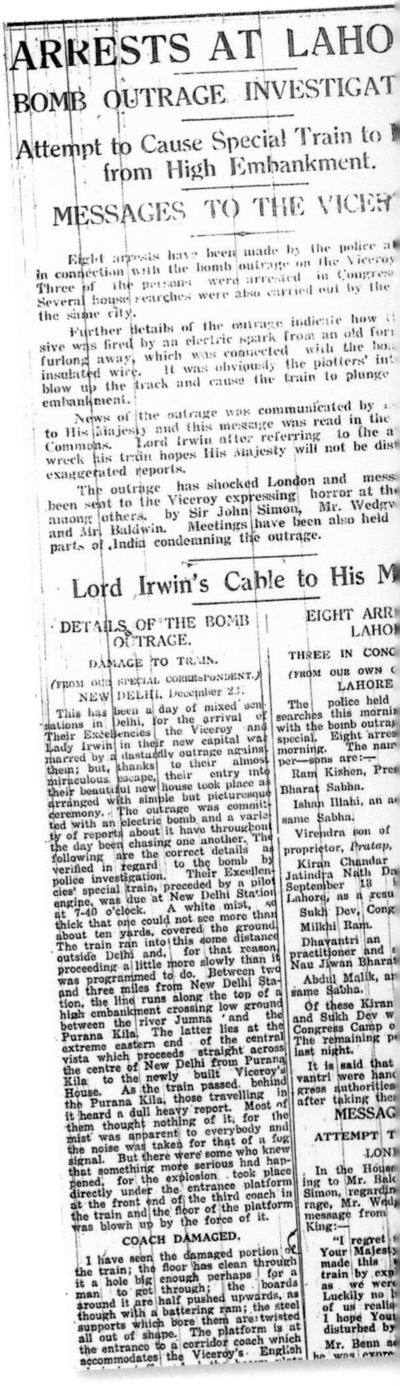

ARRESTS AT LAHO

BOMB OUTRAGE INVESTIGAT

Attempt to Cause Special Train to
from High Embankment.

MESSAGES TO THE VICE

Eight arrests have been made by the police a
in connection with the bomb outrage on the Viceroy
Three of the persons were arrested in Congress
Several house searches were also carried out by the
the same city.

Further details of the outrage indicate how
sive was fired by an electric spark from an old fort
furlong away, which was connected with the bo
insulated wire. It was obviously the plotters' int
blow up the track and cause the train to plunge
embankment.

News of the outrage was communicated by
to His Majesty and this message was read in the
Commons. Lord Irwin after referring to the a
wreck his train hopes His Majesty will not be dis
exaggerated reports.

The outrage has shocked London and mess
been sent to the Viceroy expressing horror at th
among others. by Sir John Simon, Mr. Wedgw
and Mr. Baldwin. Meetings have been also held
parts of India condemning the outrage.

Lord Irwin's Cable to His M

DETAILS OF THE BOMB OUTRAGE.

DAMAGE TO TRAIN.

(FROM OUR SPECIAL CORRESPONDENT.)

NEW DELHI, December 23.

This has been a day of mixed sensations in Delhi, for the arrival of Their Excellencies the Viceroy and Lady Irwin in their new capital was marred by a dastardly outrage against them; but, thanks to their almost miraculous escape, their entry into their beautiful new house took place as arranged with simple but picturesque ceremony. The outrage was committed with an electric bomb and a variety of reports about it have throughout the day been chasing one another. The following are the correct details as verified in regard to the bomb by police investigation. Their Excellencies' special train, preceded by a pilot engine, was due at New Delhi Station at 7-40 o'clock. A white mist, so thick that one could not see more than about ten yards, covered the ground. The train ran into this some distance outside Delhi and, for that reason, proceeding a little more slowly than it was programmed to do. Between two and three miles from New Delhi Station, the line runs along the top of a high embankment crossing low ground between the river Jumna and the Purana Kila. The latter lies at the extreme eastern end of the central vista which proceeds straight across the centre of New Delhi from Purana Kila to the newly built Viceroy's House. As the train passed behind the Purana Kila, those travelling in it heard a dull heavy report. Most of them thought nothing of it, for the mist was apparent to everybody and the noise was taken for that of a fog signal. But there were some who knew that something more serious had happened, for the explosion took place directly under the entrance platform at the front end of the third coach in the train and the floor of the platform was blown up by the force of it.

COACH DAMAGED.

I have seen the damaged portion of the train; the floor has clean through it a hole big enough perhaps for a man to get through; the boards around it are half pushed upwards, as though with a battering ram; the steel supports which bore them are twisted all out of shape. The platform is at the entrance to a corridor coach which accommodates the Viceroy's English

EIGHT ARR
LAHO

THREE IN CONC

(FROM OUR OWN
LAHORE

The police held
searches this mornin
with the bomb outra
special. Eight arres
morning. The nam
per—sons are:—

Ram Kishen, Pres
Bharat Sabha.

Ishan Illahi, an a
same Sabha.

Virendra son of
proprietor, *Pratap*,

Kiran Chandar
Jatindra Nath D
September 18
Lahore, as a resu

Sukh Dev, Cong

Milkhi Ram.

Dhavantri an
practitioner and
Nau Jiwan Bharat

Abdul Malik, a
same Sabha.

Of these Kiran
and Sukh Dev w
Congress Camp o
The remaining p
last night.

It is said that
vantri were han
gress authorities
after taking the

MESSAG

ATTEMPT T

LON

In the House
ing to Mr. Bal
Simon, regardin
rage, Mr. Wed
message from
King:—

"I regret
Your Majesty
made this
train by exp
as we were
Luckily no
of us realis
I hope You
disturbed by

Mr. Benn a
he was expre

▲ **The bombing of** Lord Irwin's special train to New Delhi was covered extensively by the media. His tenure as Viceroy (1926–31) saw tumultuous times in modern Indian history.

> “Railways were as much the **substance of state power** as they were the instrument of that power. To **contest one** was to contest the other.”
>
> IAN J KERR, “REPRESENTATION AND REPRESENTATIONS OF THE RAILWAYS OF COLONIAL AND POST-COLONIAL SOUTH ASIA” (2003)

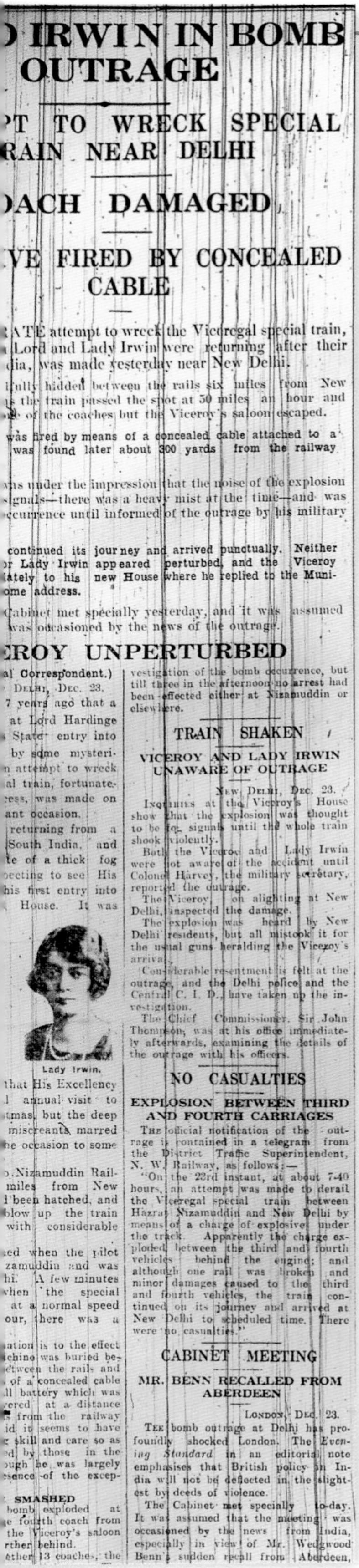

Left newspaper clipping

IRWIN IN BOMB OUTRAGE

PT TO WRECK SPECIAL RAIN NEAR DELHI

DACH DAMAGED

VE FIRED BY CONCEALED CABLE

ATE attempt to wreck the Viceregal special train, Lord and Lady Irwin were returning after their dia, was made yesterday near New Delhi.

fully hidden between the rails six miles from New th the train passed the spot at 50 miles an hour and of the coaches but the Viceroy's saloon escaped.

was fired by means of a concealed cable attached to a was found later about 300 yards from the railway

ns under the impression that the noise of the explosion signals—there was a heavy mist at the time—and was occurrence until informed of the outrage by his military

continued its journey and arrived punctually. Neither r Lady Irwin appeared perturbed, and the Viceroy ately to his new House where he replied to the Muni- ome address.

Cabinet met specially yesterday, and it was assumed was occasioned by the news of the outrage.

EROY UNPERTURBED

al Correspondent.)

DELHI, Dec. 23.

7 years ago that a at Lord Hardinge State entry into by some mysteri- n attempt to wreck al train, fortunate- cess, was made on ant occasion.

returning from a South India, and te of a thick fog his first entry into House. It was

Lady Irwin,

that His Excellency l annual visit to tmas, but the deep miscreants marred e occasion to some

Nizamuddin Rail- miles from New l been hatched, and blow up the train with considerable

sed when the pilot zamuddin and was hi. A few minutes when the special at a normal speed our, there was a

sation is to the effect chine was buried be- etween the rails and of a concealed cable ll battery which was rred at a distance from the railway id it seems to have e skill and care so as d by those in the ough he was largely sence of the excep-

SMASHED

bomb exploded at e fourth coach from e Viceroy's saloon rther behind. ether 13 coaches, the

vestigation of the bomb occurrence, but till three in the afternoon no arrest had been effected either at Nizamuddin or elsewhere.

TRAIN SHAKEN

VICEROY AND LADY IRWIN UNAWARE OF OUTRAGE

NEW DELHI, DEC. 23.

Inquiries at the Viceroy's House show that the explosion was thought to be by signals until the whole train shook violently.

Both the Viceroy and Lady Irwin were not aware of the accident until Colonel Harvey, the military secretary, reported the outrage.

The Viceroy on alighting at New Delhi, inspected the damage.

The explosion was heard by New Delhi residents, but all mistook it for the usual guns heralding the Viceroy's arrival.

Considerable resentment is felt at the outrage, and the Delhi police and the Central C. I. D. have taken up the in- vestigation.

The Chief Commissioner, Sir John Thompson, was at his office immediate- ly afterwards, examining the details of the outrage with his officers.

NO CASUALTIES

EXPLOSION BETWEEN THIRD AND FOURTH CARRIAGES

The official notification of the out- rage is contained in a telegram from the District Traffic Superintendent, N. W. Railway, as follows:—

"On the 23rd instant, at about 7-40 hours, an attempt was made to derail the Viceregal special train between Hazrat Nizamuddin and New Delhi by means of a charge of explosive under the track. Apparently the charge ex- ploded between the third and fourth vehicles behind the engine; and although one rail was broken and minor damages caused to the third and fourth vehicles, the train con- tinued on its journey and arrived at New Delhi to scheduled time. There were no casualties."

CABINET MEETING

MR. BENN RECALLED FROM ABERDEEN

LONDON, DEC. 23.

THE bomb outrage at Delhi has pro- foundly shocked London. The Even- ing Standard in an editorial note emphasises that British policy in In- dia will not be deflected in the slight- est by deeds of violence.

The Cabinet met specially to-day. It was assumed that the meeting was occasioned by the news from India, especially in view of Mr. Wedgwood Benn's sudden recall from Aberdeen.

Main body

way and bent one of the rails. The British Indian Government tried to curb this growing menace by passing the Explosive Substances Act in 1908 to stop the proliferation of explosives in the hands of dissidents and revolutionaries.

A matter of sabotage

World War I (1914–18) slowed things down considerably, but railways would once again become central to the revolutionaries, with the passing of the Rowlatt Acts in 1919. The Acts looked to curb the civil liberties of Indians under special circumstances – some political cases could now be tried without juries, and certain prisoners could be jailed without due process. In protest, there was a fresh onslaught of train sabotage. The Government of Punjab and the controversial Punjab governor, Sir Michael O'Dwyer, who would soon become infamous for his role in the Jallianwala Massacre (1919) in Amritsar, recorded a series of attacks during this period.

Railway stations were burnt, lines destroyed, and attempts were made to derail trains. There were reports of an attack on a railway workshop, a train carrying British troops, and even a mob setting fire to railway bridges at Wazirabad, near New Delhi. O'Dwyer later wrote in his autobiography *India As I Knew It* that this indicated "a prearranged design to immobilise our troops and isolate the main centres of rebellion".

In 1922, after Gandhi called off the Non-cooperation movement, there was growing dissatisfaction among revolutionary factions. It was during this time in 1925 that the Hindustan Republican Association (HRA) carried out the daring Kakori Robbery (see pp.150–51). Later reports, by way of a confession, indicated that there had been plans to blow up the Simon Commission special train (1928) as well. The Simon Commission was a group of British Members of Parliament who had been sent to India to report on constitutional reforms in

▶ **A poster of revolutionaries,** some of whom looted a train for funds in 1925. Today, they are accorded the respect given to freedom fighters and martyrs.

the country. The plan, had it succeeded, would have been rather high-profile. The railways continued to be targeted throughout the 1942 Quit India movement. A few dacoities, similar to Kakori took place at this time, in the central and eastern United Provinces. On 9 July 1940, the 170 Down Passenger train from Lucknow to Mughalsarai was stopped and its mail van ransacked for Rs 2,226 and 8 annas. The money was used to buy firearms and to print a pamphlet called "Ranbheri" (the bugle war cry).

With the clarity of hindsight, historians would later observe that the physical attacks on the railways did not mean that the people objected to the railways. In fact, everyone, even the revolutionaries and freedom fighters relied on the trains – for travel, for the swift and efficient execution of their plans, and often, in the case of some, for making quick getaways.

▼ **Indian nationalist** Subhas Chandra Bose greets his many followers as he stands in a train compartment. From meeting and greeting followers to escaping authorities, Bose's relationship with the railways in India was quite varied.

7

TEXTILE WORKERS' STRIKE

PARTIES AGREE TO INQUIRY

—

LONDON, AUG. 9.

conference of wool and textile
yers and workers has agreed to
by the findings of the Court of
ry to be appointed by the
try of Labour, but agreement
ot been reached on the question
e terms of an immediate resump-
of work, which will be discussed
to-morrow.—*Reuter.*

—

MILLION POUND FUND

—

BENGAL'S PART IN MASONIC MEMORIAL

LUCKNOW TRAIN HOLD-UP

—

MASKED BANDITS

—

PASSENGER SHOT DEAD

—

AMAZING OUTRAGE

—

A sensational report of a raid of
a train by armed and masked bandits
comes from Kakori, a station on the
Oudh & Rohilkhand Railway, eight
miles from Lucknow.
While part of a well-organized
gang of twenty stopped the train by

THE KAKORI TRAIN ROBBERY

Ever since the Revolt of 1857, the British Indian Government and Indian dissidents knew that the
railways in India were, and always had been, a soft target. In 1922, when Mohandas Karamchand
Gandhi's Civil Disobedience movement was suspended after an incident that turned violent, the
promise of self-rule through non-violent means seemed to become less and less likely. A wave
of gloom overtook young revolutionaries, who now chose to seek Independence by any means
necessary. The Kakori incident was a result of this resolve.

▲ **A newspaper article**
from *The Statesman*
reporting on the Kakori
Conspiracy, detailing
the robbery at Kakori, a
station on the Oudh and
Rohilkhand Railway.

> " With the **rapidity of an avalanche** the train was approaching. The familiar **clickety-clack** now filled the atmosphere. What had it in **store for us?** Death? Who knows? But it **no longer frightened** us. "

MANMATH NATH GUPTA RECALLING THE MOMENT THE PUNJAB MAIL PASSED BY IN THE MIDDLE OF THE ROBBERY AT KAKORI, *THEY LIVED DANGEROUSLY: REMINISCENCES OF A REVOLUTIONARY* (1969)

The 8 Down from Shahjahanpur was nearing the small town of Kakori, 16 km from Lucknow (in modern-day Uttar Pradesh). Besides passengers, the train was also carrying the railways' day's earnings from every station in the region to the railway headquarters in Lucknow. On board too were 10 men – revolutionaries who were members of the newly created Hindustan Republican Association (HRA). Armed with Mauser pistols, they waited for a prearranged signal. It was 9 August 1925 and the men were embarking on an armed robbery that would go down in the history of India's Independence movement as a daring attack against all odds.

The Kakori incident is, like several others were, what Indian historian Sumit Sarkar calls, "Swadeshi dacoities". The word "Swadeshi" in this case refers to the freedom movement that asked Indians to shun all foreign goods and buy only those made in India. The robbery's aim was to raise funds by taking from Government property. The train had become a colonizer's instrument, a symbol of oppression.

Robbery on the train
Seven members of the HRA, including Ramprasad Bismil, Chandrashekhar Azad, and Manmath Nath Gupta, had boarded a third-class carriage in the earmarked train. Three others, including Ashfaqullah Khan, were in a second-class carriage. Their task was to pull the chain and stop the train. As dusk fell and Khan pulled the chain, the train came to a screeching halt near the Kakori station. Some of the men rushed to the engine while others overpowered the guard keeping watch

over the iron safe, which contained the money. They pushed the safe onto the ground and used a hammer and chisel to break it open, but this did not work. Meanwhile, two men stood on either side of the train, instructing passengers to stay inside as they were only after Government property.

Occasionally, they fired in the air to scare the more stubborn travellers. Seeing his compatriots struggle to break the safe, Khan took charge and started hammering. "Except the clang of the hammer all was quiet. Our bullets were regularly flying to keep the passengers glued to their seat," Gupta would write later in his autobiography. Khan stopped briefly, when the Punjab Mail whizzed by, and then continued hammering. In the melee, there was one casualty, an Indian passenger, Ahmed Ali, who came out of his compartment to check on his wife and was killed by a flying bullet. The safe broke and the

men gathered the money – Rs 4,601, 15 annas, and 6 paise in all, according to the case filed later, before melting into the darkness.

The aftermath
The Government swung into action and within a month, more than 40 HRA members were arrested. Of these, 29 were put on trial, which lasted for more than two years. Eventually, all except four were sent to jail. Ramprasad Bismil, Ashfaqullah Khan, Roshan Singh, and Rajendra Nath Lahiri, were sentenced to death. Chandrashekhar Azad was never caught and died in a police encounter in 1931. The arrests and hangings ensured that the Kakori incident assumed almost mythic proportions, leaving a deep impact on the people of India. The capital punishment was seen, by some, as a disproportionate response and seemingly inspired yet more revolutionaries.

▲ **The Mauser C/96** was a preferred weapon for many revolutionaries, including Chandrashekhar Azad. This semi-automatic pistol was made in Germany in 1896–1937. Many unlicensed versions of it were manufactured in China. Reportedly, some of these were acquired and used by the Indian radicals.

◀ **The masked** revolutionaries of the HRA did not rob any Indians. This artist's impression shows them in action with their loot.

FRONTIER MAIL

With glitzy trappings and excursions into far-off lands, the Frontier Mail was a true example of the most luxurious and the exotic best the railways in British India had to offer. Launched on 1 September 1928 and operated by the Bombay, Baroda and Central India (BB&CI) Railway, it connected coastal Bombay to Peshawar (now in Pakistan) via the frontier between British India and Afghanistan. The train's name is an ode to this connection.

The express train catered to a host of passengers, including British soldiers serving in the far-flung North-West Frontier Province (NWFP), intrepid visitors travelling across the subcontinent, and Indians visiting families in far-flung cities. Ferrying both passengers and mail, it traversed from Bombay to Ratlam in central India, to Mathura and Delhi in the north, and to Lahore and Rawalpindi in the north-west, before reaching Peshawar. The North Western Railway (NWR) operated it beyond Delhi. It covered 2,335 km in 72 hours, making it the fastest long-distance train of the time. Such was the train's split-second punctuality that, when in August 1929, the train rolled into Peshawar 15 minutes late, a huge uproar ensued and the driver was asked for an explanation.

The Frontier Mail was exclusively first class. Few other modes of travel could match its charms – imported iced beer on tap, liveried waiters serving passengers in opulent dining cars on immaculate white damask tablecloths, and an à la carte menu to be devoured with silver cutlery on fine bone china. When it wasn't meal time the dining car doubled up as a lounge car for card games and light refreshments. Passengers were provided newspapers and could purchase magazines, books, and cards. Free daily news bulletins from Reuters were telegraphed along the line. Travellers could also despatch telegrams and letters en route. Later, second- and third-class sections were introduced. The train introduced "air-conditioned" coaches in 1934 when blocks of ice were placed underneath the car floor to run its cooling system.

In a daring escape in 1941, the legendary freedom fighter Subhas Chandra Bose slipped away from house arrest and journeyed from Gomoh (Jharkhand) to Delhi by the Kalka Mail and then from Delhi to Peshawar in the Frontier Mail. Today, the train is known as the Golden Temple Mail and runs from Mumbai to Amritsar, undertaking the journey in 32 hours across 33 halts.

▶ **This print from 1935** depicts the Frontier Mail crossing a viaduct as it travels through Dara Pass in the Aravalli Hills in Rajasthan on its way from Bombay to Delhi. The engine pulling the train is recorded to be a 158-tonne XC 4-6-2 steam locomotive made in the Vulcan Foundry in Lancashire, UK in 1928–29.

ANGLO-INDIANS AND THE RAILWAYS

Between the 18th and late 19th centuries, the term "Anglo-Indian" referred to British citizens who lived and worked in India. It began representing persons of mixed ethnicity with the 1911 census. Anglo-Indians, as anthropologist Laura Bear puts it, are a railway caste.

Attempts to trace the history of the railways would be impossible without unearthing its historically structured links with the Anglo-Indian community. They are deeply and inextricably linked. In 1905, the Anglo-Indian community was less than half a per cent of India's population, but made up 2 per cent of the total workforce in the railways. As such, the community serves as a living archive of the social history of the railways in India.

▼ **A European railway Institute at Jamalpur, Bihar**

Employed by the railways
From when the first tracks were laid in India, the ranks of the railways were suffused with domiciled Europeans and Eurasians. The colonial state preferentially recruited them to responsible positions, pushing the natives to the lowest levels of the hierarchy. "It will take time to qualify them for the more arduous duties of locomotive drivers, which require coolness, courage, and decision ..." wrote Juland Danvers, the Government director of the railways in India, in 1877. Indians were thus considered suitable only for working in subordinate menial positions, fixing rail lines, or repairing equipment in loco sheds, all under the watchful eyes of their white superiors.

By 1870, rising costs of European recruitment forced the railways to open up all posts to Indians. There was minimal change, however, with Indians occupying a mere 47 of the 800-odd upper administrative posts. The security of railway operations led to the collation of an Anglo-Indian workforce.

Nurtured as natural corollaries of the civilized white man, they were viewed as the ideal employees. They cost less than Europeans, their material culture was decidedly Western, viewed as more loyal owing to their genealogy, and being born in the Indian subcontinent, hardy and acclimatized.

As a result, between 1870 and 1905, almost 50 per cent of all Anglo-Indians were dependent on the railways for their economic sustenance and employed as guards, drivers, firemen, loco-foremen, and line maintenance staff.

A home of their own
The hierarchy displayed in the hiring policies of the railways made its way into the institution's social life. Railway colonies were designed, starting from 1859, to provide accommodation to European and Anglo-Indian employees. Large sprawling spaces housing quaint bungalows, neatly laid out lush lawns, and tree-lined avenues – the colonies were a reproduction of the British way of life. *The Engineers Journal* described the Cawnpore (Kanpur) railway colony in its 1858 October edition as having "good bold English architecture, something firm and solid that it does your heart good to look at."

These spaces were a sanctum preserving racial exclusivity, an escape from the degenerating influence of the dirty, diseased tropics and those who lived in it. This policy of segregation continued even after

◄ **Milk is distributed** to children at a European school in this photograph. This was one of the many facilities provided to the wards of Anglo-Indian and Eurasian railway employees.

growing Indianization forced the authorities to open up their housing policy. Indians, however, were still housed away from their European and Anglo-Indian counterparts.

A way of life

Employment in the railways also provided the Anglo-Indians with a sense of belonging. The small, tight-knit communities lived tranquil lives toeing European sensibilities, largely sequestered from Indian mores. The spatial centre of community life was the church and the Railway Institute.

Open only to Europeans and Anglo-Indians, the Railway Institute or "Inster" as the Anglo-Indians called it, were designed to be the absolute centre of social life in these isolated

townships, buzzing with dances, housie nights, costume parties, or amateur theatricals. Here, one could spend evenings dancing the foxtrot, listening to a live band play, sipping chilled beer, or playing a game of whist basking in the comforts of colonial splendour. The finer among these had card rooms and billiards rooms with a table or two. Sporting facilities, such as tennis, badminton, and squash courts, and swimming pools were also made available.

The days to mark on the social calendar, however, were Christmas celebrations and New Year nights. *Burra Din* (Big Day in Hindustani) or Christmas was the event of the year, filled with traditions and a flurry of activities – children's Christmas tree functions with teatime snacks and the arrival of Santa, the Christmas fête with a jumble sale and a raffle or two, a Christmas tableau narrating the tale of Jesus's birth, and most importantly, a fancy dress ball preceding Christmas and the New Year's Eve gala.

Margaret Deefholts, a Canadian writer with Anglo-Indian roots, recalls, "... the New Year's Eve gala was a stellar event with the women resplendent

in their *darzi*-made [tailor-made] gowns, and the men togged up in suits and ties."

Independence anxieties

The freedom movement caused upheavals in the lives of the community and were further exacerbated by Independence. Foundationally defined as the offspring of the colonial masters, and the belief that many in the community shared, of being more European than Indian, led to sharply drawn lines, leaving the Anglo-Indian reeling from social and economic prejudice. Half of the community emigrated following Independence. Today, there is a sizeable population of Anglo-Indians around the world. In India, their population has shrunk from half a million in the 1940s to about 1,50,000.

◄ **Adrian Eric Baldrey** who retired from the railways in 2008, was the last Anglo-Indian employee in Mumbai.

DURAND INSTITUTE

The first ever recreational club of the railways in India, the Durand Institute, now rechristened the Vivekananda Institute was set up in 1878 in Asansol, West Bengal by the East Indian Railway (EIR). It was named after Sir Mortimer Durand who served as India's foreign secretary from 1884 to 1894. It has a cathedral-like structure with a tower that juts out like a steeple, and Gothic arches. A picture of sophistication, it became the venue for all the major EIR social and cultural activities. High-ranking EIR officials would travel to Asansol to revel in the Institute's Christmas celebrations. Post-Independence, it suffered from neglect and decay. The Eastern Railway undertook a massive renovation exercise and restored the building to its old splendour. It was reopened on 15 August 2018, India's Independence Day.

LOCOMOTIVES

India's first electric suburban train ran from Bombay's Victoria Terminus (VT) to Kurla on the Great Indian Peninsula Railway's (GIPR) Harbour Line on 3 February 1925. A year before, in 1924, the Locomotive Standards Committee had updated and restandardized the previous British Engineering Standards Association (BESA) designs and established eight basic types of steam locomotive classes known as the Indian Railway Standards.

▲ **P-31652**

Year built	1922
Manufacturer	Ajmer Locomotive Workshop
Power	Steam
Gauge	Metre
Wheel Configuration	4-6-0

Equipped with the Walschaerts valve gear, used to regulate the flow of steam and an inside plate frame, this BESA design locomotive hauled express service on the Rajputana Malwa Railway in the west. It was originally built with 54" driving wheels. Later, it was modified with 57" wheels in order to accommodate higher speed passenger traffic.

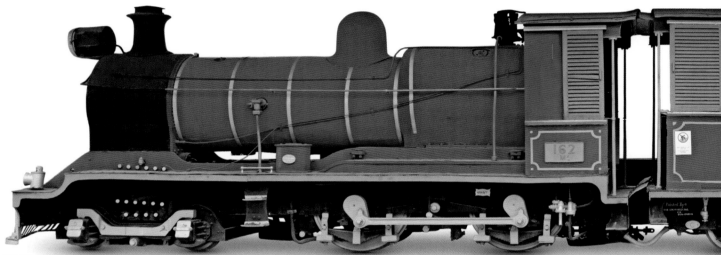

▲ **M2 162**

Year built	1923
Manufacturer	Ajmer Locomotive Workshop
Power	Steam
Gauge	Metre
Wheel configuration	4-4-0

This is the only locomotive in India to have the Joy valve gear, which helps correct inequalities while in motion. It has inside cylinders, a feature rarely seen on metre-gauge engines. Also called the *Duchess of York*, it worked the Rajputana Malwa Railway, where it hauled mail trains, and on the Bombay, Baroda, and Central India (BB&CI) Railway. It was retired in 1970.

▶ **YCG1 21900**

Year built	1922
Manufacturer	Hawthorn Leslie and Co., UK
Power	Electric
Gauge	Metre
Wheel configuration	Bo-Bo

This 640 HP electric locomotive ran on the South Indian Railway from Madras to Tambaram in the south on a metre-gauge line. In 1930, it became the first metre section to be electrified in India. This 39-tonne-locomotive had a maximum speed of 65 km/h.

▲ WCG 1

Year built 1928

Manufacturer Swiss Locomotive and Machine Works, Switzerland

Power Electric

Gauge Broad

Wheel configuration 4-6-0

Named *Sir Leslie Wilson* after the governor of Bombay in 1923–26, this electric locomotive was designed for the GIPR to transport goods. Its four 650 HP motors connected to the running wheels through a jackshaft. This component made the engine suited for work with heavy-grade trains that required extra effort while pulling. The locomotive's original classification was EF1.

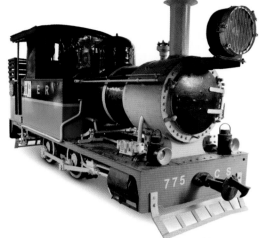

◄ CS-775

Year built 1927

Manufacturer WG Bagnall Ltd., Stafford ,UK

Power Steam

Gauge Narrow (2'6")

Wheel configuration 2-4-0

At 10.8 tonnes, this is one of the lightest locomotives. The engine, which ran on the narrow-gauge track between Shantipur and Nabadwip Ghat in the Sealdah Division of the Eastern Railway, could achieve a maximum speed of about 20 km/h. This engine stopped running in April 1986.

► XGM 911

Year built 1936

Manufacturer Beyer, Peacock and Co., Manchester, UK

Power Steam

Gauge Broad

Wheel configuration 0-8-0

This locomotive was fitted with two outside cylinders, an inside plate frame, three Ross pop valves, which prevented leaking of steam, and a Walschaerts valve gear (see p.156). It did railway yard shunting in the North Western Railway and for the Eastern Punjab Railway that ran in India's Punjab after Independence. It was rebuilt in the Mughalpura Workshop in Lahore in 1943 where its wheel arrangement was changed to 2-8-2.

▲ WCP 1

Year built 1930

Manufacturer Swiss Locomotive and Machine Works, Switzerland

Power Electric

Gauge Broad

Wheel configuration 1-Co-2

Also known as *Sir Roger Lumley*, named after the governor of Bombay from 1937–43 and originally classified as EA1, this locomotive could run at a speed of 120 km/h in 1930. It marked the introduction of high-speed trains in the Indian subcontinent. The engine was employed to haul passenger trains along the Bombay–Poona and Bombay–Manmad lines in modern-day Maharashtra.

▲ Sentinel BDR-8

Year built 1930

Manufacturer Sentinel Waggon Works, Shrewsbury, UK

Power Steam

Gauge Narrow (2'6")

Wheel configuration 4W

This steam engine served on West Bengal's Bankura Damodar River Light Railway. It was imported from a company in Shrewsbury, England that made steam-powered lorries, ships, ship machinery, railway locomotives, and even diesel engine lorries and locomotives.

BEYER-GARRATT

There is something undeniably impressive about the monsters known, quite lovingly, as the Garratts. It could be that they are among the heaviest and biggest steam locomotives ever built. It could also be because of the immense power they wielded as they hauled heavy loads, often up steep gradients. Quick and efficient, these giants could run at high speeds without causing too much damage to the tracks – especially the lightly laid ones. They were also multipurpose and could be used for passenger trains or freight.

The Garratts employed the kind of power that was quite unlike the steam locomotives of their time. They were known for their ability to, quite easily, haul a 2,400-tonne train on a 1 in 100 gradient at about 72 km/h. The articulated locomotives had three separate frames – unlike the conventional steam ones where the whole unit is carried on a single frame. This articulation allowed it to seamlessly negotiate tight curves. This was why the Garratts proved highly effective for the Darjeeling Himalayan Railway (DHR), where they were first used in 1909. The locomotives almost brought about a revolution in steam traction with these innovations.

The Beyer-Garratt had a single boiler flanked by two tenders at either end with a reciprocating engine for each tender. The power units carried the water tanks while the rear unit also shouldered the fuel supply. The boiler and firebox unit were slung between the two engine units which freed them of size constraints. The large firebox allowed for efficient fuel combustion as well, thereby increasing the transfer of heat to the boiler and helping the Garratt belt out its legendary power and tremendous performance while belching little smoke.

Garratts ran on the Anara–Bhojudih (in West Bengal) and Bhilai–Dalli Rajhara (in modern-day Chhattisgarh) sections of the Bengal–Nagpur Railway (BNR) till 1970. They also hauled iron ore in the gradient section of Dangoaposi and Tatanagar in BNR's Chakradharpur division in present-day Jharkhand. As technology improved, the engines became more and more obsolete, and some have since been relegated to museums. One is housed in the National Rail Museum in New Delhi and a metre-gauge variant is exhibited at the rail museum in Tinsukia, Assam. Another one was restored in 2008 and is now in working order at Kharagpur.

► **The magnificent Beyer-Garratt of the BNR** draws into a station in this painting, dated back to the late 1930s. More than 50 per cent of the challenging BNR line consisted of steep gradients. The powerful Garratts were also used quite successfully on the North Western Railway and the Assam Bengal Railway.

SIGNALLING

Signalling, aided by telecommunication, is a large part of the railways' safety mechanism. As the number of trains operating in the Indian Railways' circuit has grown, so has the signalling system, which has evolved over the decades. Without it, the entire rail network would be in disarray.

◄ **Railway lantern**

The initial signalling system in India was rudimentary, gradually evolving as single lines became double, the traffic increased, and the network became complex. During the 19th and 20th centuries, these changes borrowed heavily from the improvements in the Western countries, though much of the manufacturing of the signalling equipment was in-house.

▼ **A combination of semaphore signals** in operation on the Western Railway.

Early equipment

The earliest signalling equipment used on the railways in India were revolving discs or rectangular boards or semaphore signals with arms fixed on top of a pole, which were manually operated by a lever at the foot of the pole. In a lower quadrant type semaphore signal, which was widely used, a lowered arm meant that the line was clear and raised indicated

danger. Separate red and green spectacles were provided for lights for the night to indicate whether there was danger ahead or the track was clear.

While signals were erected at various locations across the network, the platform outside the station master's office had "main" or "home" signals, which consisted of two more arms on either side of the pole. Others

such as "outer" or "distant" signals, which had square-ended arms, were fitted somewhere near the facing point in each direction. The "outer" signals were really just warning indicators for forthcoming stop signals to help the driver control the speed. The two types of signals worked in tandem. The placement of signals, however, was not uniform. For instance, on the Bombay, Baroda and Central India (BB&CI) Railway sections, the "main" signals existed at both ends of the station and the "outer" signals were pushed further away. On the other hand, on the Madras Railway, the "main signals" were erected near the facing points. Signals at the end of the stations are sometimes also called "starter" signals.

Towards the end of the 19th century and the beginning of the 20th, there were revisions to signalling practices with regard to equipment. Initially, a rule indicated that all "distant" signals had to have an additional fishtailed arm. These were also changed to absolute stop signals. There were more improvisations over the years, which included adding a green light to the fishtailed arm and removing the square-ended arm.

Absolute block system
Earlier trains worked under the absolute block system, on the premise that the section between two particular stations, called the block section, should be clear for a train to leave from one station to another. Fortunately, by the time railways made their way to India, the world had already witnessed the use of electric telegraphs, which meant that the block system relied on the Morse Telegraph Instrument to transmit information on the line and whether it was safe to proceed. Once the driver received the line clear information, he received the "Paper Line Clear Ticket", which functioned as an authority pass allowing him to proceed to the next station.

Improved block instruments aided by electricity were introduced subsequently. For instance, the East Indian Railway (EIR) and Great Indian Peninsula Railway (GIPR) used the Neale's Ball token instruments on their single lines. This meant that electromechanical instruments dispensed metal balls as "tokens", such that a single token could be issued for one direction at a time. On the Madras Railway, a mechanism sensitive to train wheels was fitted on the rails such that when the wheels ran over it, the "starter" would be alerted and shift to danger. Other tokens used included the "Carsen" instrument, the Theobald key token, the Dutton-Neville Block instrument, and the Webb and Thompson electric token staff.

Additional improvements
Interlocking came up in the railways in India after an accident on the Eastern Bengal Railway in 1868. The Lonavala–Poona section of the GIPR started using it followed by the Madras Railway and Indian Midland Railway, which implemented the system in some stations. In 1892 GH List and A Morse installed interlocking apparatus at some stations on the North Western Railway. Together, they brought out the famous List and Morse system on the railways in India. In 1894, the stations between Lahore (in modern-day Pakistan) and Ghaziabad, Uttar Pradesh started using the List and Morse interlocking system. By 1910, many stations had interlocking systems in place. Initially, key interlocking was operated by the manual transfer of keys, which were eventually replaced by much faster electric key transmitters.

With the growth of traffic, there was a need for an improved signalling system. Although "cabin interlocking" existed as early as 1893, it took flight only in the 20th century. In 1912, the GIPR became the first railway to incorporate this

on the entire stretch between Delhi and Bombay with other railway companies following suit in the subsequent years.

Implementing changes
The entire system witnessed major improvements in the 20th century. In 1926, the formation of the Signalling and Interlocking Standards Committee meant standardization of all equipment and systems. The creation of a block signalling manual and rules for underground signalling cable came up in the 1930s even as improved systems were adopted. These included track-circuiting, power signalling, automatic signalling, double wire signalling, and colour light signals. All these systems minimized human intervention and helped in handling larger volumes of traffic. These technological improvements were championed by the companies in western India. For instance, the GIPR was the first to introduce the colour lighting signalling on its Harbour Branch in 1928. The BB&CI signalling installations on the Churchgate–Virar section were remarkable as well.

Post 1947, there have been many improvements in the signalling method. From route relay interlocking, multiple aspect colour light signals, wireless communication, and automatic block to the Automatic Warning System (AWS), Centralized Traffic Control (CTC), and microwave networks, the field is growing rapidly.

▲ **During the early years,** signals were manually operated by using heavy levers.

▼ **Railway traffic signal with colour lighting**

KEEPING THE RAILWAYS SAFE

The success of the railways meant an ever-growing number of passengers – a mixed blessing as this also led to increased opportunities for criminals to exploit hapless travellers. It became essential for the management to invest in security, employ forces to prevent misuse of laws, and ensure the smooth functioning of the service.

An extract from the 1921 Simla Report of the Railway Police Committee lamented the problem of thieves and robbers on rail routes: "The representative of the Tata Iron and Steel Company said that of the consignments of fruit, fish and vegetables to the industrial colony at Jamshedpur, scarcely one per cent reached their destination intact. The Mysore Chamber of Commerce states that one-half of every consignment of coal was pilfered by women who carry their spoil away openly in baskets." This is one of many from the report that is more than a litany of complaints and crimes. It also highlighted the complex role the railway police were expected to perform. They were more than just crime fighters – they protected freight, maintained public safety, enforced racial segregation, represented the arm of the British Government in India during the freedom movement, acted as strikebreakers to control labour unrest, and played a crucial part in disease control.

Private security
Initially, railway companies had their own independent security force with policing costs kept to a bare minimum. They were only concerned with the theft of freight and railway property. Provincial police forces were in charge of actual criminal investigations. The expansion of railway lines connected people and places, opened up infinite possibilities for trade and travel, and even crime. Platforms, waiting areas, and freight sheds became hubs of criminal activity – for not just theft of property, but also the robbing of passengers, who were considered easy targets. By the early 1900s, organized gangs had emerged, working across districts and provinces, robbing travellers (see pp.164–65). The railways also became a convenient tool for smugglers, counterfeiters, kidnappers, and even spies.

With a rise in crime numbers, the companies reassessed the role of their police. Costs were mounting and the changing dynamic of crimes called for greater cooperation between the district and railway police. By 1862, the Bengal Presidency had its own railway police followed by the North-Western Province (now Uttar Pradesh) in 1867, and Delhi and Punjab in 1868. A series of reviews took place over the next few years that sought to expand the railway police's function. They could also be required to work outside the purview of the railways, if needed. The railways were slowly coming under provincial management, and the companies were happy to hand over control to the Government.

Organizational changes
By 1903, the Indian Police Commission under Lord Curzon, Viceroy of India (1898–1905), recognized that the railway police and the Criminal Investigation Department (CID) would need to collaborate in order to keep up with the criminals. This led to the creation of the post of a deputy inspector general (DIG) who would supervise both the departments in a province. DIGs were on the move for at least 20 days in a month, inspecting every station or important crime scene within their province.

Due to an increase in the scope of work, the CID and the railway police would later get separate DIGs, but by then the railways had become an inextricable part of the police network. There was greater interdepartmental communication – especially during the freedom movement – the transfer of evidence and records had become smoother, and language barriers were becoming easier to navigate.

Unlike the regular police staff, the railway police staff was mostly European, even at the middle and lower levels. Only reserve inspectors and special police sergeants, who

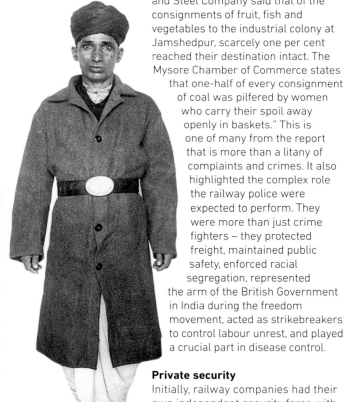

A uniformed chowkidar or guard of the railways

were usually British, investigated crimes involving European victims. They, noted American historian David Campion, acted "as a buffer between insular British communities and the Indian population – including Indian policemen."

Race and other matters

One of the key functions of the railway police was to enforce racial segregation so that the third-class passengers remained separate from the first- and second-class travellers. Patrolling constables ensured that the third class passengers (see pp.114–15) used the appropriate ticket counters, platforms, and coaches.

Often, they would work as strikebreakers, a role that came into prominence especially in 1928, during the South Indian Railway strike. Policemen, railways and otherwise, were posted at important junctions and stations and as armed escorts on running trains. Another

significant role allotted to the railway police was disease control. Given the length and breadth of the network, the railways could play a very real role in the outbreak of contagion and constables and sergeants were trained to deal with such situations. They had the authority to seal stations in case trains were going through areas that reported an epidemic. They also managed pilgrims, investigated suicides that could be potential murders, and

transported prisoners. As the freedom movement picked up momentum, the railways and its police became a symbol of the colonizers for the revolutionaries (see pp.148–49) and a useful tool for the nationalists (see pp.142–43).

"The railways," Campion wrote, "served as an essential catalyst in the growth, both in scope and sophistication, of organized crime in India as well as in the development of modern, professional law enforcement."

> ❝ Officers in charge of **railway police stations** should be given **power to search** within the limits of **district police stations** through which **their section** of railway **runs**. ❞
>
> ONE OF 24 RECOMMENDATIONS FOR IMPROVED POLICING AND SECURITY FROM THE SIMLA REPORT OF THE RAILWAY POLICE COMMITTEE, 1921

▼ **Police officers regulate pilgrims** on their way to a religious festival, in the Kurduvadi station in Maharashtra in 1930. This was one of the many duties of the railway police.

RAILWAY ROBBERIES

The railways gave birth to a brand of criminals with a unique set of skills, who took complete advantage of the new transportation system, the quick escape it offered after the commission of a crime, and the anonymity that allowed them to merge seamlessly with the seething crowds at busy stations.

▲ **FC Daly in his 1916 book** *Manual of Criminal Classes Operating in Bengal* notes that many "criminal tribes" were very clever at disguising themselves. Here, a group of robbers can be seen dressed in turbans and dhotis to avoid suspicion.

A darker, unexpected, yet inevitable, by-product of the railways was a new class of criminals. They waited for opportune moments to strike – some drugged passengers, or occasionally slit their throats, before making off with their belongings. Others conned trusting, distracted travellers or looted freight and sheds for rolling stock and goods. No one was exempt. Anyone could be a victim, even a first-class passenger. Bengal's deputy inspector general of Police, FC Daly wrote in his 1916 book *Manual of Criminal Classes Operating in Bengal*, how an ingenious thief once "lifted His Excellency, the Governor of Bombay's valuable travelling bag from His Excellency's brilliantly lighted saloon on the Southern Mahratta Railway, under the very noses of a strong body of police escorting the train."

The specialists

Railway robbers were broadly divided into three categories. The first was pickpockets or *uthaigiri* who strike fear in passengers even today. They usually worked alone and dressed well so as to not raise suspicions. Popular targets included ticket office windows and compartments.

The second category was made up of railway personnel who often took advantage of opportunities that presented themselves. For instance, in 1896–97, Bangalore saw the rise of the "Golden Gang", a group of guards who became experts at stealing silk and lace goods. Pilferage, whether by railway staff or experienced robbers, was quite common. Favourite items included cases of wine with reports of disappearing bottles becoming routine. The 1921 Simla Report of the Railway Police Committee noted that fruit thefts in the United Provinces (modern-day Uttar Pradesh) had also become "notorious". The Oudh and Rohilkhand Railway had to admit that "not a single parcel of fresh fruits can reach its destination without

suffering from the attacks of thieves", and the local government had to step in.

A third category was what the British classified as "criminal tribes" or professional groups of robbers belonging to a particular village or community. Highly decorated police officer Rai Bahadur M Pauparao Naidu in the fourth edition of his 1915 monograph *The History of Railway Thieves in India*, identified seven such classes with their own customs and modus operandi. These tribes were declassified after 1947.

The techniques

While pickpockets loitered near ticket booths to lift a wallet or bag, other thieves entered trains and waited for passengers to fall asleep or head to the dining car or refreshment room, leaving their belongings unattended. Robbers working in groups were known to rent a house near newly opened lines. They would split into teams and take turns going to the station to befriend pilgrims or passengers in trains only to rob them at night.

The stolen goods would be handed over to an accomplice or thrown out of the window, to be retrieved later. Some carried locked bags filled with rags, bundles of clothes, or steel trunks to swap with passengers' luggage. Others cut jewellery from around their sleeping victims' necks or wrists, tickling their feet with a feather to get them to turn as

needed. Usually, gangs would work a specific line until the police caught on, then moved on to other lines and towns. There were cases where passengers tried to resist or give chase. In such situations, there were horrific reports of skirmishes and travellers being thrown off trains or murdered.

Constant vigilance

Besides the watch and ward staff and recommendations for increased police presence and patrolling, the railway authorities adopted a number of measures to control rising crime. By 1921, most provinces had appointed police guards who travelled on the passenger trains.

The Eastern Bengal Railway installed a device that lit up the sides of the train if it reached a certain speed. Barred windows were introduced to prevent nimble thieves from reaching through open windows to make off with unattended coats and bags. The railway companies experimented with different kinds of locks and rivets to protect goods wagons. Compartments reserved for women had tower bolts on the inside of the doors. However, as the 1921 Simla Report of the Railway Police quoted a witness, "A flood of light is the best *chaukidar* [guard]."

▲ **Profile of a robber**
belonging to one of the tribes listed by Daly

> **66** ... **if he intends** his friends not to alight, he will scratch his head and **work his elbow in the direction** the **train** is moving. This means **'I am watched, continue your journey.' 99**

MICHAEL KENNEDY, INSPECTOR GENERAL OF POLICE, BOMBAY,
THE CRIMINAL CLASSES IN INDIA (1856)

The ticketing system for the Indian Railways has evolved by leaps and bounds over the years. From unwieldy registers to a mechanized system and then to online booking of tickets today, it has seen many variations. Seen here is a booking hall at Bombay's Victoria Terminus (VT) in 1930.

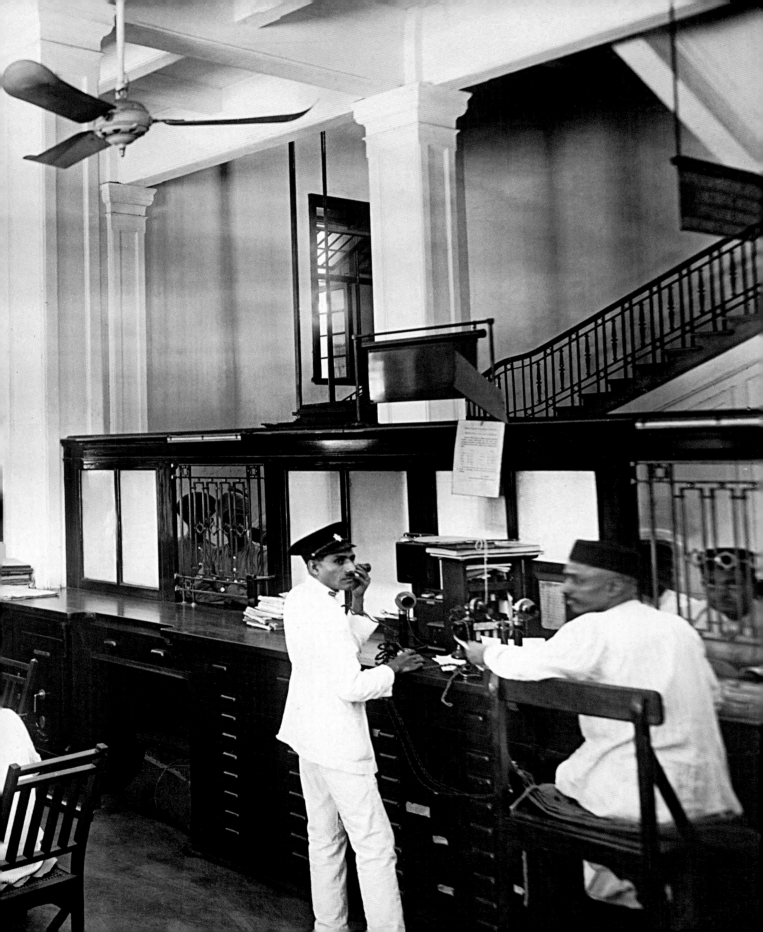

UNLOCKING THE KHYBER PASS

The British in India were convinced that the Russian Empire just across Afghanistan was looking for a chance to move in on their prized colonies in the subcontinent. Easy troop movement with a railway line through the Khyber Pass might have assuaged their fears to some extent, but, forbidden by locals and impossible to cut

An ancient trade route connecting Kabul, Afghanistan, and Peshawar (in modern-day Pakistan), the Khyber Pass had always been susceptible to invaders seeking to expand their territory into the Indian subcontinent. Crucial to the defence of the country, it was naturally a matter of grave concern. One of the biggest challenges, besides the unforgiving terrain, was the politics of the region.

Impregnable India
For long, surveys had deemed this region crucial, but unsuited for the railways. In his book *Permanent Way Through the Khyber*, British engineer Victor Bayley recounted a conversation between an unnamed commander-in-chief and the Viceroy of India: "Give me two Army Corps and a railway behind me and I'll defy the whole of Asia, and Europe too … But … a railway up to this position is impossible!" … "Until in the fullness of time," continued Bayley who had been assigned to construct the line, "came the Great War, the downfall of Russia, the war with Afghanistan, the military occupation of the Khyber and finally the genius of an engineer who in one brief season destroyed the myth of impossibility, and demonstrated … that a broad-gauge train could just be got to climb to the summit of the Pass and down again." It took five years to make that vision a reality.

Surveying the territory
The line would have to run through "Tribal Territory" – a buffer between British India and Afghanistan – that had its own set of rules. The tribes

▲ An opening ceremony programme provides details of the Khyber Pass Railway's launch, which was held on 2 November 1925.

were not answerable to British law and considered the railways "forbidden". After the Third Anglo-Afghan War in 1919, it was now even more important to build a line through; fortunately, technology had made some progress by this time. A railway system now connected Peshawar – there was a bridge over River Indus at Attock, and the North Western Railway extended into Jamrud (both in modern-day Pakistan), near the entrance to the Khyber. Colonel GR Hearn – the genius engineer of Bayley's account – conducted an extensive survey of the region to identify the best route for a line.

Building through the Khyber
Construction began in 1920. The nearly 40-km-line would begin at Jamrud and end at Landi Khana, a town in modern-day Pakistan almost 3 km short of the frontier post. It would take four reversing stations, 34 tunnels about 5-km-long, 92 bridges and culverts, and four watering stations for locomotives to

cross the Khyber. British author PSA Berridge wrote about a ruling gradient of 3 per cent between Jamrud and Landi Kotal (in Pakistan) with a rise of about 600 m in 34 km and a descent of 265 m to Landi Khana. A large part of the construction involved delicate negotiations with the Pashtun tribes. Bayley brought some of them on board as "contractors" who could employ whomever they wanted, but were also in charge of their own protection. More than 2.2 million cubic metres of material, including rock, was moved during the construction. Building material would be brought in either by motor lorries or, where there were only bridle paths, donkeys. While dynamite was brought in easily, the more unstable gunpowder for blasting shale came in tongas (horse-drawn carriages) from Peshawar. Pipes were laid for proper water supply and fortified towers built to protect the camps from feuding or raiding parties. The unpredictable weather was yet another challenge to overcome. To top it all, were some locals who would occasionally fire shots at engineers from vantage points.

Despite the challenges, the first section from Jamrud to Landi Kotal opened on 3 November 1925 and the final section to Landi Khana on 3 April 1926. *The Times* in a report from 3 November 1925, recounted a declaration by the railway member of the Governor-General's Council, Sir Charles Innes, that "the railway would stir men's imagination far beyond the limits of British India."

▼ A viaduct on the Khyber Pass Railway connects the towns of Landi Kotal and Landi Khana (in modern-day Pakistan).

> ## Impossible and forbidden, but, all the same, inevitable!

BRITISH ENGINEER VICTOR BAYLEY ABOUT THE RAILWAY GOING THROUGH THE KHYBER PASS, *PERMANENT WAY THROUGH THE KHYBER* (1939)

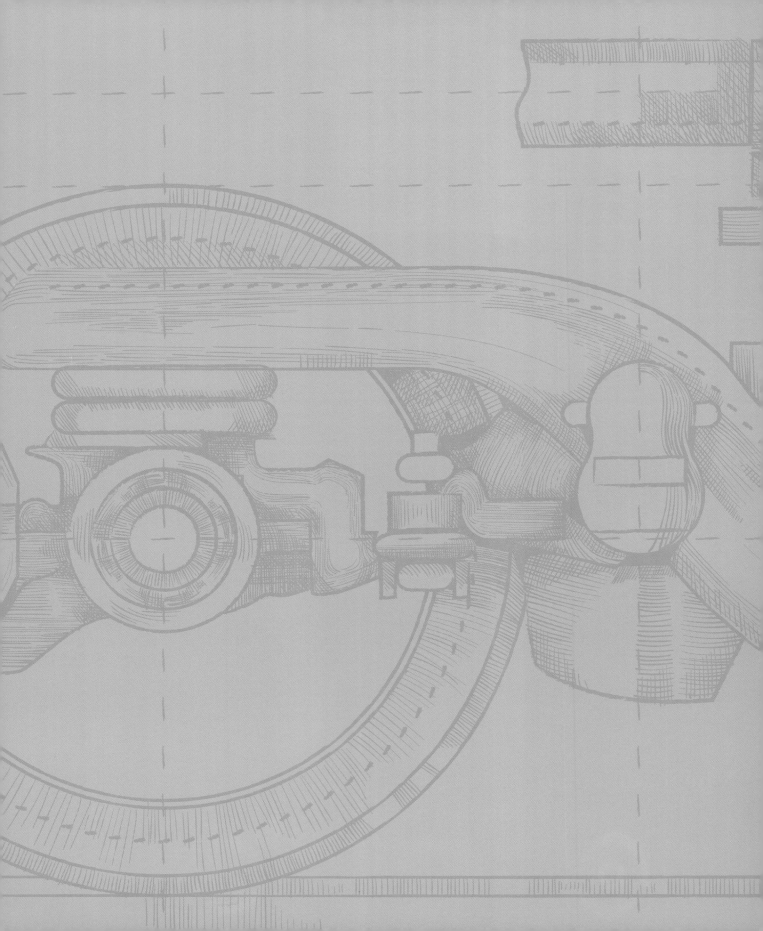

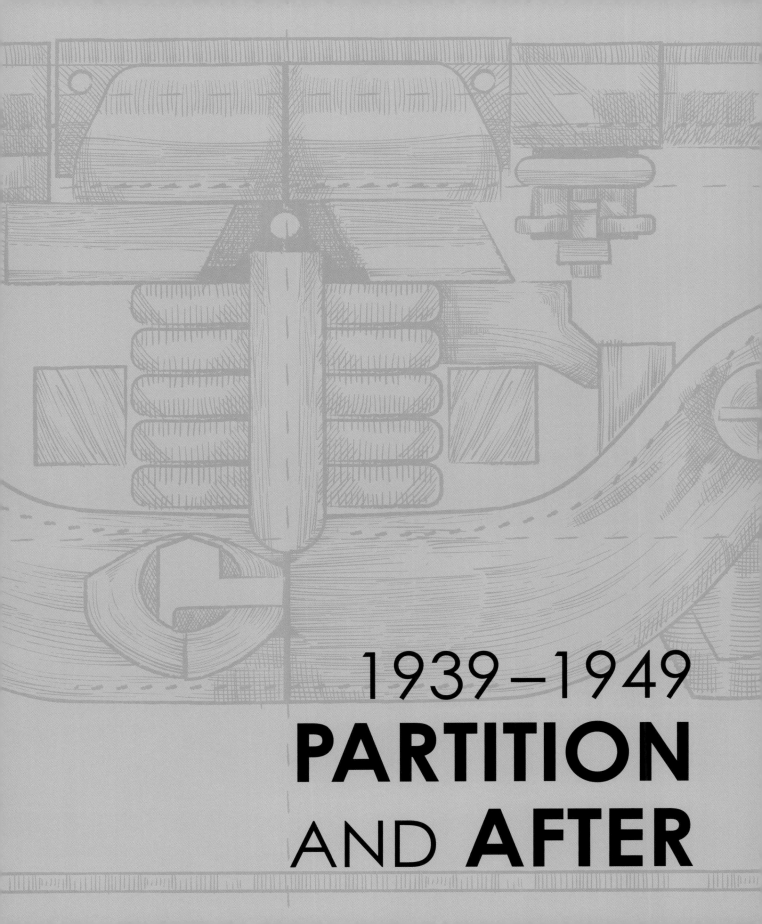

1939–1949
PARTITION
AND **AFTER**

1939–1949

If this period is known for the moment India got its independence, it also marks the immense violence that followed the partition of the subcontinent. Trains carried masses of humanity across borders, but also became sites of brutality and bloodlust. Everything was divided, even a railway network that once united a country. As a young, free India took stock, it realized that its truncated railway network was in a bad shape. It was now time to integrate and rebuild.

1939 Nazi Germany invades Poland, forcing France and Britain to declare war on Germany on 3 September, starting World War II.

1939 The Nizam's State Railway experiments with diesel railcars.

23 March 1940 The resolution demanding the creation of Pakistan is passed at the All-India Muslim League in Lahore.

17 October 1940 The Individual Civil Disobedience campaign is started by Mohandas Karamchand Gandhi. The campaign would come to an end by 1941.

July 1942 A flash flood wipes out the tracks on Chappar Rift. This route to Quetta is abandoned.

August 1942 The Quit India movement begins.

1943 A famine rages across Bengal, eventually claiming more than three million lives.

1943 The State takes over the Bengal and North Western Railway, merging several other companies to form the Oudh and Tirhut Railway.

1 October 1944 The Bengal–Nagpur Railway is taken over by the Government.

1939–40

1941–43

194

1939–45 Railways in India feel the strain of the war as workshops start making military equipment and rolling stock is taken to the Middle East.

1940s All-steel broad-gauge coaches are manufactured for the first time in India.

1939 Subhas Chandra Bose creates the Forward Bloc.

7 December 1941 A Japanese aerial attack on Pearl Harbour marks the US's entry into World War II.

March 1942 Seeking active cooperation in British war efforts, the Cripps Mission comes to India with a promise of dominion status.

1942 Most of the remaining large railway companies are taken over by the Government.

February 1943 Howrah Bridge opens, allowing the trams to connect to the Howrah route.

1944–45 The Madras & Southern Mahratta and South Indian Railway Company lines are merged and the Government takes over operations.

A report on the bombing of Poland and the start of World War II

People lining for food in Calcutta, 1943

Bombing of Nagasaki, Japan

> **If they were in India, where** on earth **was Pakistan?**
> And if they were in **Pakistan,** then how come that
> **until** only the **other day it was India?**

SAADAT HASAN MANTO, IN HIS SHORT STORY "TOBA TEK SINGH" (1955)

2 September 1945 World War II comes to an end after Japan surrenders.

October 1945 India, not an independent nation yet, becomes one of the founding members of the United Nations.

1945 The Tata Engineering and Locomotive Co. (TELCO) is formed.

6 December 1946 A Constituent Assembly is elected to write the Indian Constitution.

17 August 1947 The new borders of India and Pakistan are declared and an exodus of refugees begins. Vast networks of the Bengal Assam Railway and North Western Railway are now in Pakistan.

30 January 1948 Gandhi is assassinated.

1948 The state of Israel is established, marking the beginning of the Israel–Palestine conflict.

1948 Indian Standard Time is now observed across the country.

1949 The Railway Board adopts all-steel construction as a standard for coaches.

5 1946–47 1948–49

1945 The first all-electric interlocking is put into place at the Bandra station, Bombay.

1945 Indian Railway Standards becomes Indian Government Railway Standards.

6 August 1945 The US drops an atomic bomb on Hiroshima and three days later, on Nagasaki.

15 August 1947 India attains freedom from British rule.

November, 1947 First interim Railway Budget speech is made in free India.

1948 The Assam Relinking Project to connect it to the rest of the country via railways begins.

1948 100 WG class 2-8-2 locomotives are ordered from the North British Locomotive Company, the start of this successful class in India.

1949 The Gaekwad's Baroda State Railway and the Bombay, Baroda and Central India (BB&CI) are merged even as the Rajasthan Government takes over the Jodhpur–Bikaner Railway.

26 November 1949 The Constitution of India is adopted.

Refugees migrating to India during Partition

A locomotive built for India by Baldwin Locomotive Works

WORLD WAR II AND THE RAILWAYS

Hitler invaded Poland on 1 September 1939 and, in retaliation, the Allied forces of Britain and France declared war on Germany two days later. What started out as a European war might have stayed that way, but for France and Britain's colonial acquisitions around the world, Germany's military pact with Italy, itself an owner of colonies, and Japan, a powerful player in the East. All of the British Empire's available resources were mobilized, including the railways in India.

▶ **Railway workshops in India** during World War II were co-opted to work for the war effort. Manpower was used to build a wide variety of war equipment, from hand grenade casings to armoured vehicles. This 1942 photograph shows railway employees constructing an armoured vehicle.

Geographically, India played an indirect role in the early phases of the war as no warfare was directed against the subcontinent until 1942. Instead, men and materiel were shipped from India to support the British effort in other war zones. The railways were stripped of a vast majority of their equipment and were left with the bare minimum required for reduced civilian service.

More than 26 branch lines were dismantled and around 8 per cent metre-gauge locomotives, 15 per cent metre-gauge wagons, and 4 million sleepers were dispatched to foreign war fronts, particularly the Middle East. Railway workshops were utilized as munition plants. As priorities changed, rail repairs were delayed and the available rolling stock suffered greatly. Since one half of all senior railway positions were designated for British personnel, the conscription of European citizens meant that the railways in India were left to function without a large percentage of experienced employees.

Caught napping

The Japanese invasion of the Southeast Asian sector had begun by 1940 with an attack on French Indochina. The Japanese focus on this war theatre increased after their attack on Pearl Harbor in December 1941. The British Government in India, which had always felt threatened by the possibility of a Russian assault in the north-west region towards their border with Afghanistan, had devoted all its attention to establishing defensive infrastructures, including railway lines, to ensure rapid troop movements in that region.

The eastern front was lamentably lacking in defensive infrastructure or communication systems. Apart from river steamer services and two unmetalled trunk roads, the region had a metre-gauge line through two valleys. India's eastern frontier became the primary launchpad for the counter-offensive against Japan when the Japanese captured

Singapore in February, and then Burma in May 1942. In order to maintain command over the north-eastern rail link, the Government took over the Assam Bengal Railway Company (ABR). On 1 January 1942, the Government-owned Eastern Bengal Railway (EBR) merged with the ABR to form the Bengal and Assam Railway (BAR).

Insignia for the Bengal and Assam Railway (BAR)

Transporting refugees

The subcontinent became a sanctuary for people fleeing Burma ahead of the oncoming Japanese assault. Refugees crossed the border and poured into Assam, from where the railways transported them across India. Despite the fact that the Middle Eastern war effort had severely depleted its stock, the BAR transported more than 200,000 refugees by rail.

The staff worked continuously to prevent congestion and special trains were run for the mission. As most of the refugees were unable to pay for their train fare, the Government assumed the cost of their journey. Civilian groups gathered at the stations along the evacuation train routes, providing aid in the form of biscuits, hot tea, cheese, and jam as food was in short supply on the trains.

Military asset

Due to military activity along the eastern front, the metre-gauge railway in Assam was considered a part of the war zone and was thus controlled by the armed forces. The army's needs were prioritized over the civilians and the limited civilian passenger and goods trains running at the time were under the supervision of the military high command. Railway staff involved in the war effort were accorded army ranks. Some traffic managers were given the rank of a brigadier, station

superintendents were deemed second lieutenants, and other junior personnel were given ranks such as *subedar* major and havildar major – both senior JCO (junior commissioned officer) ranks in the British Indian Army.

Wartime rolling stock

As the war intensified, the railways became a site of battle with the Japanese attempting to destroy trains, their cargo, and the rail lines. To protect these assets, special armoured wagons were used on the lines. Mounted with machine guns and anti-aircraft cannons, these wagons chugged ahead of trains to eliminate threats from Japanese snipers or aircraft. Hospital trains were employed to transport wounded soldiers away from the battlefront. Refurbished passenger trains were fitted with a dispensary, storeroom, kitchen, and coaches for hospital staff, and could accommodate around 500 soldiers.

Transporting supplies

The railways were used to transport troops and war materiels throughout India, although the vast majority were sent to the eastern frontier. Thousands of tonnes of supplies were sent every day by rail and water routes from Calcutta to Upper Assam. From here, the supplies were taken to China via a road through Burma to aid the Chinese Army in their efforts to contain the Japanese.

When Burma fell to the Japanese in May 1942, all possible land routes were cut off and Allied forces set up a perilous airlift, known as "The Hump" that flew from Assam to reach China over the Himalayas. Now in addition to other war supplies, large amounts of concrete had to be sent by rail for the construction of aircraft runways and other projects such as an alternate land route to China. Meanwhile, soldiers would

travel as far as the train routes would take them to the edge of Assam before going the rest of the way to Burma on foot.

The extra traffic resulting from war was incredibly lucrative for the railways. This profitability, however, came at a heavy price as the railway system was worn out after being used far past its maximum capacity, with no subsequent repairs.

At the end of World War II in 1945, India's railways were in urgent need of repairs. However, the steam had gone out of the Empire in the subcontinent. The railway network was in shambles and in desperate need of renovation.

WATER, WATER EVERYWHERE!

The war effort involved innovative thinking and sometimes more indigenous solutions were found for problems. Elephants were used specially on the eastern war front, when diesel or steam power were unavailable. They would be transported in special elephant cars at the front of the train. In an interesting instance, a steam train transporting materiel to the frontier suddenly came to a halt. It had run out of water, despite having just filled the tank. Those who set out to investigate the issue immediately discovered the perpetrator— an elephant shamelessly using his trunk to suck water to give itself a bath. British soldiers on military train journeys caused similar grief to the engineers on board. Desperate for tea, but lacking a hot water source, every train stop would involve a crowd of soldiers rushing to drain hot water from the boilers.

▼ **An elephant** pushing a boxcar at Bogapani, Assam, in 1945

▲ **Timetables of private railway companies** showcased a range of graphic styles and details. Some like the GIPR promised improvements in "post-war" services, while others, such as the BB&CI, displayed sophisticated design aesthetics.

PLAN OF ACTION

Railway timetables are ephemeral publications. Once outdated, they are of little use and discarded. However, old timetables reveal a wealth of information on more than just the running time. They often include information on passenger facilities, catering, travel conditions, and tourists, making them a valuable resource for rail enthusiasts and historians alike.

The early timetables published by railway companies were quite basic, often limited to the services provided by them. So, it fell to private publishers, such as Britain's Thomas Cook and George Bradshaw, to compile and sell the more comprehensive ones. The latter, Bradshaw, was so popular that his name became synonymous with rail timetables.

India's "Newman's Indian Bradshaw" began publishing from 1868 and did much more than tell arrival and departure times. Many provided a fascinating insight into the social conditions of the time, whether it was the population of Bombay as mentioned in a timetable from 1941 (1,486,971 people) or a notice that the Frontier Mail no longer ran to the Ballard Pier station in Bombay because of uncertainty of sailings by steamers resulting from World War II.

The design
Timetables evolved over the years, encapsulating a diverse range of content, and graphic styles, and cover designs, which ranged from the very plain to elaborate full-colour illustrations. The style of the period is evident, for instance, on the cover of the Bombay, Baroda & Central India (BB&CI) Railway timetable of July–September 1945, which has an elaborate and prominent sketch of the Bombay Central railway station and a colourful bookmark promoting a film by the Hindi film director AR Kardar. Most other timetables, however, preferred a simple design.

General information
These booklets contained much more than train times and included lists of the railway's directors, managers, and members of local advisory committees. The October 1941 edition of the BB&CI timetable provided a list of dates on which various sections of the line were opened, and a calendar of fairs and festivals to encourage train travel. Also listed were dak bungalows, their distance from the stations

and their rates. To encourage tourism, it also advertised attractive circular tour tickets around India. For instance, tour number 3 covered around 8,800 km for Rs 75.

Timetables also offered a peek into the world of the European traveller planning to travel in the railways' privately chartered carriages. The October 1942 edition of the Bengal–Nagpur Railway (BNR) timetable gave details and floor plans for the two tourist carriages it provided, while the BB&CI's December 1941 edition featured details of tourist carriages, along with 16 pages of tourist information on temples, tombs, and forts, and other sites. The illustrations depicted comfortable accommodation for those who could afford it. This feature, however, disappeared during World War II.

Dining and food
The Madras and Southern Mahratta Railway's October 1942 timetable listed one broad-gauge and two meter-gauge refreshment car services, and also provided extensive details of the locations, menus, and tariffs of refreshment rooms, showing separate facilities for European, Hindu, and Muslim dining options. Its helpful advice to the traveller included, "to state whether 'boiled' or 'fried' eggs are required", and noted that "butlers will reserve seats at the Refreshment Room tables for the number of meals ordered by resting the chairs against the table." Telegraphic codes used to order meals were also given. For instance, a substantial, healthy breakfast of fish, bacon, and eggs was coded FBT (meal with tea) or FBC (meal with coffee).

▶ **As new timetables** were published, it was the norm to publicize new film releases like this still from a 1945 release found in a BB&CI booklet of the same year.

Advertising opportunities
Paid commercial advertising on the back cover, and often inside, was a common feature to help keep costs low. As new editions of timetables were published frequently, it became practical to advertise items of short-term interest, such as films, or consumer products and services, such as jewellery, watches, electrical goods, or even hotel accommodations. The BB&CI's July 1945 timetable included stills from the historical drama *Ek Din Ka Sultan* (1945), and a bound-in bookmark, printed in colour.

Effects of World War II
Day to day needs of regular travellers became the focus during World War II. Some railway companies, such as the Great Indian Peninsula Railway (GIPR), promised travellers improvements in its post-war equipment and services in its December 1942 timetable. As the war progressed, these booklets became slimmer and less detailed, though companies continued to promise better conditions to come. Its proprietors, however, had probably not envisioned that the post-war improvements would take place under an independent India.

▲ **A coloured bound-in bookmark** advertising the film *Sanyasi* (1945) and *Pahle Aap* (1944) found in the GIPR timetable of July 1945.

TOWARDS FREEDOM

The exorbitant costs incurred during World War II (1939–45) brought the Empire to its knees and its hegemony started to wane. Great Britain no longer possessed the political will or the economic might to hold on to India – the jewel in its crown. Despite a growing realization that it was the beginning of the end for British rule in India, the railways showed no signs of slowing down. Passenger traffic continued to grow as did work on expanding the railway network, which steadily fuelled India's march to freedom.

The railways in India had not been immune to the strain of World War II. The myth of benign British imperialism had meanwhile crumbled and independence became the rallying cry across the country. Canadian historian Ian J Kerr wrote in his book *Engines of Change*, "The rolling stock and infrastructure of India's railroads were badly depleted. Many British railroad men had left India to serve the British war effort and they, seeing the end of the Raj, did not return. The Indianization of the upper levels of railroad service was thereby advanced – a positive development given the severe test to which the railroads were soon to be put."

Even amid growing suspicions that these were the closing years of colonial rule in India, it was business as usual for the railways. Post-war repairs and demands for rolling stock were being addressed, matters concerning its staff were being looked into, and its capital and depreciation fund estimates were being calculated. The chief commissioner of the railways in his Budget speech for 1944–45 continued to make plans: "At the end of the war there will be much to be done in the rehabilitation of the existing assets and in the development of the railways..."

Turning a profit
The period of 1946–47 saw a significant percentage increase in upper-class and interclass passenger traffic. In fact, the continuing swell in passenger traffic made the railways curtail its expenditure

on publicity campaigns. The changing political landscape notwithstanding, the enterprise continued to make a profit. In a Budget speech for 1945–46, War Transport Member Sir Edward Benthall reported enthusiastically that the figures for the Budget were "judged by pre-war figures, phenomenal ..." and that, "the railways despite its war-usage and on the brink of finding itself in the hands of the natives had thrived and continued to grow."

The Budget speech for 1946–47 was also optimistic: "... financially the position is far sounder than it has been at any stage in the history of the railways ... Lower class travel has not been comfortable in the past because the main consideration has been the provision of cheap travel to India's impoverished masses, but improved coaching stock and other amenities together with properly coordinated road services should better the conditions of travel in the future. The railways should soon be able to meet the demand for goods traffic and will expand to meet further industrial and agricultural production." He was of the firm belief that when it came to the railways, "India has a great asset which must be carefully nursed and firmly administered."

Into the storm

The railways also investigated new lines of construction and the restoration of derailed lines. Passenger train mileage, though less than pre-war days, had shown an increase, with the railways resuming more than a thousand train services. Locomotives had been ordered, even as the construction of new locomotives was underway, and the stock of goods wagons was increased to improve service.

With a vast nationalized network, the financial stability of the railways was central to the economy of the country. The political upheaval in the follow-up to the carving of two sovereign states from a cultural and historical whole, however, created adverse conditions for its smooth functioning. Labour discontent, increased lawlessness on the rail network, inflation, and curfews threatened to derail the arduous process of returning to pre-war conditions. On 15 August 1947, India became independent and Pakistan was born. Everything was divided. The land, its people, ships, typewriters, food stock, and the railway lines. Even as the two Governments tried to come to terms with the new borders, the railways reeled from the division. A unified and cohesive system, it was never meant to be partitioned.

◀ **Engineers of the 136 Indian Railway Maintenance Company** laying down rails in Bologna a week before the German surrender in Italy in April 1945.

NEW NATIONS

On 12 August 1947, British lawyer Cyril Radcliffe sent his recommendations for the boundaries that would become India and Pakistan to the Viceroy Lord Mountbatten. Everything had to be partitioned, including the railways, and India suddenly found itself in possession of a lopsided railway system as lines, workshops, rolling stock, and even manpower were divided.

Insignia of the pre-Independence North Western Railway

Cyril Radcliffe was appointed the chairman of the two Boundary Commissions, which had been hurriedly created in July 1947 and would decide on the parts of Punjab and Bengal that would go to India and Pakistan. He and the representatives of the two main political parties, the Muslim League and the Congress, had 36 days to decide this. In June, a Partition Council had already started dividing the assets between the two new countries, from railway lines and ships to chairs and typewriters. The decision became public on 17 August.

Though expected, the ultimate division was abrupt. It left people stranded on either side of the border and administrators with the complicated job of dividing a country's assets. Journalist Ajit Bhattarcharjea in *Countdown to Partition: The Final Days* wrote: "New national and provincial boundaries had to be divided; the assets and liabilities of the Government of India and the Reserve Bank had to be divided; the jurisdiction of the superior courts had to be determined; diplomatic representation had to be arranged for both new nations. And now it all had to be completed in two weeks".

Dividing railway lines

The division changed the structure of two railway lines in particular, the North Western Railway (NWR) extended across West Pakistan, and

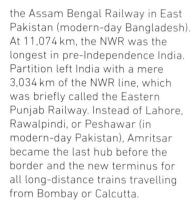

▶ **Locomotive drivers ran special trains** to relocate those Muslim residents who had opted for Pakistan following Partition.

the Assam Bengal Railway in East Pakistan (modern-day Bangladesh). At 11,074 km, the NWR was the longest in pre-Independence India. Partition left India with a mere 3,034 km of the NWR line, which was briefly called the Eastern Punjab Railway. Instead of Lahore, Rawalpindi, or Peshawar (in modern-day Pakistan), Amritsar became the last hub before the border and the new terminus for all long-distance trains travelling from Bombay or Calcutta.

The Jodhpur Railway lost 513 km to Pakistan as well. The division of Bengal raised a similar problem as only 3,125 km of 5,721 km remained in Indian territory. The main connection to Calcutta no longer existed as many of the lines were now in East Pakistan. The region of Assam had an unusual problem. The Partition of Bengal and the railways had left it isolated, linked only by a small strip of land to the rest of India. Major workshops, depots, and

stores were also divided with no contingencies. With Lahore now in Pakistan, telephone and telegraph communication between Delhi and Punjab broke down, so trains were used to despatch mail until the services were re-established in November 1947. It would be years before the system recovered from the scars of Partition.

Dividing human resources

The railway workforce was divided as well and the 1947–48 Interim Budget noted that approximately 126,300 employees opted for India and had to be accommodated and awarded new assignments. There was also the matter of, what Canadian historian Ian J Kerr called, the "communalization of the workforce". Certain roles had traditionally been taken up by members of a specific community. The division of the country affected that as well. The Budget made note of one such example from the East Indian Railway (EIR). A number of the

ngine crew opted for Pakistan. The riginal agreement was that they vould be released from their role radually. Ever-increasing communal ostilities, however, meant that this vas no longer a viable plan. As a esult, the railways, along with other epartments across the country, saw sudden drop in staff. Crews from ther railways were brought in to nsure service was not interrupted.

Working together

he 1947–48 Interim Railway Budget peech outlined how the two new overnments made temporary greements to deal with the more nmediate problems. For instance, ne new designated borders had no acilities such as stabling rooms or rrangements for wagon and coach spections, crucial for the running of trains. It was agreed that trains would go beyond the border into the other territory till the point where such facilities were available. "Working powers" were also given to Pakistan (and vice versa) for certain sections, which were isolated from the parent railway. These allowed some sections to be operated by the "other Railway". In fact, Jodhpur Railway continued to administer and operate about 513 km of lines in Pakistan until July 1948.

Among some of the biggest problems were the workshops. The key workshops in Lahore and Mughalpura were now with West Pakistan, while Saidpur went to East Pakistan. The governments tried to make special arrangements wherein the workshops across the borders would try to compensate. For instance, Mughalpura would try to fulfil the requirements of the Eastern Punjab Railway, just as the Kanchrapara Workshop in West Bengal, India, would work for the Eastern Bengal Railway within East Pakistan. A similar arrangement was attempted for the Assam Railway with the Saidpur Workshop, but this did not work out.

Lines needed repair as did the rolling stock, but facilities and manpower were limited. Goods that were previously exported through Karachi were rerouted to Bombay, which was ill-equipped to handle the extra load. There was no doubt that there were many problems, some that required urgent attention. All this, however, was nothing compared to the bloodletting that was about to ensue.

▲ **The loss of the Saidpur Workshop** hit the Assam Bengal Railway the hardest as it no longer had any recourse to repairs or maintenance of lines or rolling stock.

THE EXODUS

Every day for months after Independence, trains snaked their way across a divided Punjab, heaped with masses of humanity. Some reached their destination full of hope, depositing men, women, and children seeking to make India or Pakistan their new home. Others pulled into stations, silent carriages soaked with blood, mute witnesses to the carnage within.

▲ **Hindu and Sikh refugees** are seen waiting at the Amritsar railway station after crossing the border for trains to take them to new locations within India. This was a common scene at stations across border towns in India and Pakistan, after Partition in 1947.

People displaced in the Partition had to find some way to get to their country of choice – on foot, in bullock carts, or on trains. In the days that followed 15 August 1947, the railways became one of the most efficient ways to transport millions of people across new borders. In so doing, they became a beacon of hope, but equally a symbol of warring identities, chaos, and bloodshed.

Even as nearly 10 million refugees made their way across the border, more than a million people were massacred. Indian scholar Swarna Aiyer writes in her essay "'August Anarchy': The Partition Massacres in Punjab, 1947", that this violence should be seen within the context of the political events leading up to independence and the Partition, as two new countries tried to put in place the infrastructure that would help them make sense of the madness. No one community was at fault, each equally responsible for the sheer scale of violence that followed.

Cross-border transportation

Millions on the Move, a document issued by the Indian Government in 1949, indicated that about 673 refugee trains ran between 27 August and 6 November 1947, moving more than 23,00,000 refugees inside India and across the border. Provisions were made for evacuation from Hyderabad in Sindh via daily trains from Jodhpur. People stranded outside divided Punjab were taken in groups to railheads and then transported in trains. Between 1947 to 1948, 4 million refugees travelled across the borders in trains. They huddled wherever they could,

crammed into compartments or on roofs, even holding on to engines, where possible. A photograph from that time depicts a man at the Ambala station charging 2 annas from refugees to use his bamboo ladder to climb on to a goods train.

Floods in the region towards the end of September disrupted train services until the 101st Railway Construction Company of Queen Victoria's Own Sappers and Miners from Bangalore arrived to repair the tracks, provide military escorts, and run the trains.

Trains of death

The country had been hacked into two on religious principles, and the moving population became easy targets for zealots and religious mobs. With the news of Partition filtering in, railway stations became open to attacks as hordes of people gathered at railway stations waiting to cross the new border.

Among the initial incidents reported was the 9 August derailment of a special train of Pakistani Government officials and their families because of a mine placed on railway tracks. The Lahore railway station became the centre of violence between 12 and 18 August as people desperate to escape the city gathered there. On 13 August, 43 workers were stabbed at the Mughalpura railway workshop. On 15 August, a train in Wazirabad, Pakistan, was stopped and around 100 passengers were killed while 200 were stabbed and injured.

Trains between Lahore and Lyallpur, and Ferozepur and Bhatinda were stopped on a regular basis and

people were attacked, butchered, or raped by mobs. Retaliation followed retaliation in a seemingly never-ending cycle of violence. After an attack on the Frontier Mail on 24 August and the killing of 150 people on the Karachi Mail, train movement became sporadic. Special refugee trains started running across the borders in September, but this did not stop the mobs. As one British officer recounted: "In every carriage without exception the dead and dying were mixed up with the wounded – it was certainly a train of death."

There was some semblance of order by the end of October 1947 with better organization and an increased military presence. Wherever possible, soldiers from the Gurkha regiment – believed to be the most neutral – were stationed on trains. The repercussions of this horrific bloodshed continue to resonate across India and Pakistan in the neighbours' hostile relations today.

▲ **A convoy of Sikhs** migrate to East Punjab after Partition in this iconic image by photographer Margaret Bourke-White. Refugees commonly used roads and trains to travel across the border.

 On one side was a **train for Hindustan** packed with Hindus and Sikhs with **hundreds on the roof**. On the other was a Muslim **train for Pakistan**. In the middle was the **corpse train**. 99

NOTES FROM PARTITION OBSERVED: BRITISH OFFICIAL REPORTS FROM SOUTH ASIA, 25 AUGUST 1947

In a desperate attempt to cross the borders, refugees travelled however they could – in compartments, hanging from the engines, or even on the roof. Seen here is the Amritsar railway station in Punjab, on the border of India and Pakistan, packed with trains overflowing with refugees, in October 1947.

RESTORE, REGROUP, AND REBUILD

Even as the nation celebrated its freedom, the railways took stock of its lines and infrastructure, severely affected by Partition. As it looked towards the future, the young Indian Government began consolidating its resources and creating a true "Indian" railway network.

Indian economist John Matthai, while presenting the first Interim Railway Budget of independent India in November 1947, reflected on the many challenges they had been presented. Besides a truncated railway system, there was "depleted staff, lack of resources, the virtual breakdown of law and order, the large numbers of refugees – destitute and miserable but often very defiant and difficult – finally the wrath of the elements in the form of these unprecedented floods that have occurred." The railway staff, themselves reeling from the effects of Partition, had risen to the occasion courageously. However, it was now time to rebuild and restore, so that the railways could once again truly connect a nation.

▲ **Economist John Matthai** served as India's first minister of railways.

Restoring connections
Traffic patterns changed significantly after Partition. All traffic to northern India, which used to go via Karachi, now passed through Bombay, increasing the load on that system. Provisions were made on an urgent basis for more lines and yard facilities in that sector to handle the additional burden. An immediate issue was the rebuilding of connections to areas that were now isolated because of Partition. The state of Assam, which lost its rail link to the rest of the country with the creation of East Pakistan (modern-day Bangladesh), was of the biggest concern. It was now connected to the rest of India through a narrow 20-km-wide corridor. A massive relinking project, therefore, began in January 1948 and involved laying of 230 km of railway lines. It was completed in record time and opened to passenger traffic in January 1950 (see pp.192–93).

There were also concerted efforts to relink Kashmir. Earlier, most trains connected Rawalpindi and Jammu via Lahore, after which one continued the journey by road. Now these lines had to go through Delhi. Work began in Punjab on the Mukerian–Pathankot line in November 1949 and was opened to the public in April 1952. This changed the face of Pathankot, previously a small station that catered only to the Kangra Valley Railway. It became the hub that received support traffic from Jammu. Efforts to link Kashmir via the rail continue, even today (see pp.262–63).

Rearranging matters
While presenting the Interim Railway Budget, Matthai also emphasized the importance of regrouping the lines affected by Partition. These included the East Punjab Railway, which was under the Railway Board, East Indian Railway, Oudh and Tirhut Railway, and the Indian portion of the Bengal and Assam Railway and Assam Railway. By 1948 in Gujarat, the Bhavnagar and Kathiawar State Railways and the Jamnagar and Dwarka, Gondal, and Morvi Railways all merged under the Saurashtra Railway. The following year the Gaekwad's Baroda State Railway became a part of the Bombay, Baroda and Central India (BB&CI) Railway.

An "Indian" Railway

Matthai referred quite prominently to the "Indianization of our superior staff", a big demand of nationalist leaders during the freedom movement. In the Budget, he noted that, of the 388 European railway officers employed in important positions, about 50 per cent were due to leave or had left. Creating an Indian workforce that could take on these senior positions was of utmost urgency. A beginning had already been made towards the end of 1947 when, of six Railway Board members, five were Indian. This was a far cry from the start of that year, when four Europeans and one Indian made up the Board. The transition to a network staffed completely by Indians was seamless even as the railways continued to operate efficiently. A lack of skilled labour also became an issue to be resolved with some urgency, especially since different communities specialized in certain roles within the railways and these forces were now irretrievably divided.

"For instance," wrote Canadian historian Ian J Kerr, "Muslims often worked with locomotives or in the workshops, while Hindus and Sikhs were more common in traffic or clerical roles. The Partition led to a severe imbalance in the workforce. It would be several years before this imbalance would be properly addressed."

Independence and self-reliance

For decades, rolling stock had mostly been imported. With Independence came a renewed effort to develop an indigenous industry. Matthai reiterated its importance as, out of the available 8,400 broad- and metre-gauge locomotives, 2,900 had completed their period of service. Gradually, the availability and import of spare parts increased and was reflected in a more upbeat Budget speech the following year in 1948. This was also because Indian manufacturers were scheduled to deliver 4,050 general service wagons and expected to deliver 146 new locomotives during 1948.

The efforts slowly increased workshop outputs, efficient transportation of imported food grains, and improved the capacity of marshalling yards. Equally prominent on the Indian Government's list of priorities was to increase line capacity. Bridges were regirded for double-line traffic even as marshalling yards were extended, and sea routes were co-opted to take some of the load off the railways. The early years of independence saw a deep focus on re-energizing the railway system that had become dilapidated during the World War II era.

▲ **In an effort** to keep the railway traffic moving along the main arteries of the country, the Dufferin Bridge (later renamed Malviya Bridge) over the River Ganges in Varanasi was regirded for double-line traffic and opened by the end of 1947.

◄ **One of four locomotives completed** for India by the American firm Baldwin Locomotive Works is loaded on to the Indian freighter *Alaketu* in 1947. India started becoming self-reliant from 1948.

WP 7200

The WP class of steam locomotives were designed to be express passenger engines. With a 4-6-2 wheel arrangement and a speed of up to 100 km/h, the WP 7200 was one of the 16 prototypes imported from the Baldwin Locomotive Works in the US in 1947. It was inducted into the Indian Railway's steam fleet on 15 August 1947 – Independence Day – aptly earning the name *Azad*, meaning free. India began production of this class of locomotives in 1963 and the Chittaranjan Locomotive Works (see pp.206–07) in West Bengal became the first to manufacture them in the country. While electric locomotives were operational in and around the city of Bombay by the early 20th century, they never really reached the speed of 100 km/h.

Azad has a distinctive cone-shaped bulging nose with a gleaming silver star painted on it. Its dimensions were designed keeping in mind the poor track conditions across the country in the late 1940s. The WP class of locomotives served as the standard broad-gauge locomotives for more than four decades till they were retired in 1995.

In a bid to revive the charm of the classic steam-hauled trains and locomotives, *Azad* was restored at the Rewari Heritage Steam Loco Centre, Haryana, by a dedicated team of the Northern Railway. It began hauling a Sunday commercial steam train service between Farukh Nagar and Gadi Harsaru in Haryana in 2018. The 11-km ride is specially aimed at steam engine enthusiasts, generating tourist traffic and serving up a slice of steam heritage. On 21 November 2018, *Azad* was used to pull one of the world's most luxurious and iconic trains – Palace on Wheels (see pp.272–77) for its 12th tour – on a short trip from the Safdarjung Station to the Patel Nagar Station in Delhi. The vintage locomotive was also used to haul a passenger train for a special tour from the New Delhi Station to the Delhi Junction during the Indian Railways' 63rd Railway Week in 2018. This tour was specially curated for differently abled children.

▶ **Considered the pride of the Indian Railways,** the locomotive WP 7200 is often used to haul trains for special runs to mark occasions.

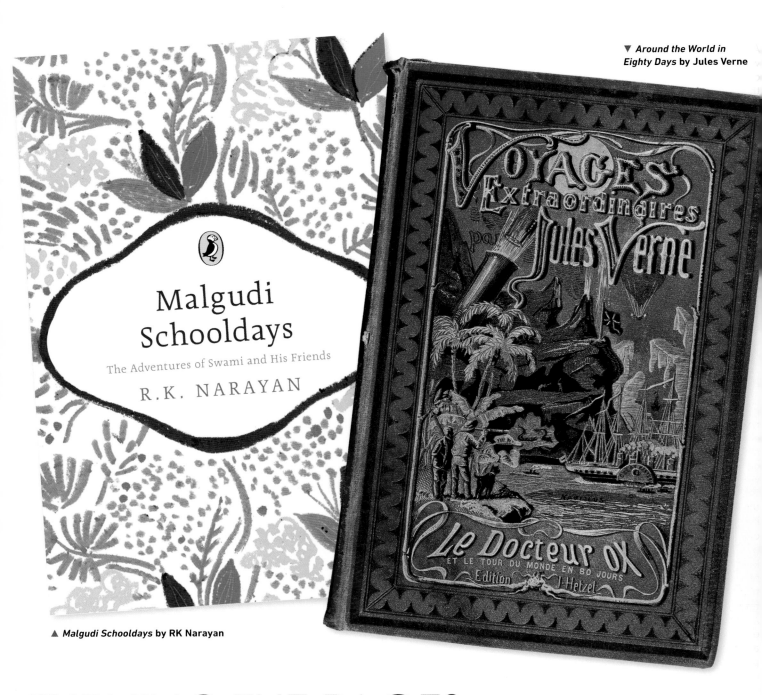

▼ Around the World in Eighty Days **by Jules Verne**

▲ *Malgudi Schooldays* **by RK Narayan**

TURNING THE PAGES

Railways were the vectors of modernity, a colonial tool, a signifier of human enterprise, and a very handy plot device for literature. Trains, their stations, a fellow traveller perhaps fleeing from his past, another on the brink of a momentous journey, with maybe a murder thrown into the mix, all made for wonderful, often familiar, tracks of writing on the railways.

Among major literary works to reference the colonial initiative of the railways in India, is French author Jules Verne's *Around the World in Eighty Days* (1872). The protagonist, Phileas Fogg's adventures around the world starts with a *Daily Telegraph* report of a new railway line laid in India, making it possible to see the world in 80 days. He makes it to Bombay and takes a train to Kholby, where the line, contrary to the news report, lies about 80 km short of completion. Verne's India, full of palanquins, tigers, holy lands, and indigo fields, has all the makings of an "Orientalist tourist brochure", notes Indian author Arup K Chatterjee in his 2018 book *The Purveyors of Destiny: A Cultural Biography of the Indian Railways*.

Verne's novel, much like most of pre-Independence writing on the railways, mirrors the colonial enterprise, where the native is the noble savage and the English, a civilizing force. So too, in English writer Rudyard Kipling's 1893 story *The Bridge Builders*, which symbolizes the triumph of colonialism and immortalizes his real-life observations of the construction of the Kaisar-i-Hind or Sutlej Bridge (in present-day Pakistan). Kipling's works, Canadian historian Ian J Kerr notes, "contributed to the British experience of railway travel" as well. More so, after AH Wheeler and Company, a chain of bookstores operating in stations across the country (see p.119), published his writings in 1888 as a part of the "Indian Railway Library".

In contrast, American author Mark Twain views India from a distinctive, non-colonial lens. In *Following the Equator: A Journey Around the World* (1897), the description of his train journeys are almost romantic. "It was a very large station, yet when we arrived it seemed as if the whole world was present –

◀ **Mark Twain's** *Following the Equator: A Journey Around the World*

half of it inside, the other half outside," he wrote.

Carriages and class

The critique of railways as an instrument of control, built to ease the plunder of colonial rule, emerged during the national movement primarily through Mohandas Karamchand Gandhi's writings. His work, *Hind Swaraj*, which was published in 1910, denounces the state of the third class and dissects the imperialist agenda of the railways. Third-class carriages had wooden benches, lacked lavatories, and people were packed in like sardines, while first-class passengers, often European, travelled in plush comfort. All the benefits of the railways accruing to the natives were happy accidents, he believed, and wrote, "Good travels at a snail's pace – it can, therefore, have little to do with the railways."

As painted stations whistle by

Despite Gandhi's criticism, the railways entrenched themselves in the nationalist's narrative. After Independence in 1947, they became an intrinsic part of India's social and economic fabric. This found face and form in Indian writing, aptly reflected in Indian writer RK Narayan's seminal 1935 *Swami and Friends*.

"As I sat in a room nibbling at my pen and wondering what to write, Malgudi with its little railway station swam into view, all ready-made, with a character called Swaminathan running down the platform," Narayan writes in his memoir *My Days* (1974). The sleepy, fictional town of Malgudi with its "little railway station", though southern in tone and texture was a microcosm for all small towns across India, a small station breathing vitality

SYMBOLS OF DESTINY

In 1947, trains transported refugees across the borders and became sites of communal violence. They brought out theatricality in the performance of violence and, though the people killed on the ground outnumbered those executed on trains, the starkness of the train killings have been seared into the collective memory of Partition.

Trains became the shorthand for writing on the violence of splitting a subcontinent into two – carrying cadavers across the border, blood congealed in its carriages, pulling into stations that reverberated with wailing, and carrying testimonials of trauma. Khushwant Singh's *Train to Pakistan*, Bhisham Sahni's *We Have Arrived in Amritsar and Other Short Stories*, Mukul Kesavan's *Looking Through Glass*, and Saadat Hasan Manto's "Hospitality Delayed" ("Kasre-Nafsi"), tell the tales of the everyday space of the train and travel and its descent into violence, narrowing our gaze on the collective madness of the Partition.

into the town, which otherwise lay frozen within its cultural homogeneity. The railway station was the signifier of alien technology, a reminder of colonial rule, and the promise of modernity. "Trains stop at Malgudi, newcomers arrive and disrupt the dreamy contentment of Narayan's heroes. Without their intrusion the novels would have no plot, and, more than that, they would have no point," writes British academic Richard Cronin.

Small towns and trains play a significant role in Indian author Ruskin Bond's work as well. He draws perhaps from his childhood holidays spent at the railway bungalow of his Uncle Fred who was a station superintendent at Delhi Main. Bond, writes Chatterjee, "is seen replenishing imagery after imagery in the quest of railway colonies situated in the Himalayan foothills, relinquishing in the process sundry romances."

▼ **Cover of Rudyard Kipling's** *The Bridge Builders* taken from a bas-relief created by Kipling's father, John Lockwood.

ASSAM RELINKED

Partition had left Assam isolated, flanked by a hostile East Pakistan at one end and Nepal on the other. As India adjusted to its new-formed freedom, it undertook a massive operation, to relink Assam by rail, while bridging turbulent rivers and navigating dense forests. It would be one of the Indian Railways' most outstanding engineering achievements.

Partition left Assam connected to India by a strip of land a mere 20 km wide. Meanwhile, the only line of communication between India and West Bengal's northern districts of Darjeeling and Jalpaiguri was a 2-ft-gauge line with limited capacity. Relinking Assam, the gateway to the north-east and crucial to Indian interests, had become a matter of urgency. As a Ministry of Railways memorandum to the Cabinet noted, it was an "absolute necessity both strategically and administratively. India cannot depend for passage to Assam on the goodwill of Pakistan." Construction began immediately in January 1948 with engineer-in-chief Karnail Singh at the helm of what was to be a formidable assignment.

By the time it was complete, the 228.5-km-long Assam Rail Link Project (ARLP) cost about

Rs 93 million and took less than two years to complete, opening for passenger traffic on 26 January 1950.

Reconnaissance

The best way to establish a connection was by linking the metre-gauge lines of the Oudh and Tirhut Railway with the Assam Railway. This meant connecting Kishanganj in Bihar with Amingaon in Assam. The project was divided into four key sectors. Surveys were conducted – first by air and then on the ground – before work commenced. The lines ran through Bihar's Purnea district for about 64 km, West Bengal's Darjeeling and Jalpaiguri districts for 125.5 km, and Cooch Behar for 8 km, and Assam's Goalpara district for about 35 km.

Given the lack of time and the seemingly impossible deadline, surveys were quick but quite promptly revealed several

potential problems, including bridging the Rivers Tista and Torsa. Weather played a huge role as the monsoon, the surveyors realized, lasted for more than six months in the region. The deadline for the completion of the project was January 1950. This left engineers 11 months of working time.

▼ **The bridge over the River Tista** was one of the most difficult ones to build due to strong currents and high waves.

Easier said than done

The first step was replacing, and not converting, the 190-km, 2 ft-gauge line between Kishanganj and Siliguri into metre gauge as it was laid like a tram line. This section came under the Darjeeling Himalayan Railway (DHR), so in October 1948, the Indian Government bought the DHR's main line and its extensions, handing its operations over to the ARLP. This was one of the easier problems to solve.

The second section proved more complicated. The 35-km stretch between the Siliguri junction and Gish Bridge near Bagrakote, both in West Bengal, required bridging many small streams and rivers. However,

> ## " Turbulent **rivers were bridged,** jungles cleared, and the **monsoon outwitted.** "
>
> *THE STATESMAN*, 11 DECEMBER 1949

it was the one over the Tista, a tributary of the Brahmaputra, which proved the most challenging. One of the most turbulent rivers in the area, the Tista has unmanageable waters between June and September because of the monsoon and meltwater from the glaciers. It is also susceptible to sudden course changes and flooding, with waves that rise as high as 4.5–6 m. The bridge at Sivok took all this into consideration. Wells, nearly 14-m-deep, were sunk into the riverbed and the structure that was built had one central span of about 76 m and two 45 m spans on either side. When a flood of 0.65 million cusecs breached the east guide bund in June 1950, the bridge was extended by three spans of 45 m on the east.

The Madarihat–Hasimara section was about 14-km-long, but deceptive in its distance, for it involved bridging the Torsa, a fierce river, originating in Tibet and known for its floodwaters. CAH Edwards, engineer-in-chief, surveys and construction, Eastern Bengal Railway, had observed in his 1927 report to the Railway Board that "the velocity of the floods is very great and destructive." Its width and flotsam from uprooted Sal trees added to its untameable nature. In fact, the earlier line avoided the Torsa with a 320-km detour via

Lalmanirhat (a part of East Pakistan, now Bangladesh). In his 1951 book, *A Complete Story of the Assam Rail Link Project*, Karnail Singh wrote that the river would have remained unbridged had it not been for the Partition. Surveyors and engineers had no option but to bridge the Torsa. River training involved using elaborate guide bunds and well foundations sunk to nearly 18 m. The bridge itself was nine spans of 45 m each.

The final section of Alipur Duar to Fakiragram was comparatively uncomplicated, barring a portion of 8 km in Cooch Behar, which involved navigating through the impenetrable, malarial Buxa forests, accessible only by elephants and crossing the Rivers Sankosh and Raidak.

During the course of the construction, 379 channels, spread over 402 km, were bridged, some that remained accessible for only five months in a year. Of these, 22 rivers, including the Tista, Torsa, and Sankosh needed deep well foundations. For the first time, prestressed concrete girders of around 18 m and 12 m spans were used to bridge across the three rivers.

KARNAIL SINGH (1904–76)

A graduate of Thomson Engineering College in Roorkee, Uttarakhand, Karnail Singh was no stranger to challenges. He started his career with the North Western Railway (now in Pakistan) in 1928, focusing mostly on special projects, such as the reconstruction of the Quetta line after the 1935 earthquake and building the lines to Hindubagh–Fort Sandeman and Fort Abbas–Hotwala in Bahawalpur. However, it was the Assam Rail Link Project, completed in a record time of two years, which proved to be his greatest achievement. He was involved in the construction of the Saraighat rail-and-road bridge over the Brahmaputra as well. He was appointed as chairman of the Railway Board in April 1960.

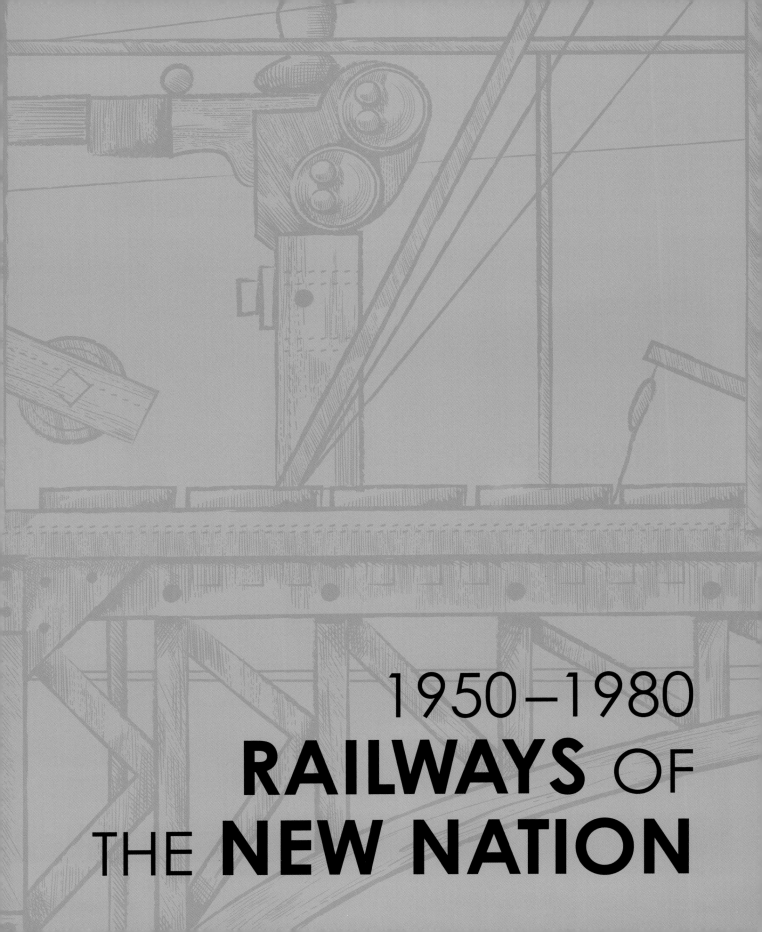

1950–1980
RAILWAYS OF THE NEW NATION

1950–1980

Buoyed by new nationhood, these decades saw a fresh start for the Indian Railways. The political obstacles that had existed under colonial rule had disappeared and a major reorganization of the railways was undertaken, starting with its division into six zones. This period also saw several new technological and institutional changes, a move towards modernization, phasing out of steam, and setting off on the path to electrification.

26 January 1950 The Constitution of India comes into effect, formally establishing India as a Republic. On the same day, Chittaranjan Locomotive Works (CLW) is inaugurated and the Assam Rail Link is opened to passenger traffic.

25 October 1951 The first general elections of India are conducted.

1954 Sleeping accommodation is introduced in third-class coaches.

1956 The first fully air-conditioned train, popularly known as the AC Express, is introduced between Howrah and Delhi.

1959 Fans and lights become standard fixtures in all passenger coaches, including the third class.

20 October 1962 China invades Ladakh and the North East Frontier Agency, starting the Sino-India war.

14 November 1963 CLW rolls out *Bidhan*, the first entirely India-built electric locomotive.

1950–55   1956–61   196

14 April 1952 The Eastern, Northern, and North Eastern Railways are formed.

1955 Integral Coach Factory at Perambur, Tamil Nadu, is inaugurated, the South-Eastern Railway is formed.

15 January 1958 The Northeast Frontier Railway is formed by splitting the North Eastern Railway.

1961 The CLW starts manufacturing electric locomotives and the Diesel Locomotive Works is set up at Varanasi, Uttar Pradesh.

21 November 1962 The Sino-Indian war comes to an end.

1951 The zonal grouping of the railways starts with the creation of the Southern, Western, and Central Railways.

1957 The Indian Railways decides to adopt 25 KV AC system for electrification. In the same year, the Research Designs and Standards Organisation (RDSO), the Indian Railway Institute for Signal Engineering and Telecommunication (IRISET), and the Railway Protection Force (RPF) are established.

1951 general elections in India

An inauguration at the Chittaranjan Locomotive Works

Locomotive *Bidhan*

> " ... it was **a marriage between the old and the new.** This **marriage was essential** because India could hardly live in an old age. When science was making very **fast progress,** India ... was making an effort to achieve progress through **electrification.** "

JAWAHARLAL NEHRU AT THE INAUGURATION OF THE ELECTRIC TRAIN IN CALCUTTA ON 14 DECEMBER 1957

April 1965 Following Pakistan's Operation Gibraltar, India and Pakistan go to war.

3 March 1969 The Rajdhani Express, the first high-speed all-AC train, runs between Howrah and New Delhi.

16 December 1971 End of the third Indo-Pak war, which marks the formation of the new nation of Bangladesh.

1974 The Rail India Technical and Economic Services (RITES) is incorporated as a public limited company.

26 June 1975 President Fakhruddin Ali Ahmed declares a state of internal Emergency in the country.

1965 Fast freight services or the "Super Express" are introduced on several routes.

1971 The Indian Railways formulates its gauge conversion policy.

1972 Construction of the Calcutta Metro begins.

21 March 1977 The Emergency in India comes to an end.

1979 The Central Organisation for Railways Electrification (CORE) is formed.

7

1968–73

1974–80

September 1965 The second Indo-Pak war ends in a ceasefire.

3 December 1971 India goes to war against Pakistan in support of the Bangladesh Liberation War.

1 February 1977 The National Railway Museum (NRM) opens to the public.

1977 Abolition of third-class railway travel. Wooden-slat seats are abolished and a cushioned second-class seating system is made the minimum standard.

1964 The CLW builds its first AC locomotive, a WAG-1.

1971 The Farakka Railway Bridge and the Pathankot–Jammu Tawi section is opened.

1973 CLW stops production of steam locomotives.

1966 The first container service in India starts between Bombay and Ahmedabad and the South Central Railway is formed.

20 July 1969 Apollo 11 lands on the moon and Neil Armstrong and Edwin Aldrin Jr are the first people to walk on the moon.

3 May 1974 The All India Railwaymen's Federation, led by its president George Fernandes, launches a total strike. The strike is one of the factors that contributes to the imposition of the Emergency in India.

Indian soldiers during the 1971 Indo-Pak war

Builder plates at the National Rail Museum, New Delhi

THE PEOPLE'S RAILWAYS

The railways picked up the pieces after Partition and looked towards a young, free India as it sought to actively be a part of nation-building. To do so, however, it first had to go through the long process of restructuring its operational units and build new lines to properly connect the country so that it could truly become the "Lifeline to the Nation" – its slogan today.

The early decades following Independence saw the railways' transition from a colonial tool to an enterprise that contributed to the larger agenda of nation-building, all the while serving the interests of India and its people. This was the time that the country's "greatest national asset" – as Jawaharlal Nehru, the first prime minister of India, called the railways in April 1952 – experienced a rebirth that helped it become a true lifeline to the country. If the 1950s were a time of integration and reorganization for the railways, the 1960s and 1970s were about modernization, increasing capacity, and building new lines.

FATEH CHAND BADHWAR (1900–95)

Independent India's first Railway Board chairman, Fateh Chand Badhwar, began his career with the East Indian Railway (EIR) Company in 1925. As the chairman, he presided over the successful unification of the lines, including those belonging to the Princely States. He also promoted the process of industrialization and modernization to ensure lesser dependence on Britain for rolling stock. The Research Design and Standards Organisation (RDSO), which focused on development, was established during his term. He was awarded the Order of the British Empire in 1946 and the Padma Bhushan in 1955.

A matter of zones

One of the earliest steps was to reorganize and better integrate its operational centres, which served 42 different railway systems. These included 13 Class I railways, so designated because of annual gross earnings of Rs 5 million or over, and 10 that belonged to Class II with earnings of Rs 1–5 million. There were 19 systems designated as class III with earnings under Rs 1 million. Of these, 32 belonged to former Princely States, including 2,247 km of the Nizam's State Railway (see pp.74–75). It was important to bring all of these lines under one management for the larger purpose of unification. This thought process mirrored the general trend in other countries, including Britain, France, Germany, Canada, and the US.

Justifying this decision, the minister of railways, transport, and states, N Gopalaswami Ayyangar, said in a 1951 speech, "A multiplicity of railway administrations, varying in size and standards, viability and efficiency has, for many years, been a clog on industrial development and general economic advancement in large parts of the country." It was, therefore, essential to regroup "the large number of small administrative units into a small number of larger ones." The regrouping was done all the while keeping in mind that the new systems served a compact zone, were large enough to support the headquarters, could implement improvements, and were equipped with adequate workshops and training facilities. It was equally important that the regrouping cause minimal dislocation and disturbance to existing arrangements.

Between April 1951 and 1952, six zones were created – Southern, Western, Central, Eastern, North Eastern, and Northern. This became eight when the Eastern Railway was split because of increased workload to create the South Eastern Railway. The number went up to nine in 1966 when portions of the Southern and Central Railways were carved out to form the South Central Railway to streamline

and improve the efficiency of the service to the southern states. Today, there are 17 zonal administrations, which do not include the Konkan Railway (see pp.248–49).

Management matters

The year 1951 saw changes in the Railway Board as the post of chief commissioner was abolished and the chairman was appointed the most senior functional member. There was further reorganization in 1954 with an increase in the number of members to five to work alongside the chairman and the financial commissioner. More power was also given to the former, who was now responsible for technical and policy matters. Today, the Railway Board consists of eight members in addition to the chairman. The Board manages the administrative role under the purview of the Union Cabinet minister of the Indian Government. Each zone, in turn, is under the command of a general manager.

New places, new lines

Partition necessitated the building of two lines on an urgent basis and both started almost immediately in the years following Independence. The first, the Assam relinking project, was a mammoth endeavour (see pp.192–93), which was

completed in record time. The second, the Mukerian–Pathankot line in Punjab, proved to be of immense strategic importance amid growing hostilities with Pakistan. Within months of Independence, the countries fought a war over Kashmir; they would go on to fight again in 1965, 1971, and 1999.

Work on the 43-km-long line began in November 1949. It required extensive bridging and opened in April 1952. While it reduced the distance between Delhi and Pathankot by 70 km, Jammu in the north-west was still far away, so construction began to extend the line to Kathua, about 80 km short of Jammu. The attempt to complete the line all the way to Jammu continued through the 1960s, slowing down considerably because of the 1971 Indo-Pakistan war. It finally opened to passenger traffic in December 1972. Work continues today to connect Delhi and Kashmir (see pp.262–63).

Rajasthan was another region that saw key railway construction for military and strategic reasons. A rail link to Jaisalmer, a sprawling town in the heart of the Thar Desert at the edge of the India–Pakistan border, had always been under consideration. It became a matter of importance after the 1965 Indo-Pakistan war and work began in full swing in 1966. The 106-km-long Pokhran–Jaisalmer link opened a year later in 1967. The 233-km-long Jhund–Kandla, later

▲ **The Camel Corps** of the Rajasthan Armed Constabulary patrol the border areas during the 1965 war. Connecting this area via the railways became a matter of utmost urgency.

Gandhidham, line in the Saurashtra region of Gujarat opened in 1969. A section crosses the quicksands of the Rann of Kutch via a 6-km-long bridge. The line was built to reduce the load on the Bombay port and railways after Partition and also increase connectivity to the Kandla port, an important hub for import and export traffic.

Another significant line constructed at this time was the Khandwa–Hingoli project that ran through the states of Madhya Pradesh and Maharashtra, crossing the Satpura, Melghat, and Ajanta hill ranges. The line crosses four rivers, including the Tapti. Construction through Melghat was particularly treacherous with one section of the line making a complete spiral in order to gain height. It integrated the metre-gauge sections of western and southern India.

▼ **The palatial Churchgate station** building in Mumbai serves as the main office of the Western Railway, created by merging Bombay, Baroda and Central India (BB&CI) Railway with several other lines.

The Kothavalasa–Kirandul line passes through many scenic valleys and tunnels in the Eastern Ghats.

IRON STRENGTH

The Bailadila Hills of the Dantewada district in the Bastar area of modern-day Chhattisgarh remained isolated until 1956 when an agreement with the Japanese for the export of 4 million tonnes of iron ore led to a flurry of exploration and construction. Over the course of four years, the railways laid a complex line that crossed the Eastern Ghats. Its sole purpose was to transport iron ore.

Dandakaranya, a sparsely populated, dense forest in the heart of central India, finds a place in Hindu mythology as the home of Rama, the main protagonist of the epic *Ramayana*, during his 14-year exile. Extending to nearly 92,000 sq km and into parts of Andhra Pradesh, Telangana, Odisha, and Chhattisgarh, the area became recognized for its rich resources in the late 19th century when reputed geologist PN Bose discovered iron ore in the hills of Bailadila.

The area had always been rich in minerals with extensive reserves of haematite, but the rugged terrain and inhospitable climate deterred even the most determined explorer seeking to exploit its wealth. Until the 1960 deal with Japan, this region remained cut-off; it took about a week to reach the area from its nearest railhead in Raipur or Visakhapatnam.

Boosting business
The new agreement led to the laying of three new railway lines, which connected the region and ensured a seamless transfer of iron ore from the mines to the Visakhapatnam port in Andhra Pradesh.

The 41-km Kiriburu–Bimlagarh link and the 182-km Sambalpur–Titlagarh line transported ore from the Kiriburu mines. The 448-km-long Kothavalasa–Kirandul line connected the Bailadila mines at Kirandul with the South Eastern Railway's main line at Kothavalasa, 27 km from Waltair, the port head of Visakhapatnam and a key freight transit point.

The challenges
The first two lines, Kiriburu–Bimlagarh and Sambalpur–Titlagarh, both in Odisha, opened for use in April 1963. Kothavalasa–Kirandul, also known as the K–K line, proved to be an engineering challenge.

Passing over the Eastern Ghats, the line has the distinction of being the highest broad-gauge line in the world as it gains an altitude of 997 m above sea level. The difficult terrain in the Ghat section necessitated gradients of 1 in 60 and curves as sharp as eight degrees (radius 218.38 m). The construction of the line involved boring 46 tunnels and building 87 major and 1,236 minor bridges.

Tunnels proved to be particularly challenging. The oldest hill range in India, the Eastern Ghats are formed from a foliated metamorphic rock called khondalite. So, work on them required high technical competence as the boring involved cutting through broken, stratified, and weathered strata. Invariably, the top heading had to be constructed and supported by steel ribs with the benching through underpinning operations.

Chimneys, domes, and vaults occurred in some of the tunnels, reducing access and making it difficult for workers to carry heavy machinery. Regardless of the challenges, work carried on manually. Engineers had to battle frequent landslides and steep hillsides, which often resulted in the construction of bridges on steep, eight-degree curves. This meant that the erection of girders on the alignment became

a problem. In some cases, gorges were bridged using 40.26-m-high piers. The one over the River Kolab is a good example where a long steel-work weighing 1,315 tonnes had to be assembled and set over piers as deep as 26.8 m.

At great cost
The entire K–K line cost Rs 553 million and was built manually with the help of 30,000 labourers. In fact, the only mechanical equipment used was an air compressor. It took about four and a half years to complete the construction and the line opened for freight traffic in May 1966. The movement of iron ore finally began the following year in May 1967.

Today, the K–K line is celebrated for its breathtaking views as it passes through the Borra Guhalu station, named after the prehistoric caves below it, and the Araku Valley in the Visakhapatnam district of Andhra Pradesh, home to many rare and endangered birds and plants.

▲ **The large-scale, open cast iron ore mines** of Bailadila are among the first of its kind in India. They have the unique distinction of having a down-the-hill convoy system that passes through a tunnel to move the iron ore from a crushing plant to the processing plant.

▼ **The Kothavalasa–Kirandul line** is the lifeline for many steel plants in India, as many of them rely on the iron ore supply from the mines of Bailadila.

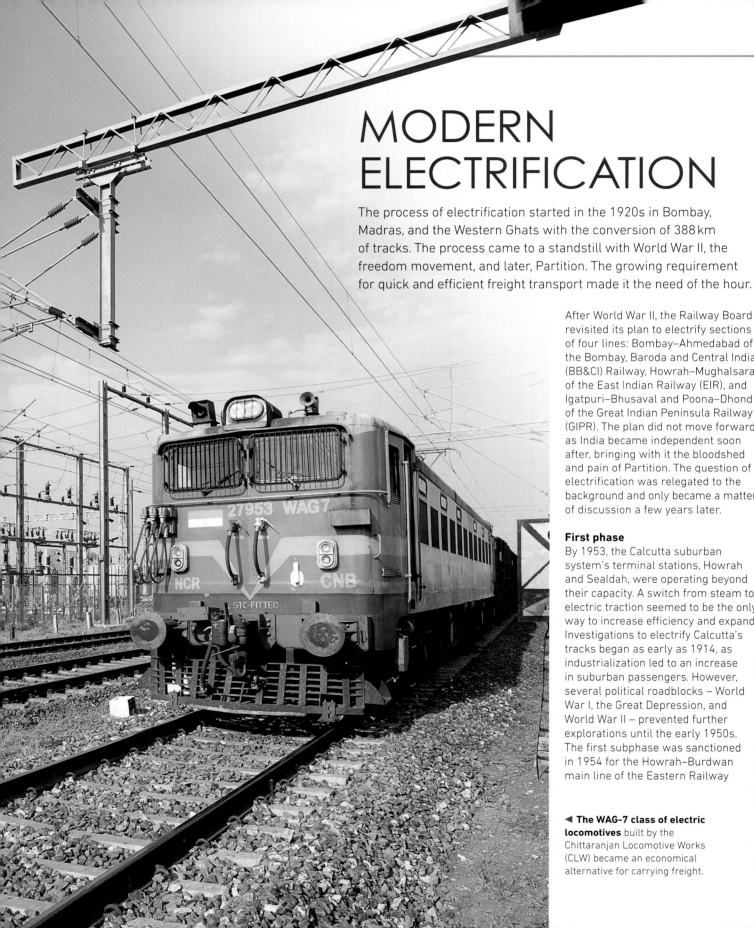

MODERN ELECTRIFICATION

The process of electrification started in the 1920s in Bombay, Madras, and the Western Ghats with the conversion of 388 km of tracks. The process came to a standstill with World War II, the freedom movement, and later, Partition. The growing requirement for quick and efficient freight transport made it the need of the hour.

After World War II, the Railway Board revisited its plan to electrify sections of four lines: Bombay–Ahmedabad of the Bombay, Baroda and Central India (BB&CI) Railway, Howrah–Mughalsarai of the East Indian Railway (EIR), and Igatpuri–Bhusaval and Poona–Dhond of the Great Indian Peninsula Railway (GIPR). The plan did not move forward, as India became independent soon after, bringing with it the bloodshed and pain of Partition. The question of electrification was relegated to the background and only became a matter of discussion a few years later.

First phase
By 1953, the Calcutta suburban system's terminal stations, Howrah and Sealdah, were operating beyond their capacity. A switch from steam to electric traction seemed to be the only way to increase efficiency and expand. Investigations to electrify Calcutta's tracks began as early as 1914, as industrialization led to an increase in suburban passengers. However, several political roadblocks – World War I, the Great Depression, and World War II – prevented further explorations until the early 1950s. The first subphase was sanctioned in 1954 for the Howrah–Burdwan main line of the Eastern Railway

◄ **The WAG-7 class of electric locomotives** built by the Chittaranjan Locomotive Works (CLW) became an economical alternative for carrying freight.

and the Seoraphuli–Tarakeswar branch line of the Howrah division. The electrification of the Howrah–Bandel section, including the branch line, took place in 1957. The Calcutta section used the DC (direct current) 3000 V system, which had proved quite beneficial in Europe, specifically Italy, as opposed to Bombay and Madras, which used the DC 1,500 V system.

Need of the hour

Electrification and dieselization became a matter of urgency with the Second Five Year Plan (1956–61), which prioritized industrialization, unlike the first plan (1951–56) that focused on rehabilitation. The east saw a visible change with this policy of industrial growth. Three new steel plants were set up at Rourkela, Odisha, Bhilai, Chhattisgarh, and Durgapur, West Bengal. Production increased in the steel plants of Tatanagar, Jharkhand, and Burnpur, West Bengal.

To facilitate the development of heavy industries, Bengal and Bihar's coal belts were exploited. Provisions had to now be made for the efficient transportation of materials, such as iron, steel, and coal, as this would entail large-scale movement of freight traffic along the tracks of the Eastern and South Eastern Railways. This was beyond the power of steam traction and electrification seemed inevitable.

Initially, the scheme was drawn on the direct current system, based on the already-electrified Bombay and Madras sections. However, seeing the success of the alternating current system on the Société Nationale des Chemins de fer Français (SNCF) or the French National Railways, India decided to explore its feasibility for the main lines. Electrical engineering experts from the SNCF investigated the prospects of electrification on 25 KV AC 50 cycles Single Phase and recommended it. By 1958, the Indian Railways adopted the system because of operational and financial benefits. The first steps involved the electrification of the Eastern Railway's Bardhaman–Gomoh section, Igatpuri–Bhusaval on the Delhi–Bombay line of the Central Railway and Tambaram–Villupuram on the Southern Railway. It was extended from Gomoh in Jharkhand, to Mughalsarai in Uttar Pradesh, on the Eastern Railway. Priority was given to Asansol–Tatanagar and Rourkela and Rajkharswan–Barajamda on the South Eastern Railway. Until 1970, expansion was carried out rigorously in the coal–steel belt of the east. The focus then shifted to the Delhi–Bombay and Bombay–Ahmedabad lines of the Western Railway and the Jolarpettai–Olavakkode section of the Southern Railway.

Railway Minister Kengal Hanumanthaiya hailed the electric traction in his Railway Budget speech for 1971–72. He said: "Steam engines have lower speeds and acceleration, less thermal efficiency and hauling capacity ... they require coaling and watering facilities en route. Diesel and electric engines with higher speed, better acceleration, greater hauling capacity and less need for servicing en route are able to achieve improved operation and substantial savings in working expenses."

Way forward

The complex process of electrification necessitated major overhauling of equipment and systems as well, such as signalling, telecommunication, and the import of new types of locomotives. This was, in a way, the beginning of a technological boom for the railways and paved the way for several initiatives. For instance, in a first in the world, the Diesel Locomotive Works (DLW) in 2018 successfully completed the conversion of a diesel locomotive to an electric one in 69 days at half the cost. Additionally, the railways commissioned the longest electrified tunnel in the country at 6.6 km in Andhra Pradesh in 2019.

The process of electrification continues even today with the aim to create a zero carbon-emitter railway within the next decade or so.

ORGANIZING RAILWAY ELECTRIFICATION

In the 1950s, the Project Office for Railway Electrification (PORE) was set up in Calcutta to monitor the electrification of the Howrah–Bhardaman section. It merged with the Main Line Electrification Project the following year under a general manager headquartered in Calcutta, and administered the Eastern and South Eastern Railways projects. It was decommissioned in 1968 after work came to an end. The Northern Railway Electrification office, under an engineer-in-chief, was constituted in 1961 at Allahabad, Uttar Pradesh for the Mughalsarai–New Delhi section. A specialized organization came up in 1978 after the J Raj Committee submitted its report, which led to the creation of the Central Organisation for Railway Electrification (CORE). Headquartered in Nagpur, Maharashtra, till 1984 and then Allahabad, its mission is the successful and effective execution of all railway electrification projects.

▼ **Rolled out in 1983-84**, the first phase of the Chennai Mass Rapid Transit System (MRTS) included the 8.55-km-stretch from Chennai Beach to Thirumayilai, crossing the Chennai Fort. This suburban passenger service uses Electrical Multiple Units (EMUs), which are fast and cause less pollution.

THE ROAD AHEAD

The makers of an independent India knew that they needed a clear roadmap in order to have a modern and efficient railway system. As a result, during the first decade after Independence, the Indian Railways focused on building self-sufficiency and development.

Post-Independence, India embarked on a planned development programme for its economy with a series of Five-Year Plans, drawn by the Planning Commission, an institution set up by the Indian Government in March 1950. While the plans focused on socio-economic dimensions, the railways occupied an overwhelming portion as the policymakers recognized its crucial role in driving economic growth.

Plan of action
Every Five-Year Plan concentrated on a specific aspect of developing and strengthening the railways,

wrote author MA Rao in his book *Indian Railways*. The First Five Year Plan (1951–56) looked at fortifying and reconstructing the crumbling railway system, a legacy of World War II and Partition. Emphasis was placed on the development of the indigenous capacity for the production of railway equipment. However, even though the Government adopted several successful measures to develop the domestic capacity, the limited supply was unable to keep up with the ever-increasing demand for rail transportation. The Second Five Year Plan (1956–61) sought to correct this

▲ **The WAG1 20710 or** *Bidhan* was built in the Chittaranjan Locomotive Works in 1963. This was the first indigenous electric freight locomotive.

severe mismatch between demand and supply through policies that aimed at handling increased traffic through capacity expansion and modernization. The extensive measures did have a significant impact in narrowing the demand and supply gap, yet, towards the end of 1961, there were still many pockets of paucity. The Third Five Year Plan (1961–66) and the

▶ **India's first air-conditioned suburban local train for Mumbai** was manufactured in Chennai's Integral Coach Factory (ICF) and introduced on 5 April 2016. These trains ply on the Harbour line of the Central Railway, have 12 coaches, and can carry 1,028 seated and 4,964 standing passengers.

consecutive Annual Plans of 1966–67 and 1968–69 attempted to bridge this gap once and for all while undertaking measures for the mechanization of spaces and practices. By the end of the plan period, the railways achieved its objective of a supply capacity in excess of demand. The Fourth Five Year Plan (1966–71) saw huge expansion and development in production capacity. By 1971, after many turbulent years, the railways finally achieved a degree of stability and strength. The Fifth Five Year Plan (1971–76) aimed at consolidating and building upon the gains made during the Fourth plan while the manufacture of diesel and electric locomotives alongside coaches, wagons, and Electric Multiple Units (EMUs) continued on the same scale.

Going local

The initial years were all about becoming independent and to avoid importing equipment, including locomotives. During the British rule,

workshops, such as Jamalpur and Ajmer, produced locomotives, albeit in lesser numbers, and the railways imported most of the equipment from Britain. After Independence, low reserves of foreign exchange and the risk of further burdening India's economy meant that the railways could no longer afford to import locomotives and other machinery. British engineer and railway historian OS Nock in his book *Railways of Asia and the Far East* explained that it was essential to source fuel locally and capitalize on India's "large deposits of coal".

Becoming self-sufficient

In the move towards self-sufficiency, large production facilities were set up in various parts of the country. The construction of a locomotive building factory at Chittaranjan began in 1948 and it went into production in 1950. In 1955, the Integral Coach Factory or ICF was established in Chennai, Tamil Nadu, to produce "integral" coaches. The addition of a furnishing division in 1957 meant that it now rolled out complete passenger coaches. The Diesel Locomotive Works (DLW) came up in Varanasi, Uttar Pradesh in 1961, which, in its initial years assembled locomotives from imported parts. It soon started manufacturing complete diesel locomotives.

In the late 1980s, two more production units were established in Punjab. These included the Rail Coach Factory (RCF) at Kapurthala to meet the increasing demand of coaches and the Diesel Component Works (now Diesel Loco Modernization Works) at Patiala to manufacture spare parts for diesel and electric locomotives. Manufacturing plants for wheels and axles and coil springs were set up in Bengaluru, Karnataka, and Gwalior, Madhya Pradesh. Modernization became a point of focus to inject efficiency into the production system and this was done with the help of the Central Organisation for Modernisation of Workshops (COFMOW), which was formed in 1979.

RAILWAY STAFF COLLEGE

After 1949, conversations for a central training institute gained momentum. In 1952, the Railway Staff College, housed in the Pratap Vilas Palace in Vadodara, opened. Its training methods included classroom lectures, practicals, and field visits. By the middle of the 1960s, railway training was established as a distinct discipline. The following decade saw it expanding to incorporate advanced courses, such as scientific management. The college has remodelled itself over the years in order to keep pace with changing times. Several other institutions for technical training have been established as well, such as the Training School in Pune, also known as the Indian Railways Institute of Civil Engineering, and the Indian Railways Institute of Signal Engineering and Telecommunications in modern-day Telangana.

The Railway Staff College at Vadodara is now known as the National Academy of Indian Railways.

Setting standards and guidelines

It was only a matter of time that there would be a need for applied research in the development of railway technology. The Indian Railway Conference Association (IRCA) and the Central Standards Office (CSO) were both remnants of a colonial past. In 1952, the Research Section of the CSO was rechristened the Railway Testing Research Centre (RTRC) and assigned to provide new designs, test prototypes, and conduct research to resolve technical issues. In 1957, the CSO and RTRC merged into the Research Design and Standards Organisation (RDSO), and became the technical advisor to the Railway Board, various zonal railways, and manufacturing units. Over the years, its scope has expanded from being an independent research and development centre to providing consulting services to non-railway organizations and railway projects in countries across the world.

The Chittaranjan Locomotive Works was Jawaharlal Nehru's (third from left) dream project. During a visit to the workshop in 1963 for the inauguration of *Bidhan*, he said that it "stood as a symbol of India's progress in the field of science and technology."

CHITTARANJAN LOCOMOTIVE WORKS

The setting up of the Chittaranjan Locomotive Works (CLW) marked India's first step towards becoming self-sufficient in locomotive production. Originally called the Loco Building Factory, it was renamed as a tribute to the freedom fighter, Deshbandhu (friend of the nation) Chittaranjan Das.

Production began on 26 January 1950 and five types of steam locomotives were built until 1973–74. The factory began manufacturing diesel hydraulic locomotives from 1968, building 842 vehicles of seven types until 1993–94. Some important electric engines produced by the CLW included *Lokmanya* (WCM5), commissioned by India's first prime minister, Jawaharlal Nehru, in 1961, *Bidhan* (WAG-1), the factory's first indigenous locomotive, *Navyug* (WAG-9), one of the most powerful freight engines built in 1998, and *Navikaran* (WAP-7), the three-phase AC electric passenger locomotive, which was released in 2000. Government figures indicate that the workshop produced 6,791 electric locomotives between 1961 and 2019.

Several additions were made to the CLW, starting from 1955, with the installation of a plant for galvanizing steel masts. By 1969, almost 50,000 tonnes of steel masts had been galvanized and used on electrification projects. A steel foundry was established in 1961 to make the production of steel castings more self-sufficient and manufactured intricate steel castings weighing up to four tonnes. Prior to this, steel castings were imported from the US. An electric locomotive shop (1962) and traction motor shop (1966) also came up.

The industrial town of Chittaranjan in West Bengal, which stood on 1,800 hectares of land, was built to accommodate life that would grow around this manufacturing unit. The township is divided into colonies with playgrounds, dispensaries, children's parks, schools, social centres, staff institutions, a central hospital, a technical training school, and a vocational training centre.

Today, the CLW, a symbol of a self-reliant, industrial India, has become one of the largest manufacturers of modern, high-powered electric locomotives.

A postage stamp illustrating an engine being serviced at the CLW was issued in the year 1955.

CLASS WP NO.7161

Imported until 1959, the Class WP was manufactured in India between 1963 and 1967 at the Chittaranjan Locomotive Works (CLW) of West Bengal. The heritage locomotive Class WP No. 7161 was built in 1965 to run on the Northeast Frontier Railway. It is now based at the Rewari Steam Locomotive Shed, where it was named *Akbar* after the third Mughal Emperor (1556–1605).

A LEAGUE OF ITS OWN

When the Class WP of sleek, bullet-nosed, mainline steam locomotives was first introduced, it set the standard for the Indian Railways and became the mainstay of broad-gauge passenger operations for the rest of the 20th century. Known for free steaming, high fuel economy, superior riding characteristics, and without the tail wag of the earlier X classes, its arrival marked the change of the broad-gauge coding from X to W.

The first 16 Class WP steam locomotives – W for the 1.67-m-broad gauge and P for passenger – arrived in India in 1947 from the Baldwin Locomotive Works in the US. However, in 1963–67, 259 engines were built in the CLW. Requiring a crew of three – a driver and two firemen – these locomotives hauled most of the prestigious passenger trains on the Indian rail system for the next 25 years. They established a sound reputation during their time in service, with their good performance earning them the title "Pride of the Fleet".

FRONT VIEW

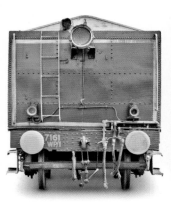

REAR VIEW

Heritage shed
Converted to a heritage museum by the Indian Railways in 2002, the Rewari Steam Loco Shed houses some of India's last surviving steam locomotives.

SPECIFICATIONS			
Class	WP	**In-service period**	1965–96 (No. 7161)
Wheel configuration	4-6-2	**Cylinders**	2
Origin	India	**Boiler pressure**	14.78 kg/sq cm
Designer/builder	Chittaranjan Locomotive Works	**Drive wheel diameter**	1,702 mm
Number produced	755 (259 in India) Class WP	**Top speed**	109 km/h

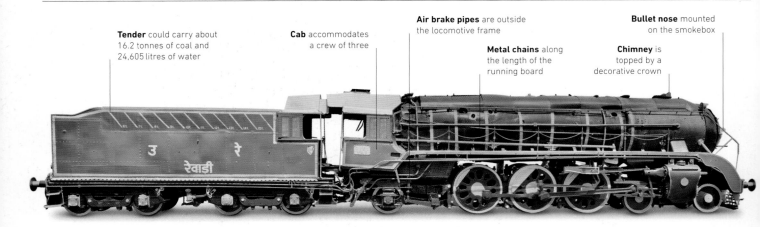

Tender could carry about 16.2 tonnes of coal and 24,605 litres of water

Cab accommodates a crew of three

Air brake pipes are outside the locomotive frame

Metal chains along the length of the running board

Bullet nose mounted on the smokebox

Chimney is topped by a decorative crown

India's star locomotive
The bullet nose bears a silver star
and is the most distinctive feature
of the locomotive. A nameplate
with the name *Akbar* sits centrally
below the nose.

LOCOMOTIVE EXTERIOR

With its distinctive bullet nose, a crown on top of the chimney, a 4-6-2 wheel arrangement, and a side profile that includes chain-decorated footboards along the length of the boiler, No. 7161 is regarded as one of the most majestic locomotives that has ever run on the Indian Railways. These features have proved popular with railway enthusiasts and tourists.

1. Hand-painted name on plaque at front **2.** Brass crown decorating top of chimney **3.** Headlight in the centre of a metal star **4.** Pilot light lamp, one positioned on either side of engine **5.** Cattle guard **6.** Steam chest valves **7.** Steam chest **8.** Driving wheels with balance weight and connecting rod **9.** Big end and motion **10.** Rear carrying wheel **11.** Steps leading into cab interior **12.** Entrance to cab with wooden-slatted windows **13.** Light at the back of the tender, or the coal car **14.** Engine number **15.** Rear buffer **16.** Ladder at the back of the tender

CAB INTERIOR

The cab is spacious enough to house the engineer and two firemen. The extra space also allows the firemen to stoke coal using shovels that are larger than those used in earlier locomotives. The red-painted handles for operating the locomotive and the monitoring gauges are positioned for ease of use.

17. Interior of engineer's cab   **18.** Lubricator box
19. From left to right: injector steam cock handle, dynamo cock, main cock, vacuum steam cock, and injector steam cock handle   **20.** Firehole door
21. Reverser wheel   **22.** Steam pressure gauge
23. Rocking grate   **24.** Front of tender

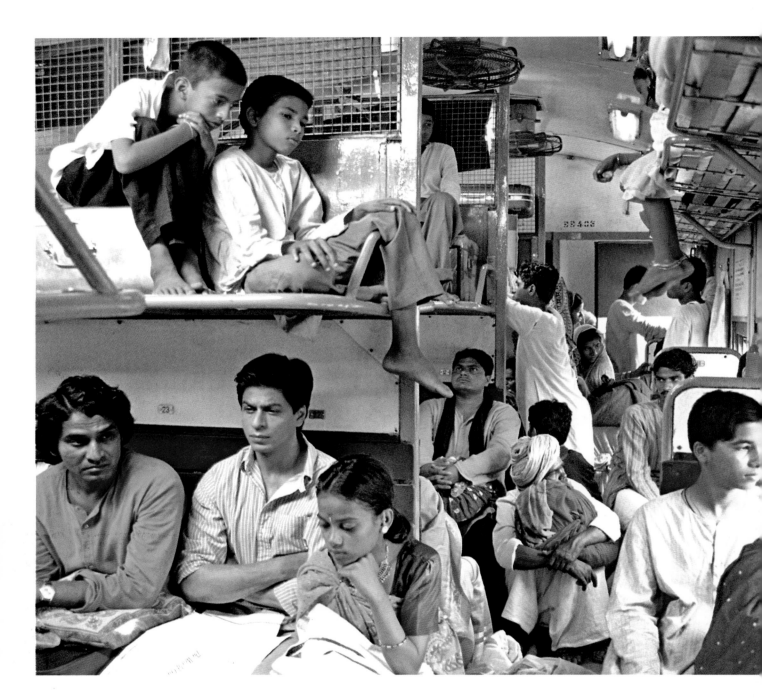

IN REEL LIFE

Cinematic narratives have often employed trains to twist and turn a plot, writing them into the very grammar of the movies. They star in girl-meet-boy romances, are seen in movie montages, provide edge-of-the-seat action, and signal a change of place, time, and pace.

▲ **The motif of trains** is quite common in many Indian films. Scenes are often re-created from stations and passenger coaches. Seen here is a still from the Hindi film *Swades* (2004) starring Shah Rukh Khan.

क्र.	फिल्म का नाम	शूटिंग माह/वर्ष	स्टीम इंजन नं.
1.	गदर एक प्रेम कथा	09-2000	7015WP/7161WP
2.	वृत्तचित्र (टेलीफिल्म)	06-2004	7161WP
3.	गांधी माई फादर	04-2005	15005 WL
4.	रंग दे बसंती	08-2005	7200WP
5.	पार्टीशन	10-2005	7161WP
6.	गुरु	04-2006	7200WP
7.	लव आज कल	09-2008	22907 AWE
8.	वीर	05-2009	22907 AWE
9.	प्रणायम (मलयालम फिल्म)	06-2011	7161WP
10.	गैंग्स ऑफ वासेपुर	02-2012	7161 WP
11.	भाग मिल्खा भाग	10-2012	7161 WP
12.	स्टीम पेनत्रवी (मलयालम फिल्म)	07-2013	22907AW
13.	रुक श्री चन्द्र, रुक श्री सुधा (टी.वी. धारावाहिक)	02-2014	7161 WP
14.	जंतीसार	05-2015	EIR 22
15.	की एण्ड का	09-2015	7161WP
16.	सुल्तान	04-2016	7161 WP
17.	करीब करीब सिंगल	02-2017	EIR 22
18.	विजय 61 (तमिल)	04-2017	7161WP
19.	राइफलमैन जसवन्त सिंह रावत	12-2017	7200WP

Before making their debut on reel, trains were synonymous with speed, enterprise, and modernity, and came to motion pictures imbued with meaning. As Indian author and journalist Jerry Pinto wrote in an essay for *India Junction*, these were "liminal spaces", which symbolized change, "disrupted social order", and a place where "one might go to die" or even "come back to life". There was no doubt, "you only had to catch sight of a train passing and everyone knew that something drastic had happened".

Sites of adventure and change
The first few Indian movies converted the thrill and speed of a train shooting down its tracks into a live site of action and adventure. *Miss Frontier Mail* (1936), *Deccan Queen* (1936), *Toofan Mail* (1934), *11 O'Clock* (1948), *Punjab Mail* (1939) — it was as if the sense of adventure of being on a train journey, its speeding whirl, were reified on screen. The visual trope of the train as a site of a waylaid robbery became common through the 1970s and 1980s. Perhaps the most iconic was Ramesh Sippy's *Sholay* (1975), which introduced the protagonists, Jai and Veeru, as they fought horsebound dacoits on a moving freight train. Climactic chase sequences and impending disasters were a popular theme, such as *The Burning Train* (1980). It told the story of a newly introduced Super Express being threatened by the possibility of a bomb exploding, the imagery of crash and rescue at play.

In other films, the railways served as the archetype of change and modernity, such as in Satyajit Ray's *Pather Panchali* (1955), as little Apu and Durga ran through tall, swaying, white *kashphool* (type of grass) just in time to catch sight of a steam train hurtling by. In Mani Ratnam's *Guru* (2007), the train marked the separation from home and setting out to earn one's fortunes, while the train in Anil Sharma's *Gadar: Ek Prem Katha* (2001) drove home the pain and violence of Partition.

Tale of the common man
Part of the larger cultural memory of the country, Indian cinema served as the reserve of collective stories we love and know. The railways were backdrops, as a site of representation of the common man, and part of an ensemble moving the plot along. Actor Amitabh Bachchan channelled the angry young man in *Coolie* (1983), where he portrayed a railway coolie rallying against injustice. Decades later, the humbling poverty and want that continued to coexist with a booming image of urban India was on display in the third-class compartment of *Swades* (2004), bringing the US-returned Mohan to the reality of the homeland he was trying to navigate.

The Mumbai local finds a place as well, a part of everyday hustle, its chaos celebrated in movies, such as the Irrfan Khan-starrer *The Lunchbox* (2013) and Danny Boyle's *Slumdog Millionaire* (2009).

Spot of romance
Iconic celluloid romances were brought to life on trains as well. Director Mani Ratnam used the railways to great effect in his Tamil films, from the hero spotting the heroine on a railway platform *OK Kanmani* (2015) to trains serving as sites for declarations of love in *Mouna Ragam* (1986) and *Alaipayuthey* (2000). In Hindi cinema, Aditya Chopra had his protagonists meet, fall in love, separate, and finally move on to their happily-ever-after on trains across Europe and

◀ **A board at the Rewari Steam Loco shed** in Haryana lists all the Indian films that star the steam engines from the shed.

India in *Dilwale Dulhania Le Jayenge* (1995). The intimate setting of the train compartment became a tool for love at first sight in Kamal Amrohi's *Pakeezah* (1972) as did a nondescript, isolated railway station in Mani Ratnam's *Dil Se* (1998).

To a tune
The chugging and whistling of a train, its form twisting into a tunnel has been a visual for some of Indian cinema's greatest songs as well. Rajesh Khanna driving along the Darjeeling Himalayan Railway (see pp.86–87) singing "Mere Sapnon ki Rani" from *Aradhana* (1969), Saif Ali Khan aboard the same humming "Yeh Hawayein Gungunayein" in *Parineeta* (2005), Prabhu Deva shimmying to "Chikku Bukku Rayile" set to the rhythm of a moving train continue to be enduring reel images.

▼ **A still** from the film *Aradhana* (1969) (top); poster of the 1936-Mehboob Khan classic *Deccan Queen* (bottom).

AGAR MOVITONE
ARUNADEVI · SURENDRA
MEHBOOB

DECCAN QUEEN

Based on the 1954 novel *Bhowani Junction* written by a British army officer, John Masters, this eponymous film was released in 1956. It stars Ava Gardner as Victoria Jones, the daughter of a British railway man living in the imaginary town of Bhowani. Shot in both England and Pakistan, the film gives a peek into the lives of the British and Anglo-Indians of the railway community and the challenges they faced before India's Independence.

A FLAM

M

STE

with **BILL TRAVERS**

Screen Play by **SONYA LEVIEN** and **IVAN MOFFAT**   Based On the Novel by JOHN MASTERS   Photographed in EASTMAN

LOVE STORY ON A BACKGROUND
OF TURMOIL AND REVOLT!

BHOWANI JUNCTION

Filmed in Pakistan. Cast of Thousands.

AVA GARDNER
ART GRANGER

in
CINEMASCOPE and COLOR

HAM SOFAER

ted by GEORGE CUKOR   Produced by PANDRO S. BERMAN

B
58/473

RAILWAYS IN WARTIME

The Indian Railways, its resources and people have always been co-opted to aid the war effort. They have supported the armies at the frontlines, provided supplies, and even run trains in enemy territory, often at great risk to themselves.

The railways played a crucial role in the country's defence during the colonial era. The Railway Volunteers, as they were called, were made up exclusively of European and Eurasian railway employees who attended annual camps and received basic training. The Indian Railways' Territorial Army (TA) was formed in 1949 as an auxiliary unit to maintain essential rail transportation in peacetime and to ensure links and communications in hostile territory during wars. From repairing lines in conflict zones or providing supplies to the armed forces during wartime, the Indian Railways and its army have been at the frontlines for all conflicts since then.

Fighting Pakistan in 1965
In April 1965, fighting began along the border in the Rann of Kutch, Gujarat. Increasing hostilities and a subsequent Pakistani incursion led to full-scale war in September. On 10 September, three locomotive "pilots" and 14 railway constables entered the war zone along the Indo-Pakistan border in Barmer, Rajasthan. They were in a six-wagon train loaded with rations and

▲ **Following Pakistani incursions** into Indian Kashmir in 1965, India declared war on 6 September. Seen here is the front page of the Canadian newspaper *Globe and Mail*, dated 7 September 1965.

ammunition meant for the 13th battalion of the Grenadiers who were running short of supplies. The Pakistani Air Force was strafing the area, but the road was riskier. As the train inched forward, it was

▼ **Members of the Railway Territorial Army** working on rail tracks in Pakistan in 1971.

intercepted at Gadra Road in Barmer, about 3 km from the railway station and bombed. The engine boiler exploded and all 17 men died. Today the spot is a memorial and trains passing by often slow down or stop to pay tribute.

Fighting on two borders

During the 1971 war, the railways serviced the eastern and western border. It ran 2,000 special trains to move forces and equipment; 9,000 members of TA units were mobilized to help with train movement and damage restoration and during the course of their duties in the border areas, 13 railwaymen died, and 26 were wounded. The contribution of the Northern Railway was especially significant, as between October and December, it ran 755 special trains along with 41 ambulance specials, besides others that carried supplies.

The 1033 Railway Engineers, made up of railwaymen from the Western Railway Zone, were despatched to the Barmer, Rajasthan sector, in December 1971. They were to support the Indian forces who had made their way across the border past Khokhrapar, a border town towards Sindh about 6 km inside Pakistan. The assignment was to link the lines between Khokhrapar and Munabao, the last railway station at the Indian border in Rajasthan, to ensure reliable supply of food, water, and ammunition. They did this in 48 hours, despite continuous air raids and strafing and even extended the railway line past the border by 10 km. The first train to Khokhrapar left Munabao on 7 December, less than a week after the war started. For his wartime contribution, a railwayman was awarded the Vir Chakra, a gallantry award. Two others received the Vishisht Seva medals (Special Service medals). Jodhpur's divisional superintendent and divisional engineer received the Padma Shri, the fourth highest civilian award in India, and five railway employees in Punjab were awarded the Shaurya Chakra (for gallantry other than in the face of the enemy).

Apart from aiding the evacuation of refugees, the railways helped Bangladesh repair four major bridges that had been destroyed by Pakistani forces, and supplied material for the restoration of damaged rail tracks.

> ### THE WARS BETWEEN INDIA AND PAKISTAN
>
> From its Independence in 1947, India's borders in the north and the north-east have experienced regular skirmishes. However, it has also seen three wars with Pakistan, one of which led to the formation of Bangladesh. The first, in 1947–48, started after armed tribesmen from Pakistan entered Kashmir. The Maharaja of Kashmir acceded to India in exchange for military assistance. A ceasefire was announced in January 1949. The second war began in 1965, after Pakistani troops and civilians crossed the border into Kashmir in a manoeuvre codenamed Operation Gibraltar. This started a 17-day war that ended with a UN-brokered ceasefire and the 1966 Tashkent agreement. The 1971 war began after Indian troops entered East Pakistan following the outbreak of a civil war, in support of the people there. The war came to an end in 1971 after East Pakistan became the independent nation of Bangladesh. Since then there have been several skirmishes along the Kashmir border, including the 1999 conflict in Kargil, Ladakh.

Peacetime endeavours

The TA has also been mobilized during civilian disruptions, such as the 1974 railway strike when they drove trains and fulfilled key roles to ensure smooth operations. It was renamed the Railway Engineers Regiment in 1977.

The present-day six regiments (in Kota, Chandigarh, Hyderabad, Jamalpur, Jhansi, and Adra) have railway personnel with a small nucleus of permanent staff drawn from the Indian Army. As a part of their role, they attend an annual training camp for compulsory arms, ammunition, and defence training.

▼ **Railway engineers** ensured vital supplies of food, water, and ammunition during the military confrontation between India and Pakistan during the 1971 war.

GOLDEN KATAR SPECIAL

> The **desert has no place** to take cover, so we **lay motionless (a hundred of us)** waiting for the **worst, but the bullets** missed us by a few inches. **What saved us** was a **single anti-aircraft gun** we had **mounted on the train** as a last minute innovation. "
>
> LT COL (RETD) ML KHANNA, COMMANDING OFFICER, 1033 RAILWAY ENGINEERS (TERRITORIAL ARMY) ON HIS EXPERIENCES DURING THE 1971 INDO-PAKISTAN WAR

GODAVARI BRIDGE

The River Godavari has the distinction of having three distinct bridges spanning its breadth, each built during different periods of the 20th century. For the railway builders of colonial India, this may have seemed like an inevitable task. After all, the Godavari was one of the longest rivers in the country at 1,465 km, traversing four states before making its way to the Bay of Bengal.

The first, Havelock or the old Godavari Bridge, which was designed by British engineer FTG Walton, came up in 1900 at Rajahmundry in Andhra Pradesh. The 2,950-m-long masonry pier and steel girder bridge served rail traffic along the Chennai–Howrah line.

The second bridge was commissioned after India's Independence during the Third Five Year Plan (1961–66) when most of the Chennai–Howrah track was doubled, barring the Kovvur–Rajahmundry stretch, which required bridging the 3-km-wide river. The local population's demand for a road bridge led to the construction of the Kovvur–Rajahmundry Bridge in 1974. The double-decked, steel girder bridge caters to road and rail traffic. The bridge was constructed using the pneumatic well technique. While the lower deck functions as a single-track rail link between Rajahmundry and Kovvur, the road deck running on top of the girders provides passage to cars. At the time of its construction, it was the longest rail–road bridge in the country, a position now usurped by the Bogibeel Bridge over the River Brahmaputra in Assam.

The unique Godavari Arch Bridge, opened for rail traffic in 1997. It replaced the Havelock Bridge nearby, which was decommissioned the same year after being operational for nearly 100 years. Built with prestressed concrete with a bow-string arch girder superstructure, the 2,745-m arch bridge has 28 spans of about 97 m each.

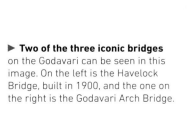

▶ **Two of the three iconic bridges** on the Godavari can be seen in this image. On the left is the Havelock Bridge, built in 1900, and the one on the right is the Godavari Arch Bridge.

SERVING A NEW COMMUNITY

The railway enterprise that emerged post-Independence broke away from the legacy of its past. Rising from the ashes of Partition and its aftermath, it had new vigour and was dedicated to provide people what they deserved. Not just a symbol of growth and modernization, the railways had become a way of life for millions.

During the colonial rule, railway management was controlled entirely by the British. It was only post-World War I that Indians started occupying administrative positions, limited to those in the middle level. "One of the greatest changes post-1947," Canadian historian Ian J Kerr in his 2006 book *Engines of Change* notes, "was the complete Indianization of the railroad workforce in full realization of a long-standing nationalist demand". The number of people employed by the Indian Railways remained high even after Independence. While senior staff members were recruited by Railway Service Commissions, high-ranking officials were appointed through the government-run public service commissions. The labour workforce was hired by local committees. Although some of the labour force remained casual, the Indian Railways, as a Government-owned employer, provided many amenities to its employees. These included housing units, schools, and medical and travel facilities. As with most enterprises, there were some troubles with the labour unions, but overall the condition remained satisfactory.

▼ **The number of passengers** using the railways kept soaring after Independence and the Indian Railways strived to improve facilities.

PRESIDENTIAL SALOON

In 1956, a twin-carriage red saloon was built for the President of India for his or her rail journeys. It constituted a dining room, a lounge, a bedroom, a kitchen, and chambers for the President's staff. With teak furniture and silk upholstery, it was designed to incorporate luxury and comfort. In 2003, the saloon was modified to accommodate modern facilities, such as Wi-Fi. After being in service for more than five decades, the saloon was finally decommissioned in 2008 owing to safety concerns.

Passenger services

While railway travel had always been popular during India's colonial period, the number of passengers increased by 1,147 million between 1950–51 and 1970–71 and showed an upward trend throughout the last quarter of the 20th century. Independence also paved the way for a national railways committed towards providing good

वातानुकूलित 2 टियर
AC TWO TIER

◀ **Towards the end of the 1970s,** the Indian Railways adopted AC two-tier coaches, followed by AC three-tier ones in 1993 when ordinary sleeper coaches were also introduced.

and affordable service to every Indian, unlike earlier, when its objective was making a profit.

Fares, which were inconsistent across different railways and did not always correspond to the amenities provided, improved as well. From 1948, the railways adopted a uniform fare structure. Any increase during the revisions was in direct proportion to the provision of additional facilities.

There was a marked shift in the passenger travel experience as well. The pre-existing four passenger classes were discontinued in 1955. There were not many takers for the first class and therefore, there were economic disadvantages to running it. Hence, it was abolished. The second, inter, and third classes were renamed as first, second, and third classes, respectively. Even before this

restructuring, efforts were made to alleviate the condition of third-class coaches by introducing sleeping facilities on some fast trains. Cleanliness became a priority for these coaches; in 1956 third-class passengers got access to the dining car, and by 1959 all coaches had fans and lights.

Air conditioning
British author JN Westwood in his 1974 book *Railways of India* links the growth of air-conditioned travel to the multiplication of classes. He lists seven passenger classes in the early 1970s: air-conditioned, first class, air-conditioned chair car, second class in express as well as in ordinary trains, and third class in express as well as in ordinary trains. More categories were inserted and some replaced to extend better services to the passengers and make air-conditioned travel accessible. Of these, AC two-tier and three-tier have been extremely popular with the passengers and the corridor-type first-class coaches are gradually giving way to air-conditioned sleeper coaches. Amenities at stations underwent a sea change as well with the addition of more waiting halls and retiring rooms, provisions for clean drinking water and food, and sheltered platforms.

New trains
Affordable services became almost a byword during this period, beginning with the introduction of the Janata Express for third-class travellers in 1948. In British India, third-class passengers were forced to travel by trains that were extremely slow. Now they could travel with affordable prices to mail train schedules. In 1956, the Kanpur–Jhajha (Bihar) Janata Express got a buffet-cum-cinema car.

In 1972, the Rajdhani Express, a fully air-conditioned train, a first of its kind in India, started running between Howrah and New Delhi as part of a new series of trains (see pp.222–23). Since then, different types of trains have been introduced, including the Shatabdi Express (see pp.232–33) and Duronto Express (see p.280).

Safety
New challenges emerged as the very fabric of the network changed. Safety became an increased priority as speed increased. Recommendations of three committees went a long way in improving the safety regulations. For instance, the 1962 Kunzru Committee suggested the formation of a safety organization on each railway, under the close supervision of the Railway Board. It laid emphasis on improving the staff's job knowledge, conducting regular inspections, and introducing modern technical safety and signalling aids. The 1968 Wanchoo Committee in its report, while re-emphasizing the Kunzru Committee's recommendations, placed in perspective some failures that may have occurred while managing such a vast network. The Sikri Committee in 1978 was appointed to review the implementation of these suggestions to inspect the existing safety regulations in place, and provide additional recommendations. With an increased focus on safety, the Indian Railways was successful in reducing the number of mishaps.

▼ **The Railway Board** instituted Accident Free Service Awards to felicitate the staff. Pictured here is the Station Superintendent of Joginder Nagar station in Himachal Pradesh, YR Malhotra, receiving the award.

RAJDHANI EXPRESS

The introduction of the Rajdhani Express towards the end of the 1960s ushered in an era of speed, comfort, and luxury for the Indian passenger. Named to reflect its journey that began or ended in Delhi, the capital or *rajdhani*, these trains were the pioneers in the introduction of WAP electric locomotives, air-conditioning equipment innovations, and emergency lighting. Additionally, they set the standards for comfort and accessories that are now the norm in passenger coaches.

Making its maiden run between Howrah and New Delhi on 3 March 1969, the first Rajdhani Express covered the 1,145 km inter-city distance in 17 hours and 20 minutes. A single WDM-4 hauled this biweekly, eight-car train at a maximum permissible speed of 120 km/h. Initially, there were several objections to the train overshooting the speed mark as express trains mostly ran at speeds of 100 km/h. The Railway Board and the zones were opposed to the maximum speed limit, raising safety concerns and doubts about the tracks and the locomotives being able to support the high speeds.

However, this did not affect its popularity and a second 18-coach Rajdhani Express started operations between New Delhi and Bombay on 17 May 1972 and a third, which was added several decades later in 1992. In 1971, Kanpur was introduced as the first passenger stop and more halts were added to the route subsequently. The early Rajdhanis had first-class and AC chair car options, and other travel options, such as sleeper accommodation and two and three tier coaches, were added later. It also serves meals, the cost of which is included in the ticket price.

Created when airplane tickets were exorbitant and out of reach for the middle-class Indian, the Rajdhani proved to be the ultimate means of fast, comfortable, and affordable railway travel, especially since it was one of the first fully air-conditioned trains of the time.

Today, it is no longer viewed as the novel experience it used to be, yet, the Rajdhani's reservation-only accommodation, restricted number of stops, operational priority, and good-quality equipment make it one of Indian Railways' most profitable express trains and a popular choice for train travel.

◄ **One of the longest running Rajdhani Express** service is the Thiruvananthapuram Rajdhani, which connects New Delhi to Thiruvananthapuram, or Trivandrum, in Kerala and covers a distance of more than 3,149 km.

PUBLIC SECTOR UNDERTAKINGS

It is no mean feat that a nation once drained of its resources contributed in a significant way to the rebuilding efforts of other nations with shared experiences. In this, the railways and its Public Sector Undertakings (PSUs) played a significant role. In a way, the PSUs have helped railways move with the times.

▲ **RITES** has been a consultant in many metro projects, such as the Bangalore Metro Rail Corporation (BMRC).

By the last quarter of the 20th century, the railways had recuperated from the strains of Partition and made several advances, its system firmly established and supported by the pillars of indigenous technology and expertise. The refashioning of the railway system is perhaps a paradigm of how a developing nation, once a colony and severely marred in its freedom movement, successfully rebuilt its infrastructure and bounced back on its feet. Impressed by India's transition to Independence, many other developing nations looked at it for a helping hand. Thus, in the 1960s, India provided technological assistance and expertise to countries such as Ghana, Nigeria, Zambia, Iraq, and the Philippines. The collaborations were perceived to be advantageous. The countries shared similar histories and thus similar requirements, such as rebuilding programmes at a low cost.

▼ **Dedicated Freight Corridor Corporation of India's** newly constructed and highly advanced Eastern Dedicated Freight Corridor's operation control centre is situated at Prayagraj in Uttar Pradesh.

Early attempts

This was not the first time that India had extended support to foreign parties. In the 19th century, Indian labourers built a line in Abyssinia (part of present-day Ethiopia). Even without being an active participant in the two world wars, India made significant contributions in terms of men and materiel. However, these were channelized under the British. The context, mechanisms, and motivations were far different when India assisted other newly independent nations in building their railways. There was little vested interest and the idea was, as author RR Bhandari wrote in *Indian Railways: Glorious 150 Years*, "promoting technical cooperation amongst developing countries for achieving individual and collective self-reliance". This transfer of technology, sharing expertise, and providing consulting services was not streamlined, but through what author and railwayman MA Rao calls "ad hoc arrangements of the Railway Board".

A new trend

Increasing demands for railway assistance from India led to organizing the railways' consulting services through Government-owned enterprises, popularly known as Public Sector Undertakings (PSUs), under the control of the Ministry of Railways. The Rail India Technical and Economic Services (RITES) Limited and the Indian Railway Construction Company Ltd (IRCON), were created in 1974 and 1976, respectively. This heralded a new phase in the organizational

structure of the Indian Railways. Canadian historian Ian J Kerr wrote in *Engines of Change*: "In a dramatic reversal of the dependence during the colonial period on foreign equipment and foreign experts India has become an exporter of railroad equipment and technical and managerial expertise".

RITES and IRCON

As the first PSU of the Indian Railways, RITES was successful from the beginning, recording profits in its first operational year. Since then, it has worked with many countries, such as Ghana, Nepal, Malaysia, and Syria. Countries struck by war, such as Cambodia and Vietnam, have turned to it for help with the reconstruction of their railways. Initially, the scope was limited to rail consultancy services. Over time, it has branched out to specialize in other transportation areas, provide quality inspections, export rolling stock and other equipment to Southeast Asian countries, and contribute to metro services in Delhi and Bengaluru. It continues to expand and diversify and has participated in domestic matters as well, such as developing a model to enable heavy industrial units to lease locomotives for their use and providing guidance for the Udhampur–Srinagar–Baramulla Rail Link (see pp.262–63). In 1995, IRCON, renamed Ircon International Ltd, was involved in a range of activities, such as the construction of new lines, railway electrification, establishment of production facilities, and testing telecommunication systems. It has

also expanded its operations to include other transportation facilities and infrastructure development. It established the Rail Coach Factory (RCF) in Kapurthala, Punjab, and provided services to countries, such as Malaysia, Sri Lanka, and Saudi Arabia.

CONCOR
The Container Corporation of India Ltd (CONCOR), a Navratna CPSE under the Ministry of Railways, handles multimodal logistical support (road and rail) of domestic and international cargo from the production centres or ports to consumption points. It does so by operating terminals of various kinds. It started with seven inland

container depots or "dry ports" established in the interiors, which now number 84. It also owns 15,303 wagons, 30,157 owned and leased containers, 111 reach stackers, and 16 gantry cranes. It manages air cargo complexes and provides value-added services, such as warehousing at the terminals. With an aim to support the country's increasing trade, it has embraced technology. From the VSAT-based network, the Terminal Management System for Domestic (DTMS) and Export Import (ETMS) to E-Office and Oracle ERP, CONCOR has continued to move with the times.

It runs double stack container trains from Khatuwas terminal (Rajasthan) to the Mumbai port and has also ventured into coastal shipping. Its services from Kandla Port to Tuticorin have been key in the expansion of the domestic movement of cargo. CONCOR also runs many programmes through its CSR (corporate social responsibility) policy.

PSUs for specific purposes
Over time, several PSUs have been set up for specific areas. In 1986, the Indian Railways Finance Corporation (IRFC) was incorporated to fund projects through market borrowings. The Indian Railway Catering and Tourism Corporation Ltd (IRCTC) (see pp.250–51) was formed to provide better catering and ticketing services. In 2003, Rail Vikas Nigam Ltd (RVNL) was incorporated for planning, developing, and executing projects relating to railway infrastructure, which were to be processed on a fast-track basis. The Konkan Railway Corporation Ltd (KRCL) and the Mumbai Railway Vikas Corporation Ltd (MRVC) focussed on the Konkan Railway and suburban railway projects in Mumbai, respectively. The loss of freight traffic to road and improvement in freight facilities led to the incorporation of the Dedicated Freight Corridor Corporation of India Ltd (see pp.258–59) in 2006.

▼ **Set up in September 1993**, the Inland Container Depot at Tughlakabad, New Delhi, was the first terminal of CONCOR. It is also the biggest dry port in India.

1981–1999
A TIME OF TRANSITION

1981–1999

The 1980s saw the phasing out of steam and a solid move towards electrification with several advances in technology, including computerization, in the following decade. Trains on the Indian rail network became faster. The railways in these decades reflected the socio-economic and political realities of India's democracy, including the shift in its economic policy towards liberalization.

October 1981 A manufacturing unit called the Diesel Component Works (DCW) is established in Patiala, Punjab, to undertake production of locomotive components.

July 1984 The Railway Reform Committee recommends the creation of four new railway zones.

February 1983 In order to promote tourism, a tourist train called the Great Indian Rover, which makes journeys to sacred Buddhist sites, is launched.

1985 A pilot project for the computerization of the Passenger Reservation System (PRS) through the Integrated Multitrain Passenger Reservation System (IMPRESS) is introduced in New Delhi.

1987 Early computerization reservation systems begin operations in Mumbai, Chennai, and Kolkata.

July 1988 The first Shatabdi train is introduced between New Delhi and Jhansi.

1989 Work on Konkan Railway begins.

1990 The first Self-Printing Ticket Machine (SPTM) is introduced in New Delhi.

1981–84

1985–88

198

1983 Steam is eliminated by Southern Railway.

June 1984 The Indira Gandhi-led Government begins Operation Bluestar.

October 1984 First metro service opens for the public in Kolkata.

1986 The Rail Coach Factory is established at Kapurthala, Punjab.

July 1987 First solid-state interlocking (SSI) system is introduced at Srirangam, Tamil Nadu.

1988 CONCOR is created.

June 1989 The Railways Act, 1989, comes into effect, replacing the Railways Act, 1890.

A WM class steam locomotive hauling a train

Interiors of a Shatabdi Express

A train on the Konkan Rail

" It is the **Indianness of the IR experience** that makes for its **easy running** and provides positive examples of the **bigness of character** of the Indian railwayman. **Meticulous, reliable and scientific,** he is everything the **tourist is taught** to believe the **Indian is not.** "

BILL AITKEN, *EXPLORING INDIAN RAILWAYS* (1994)

July 1991 India shifts to a new Industrial Policy, a move towards liberalizing the economy through private participation.

1993 Air-conditioned (AC) 3-tier coaches and the sleeper class are introduced along with the establishment of the Railway Capital Fund.

1997 Third Godavari bridge is built.

April 1999 The Darjeeling Himalayan Railway (DHR) is declared a World Heritage Site by UNESCO.

1995 The first WDP-1 and WDG-2 locomotives are commissioned.

26 January 1998 The first passenger train on the Konkan Railway is flagged off.

2   1993–96   1997–99

1992 The Indian Railways adopts the Unigauge Policy.

1994 The IVRS telephone-based inquiry comes into being.

October 1998 The Guinness World Records awards *Fairy Queen* with the record of being the oldest working steam locomotive in the world.

21 May 1991 Rajiv Gandhi, the former Prime Minister of India, is assassinated in Sriperumbudur, Tamil Nadu.

1996 Victoria Terminus (VT) renamed Chhatrapati Shivaji Maharaj Terminus (CSMT) and six new railway zones are proposed. Cabinet approves the first phase of the Delhi Metro.

October 1997 The *Fairy Queen* is brought back in regular revenue service.

September 1999 The Indian Railway Catering and Tourism Corporation (IRCTC) is incorporated.

Delhi Metro

The *Fairy Queen*

A TIME FOR MODERNIZATION

The end of the 20th century saw some remarkable changes in the Indian Railways, which led to a quiet revolution. While the system was administered with new blood in the form of new-age projects, such as computerization, some of the old practices and policies were reviewed.

◀ **Automatic Ticket Vending Machines** in later years further eased the ticketing system. These touchscreen machines are operated by using a smart card.

The focus of the Indian Government during the last two decades of the 20th century was to aid modernization and bring about economic and technological self-sufficiency. This period, therefore, saw a lot of structural changes in the Indian Railways, which mostly arose as a result of outdated policies dating back to the British era. These changes, however, need to be seen within the context of India's shift towards economic liberalization in the 1990s, when the railways found itself close to losing its monopoly over the transportation system.

▼ **In the 1970s,** the Indian Railways pioneered the use of IBM 1401s. It was one of the few organizations to have more than a dozen of these computers.

Computerization

The railways has always had to devise ways to stay efficient in the face of an ever-increasing volume of workload. The 1920s introduced mechanization through punch card equipment for data processing, which continued to be in operation for many years post-Independence. This soon proved to be limited in its capacity when the railways witnessed a significant increase in traffic and statistical data. The system transitioned to unit-record equipment in the early 1960s, but were phased out within a few years. The idea of a comprehensive management information system first came up around this time, wherein all subsystems could be integrated, for quick access to data, which would help in faster decision-making. This required improvement in the data processing equipment.

Thus, electronic computers made their way into the system in the mid-1960s. Nine zonal railways, three production units, and the Railway Board office were given second-generation computers, the IBM 1401s. Passenger revenue, financial management, and goods accounting were computerized. Soon, the further increase in traffic

necessitated upgradation. By the mid-1980s, second-generation computers gave way to third- and fourth-generation ones, in tandem with the Seventh Five Year Plan (1985-90), which laid emphasis on modern technology. During this phase, the Passenger Reservation System (PRS), the Freight Operations Information System (FOIS), locomotive sheds, stores, workshops, and divisions were all brought under the computerization scheme.

Reservations

Starting with a pilot project in New Delhi in 1985, the computerized PRS system, based on a software developed indigenously by Computer Maintenance Corporation (CMC) for the Indian Railways brought about a revolution. Passengers no longer had to face long queues to get to the reservation desk and the clerk at the counter was freed of cumbersome, lengthy ledgers. It increased staff productivity and administered speed and accuracy into the system. Computerization did not have an adverse effect on labour relations either, with no downsizing of staff. On the contrary, the use of advanced applications and opening up of more counters in remote locations created more demand for a skilled workforce.

The implications of the success of PRS was huge. Academic and author V Rajaraman in "History of Computing in India, 1955–2010" noted that "there was an attitudinal change among both the general public and the white collar workers about computerization. This was the beginning of the acceptance of computers and the realization that in a country which has large volumes of data to be processed the use of computers is inevitable."

Legislation

In 1973, the Government recognized the obsoleteness of the Indian Railways Act, 1890, and the few amendments that had been made to it since its enforcement. The minister of railways mentioned in the Budget

"RO-RO"

In the late 1990s, there was a slight decrease in the freight operations on the Indian Railways. As an innovative measure to improve the freight traffic, the Indian Government introduced the concept of the "Roll-On-Roll-Off" (RO-RO) service. Introduced on the Konkan Railways' diesel route in 1999, this scheme involves rolling loaded goods trucks onto flat wagons and transporting them via rail to their destination. Over the years, the service has been extended to other territories. This multimodal service is fuel-efficient and has also helped in decongesting cities while easing the transportation process for truck operators with no detentions and less paperwork.

Trucks moving on a railway bridge in the Konkan region as a part of the "RO-RO" scheme

of 1973–74 that "the objective is to bring this old statute into accord with the present day conditions and make it a more flexible instrument of regulation." Changes were sought in many sections, including compensation for accident victims and incidents related to unwarranted chain pulling, trespassing, and destruction of railway property and equipment. By 1977, a second draft was formulated "keeping in view the changed circumstances in which Indian Railways have to function in free India." By 1978, the final draft of a Bill for re-enactment of the Indian Railways Act was completed and placed for review with the Ministry

of Law. Following due process, the Act came into force from 1990. The Railways Act, 1989, lays down comprehensive legislative measures relating to the railways in independent India. The topics covered include the role of the Central Government vis-à-vis Zonal Railways, appointment and duties of a chief commissioner of railways safety, provisions for executing necessary works, rules for opening of the railways, constitution of Railway Rates Tribunal, regulations for the carriage of passengers and goods, railway accidents and liabilities of the administration with respect to victims, and offences and penalties, among other issues.

 The **reservation** system using **computers** was an **eye opener** to the **general public** as it demonstrated the **advantages** of using computers.

V RAJARAMAN, "HISTORY OF COMPUTING IN INDIA, 1955–2010"

SHATABDI EXPRESS

Modelled after intercity express trains that shuttled business executives travelling between cities, almost mimicking same-day return flights, but with more economy, the advent of the Shatabdi Express represented a turn towards greater functional speeds on the Indian rail network. With express speeds, punctual arrival and departure times, and quality service, these passenger trains usually plied on high-density routes and were established to connect main cities across the country.

Introduced in July 1988, the first train ran between New Delhi and Jhansi, a route that was extended by almost 300 km to Bhopal in 1989. Today, there are over 20 Shatabdi trains connecting almost every part of the country. Popular among travellers, they are hauled by powerful electric or diesel locomotives of 3,500 to 5,000 horsepower and can reach speeds of up to 160 km/h. With no unreserved accommodation, this class has few intermediate stops and is often prioritized over other trains, ensuring faster connectivity. Air-conditioned, superfast, and premium, they are priced higher than other passengers trains on the same route. This is why several variants have emerged over the years, including the Jan Shatabdi Express with non-AC coaches making it more affordable. These trains, which return to their station of origin on the same day, do not have berths but chair seating in executive or chair car coaches.

An interesting piece of political manoeuvring is at the heart of the name of this class of trains. The Indian Railways follows a strict policy of not naming trains after personalities. But the Shatabdi, meaning "century" in Hindi, was so named to commemorate the birth centenary of Jawaharlal Nehru.

Once given the title of the fastest train, it has since been dethroned, losing its position to the Tejas Express, India's first semi-high speed, AC train, which began operations in 2017 and the more recent Vande Bharat Express (see pp.282–83) that plies between Delhi and Varanasi and began service in February 2019.

The Aurangabad-bound Jan Shatabdi Express crosses a viaduct through the Thul Ghats, Maharashtra.

N RAILWAYS

प.रे

डब्ल्यूएपी5 30061

वडोदरा

A WAP-5 locomotive hauls
the high speed Mumbai
Central–Ahmedabad
Shatabdi Express.

DIESEL AND ELECTRIC LOCOMOTIVES

The changing fabric of economy and society in India post its Independence required a remodelling of the rail transportation system. Shifting from steam to diesel was the only way to meet the demand of this rapidly growing network. Though imported earlier, they were soon being manufactured in newly established workshops in India.

▶ WDM-2

Year Introduced	1962
Manufacturer	American Locomotive Company (ALCO); Diesel Locomotive Works (DLW)
Power	Diesel-electric
Gauge	Broad
Wheel arrangement	Co-Co

In 1958, the Indian Railways bought 100 WDM-1 class locomotives from the ALCO, primarily for coal transportation on the Eastern and South Eastern Railways. They soon became inadequate for freight transportation. The Indian Railways were keen to manufacture locomotives based on technology transfer from a foreign manufacturer. After the establishment of the DLW, these were assembled from kits sent by the ALCO. This class was so successful that some locomotives were also exported to Bangladesh and Sri Lanka.

◀ WAG-5

Year Introduced	1988
Manufacturer	Chittaranjan Locomotive Works (CLW); Bharat Heavy Electricals Limited (BHEL)
Power	AC Electric
Gauge	Broad
Wheel Arrangement	Co-Co

Highly successful, more than 1,100 units of this locomotive have been produced. With 4360 HP, the locomotives could run at 100 km/h. Over the years, many variants have been produced. The differences in the variants range from speed to gearing. Many variants built by the BHEL have been produced by CLW. Although WAG-5 are freight-dedicated locomotives, with the arrival of WAG-7 and WAG-9 variants, it operated on local trains.

▶ WDG-4

Year Introduced	1999
Manufacturer	General Motors and Diesel Locomotive Works
Power	Diesel-Electric
Gauge	Broad
Wheel Arrangement	Co-Co

The first WDG-4 locomotives were imported, some fully built, and others in kit form to be assembled in India. Compared to WDM-2, these locomotives have lower fuel requirements and maintenance cost. With 4,000 HP, they can achieve a maximum speed of 100 km/h and work well in steep terrain. In 2010, a modified version of this class, WDP-4B, was introduced for passenger service.

◄ YDM-1

Year Introduced 1955
Manufacturer North British Locomotive Company, Glasgow, UK
Power Diesel (Hydraulic transmission)
Gauge Metre
Wheel Arrangement B-B

The first diesel locomotives to haul main-line trains in India, they were used for freight operations around Gandhidham, Gujarat, on the Western Railway, where there was no provision of water for steam locomotives. Later, they ran on some parts of the South Central Railway. Weighing 44 tonnes, they could run at 88 km/h. They were phased out of service at the end of the 20th century. They are preserved at the Regional Rail Museum, Chennai and the National Rail Museum, New Delhi.

▲ YAM-1

Year Introduced 1964
Manufacturer Mitsubishi, Japan
Power DC Electric
Gauge Metre
Wheel arrangement B-B

This class of locomotives worked on the Southern Railway line in the Chennai region, especially on the section between Tambaram and Villupuram. They were withdrawn from service in 2004 after gauge conversion. Weighing 52 tonnes and with a power output of 1,740 HP, they could run at 80 km/h. In all, 20 units, numbered 21904–21923, were imported. While most locomotives are stationed at Tambaram, locomotive number 21912 is with the CLW.

▲ WAP-4

Year Introduced 1994
Manufacturer Chittaranjan Locomotive Works
Power AC Electric
Gauge Broad
Wheel Arrangement Co-Co

The WAP series was extensively used for passenger trains, of which WAP-4 is the most common. The 1990s were a period when the express trains were becoming common. The earlier WAP-1 were limited in their ability to haul trains with increased number of coaches. This class has been so successful that many units of WAP-1 and WAP-6 have been converted to WAP-4. The locomotives could run as fast as 140 km/h.

▲ WAM-4

Year Introduced 1970
Manufacturer Chittaranjan Locomotive Works
Power AC Electric
Gauge Broad
Wheel Arrangement Co-Co

Fondly called "The Old Monk", this class is the first locally designed and built electric locomotive in the country. With 3,850 HP, these could attain a speed of 120 km/h. Till the mid-1980s, WAM-4 engines were the mainstay of passenger service in the Indian Railways. Many locomotives, such as WCAM-1, WCG-2, and even some WAPs, were inspired by this class.

GOODBYE STEAM

By the late 1990s, steam locomotives almost disappeared from the Indian landscape.
Once a symbol of connectivity and progress, today they are an important part of the
railway heritage, fired up on special occasions as a romantic link to the past.

▲ **In January 2007,**
the iconic 1947-built
WP 7200, or *Azad*,
was steamed up for a
60 km-run in New
Delhi as part of the
"Rail Heritage Month".

In June 1970, the WG10560, a broad-gauge steam locomotive, rolled off the factory floor at the Chittaranjan Locomotive Works (CLW) in West Bengal (see pp.206–07). Its manufacture marked the end of an era. The locomotive, called the *Antim Sitara*, or last star, was the last of its kind to be built in India, its name inspired by the *Evening Star*, the last steam locomotive to be manufactured in Britain.

Once known as the iron horse or the *butcha* (child) of a monster, the steam locomotive had imprinted itself in public memory, as it hauled heavy trains across the countryside, spewing white smoke and changing India's landscape. Practical matters of economy and service, however, ensured that the end was around the corner.

Better than steam

Author and railwayman MA Rao noted that the growing expense of coal and increasing demand for efficiency meant that electric and diesel traction were given preference. Steam faced several challenges, which included low speed, slow acceleration, and time lost on watering, coaling, maintenance, and turning the locomotive after it reached its destination. All this cut into its usage time – steam locomotives could run for about 12 hours a day while the diesel or electric ones could be used for up to 21 hours.

Rao further wrote that the thermal efficiency of a steam locomotive was 7–12 per cent while diesel was at 28–32 per cent and electric at 50 per cent. High operating and maintenance costs sealed the fate of steam locomotives. By 1970–80, Rao wrote, diesel and electric did not make up even half of the total locomotives in use, and yet hauled "88.6 per cent of the total gross tonne kilometres of goods against only 11.4 per cent hauled by steam locomotives". He added that the "engine kilometres per day per engine on line were

three to four times those of steam locomotives and the speeds nearly double, on the broad gauge".

By the late 1990s, steam had practically gone out of circulation. "The age of steam engines is ending in India," lamented a 1993 article in the British newspaper *Independent*. "By 1996, all of India's remaining steam trains will be replaced by diesel ones, which cost less to maintain and are faster and more muscular". Another enthusiast wrote, in a 1994 letter to the Indian newspaper *Times of India*, "Please keep some steam for me when I come next year". In April 1997, a mere 75 steam locomotives were running across the country. Today, there is a small fraction of that number. Most run in the hill railway system or have become a part of the railway heritage.

Remembering the black beauty

The steam locomotive, railway enthusiast Joydeep Dutta wrote in an essay for the Indian Steam Railway Society's annual magazine, "was the most human machine ever designed. It has a personality of its own". It is perhaps why steam locomotives have managed to stay on in public memory.

Despite the fact that many engines were later sold as scrap, others made their way to museums as an important part of railway heritage. The *Antim Sitara* today finds pride of place at the CLW locomotive park as does the *Deshbandhu*, India's first indigenously produced steam

engine. The Rewari Railway Heritage Museum in Haryana and the National Rail Museum in New Delhi have preserved several steam locomotives, including the iconic *Fairy Queen* (see pp.34–35).

Heritage runs are made across the country regularly, such as in 2010 when the EIR 21 (see pp.36–37), hauled one coach between Chennai Egmore and Kodambakkam in Chennai. This locomotive, last operated in 1909, was displayed at the Jamalpur Locomotive Workshop and Howrah for more than a century before its revival.

> The **dense and murky clouds** out-belching from **thy smoke-stack**, / Thy knitted frame, **thy springs and valves,** the tremulous **twinkle of thy wheels,** / Thy train of cars behind, obedient, **merrily following** …

WALT WHITMAN, POET, "TO A LOCOMOTIVE IN WINTER"

▼ **The WM Class**
2-6-4T tank locomotives were built by the Vulcan Foundry, starting in the 1930s. Seen here is a locomotive of this class hauling a train between Jamalpur and Monghyr in 1981.

13022

PRESERVING THE HERITAGE

The railways in India is a long and continuing tradition and the preservation of its heritage forms a beautiful link with the past, establishing continuity and providing a sense of growth and identity in changing times and modern technology.

The lines traversing the Western Ghats, the railway towns, such as Kharagpur and Jamalpur, the locomotives, tickets, stamps, and government reports, are all relics of India's long and continuing tryst with the railways. Some are tangible, as small as a metal pass or as large as a bridge. There are intangible relics as well that contain skills, knowledge, and memories, which transcend the physicality of railway heritage.

Among some of the most visible examples of the railway's rich legacy are its stations. Author and journalist Gillian Wright in her essay "Railways: A 160-year Heritage" writes: "Across the land, even the humblest branch line stations with their rows of thick-boled shade trees along the length of the platforms, have their history as well as immense charm. And then, there are the half-timbered cottage stations of India's narrow-gauge hill railways and the varied

architecture from – Rajput to Nawabi – of railways of India's erstwhile Princely States." Yet, the most renowned are the four UNESCO-declared "World Heritage Sites". These include the Darjeeling Himalayan Railway (see pp.86–87) inscribed in 1999, the Victoria Terminus (see pp.120–21) building inscribed in 2004, the Nilgiri Mountain Railway (see pp.92–93) inscribed in 2005, and Kalka Shimla Railway (see pp.90–91) inscribed in 2008.

▼ **Workers undertaking** repairs at the Steam Loco Shed in Rewari, Haryana.

▲ **An antique valve gear model**

> " Much like India itself, the **Indian Railways** has a bit of both, **heritage** and **modernity** ... enchanting **vintage trains** ... services like **Vande Bharat** ... breathtaking new **bridges** ... dramatically further the railways' **reach** and **connectivity**. "

VINITA SRIVASTAVA, EXECUTIVE DIRECTOR, HERITAGE DIRECTORATE, RAILWAY BOARD

While some of the historical elements, such as stations, bridges, and tunnels, have been seamlessly incorporated into the modern railway system and continue to be in active use, there are others that have become outdated and relegated to the annals of history.

Railway sanctuaries

Museums are the most common way to preserve and conserve heritage and help keep history alive in the public imagination. New Delhi's National Rail Museum (see pp.240–41) was the first railway museum in India. Its popularity since its inception has been instrumental in the creation of other similar spaces, each with its own unique history. These include the Heritage Park at New Tinsukia, Assam, the Heritage Model Room at the Jodhpur Workshop in Rajasthan, and the rail museums in Trichy (Tamil Nadu), Howrah (West Bengal), and Mysore (Karnataka). These spaces provide people an opportunity to turn back the pages of history and relive the Indian Railways' glorious past.

The Steam Loco Shed at Rewari needs special mention as does the Golden Rock Workshop at Perambur, Tamil Nadu, which undertakes periodic maintenance of steam locomotives. Remodelled as a heritage space, the Loco Shed at Rewari houses some of the most iconic steam locomotives in India. The famous *Fairy Queen* and other locomotives, such as *Akbar*, *Azad*, *Angadh*, *Virat*, *Sher-e-Punjab*, *Sahib*, *Sindh*, and *Sultan*, are all kept here with some that are operated for heritage runs.

Conserve and preserve

The conservation and preservation of railway heritage includes preliminary and detailed examinations, scientific as well as historical knowledge, funding, repairing, and maintenance. The actual restoration work may also have its own challenges. Sometimes, maintenance practices, artisanal skills, and traditional materials disappear with an older generation, making it tricky to replicate original designs. Old steam locomotives often have missing and broken parts, which require expertise to rebuild and recreate.

At times, modern equipment is added to ensure that they can operate. For instance, the Perambur Loco Works undertook the renovation of EIR 21 (see pp.36–37) and added advanced technological elements, such as a GPS-based speedometer.

There are several other instances of extensive reconstruction as well, especially for buildings, such as the East India Company (EIC)'s Burlington building, the oldest hospital in Asansol, West Bengal. It required extensive waterproofing of the roof, careful preservation of the old curved tiles, new electrical wiring, and even weatherproof painting.

For the people

In recent years, the Ministry of Railways has initiated several measures for railway preservation including public awareness programmes, workshops, and exhibitions. Its Heritage Directorate recently collaborated with Google Arts and Culture for a virtual documentation of railway heritage, titled "The Lifeline of a Nation". Combining journeys, people's stories, engineering marvels, and heritage, the railways come alive with just a click. There have also been many remarkable private initiatives as well, such as the Indian Railways Fan Club Association (IRFCA). The website, set up by a group of rail fans engaged in documenting railways, is a goldmine of information related to the Indian Railways.

▼ **Austin Car,** which was used as an inspection carriage, is now displayed at the Railway Museum, Mysore.

NATIONAL RAIL MUSEUM

The special thing about museums is that they construct a time gone by into a living space as in the case of the railways in India. Its long history and romance is painstakingly preserved and celebrated in the National Rail Museum (NRM) in New Delhi. Its sprawling 11 acres houses rare operational exhibits, such as the Patiala State Monorail Tramway (see pp.110–11), the John Morris Fire Engine, and some of India's famous locomotives. These include the Bengal–Nagpur Railway's 91-ft-long Beyer-Garratt, *Hasang*, the smallest locomotive, and *Sir Leslie Wilson*, one of India's first-generation electric locomotives.

It was initially conceptualized as a museum to commemorate India's transport history and opened to visitors as the Rail Transport Museum in 1977. It was renamed as the NRM two decades later in 1995. The man credited with the work was railway enthusiast Michael G Satow, who was approached by the curator of London's Clapham Railway Museum, looking for help to move a coach built in 1870 in Lucknow, to the Transport Museum in India. This began Satow's long association with the NRM when he joined the project as an honorary advisor to the Ministry of Railways for the Rail Transport Museum in 1970.

Home to a range of exhibits, it today includes life-size rolling stock, vintage locomotives, saloons, exquisite miniature train models, and rare photographs. Railway simulators provide interactive experiences to visitors as do 3D virtual reality tours. Train rides around the Museum give a bird's eye view of the locomotives on display in the outside area. The NRM has taken on the role of preserving history and has undertaken restoration work for the Patiala State Monorail and the Mysore Maharaja's Saloon (see pp.78–81). It preserves archival documents, maps, and drawings as well, making the museum a treasure trove for the history of the Indian Railways.

A 1977 poster advertising the Rail Transport Museum, now known as the NRM. It remains closed on Mondays even today.

A sprawling 11-acre museum, NRM's outdoor open space is modelled to represent a railway yard featuring rare locomotives. A train, with open and closed carriages, takes visitors around the outdoor display area.

डब्ल्यू. डी. एम 2 WDM 2
1963

INDIA
भारत

6·00

DHR (DARJEELING)

डी एच आर (डार्जिलिंग)

बी B 1889

1993

RAILWAY CENTENARY

2 AS
आ

1853   1953

INDIA POSTAGE

0.10

ELECTRIC LOCOMOTIVE

विद्युत इंजन

भारत INDIA

पूर्व रेल शताब्दी

भारत
INDIA

4·00

...NARY OF SOUTH EASTERN RAILWAY 1887-1987

भारत
INDIA

25
YEARS

1971-1996

5·00

रजत जयन्ती राष्ट्रीय रेल संग्रहालय
SILVER JUBILEE NATIONAL RAIL MUSEUM

1996

The Indian Railways has had a long life, with many remarkable events and moments along the way. It traditionally releases vibrant commemorative stamps as an endearing reminder of the illustrious journey of the railways in India.

भारत INDIA

KONKAN RAILWAY

भारत INDIA

5.00

कालका – शिमला रेल के 100 वर्ष
100 Years of Kalka - Shimla Railway

INDIA POSTAGE

4 A.S.

MAIL TRAIN

जी आई पी न.1 GIP No. 185

2.00

1976

भारत
INDIA

भारत
INDIA

ARY OF DARJEELING HIMALAYAN RAILWAY

भारत
INDIA

100

NERAL MATHERAN

1993

एम एल ML 1905

डब्ल्यू. पी. /1 WP./ 1963

100

1976

भारत
INDIA

एफ्/1 F/1
1895

R M R

भारत
INDIA

दक्षिण पूर्व रेल शताब्दी

भारत IND

15

691

CENTENARY OF SOUTH EASTERN RAILWAY 1887-19

1887

HIDDEN FACES

There's more to the Indian Railways than its locomotives, architecture, history, bridges, and tunnels. The real story lies behind the scenes with its massive workforce that works tirelessly to keep the network connected and in rapid motion.

▲ **Railway employees** work relentlessly to improvise and upgrade equipment and ensure smooth running and safety. Here, rail workers in Amritsar, Punjab, convert the traditional lever frame to a new electronic interlocking system.

The Indian Railways has grown by leaps and bounds and has become, as its slogan says, the "Lifeline of the Nation". It encompasses modern technology, elaborate policies, and huge monetary investment. The real driving force behind its success, however, is its workforce – women and men who work in maintenance, manage tracks, technicians, engineers, and stations and track officials. They manage lines, no matter how remote, to ensure the safety and efficiency of the railways.

Right on track

Intertwining tracks on the Indian landscape make for a powerful picture. They are visible symbols of the material presence of railways connecting even remote areas. The tremendous work that goes into constructing and maintaining them, however, often remains unreported and undocumented.

Key on-ground staff, the track maintainers and keymen, focus on walking along the lines assigned to them, inspecting sleepers, fittings, and every nut and bolt. A major part of their duty is to alert the driver in case of any fault and the job often continues well into the night regardless of the weather. Their tools include a hemp cord, hammer, spanner, red and green flags, and detonators. Those that inspect civil engineering structures,

◄ **Conductors' or ticket collectors'** duties include checking tickets, providing correct information, and prompt guidance to commuters.

such as bridges and tunnels, use manual carts to move along tracks. They keep an eye on the tiniest of faults and assess the need for repairs or additional structures. In certain areas of the country, they battle challenging circumstances, threats from wildlife and dangerous terrain.

There are many others who keep the railways constantly operational, from gatemen stationed in small cabins at level crossings and ticket collectors, dressed in their characteristic white shirt, black trousers and coat, to the metal cutters, blacksmiths, engravers in production units, and sectional controllers at control rooms. Each one of them makes a significant contribution to the success of one of the biggest rail networks in the world.

Breaking barriers

Traditionally, life in the railways was seen as appropriate for men, and women were not a part of the workforce. However, the Indian Railways has the remarkable capability to transform itself. Since 1947, there has been a significant increase in the induction of female staff.

From working on the tracks to becoming locomotive pilots, no role is out of bounds and women have successively broken barriers. Some of them, the "first ladies", a term coined by JL Singh, retired railwayman and secretary of the Rail Enthusiasts' Society, have been lone warriors. For instance, Priya Prakash became a part of the Accounts Service as early 1957. Jaya Chauhan became the first woman officer of the Railway Protection Force (RPF), a part of its 1984 batch. When M Kalavathy joined the Indian Railway

Service of Signal Engineers, and Manju Gupta became a member of the Indian Railway Service of Electrical Engineers, both were the first women to do so. Surekha Yadav was the first-ever female train driver. More recently, Vijaylakshmi Viswanathan became the financial commissioner in 2002.

THE UNSUNG HEROES

There's a slogan within the rail community: "Once a railway person, always a railway person". This is truly reflected in the role that the railways played in saving countless lives during the Bhopal gas tragedy in 1984. Ex-Member (Staff), Railway Board, Manoj Pande, was Assistant Personnel Officer in Jhansi at the time and was deputed to help with the relief. He recounts how the general manager's inspection special on its way back to Bombay from Jhansi was detained at Sukhi Sewaian, a station short of Bhopal. Sensing the gravity of the situation, the general manager and a few other officers, went on the engine to the Bhopal railway station. They were met with chaos. The station was flooded with people, injured and in pain. Staff, officers, and medical personnel from the nearby towns of Bhusawal and Jhansi also reached there. A makeshift hospital was set up as well, as railway employees worked tirelessly in the hazardous situation. There was a huge exodus from the city, but railway services continued. Its employees stood firm, even though 45 colleagues, including Harish Dhurve, the station master, succumbed to the toxic gas. Their courage is representative of the love most railway personnel feel for the system.

► **A plaque commemorates** the victims of the Bhopal gas tragedy.

▼ **M Kalavathy from the 1981 batch** paved the way for more women to join the technical departments. Today, she works as the chief signal engineer in the Southern Railway.

SPORTS STARS

The Indian Railways is among the few dominant forces fostering the national sports scene, supporting women and men in search of sporting glory. By providing them with institutional support, job security, and funding, the railways have made it easier for them to achieve their and the nation's dream.

The Wembley stadium in London was packed with 25,000 spectators on 12 August 1948, all gathered to watch England play India in the final of the men's Olympic hockey tournament. Over the course of the match, India scored a whopping four goals over England's zero to win its first gold since Independence on 15 August 1947. At the helm, as captain, was Bombay, Baroda and Central India (BB&CI) Railway employee Kishan Lal, who is today considered one of the greatest right wingers of the game. He has,

however, not been the only railway employee to bring glory and acclaim to the country. The Indian Railways has had a long association with sportspersons, nurturing and supporting their talent, no matter what their specialization.

Promoting athletes

The Indian Railways Athletic Association, the first formal body for the organization of sports in the railways, established as early as 1928, was renamed, and finally rechristened the Railway Sports

Promotion Board (RSPB) in 1998. This was done to reflect the Board's role in promoting sports at national and international levels. An apex body, the RSPB coordinates and builds liaisons with different national sports federations and 30 railway sports associations. It is treated as a separate national sports organization, as it is affiliated to the Union Sportive Internationale des Cheminots, and is also a member of the Board of Control for Cricket in India (BCCI). In 2009 and 2012, it was awarded the Rashtriya Khel Protsahan Puraskar by the

▼ **In this picture from the London 1948 Olympic Games,** the Indian hockey team is seen playing against the Spanish team in a hockey match at Chiswick.

Ministry of Youth Affairs and Sports, for "Employment of Sportspersons and Sports Welfare" and "Financial Support for Sports Excellence".

Talent management

The Indian Railways, recognizing the importance of developing sports talent in their ranks, has taken an active interest in building a strong sports cadre. It offers innumerable opportunities to sportspersons interested in participating in national championships, including civilian awardees who have been honoured with the Padma Shri, Arjuna, Dhyan Chand, Dronacharya, and the Rajiv Gandhi Khel Ratna awards.

It also ensures steady employment, training, and coaching facilities. Their goal to build a sports cadre has meant that the Indian Railways have instituted recruitment policies especially for sporting talent, as well as several measures such as special casual leave to ensure uninterrupted training throughout the year, and out-of-turn promotions and incentives for high-performing athletes. The railway calendar now recognizes 28 sport disciplines.

Making a name

After the success at the 1948 London Olympics, India went on to win many more medals internationally with the men and women from the railways playing a significant role. In fact, the 81-member Indian contingent at the 2012 London Olympics had 12 railway sportspersons, while the 2016 Rio Olympics had 35 out of the 121-member contingent.

Hockey has always seen a good representation of railwaymen, and more recently women. Leslie Claudius, Mohinder Lal, and Harbinder Singh were all part of teams that won Olympic medals, including the gold on three occasions.

Boxer Vijender Singh and wrestler Sushil Kumar, both Olympic medallists, began their careers with the Indian Railways. Incidentally, Kumar is the only Indian double

◀ **In the 1986 Asian Games in South Korea,** PT Usha completed the women's 200-m-race in a record time. She won four gold medals and one silver medal in various events, bringing remarkable glory to India.

medallist at the Olympics from the railways – winning the bronze at the 2008 Beijing Olympics and silver at the 2012 London Olympics in freestyle wrestling.

Cricket, of course, is never far behind. The railways have produced cricketing giants who went on to become a steady part of the sport. Among the most successful are former Indian captain, Mahendra Singh Dhoni, who worked as a Travelling Ticket Examiner (TTE) with the South Eastern Railway in West Bengal, and Nanik Amarnath Bhardwaj (popularly known as Lala Amarnath), the first Indian to score a 100 in a Test match and the captain of the first Indian Railways' Ranji Trophy team. Murali Kartik, a familiar name in domestic and English county games, Sanjay Bangar, and Chennai Super King's Karn Sharma are products of the Indian Railways as well.

Women in sports

Women's rise in sports in India has often been arduous with access and opportunities hard to come by. The Indian Railways have a stellar record at providing sporting opportunities to women and have made major strides in levelling the playing field for women in sports, including the more

unconventional ones. For instance, the Northern Railway's Rachel Thomas became the first Indian woman to skydive on the North Pole in 2002 and the RSPB became one of the first organizations to encourage a women's wrestling team in India. More recently, wrestler Sakshi Malik brought bronze honours to India at the 2016 Rio Olympics.

Perhaps the best known is Pilavullakandi Thekkeparambil Usha, better remembered as PT Usha, who was nicknamed "Payyoli Express", the track and field athlete instrumental in taking Indian athletics to the world stage. Amongst others are Arjuna-awardee Dola Banerjee, sprinter Dutee Chand, cricketers Mithali Raj and Harmanpreet Kaur, and badminton player Madhumita Bisht. The Indian Railways' commitment to fostering female sporting talent can be attested by the fact that the Indian women's hockey team at the Rio 2016 Olympics comprised almost entirely of railway players, as was the 15-member Indian women's squad for the 2017 Women's Cricket World Cup, which had 10.

▼ **In the late 1990s,** Dhoni was selected to play as part of the South Eastern Railway cricket team. He was appointed as TTE from the sports quota.

LINKING THE WEST COAST

Designed and built over seven years, the construction of the Konkan Railway was one of the tallest challenges taken up after Independence. Connecting the Konkan region with railways meant seamless access to the south-western coast of India, encouraging trade, progress, and tourism within the region.

The Western Ghats had always seemed daunting to intrepid British railway engineers seeking to make inroads into India. The death toll and technical challenges that came with laying the lines at the Bhore and Thul Ghats (see pp.50–51) only underlined their treacherous nature. As a result, the Konkan coast remained untouched by the railways for a long time, flanked as it was by the intimidating Sahyadri Hills, or the Ghats, and the Arabian Sea. There were several proposals, some in the 1880s, with one even called "unproductive" and "absurd".

In 1952, Arjun Balwant Walawalkar, chief draftsman of the Bombay, Baroda and Central India (BB&CI) Railway, put together a proposal in the form of a booklet titled "Konkan Railway Project". This was the first real push towards building a line along the coast. Walawalkar is today considered one of the pioneers of the project. Though the idea remained on paper, it gathered momentum through the 1970s with scattered surveys in the 1980s, until political will made it a reality in the 1990s. It was obvious that the line would be financially viable because of high freight and passenger traffic, and also reduce crucial travel time between Mangalore and Mumbai by 26 hours.

Unorthodox methods

The Konkan Railway project is considered an archetype of a modern Indian railway project because of its innovations, not just in technology but also the way it was financed and managed. Mostly unhindered by bureaucratic red tape and fairly insulated from the political turmoil of the period, the construction was completed in a record seven years – a mere two years off the mark.

The formation of the Konkan Railway Corporation Limited (KRCL) in July 1990 as a public limited company was a significant departure from the norm, as the Government at the time, controlled all railway projects. The railways ministry took over administrative control while Maharashtra, Goa, Karnataka, and Kerala, as beneficiary states, provided equity capital, and additional funds were raised with the sale of tax-free bonds. Railwayman and engineer E Sreedharan took charge of the project as chairman and managing director.

The line was divided into seven sectors, each about 100 km, headed by chief engineers with enough authority to allow them to cut through the bureaucratic red tape. Sreedharan believed that five years was enough time to complete a 100–120-km-line. Additionally, there was a small team of experienced officers who provided their expertise to the different sectors with 400 freshly recruited engineers on the ground. These young survey engineers were given motorcycles, modified to carry survey equipment, to travel across Goa quickly to work on alignments and collect data. The organization remained small with about 2,400 people in its employ at its peak.

The construction

Laying the 738.9-km-broad-gauge line across three states, while crossing the Sahyadri Hills was a formidable task with rocky hills, treacherous soil conditions, innumerable rivers, big and small, and an intense annual monsoon added to the mix. "The saga of the construction of Konkan Railway is one of boring, drilling, cutting, and dynamiting your way through (the)

▼ **To construct tunnels,** huge rocks had to be blasted. Seen here is a profile marking on a rock before the initial blast.

The Konkan Railway has thousands of bridges across the rivers on its way. Some of the views are breathtaking.

arms and tentacles of the Western Ghats that came in the path of the rail line," wrote Joseph George, the general manager of the KRCL in an article.

Today, the line with 342 curves, crosses 67 stations across 1,880 bridges, the longest of which is across the Sharavati River in Honnavar, Karnataka at 2,065.8 m. Maharashtra's Panval Nadi is the tallest viaduct, nearly 423-m high, built using prestressed concrete girders to cross a ravine, as was the norm for this line. The viaducts used incremental launching by building the bridge from one end and pushing it forward, in a first for India. Welded steel triangular girders were also used for the bridges built over water. The tracks laid could accommodate high-speed trains that run at 160 km/h.

Building tunnels
The greatest challenge however lay in the tunnels, 91 in total, with the Karbude tunnel near Ratnagiri in Maharashtra as the longest at 6.5 km. The problem arose between Sawantwadi and Canacona in Goa where soil conditions threw engineers for a loop as did constant roof collapses and cave-ins. The soil, Sreedharan said, "became like toothpaste"; so agility with solutions and construction strategy proved to be the key. For the first time, tunnels had low-maintenance ballastless tracks, which use concrete or asphalt. Artificial ventilation, jumbo drills and electrohydraulic digging arms and loaders were imported from Sweden. Soft soil, particularly in the Pernem and Old Goa Tunnels in Goa, led to tunnel collapses, causing many delays, which were finally overcome.

The entire Konkan Railway line became operational in January 1998, changing the face of railway construction in India as engineers took their experience to other projects, such as the Delhi Metro and the Kashmir Link project (see pp.262–63).

E SREEDHARAN

Known as "India's Railwayman" and Delhi's "Metro Man", E Sreedharan was a part of the Indian Railways Engineering Service and has some turnkey infrastructure projects to his name. During his time in the railways, he was in charge of successfully rebuilding the Pamban Bridge in 64 days after its destruction during the 1964 cyclone in Rameswaram. After his retirement in 1990, he took charge of building the Konkan Railway and the Delhi Metro. He was awarded the Knight of the Legion of Honour in 2005 by the French government, the Padma Vibhushan, an Indian civilian award, in 2008, and the Order of the Rising Sun, Gold and Silver Star by the Japanese government, in 2013.

▶ E Sreedharan (right) receiving the Institute of Company Secretaries of India (ICSI) Corporate Governance Award in 2008.

THE BIRTH OF A BRAND

The coming of the Indian Railway Catering and Tourism Corporation Limited, or IRCTC, in 1999 changed the way the railway industry looked at service, for not only did it improve and professionalize catering and hospitality services, it redefined the way value-added services were provided to passengers.

▲ **Meals served on trains and stations** are sourced from IRCTC's "base kitchens", which are equipped with modern amenities. Seen here is an IRCTC employee carrying hygienically packed food in a food cart from the base kitchen in New Delhi.

When the IRCTC was formed, it was unimaginable that it would unleash a revolution in the Indian Railways. At the heart of its enormous success and popularity is the idea that it has constantly evolved and has successfully managed to keep pace with the rapidly changing character of its customer base. However, what has not changed over the years is its founding principle, which is as simple as providing efficient and quality services to the customers while following the industry's best practices.

This intention had been carefully woven into its business model and in doing so, the IRCTC redefined the relationship between the government as a service provider and the population as the consumer. The Indian Railways now has a corporate face focused directly on customer needs and satisfaction, with an anticipation that it could open pathways to greater returns.

Food on the go

Prior to the advent of IRCTC, railway passengers had to disembark at stations and rely on food available. Often, the quality of food at the stations was dubious but passengers, mainly those travelling considerable distances, had little choice. The IRCTC rapidly took over departmental and staff catering from 2001 and completely revamped the facility. It built the required infrastructure, such as mega base kitchens, food courts and food plazas, and injected order into the system.

However, its real pioneering effort lay in the railways' food service, when it introduced in-transit catering through pantry cars attached to the trains. Now all passengers, no matter which class they had opted for, had access to hygienic food.

An element of risk

The IRCTC's next foray was into the world of ticket reservation in 2002 when they started offering online booking. In India, the internet was still in its infancy, e-commerce was uncharted territory, so customer reaction was bound to be quite unpredictable. This did not stop the IRCTC, which took all the challenges in its stride and launched what turned out to be hugely successful digital services for ticketing. It moved towards next generation e-ticketing with the launch of the IRCTC Rail Connect mobile application in 2014, which increased booking capacity to over 20,000 tickets per minute.

Collaborations

While consolidating its services, the IRCTC has never shied away from inventing and reinventing its business

▲ **To enhance the** overall standards of service, professionally trained lady stewards have been introduced on some trains.

model and has actively encouraged private and public partnership in order to expand its reach. For instance, milk and milk products are purchased from dairy units in the cooperative sector and IRCTC has even collaborated with global food chains, private restaurants, and online ordering platforms.

One of the most important projects in this area has been the creation of the brand "Rail Neer", to provide clean, hygienic potable water to all passengers. Prior to its introduction, most passengers struggled to easily access clean drinking water. The IRCTC solved that problem of availability and took on the entire cost of the project, without placing any additional strain on railways' finances. Today, its plants produce over 11,00,000 bottles per day.

▼ **Physical tickets were earlier sent to** customers, but are now digital. Confirmations are done directly through emails and mobile phones.

◀ **The IRCTC has set up** manufacturing plants to produce packaged drinking water, sold exclusively on all railway premises and trains.

2000 ONWARDS
THE **NEW**
MILLENNIUM

THE NEW ERA

Liberalization and the new millennium brought with it a multitude of challenges for the railways. From trying to remain relevant in an age of affordable airfare and quick travel to providing efficient freight services and staying environmentally conscious, the Indian Railways has its share of work cut out.

Liberalization in the early 1990s changed the face of the Indian economy and the railways, which operated under the direction of the Indian Government. By the time the millennium came around, the Indian Railways had a new set of challenges, from modernization and changing technologies, to competition from airlines offering cheap fares and discerning travellers seeking speedy, comfortable, and competitively priced travel. Equally important was the need to make freight services profitable once again.

Top on the railways' list was the need to adapt and stay relevant while transforming itself, as authors V Nilakant and S Ramnarayan wrote in their book *Changing Tracks: Reinventing the Spirit of India*: " ... from a colonial workhorse and social equalizer into a modern piece of critical infrastructure carrying India into the 21st century ... ". It is no wonder that the Indian Railways' Vision 2020 statement was to "reinvent" the system so that it was "fast, punctual, comfortable, clean, and indeed, memorable". Alongside key infrastructural changes, there were legislative decisions as well that have impacted the system.

Changing legislation

An interesting, yet significant, change took place in 2012 in the British Parliament with the phasing out of 38 Acts that were put in place during the British rule. They were considered "as being spent, obsolete, unnecessary or otherwise not now of practical utility".

More recently, in 2017, the Indian Government ended the 92-year-old practice of maintaining two separate Budgets – Railways and General. The practice began in 1924, following the Acworth Committee Report recommendations (see pp.134–35). Yet, it was believed that over the decades, it had become a mere "ritual" with no real advantages. It was becoming apparent that the railways was trying to leave its colonial past behind. A merged budget meant that the Indian Railways could now increase its capital expenditure and focus on generating revenue, while its functional autonomy remained unaffected.

Speed

Punctuality and speed has always been a matter of importance and the focus on increasing the speed of long-distance trains and the Vande Bharat Express (see p.282–83) is proof of this. Studies are being conducted to set up high-speed rail corridors to provide bullet train services across the country with work underway to develop a Mumbai–Ahmedabad corridor.

Carrying freight

Equal emphasis is being laid on freight services as the railways has always lost out to the road sector, leading to a significant decrease in the market share. Dedicated freight corridors, however, seek to change that (see pp.258–59) as they will increase the railways' capacity to meet demand and improve the quality of services. Efforts are on to improve the railways' connectivity to ports as well and to modernize and upgrade the systems to allow cargo tracking and punctual deliveries.

◄ **Solar panels on trains** are an eco-friendly way to power many passenger facilities within carriages. Seen here is solar-powered DEMU at Sarai Rohilla station, New Delhi, in 2017.

Going green

The Indian Railways has announced often that it aims to become a "net zero" carbon emitter by 2030. The process of electrification has been underway in order to make the railways run on electricity completely. In 2018, the railways commissioned its first state-of-the-art 12,000 HP electric locomotive as a part of the "Make in India" project.

In another first, the Diesel Locomotive Works (DLR) in Varanasi converted a diesel locomotive into an electric one. The railways has undertaken compressed natural gas (CNG) substitution for Diesel Electric Multiple Unit (DEMU) trains and even introduced solar energy-based DEMUs.

Bio-toilets have also been introduced to trains as have solar panels over station and service building rooftops. Steps are also being taken to make railway stations greener and more energy-efficient.

BOGIBEEL BRIDGE

The 4.9-km-long Bogibeel bridge over the Brahmaputra River, connecting the Assamese cities of Dibrugarh and Silapathar, about 6 km from Arunachal Pradesh, opened for use in December 2018. It has a two-line track on the lower deck and a three-lane road on the top deck. Work began in 2002 about six years after its foundation stone was first laid in 1997, but progress slowed substantially, mostly because of the weather. The bridge has reduced the travel time from Assam to Arunachal Pradesh to four hours. It is considered extremely important for improved access to the north-east region and for its proximity to the India–China border.

The Bogibeel bridge is Asia's second longest rail- and road- bridge.

THE FREIGHT STORY

Freight traffic has historically been central to the railways, which was driven by colonial trade interests. Even when the railways acquired strategic and military importance, freight remained its mainstay. Its importance has grown manifold in contemporary times as it forms a major revenue source for the railways and is a major contributor to the country's economic prosperity. In many ways, it is the way forward for the Indian Railways.

▲ **A block rake train** loads iron ore for TISCO at Gorumahisani, Odisha, from the nearby mines.

The port towns of Calcutta, Bombay, and Madras were of utmost commercial significance to the British Empire, as much to export raw materials back to England as they were to import finished products. It was imperative, therefore, to link them via an extensive railway network. By 1870, Calcutta and Delhi were directly connected, as were Calcutta and Bombay through Jubbulpore (Jabalpur), while Bombay and Madras had railway lines through Sholapur and Raichur. With this, the ports were connected to India's major cotton fields. The line to Raneegunge and its coal mines meant that the railways met the coal needs of not just Calcutta, but northern, western, and central India as well.

Trade purposes

During the colonial period, the railways carried all types of freight, from coal, cotton, jute, leather, hide and skin to fruits, wine, tea, and even food grains for export. By 1866, 23 per cent of wheat imported to Britain was from India. Academic John Hurd in his 1975 essay "Railways" noted a visible increase in total net tonnage of freight, from 3.6 million in 1871 to 42.6 million in 1901 and 54 million by 1904. This was because the railways provided reliable and speedy movement of goods as compared to the traditional forms of bullock cart and riverine transport.

The emergence of the Tata Iron and Steel Company (TISCO) and the Indian Iron and Steel Company (IISCO) heralded a new era. Increase in steel production created a demand for quick

and efficient transportation of raw material and finished product. Soon, it proved to be the new captive traffic for the railways. The Bengal–Nagpur Railway (BNR) undertook several initiatives, including production of wagons to carry steel and iron ore in bulk. It also commissioned and constructed the Inner Harbour at the Visakhapatnam Port in 1933 to facilitate the export of manganese ore from the Central Provinces.

Challenges

Post-Independence, it became necessary to ensure smooth and efficient freight services, as India embarked on a programme of planned economic development. As freight facilitated economic growth, there was a multiplier effect on it. Commodities such as coal, fertilizer, cement, petroleum products, food grain, iron ore, raw material to produce steel, and steel itself were criss-crossing the country on rail tracks in a bid towards economic development through an industrial boom. There were instances when lines were laid specifically for freight. In one such example, three lines were constructed from the Bailadila mines (in present-day Chhattisgarh) to move 6 million tonnes of iron ore to Visakhapatnam for export to Japan (see pp.200–01).

However, outdated and limited rolling stock, such as wagons with vacuum brakes and incompatible couplings, and complex, time-consuming procedures, such as the option of booking individual wagons to transport materials, restricted the railways from truly utilizing freight

transport. These cut severely into train operations, leading to long delays in freight and passenger movement. The Indian Railways sought innovations in its freight operations.

Beginning of change

Canadian historian Ian J Kerr notes two key innovations in freight transportation in independent India. One lay in enhancing capacity equipment and the other in improving policies and practices.

In a major policy change, a uniform rate structure was implemented in 1948, which has since been continuously improved and simplified to provide better services to customers. Equipment change entailed hopper cars, tanker wagons, rail flat cars, and units with improved technology, such as refrigeration and air brakes. In the mid-1960s, the introduction of containerization revolutionized the way freight moved. It not only integrated road and rail transportation, but also provided speedy and safer services for freight.

The early 1980s saw another significant change, under the Railway Board chairman MS Gujral. During this time, homogenous wagons were linked together, reducing the time taken in train formation and increasing efficiency. This period also saw the introduction of block rakes where entire trainloads of consignments such as coal were booked making freight movement efficient and effective. The impact was immediate with the railways registering a marked growth in goods transportation in 1981–82 when it went up by 13 per cent to 221 million tonnes.

CONCOR's role

The end of the decade saw the formation of the Container Corporation of India (CONCOR) in 1989, as container traffic – export–import and domestic – set new trends in railway freight traffic. CONCOR, a Public Sector Undertaking, played a significant role in subsequent years. It took charge of the inland container depots that were previously with the Indian Railways and commissioned several more to meet the growing demand. It acted as a carrier, while providing 94 per cent of the transport through the railway network, and as a terminal and warehouse operator.

Today, the Indian Railways operates up to 7,000 freight trains daily and the traffic accounts for nearly two-thirds of its revenue.

Increasing innovations in operating practices, new wagons, improvements in track structures with enhanced safety parameters have also contributed to a steady increase in profits from freight. The upcoming dedicated freight corridors (see pp.258–59) and an increased focus on freight will boost CONCOR's purview, as it provides ready infrastructure and easy connectivity between the ports and the hinterland.

▼ **Front-loaders arrange** stacks of coal on a freight train parked at Krishnapatnam Port in Andhra Pradesh.

DEDICATED FREIGHT CORRIDOR

The Indian Railways has mostly had a mixed traffic of freight and passenger trains plying on its tracks. Now, work is on to create a distinct, dedicated network to carry freight across the country. Not only will this enhance capacity and efficiency, and reduce congestion, it will also increase the railways' freight share by a significant margin.

Bringing this together is the Dedicated Freight Corridor of India Limited (DFCCIL), a Public Sector Undertaking, formed in 2006 with the aim to plan, build, operate, and maintain freight-carrying corridors across the country.

The decision to build dedicated freight corridors came about under the Eleventh Five Year Plan (2007–12), which focused on "inclusive growth". The plan referred to the massive strain placed on the Delhi–Mumbai and Delhi–Kolkata routes because of the "rapid rise in international trade and domestic cargo". The first step to easing this strain lay in building dedicated freight corridors along "high density routes", starting with two in the west and east sectors, respectively. This involved constructing 7,201 km of new rail tracks. "This will help to decongest the two routes for freight movement and also increase the economic potential of the hinterland areas, which will benefit from the reduced cost of transport. It will also provide spin-off benefits in terms of the location of industrial clusters along the new corridors, thereby attracting potential investment in a number of states," the plan stated.

The DFCCIL is now in the process of constructing five freight corridors that span the length and breadth of India, of which two are under construction and surveys are underway for two others. These will be laid east to west with Kolkata–Mumbai (2,328 km), north to south with Delhi–Chennai (2,327 km), along the east coast with Kharagpur–Vijayawada (1,115 km), and along the south-west Chennai–Goa corridor, which is still under consideration. Apart from easing the strain on the existing infrastructure, these corridors are expected to integrate the domestic market and provide an industrial boost to the economy.

◀ **Aerial view of a double-stack freight train** as it moves on the Ateli (Haryana)–Phulera (Rajasthan) section of the Western Dedicated Freight Corridor (WDFC) during its inaugural run on 15 August 2018.

▲ **In June 2015,** Indian travelled in a special train to Lahore to attend the death anniversary of Maharaj Ranjit Singh (1801–39 ruler of the Sikh Empire o Punjab. They are seen her at the Wagah station

CROSSING BORDERS

From reviving its rail links with Pakistan and Bangladesh to building new ones with Nepal, the Indian Railways' international connections have played an important role in healing wounds, fostering bilateral relationships with its neighbours, and building a bridge of friendship.

Until 1947, the railways connected almost every corner of the Indian subcontinent, promoting the economy, fostering trade, helping protect its distant frontiers, and carrying people. The drawing of borders and Partition changed everything. The railways, a service that was never meant to be partitioned, split in two. Since then, for many decades, India and its neighbours have made several efforts to reconnect the lines in an effort to heal wounds and foster bilateral relations.

Train of accord
After Independence, hostilities between India and Pakistan put paid to any hopes of easy train travel between the two countries until the end of the 1971 Indo-Pakistan war and the creation of Bangladesh, formerly East Pakistan. According to one of the outcomes of the 1972 Simla Agreement, a peace treaty between India and Pakistan, the Governments would promote travel facilities for the citizens of both countries in an effort to "restore and normalize relations".

This was furthered by the Samjhauta Express, which means accord or compromise in Hindi and Urdu, which started services on 22 July 1976, running between Amritsar and Lahore. In the late 1980s, increased security concerns saw the train from India terminating at Attari, a town 3 km from the India–Pakistan border at Wagah in Punjab. Here, passengers disembarked, went through customs and immigration, and then boarded a Pakistan Railways train for their ultimate destination.

Prior to this, a through service between Jodhpur in Rajasthan and Karachi did exist, but was discontinued around 1965. It restarted in 2006, but did not provide a direct connection. Passengers travelled from Jodhpur to Munabao, a village near the desert town of Barmer on the Indian border, went through customs and immigration, before being taken to the Zero Point Station in Pakistan. There, they boarded the Thar Express to Karachi. This line sought to revive the train that once ran between Ahmedabad, in Gujarat, and Pakistan's Hyderabad, during British rule.

However, services on both these trains have been quite inconsistent, given the tenuous nature of diplomatic relations between the two countries.

Fostering friendship
The people of Bangladesh and India waited for a train connection between the two countries for 42 years. There were direct buses and flights, but the railways carried a deeper connection, symbolic of a time when the two countries were part of a whole. In fact, before Partition, a regular overnight train ran from Kolkata to Goalanda and Dhaka, both in Bangladesh. Until the 1965 Indo-Pakistan war, three trains ran between India and East Pakistan, including the East Bengal Mail, East Bengal Express, and Barishal Express.

In April 2008, the train called Maitree or Friendship Express began service, travelling 500 km from Kolkata to Dhaka. It was a result of bilateral talks between India and Banglaesh. A second line was inaugurated in 2017 connecting Kolkata with Khulna, a city in Bangladesh, an attempt to revive the Barishal Express route. Called Bandhan (or bond) Express, the train travels 172 km and makes three stops.

BOAT MAIL
Until 1964, India and Sri Lanka were linked, not directly, but by train and boat when the Indo-Ceylon Express ran services from Madras (now Chennai) to Colombo. Passengers would board the Rameswaram Express (or Boat Mail) from Madras Egmore and travel through Pamban to a pier at Dhanushkodi, a small village at the very tip of the island of Rameswaram. Here, they would board a ferry run by the Southern Railway, which would take them across the open sea to board a connecting train at Talaimannar in Sri Lanka. The December 1964 cyclone with almost 7-m-high tidal waves, one of the fiercest storms to hit India, destroyed Dhanushkodi, washed away the Pamban bridge, tore up the railway line, and swept away the Pambam–Dhanushkodi passenger train. While international ferry services continued briefly until the mid-80s, the tracks were never repaired.

Remains of the Dhanushkodi town

New routes
The most recent international connection has been a 34-km-line that will run from Jayanagar in Bihar to Janakpur in the neighbouring mountain state of Nepal. Earlier, a 2.5 ft narrow-gauge line existed here, built during the British rule to transport timber from Nepal, which stopped running in 2014. Construction for the line has begun and train services are expected to start soon. A 39-km-long line from Raxaul, Bihar in India, to Birgunj, a city in Nepal also existed – built in 1924–27, but mostly to move freight, and it stopped service in 1965. Since then, the tracks on the Indian side have been converted to broad gauge.

There have been several other feasibility studies as well, looking at ideal train connections between countries. Notable among these was a proposal to link parts of Bhutan with Assam and West Bengal. However, there has been no movement on this plan.

▼ **Maitree Express** ready for departure from the cantonment station in Dhaka in April 2008 amid cheers from the crowd.

KASHMIR CONNECTION

The Jammu–Srinagar link has been in the works for decades, battling non-stop challenges, from unforgiving terrain and construction issues, to political troubles. Yet, the completion of each phase has improved connectivity and furthered the attempt to integrate a region that has for long been crucial to India's strategic interests.

Sir Pratap Singh, the Maharaja of Jammu and Kashmir (1848–1925), ordered the first surveys to explore a railway link to the Kashmir Valley in 1902. There were two possibilities: Abbottabad (in present-day Pakistan)–Srinagar and Jammu–Srinagar through Banihal. Both proved to be expensive endeavours and were abandoned.

Therefore, until 1947 and Independence, visitors to Kashmir followed a circuitous route that involved train travel until Rawalpindi (in present-day Pakistan) or Jammu and then a road journey into the Valley. Partition made matters even more complicated. Sialkot, the city that once provided the sole railway link to Jammu via a 43-km broad-gauge line operated by the North Western State Railway, became a part of Pakistan. By September 1947,

train services were suspended and it fell upon the Indian Government to re-establish links with Jammu and Kashmir (J&K).

Early links
The nearest railhead was in Punjab so work began on the Mukerian–Pathankot route, which opened in 1952. By 1966, the line extended to Kathua, a town on the edge of the Jammu–Punjab border about 5 km from Pathankot. Jammu, however, was still about 77 km away. Work picked up pace as relations between India and Pakistan deteriorated and continued through the 1971 war between the two countries. A year later, the Kathua–Jammu section opened for passenger use. As the Srinagar Express, now known as the Jhelum Express, pulled into the station on 2 December 1972,

it proved to be a momentous occasion. For the first time in the 25 years since India's Independence, Jammu was connected via a railway line.

Pushing inwards
It took the Indian Railways almost three decades to push beyond Jammu to Udhampur, 53 km away. The project was sanctioned in 1980–81 and work began in 1983, but it took far longer to construct than the earlier estimates of five years. Bridging the Tawi River and cutting through unstable terrain and the Shivalik Hills had proved to be quite a challenge and the line could only open for use in 2005. The track today includes 158 bridges (including 36 major and 122 minor ones) and 20 major tunnels. In the meantime, the Indian Government approved a proposal to construct a line from Udhampur

to Baramulla, a town close to Srinagar in the Kashmir Valley, much like the 1902 proposal. It was an ambitious project propelled by India's strategic interests in the region and an attempt to integrate Kashmir with the rest of the country. As a result, it was identified as a project of national importance with funding by the Central Government. The Konkan Railway Corporation Ltd (see pp.248–49), and the Indian Railway Construction Company (IRCON), a Public Sector Undertaking specializing in infrastructure, began work on different sections of the line.

Udhampur to Baramulla
Work began in three sections or "legs" as it was called, each throwing up its own peculiar geographical challenges, with insurgency taking its own toll on the construction.

The first leg, 25 km long, connected Udhampur to Katra, a small town popular with Hindu devotees and the starting point of a trek up to the holy temple of Vaishno Devi. Scheduled to open in 2007, it involved the construction of 11 km of tunnels, 36 major and minor bridges, and traversing sharp curves. This included the country's longest steel girder bridge over the River Jhajjar,

85-m-high. There were substantial delays because of extensive seepage and the swelling of soil, where soil increases or shrinks according to its moisture content. A subsequent tunnel collapse meant that extensive survey and redesigning was required to be done before construction commenced. The line finally opened in 2014.

There have been several difficulties in the second leg of construction, which began in 2008. The iconic Pir Panjal Tunnel, which became operational in 2013, belongs to the complicated and daunting second leg – the 129-km-long Katra–Qazigund section. At 11 km, this is the longest transportation tunnel in the country. The tunnel is perhaps one of the trickier sections with the highest "overburden" of soil strata of 1,100 m in the country. Straight and running in a north–south direction, the tunnel is 440 m lower than the road tunnel, making it less vulnerable to snow.

Author and Indian Railways expert, Vinoo Mathur in his book *Bridges, Buildings and Black Beauties*, notes that the route is extremely challenging because "the mountain is young, geologically unstable, the rock structure extremely fragile and the line has to be built across four different thrust zones". That is why,

he writes, "each stretch of the line provides a new challenge to the railway engineer." In fact, 108 km of the track is expected to pass through tunnels with remaining lines crossing at least 70 bridges, including the record-breaking Chenab Bridge (see pp.264–65). Work is still underway and the new target for completion is 2021.

The designated third leg of the stretch, the 118-km-long Qazigund–Baramulla section in the Kashmir Valley, began operations far earlier, in 2008. A Diesel-electric Multiple Unit or DEMU presently runs between Banihal and Baramulla via Srinagar.

▲ **The Jammu to Udhampur** section of the rail bridge is made of concrete.

The famous V-shaped Chenab River Gorge that the train will cross once the bridge is constructed. The beginnings of an arch can be seen on either side.

CHENAB BRIDGE

The massive steel edifice being constructed across the Chenab River Gorge, Jammu, at 1,315 m and spread over 17 piers may not be the longest in the country. Yet once it is built, the innocuously named Bridge No. 44 will be the most crucial component in the Katra–Banihal section of the Udhampur–Srinagar–Baramulla Rail Link (USBRL). It will also hold the distinction of being the highest steel arch railway bridge in the world. The centre of the arch rises 359 m above the river bed level, which is 35 m taller than the Eiffel Tower in Paris and almost five times the height of the Qutb Minar in Delhi. The span of the arch is 465 m.

Given the politically volatile nature of the region, the Indian Railways worked closely with the Defence Research and Development Organization (DRDO) to design the bridge, which uses special blast-proof steel and can withstand a bomb blast. It has been constructed to withstand seismic forces likely in earthquake Zone V or of Very Severe Intensity, even though this area falls under Zone IV or of Severe Intensity. Sufficient redundancy has been built into the design to ensure that the bridge will not collapse even if one pier is removed. Wind tunnel tests were conducted to ensure that the bridge would withstand powerful gusts and, as a result, it can endure winds up to 266 km/h.

The geologically fragile nature of the region and its remote location has been challenging for the Konkan Railway Corporation Ltd (KRCL), which is at the helm of the project. The USBRL built 22 km of roads for construction of this bridge alone. The danger of landslides meant that the two ends of the gorge, where the arch foundations are placed, were stabilized using, among other means, rock bolts that are 11 m long and 32 mm in diameter.

A long viaduct leads up to the Kauri end of the bridge. The area near the viaduct also houses the staff settlement of the railway project.

CITY CONNECTIONS

Intracity transport has always struggled to keep up with expanding urban areas and growing populations by constantly improvising and upgrading its transport facilities. The metro rail projects across India's metropolitan cities have tried to do exactly that and have revolutionized everyday travel, so much so that life in many cities is unimaginable without this service.

Author and railwayman MA Rao in his book *Indian Railways* argues that the rapid industrialization that followed India's Independence was not uniform across all regions, with the four metropolitan cities of Delhi, Kolkata, Chennai, and Mumbai witnessing far more rapid development. It was inevitable that people from different parts of the country converged on these cities in search of employment, which in turn led to a surge in their populations. Soon, the strain on public transport was visible with limited road capacity and inadequate bus services.

In the "City of Joy"
As early as 1949, the Government of West Bengal toyed with the idea of an underground transport system in Kolkata. A team of French specialists

explored the feasibility of such a system, recommending certain sections. However, there was no further movement in the project. Efforts to expand roads did not yield favourable results and the situation continued to worsen.

In 1969, the Metropolitan Transport Team of the Planning Commission recommended a rapid transport system and by 1971, a plan was in place to build three lines – Dumdum–Tollygunge, Bidhannagar–Ramrajatala, and Dakshineswar–Thakurpukur. The highest priority was given to the Dumdum–Tollygunge section and construction began in 1972. By 1984, the stretch between Esplanade and Bhowanipur was opened for service and the entire north–south line became operational by 1995. In recent

years, the line was extended to Noapara on one side and New Garia on the other.

The construction of the second line, or the east–west metro corridor, between Salt Lake Sector V and Howrah Maidan, started in 2009. Although implemented by the Kolkata Metro Rail Corporation (KMRC), the project will be operated by the Metro Railway, Kolkata, the only metro under the Indian Railways. Still under construction, the east–west line is unique because its section between Lal Dighi and the Howrah station would pass under the Hooghly River, making it the first underwater metro in India. Several other lines have been sanctioned as well, including Joka–Esplanade, Noapara–Barasat, and Baranagar–Barrackpore. There are also plans to provide connectivity between the main city and suburbs

The capital

Delhi followed Kolkata's lead to implement the Mass Rapid Transport System (MRTS) across the city with the formation of the Delhi Metro Rail Corporation (DMRC) in 1995, which was jointly owned by the Central Government and Government of the National Capital Territory of Delhi. The first metro stretch opened in 2002 between Shahdara and Tis Hazari. The network has diversified considerably over the years, not just within the city, but even to surrounding areas, such as Ghaziabad, Noida, Gurugram, and Faridabad. Various other bodies engaged in metro construction have drawn upon its success and the DMRC has acted as a consultant for several other metro projects in the country.

Developments in other cities

Following the success of MRTS in Delhi, metro services were introduced in many other regions. Gurugram's Rapid Metro, India's first fully privately financed metro system, began operating in 2013. Keeping in mind the large numbers of passengers shuttling between Delhi and Gurugram, the Rapid Metro

is also connected to the Delhi Metro. In Mumbai, different lines of the rapid transit system are being developed by different bodies. These include the Mumbai Metropolitan Region Development Authority (MMRDA), the Metro One Operation Pvt Ltd (MOOPL), and the Mumbai Metro Rail Corporation (MMRC). The first line, Versova–Andheri–Ghatkopar, entered operations in June 2014.

Chennai's metro also started services in June 2015 with the Chennai Metro Rail Limited (CMRL). In Noida, the metro service was developed by the DMRC on behalf of the Noida Metro Rail Corporation (NMRC) and it opened to commercial service in January 2019. In Ahmedabad, the metro service, developed by the Gujarat Metro Rail Corporation, opened to the public in March 2019 between Vastral Gam station and Apparel Park station. Other cities, such as Bengaluru, Hyderabad, Kochi, and Jaipur, have established their rapid transit system as well.

The construction

Metro services have mostly been introduced as alternatives to strained road transportation.

Therefore, lines are either elevated or underground. This requires complex construction techniques, ranging from cut and cover method and ballastless tracks to heavy tunnel boring machines (TBMs) and box pushing technology. There has also been rapid technological improvement, for instance, with some trains on the Delhi metro network fitted with Unattended Train Operation technology, eliminating the need for manual operations.

Advantages

The metro services provide an affordable and comfortable means of everyday travel. The trains are fully air conditioned and stations are equipped with modern facilities, such as escalators, vending machines, and shopping avenues. With the introduction of smart cards, passengers do not even need to stand in queues to buy tickets.

Metro services not only provide a huge carrying capacity, but are also environmentally friendly means of transportation. The Delhi Metro has even been certified by the United Nations as being the first metro rail system to reduce greenhouse gas emissions.

▲ **For the people living in Delhi and the NCR,** the metro service is a lifeline. It helps people travel across the city in safe and comfortable conditions.

Time and again, the Indian Railways has proved to be a pillar of strength to the nation in times of crisis. In one such example, when Chennai faced a major water shortage in 2019, the Indian Railways stepped up to provide support. Seen here are workers collecting water from a special train with 50 wagons that carried 2.5 million litres of water for the city.

A TASTE OF LUXURY

In 1982, India's first luxury tourist train, the Palace on Wheels, rolled out of Delhi, packed with tourists eager to experience the lavish, opulent lifestyle of India's royals. It changed the way Indians looked at train travel, which was no longer a utilitarian tool, but offered opportunities of unparalleled luxury, a way to live life king-size.

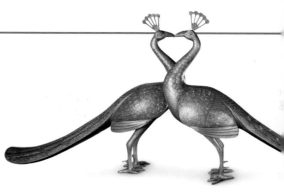

▲ **Decorative peacock** statues in the restaurant of Maharajas' Express.

"... at midnight the Prince drove to the Special Train stabled at Kirkee where the servants had arranged luxurious beds in the carriages, and in half an hour more they were rattling away from the former capital of Peshwas, on their return trip to Bombay, sleeping as securely as they were at home," recounted William Howard Russell, the honorary private secretary of the Prince of Wales, Albert Edward, who was touring India in 1875. This was his first trip to India and he was suitably impressed by the "Special Train". Almost a home away from home, the East Indian Railway (EIR) built it for the occasion, surpassing itself in

1905 during the next royal visit when it built nine saloon carriages, of which seven were longer than what ran in England at the time. Full-sized baths with showers and douches, a first, were also added.

In the pre-Independence era, luxury trains were used mostly by the affluent and royals. Elaborate, opulent coaches were the norm for the Viceroys and a source of pride for the royalty, whether it was the Gaekwad of Baroda, Maharajas of Jaipur and Jodhpur, or the Nizam of Hyderabad.

The monopoly of the royals over luxury ended towards the end of the 20th century with the introduction

of the Palace on Wheels in 1982. The tourist train drew inspiration from its royal past and proved its potential as a tool of profit. Luxury rail travel was now available to those willing, and able, to pay for it.

A touch of the old

The lifestyle of pre-Independence Princely States and their love for plush saloons deeply influenced the Palace on Wheels (see pp.272–77). Western Railway assembled and the Ajmer Workshop rebuilt the 20 cars, including 12 vintage saloons and dining, lounge, and service cars. A precursor of all the luxury trains in India, it was fully booked on its

inaugural run and earned around $1 million – a princely sum in the 1980s. The modern broad-gauge train later replaced this metre-gauge version and continues to run today.

In the lap of luxury
There was no doubt that luxury train travel had immense potential in the Indian market, and it was only a matter of time that the Palace on Wheels would soon have competition.

In 1994–95, Gujarat Tourism and the Indian Railways launched the Royal Orient, which took its passengers on a tour of Gujarat and Rajasthan in palatial carriages named after Rajput kingdoms of old. The one-of-a-kind Deccan Odyssey followed in 2004, inspired by the travelling saloons of the Maratha rulers, with royal blue coaches that took their names from Maharashtrian sites and monuments. The Golden Chariot, which traverses south and south-west India, flagged off in 2008 and was followed by the Royal Rajasthan on Wheels in 2009. Each train had its own route and identity.

The goal, though, was the same – to offer unforgettable, experiential travel, something ordinary passenger trains could not.

Like kings and queens
While the Palace on Wheels had always been the premier name in luxury trains, the Maharajas' Express went a step further. Inaugurated in 2010, it wove the elegance and opulence of India's kings and queens with the country's history and heritage. With guest saloons named after the nine precious gemstones or *Navratnas*, this award-winning train blended tradition with modern facilities. It travels on four different routes, taking the traveller from the hot deserts of Rajasthan to the glory of the Taj Mahal, the ghats of Varanasi, and the World Heritage Site at Khajuraho.

Operated by the Indian Railways Catering and Tourism Corporation (IRCTC), the train won the prestigious World's Leading Luxury Train Award at the World Travel Awards for seven consecutive years, starting in 2012.

FOLLOWING THE BUDDHA
This spiritual journey, based on the prominent Buddhist text, *Mahaparinirvana Sutra*, was commissioned in 2007 as Mahaparinirvana Express. It was later renamed the Buddhist Circuit Special Train. The train travels to key Buddhist sacred sites, including Lumbini, where Buddha was born, Bodhgaya, where he gained enlightenment, Sarnath, where he taught, and Kushinagar, where he attained nirvana. In 2018, the train got a new rake with modern facilities and a kitchen.

1. The lounge carriage inside the Palace on Wheels **2.** The exterior of the Maharajas' Express **3.** A uniformed attendant outside the Deccan Odyssey **4.** A delectable plate of food served in the Maharajas' Express **5.** The Safari Bar in the Maharajas' Express **6.** Musicians welcoming guests to the Golden Chariot

PALACE ON WHEELS

Travelling in the style of a Maharaja through India's most evocative destinations is one of the most luxurious railway experiences. The Palace on Wheels, one of the world's top five luxury trains, is a reconstruction based on the personal carriages of the rulers of Rajputana and Gujarat, the Nizams of Hyderabad, and the Viceroys of India. Each carriage is named after a Princely State of Rajasthan, with interiors that reflect its history through paintings, furniture, and handicrafts.

ASPIRING TO ROYALTY

In 1982, the Indian Railways teamed up with the Rajasthan Tourism Development Cooperation to provide a luxury metre-gauge service with plush carriages that emulated the grand decor of an earlier age. In the 1990s, the service was switched to broad gauge and the accommodation was replaced with air-conditioned cabins and attached bathrooms. Still running today, the train is made up of 14 saloons, a kitchen car, two restaurants, a bar with a lounge, and four service cars. To add a further touch of royal experience, the train offers personal *khidmatgars* (attendants), who are available to serve guests around the clock.

STEAM ENGINE

DIESEL ENGINE

Trip of a lifetime
The week-long trip on the Palace on Wheels takes passengers through north-western India on a nostalgic journey to some of the most popular tourist spots in the Golden Triangle.

SPECIFICATIONS			
In-service	1982–present	**Route**	Rajasthan and the Golden Triangle (Delhi–Jaipur–Agra)
Passenger capacity	Approx. 80	**Coaches**	14

Windows run on the full length of the carriage

Exterior paintwork is identical on every saloon carriage

Coat of arms identifies the Princely State that inspired the interior decoration

Painted sign shows the name of the saloon carriage

Passenger doors at each end with stylized oval windows

Dining in the lap of luxury
The two restaurant cars on board the Palace on Wheels are called Maharaja (shown here) and Maharani. Guests are served fresh food prepared in the attached kitchen car.

JAIPUR SALOON AND BEDROOM

The Jaipur saloon is decorated in colours that represent the former Rajput State of Jaipur, while the exterior of the carriage bears its coat of arms. The ceiling is adorned with the region's famed *phad* (foil work) and illustrates religious festivals such as Teej, Holi, Gangaur, and Diwali. Each saloon consists of four coupés (sleeping rooms) and a bathroom. A mini pantry and a lounge provides additional comfort.

1. Name of car embossed on metal plate   **2.** *Phad* (foil work) on ceiling depicting festivals celebrated in Rajasthan
3. Glass and gilt ceiling light   **4.** Saloon with banquet-style sofas and painted fresco ceiling   **5.** Metal hand plate on door
6. Coupé   **7.** Carriage corridor   **8.** Mirror inside the coupé   **9.** Private bathroom with elegant modern fittings and mirror
10. Switches for light and music.

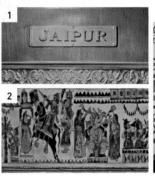

PALACE ON WHEELS BAR

The lounge bar is designed to reflect a contemporary royal style with flourishes that hark back to the Princely State Rajput era. With its wood, marble, and brass fixtures, the bar area epitomizes the aesthetic of the time. A selection of antique pitcher designs ornament the front of the counter area, depicting some of the drink-pouring vessels the Maharajas would have used.

11. Bar and lounge carriage   **12.** Marble-top bar counter   **13.** Antique pitcher design in marble, with gold inlay work, on front of bar counter   **14.** Emergency stop chain   **15.** Chandelier   **16.** Peacock motif in tinted glass   **17.** *Jaali* (latticework) teak panel
18. Armchairs with *patra* (oxidized white metal) work on borders   **19.** Deep-cushioned sofa with raw silk upholstery   **20.** Intricately carved elephant head design – a symbol of prosperity – at end of armrest

MAHARANI RESTAURANT

The Rajasthani theme continues in the interior design of the Maharani dining cabin, with floral carpets and curtains, and featuring framed art from the Mughal period hanging on the walls. The most opulent touch is arguably the mirrored and teakwood-panelled ceiling.

1. Sumptuous dining room with mirrored ceiling   **2.** Mughal art in marble, created with vegetable colours, on carriage wall   **3.** Silk-embroidered drapes with floral design   **4.** Tree motif in stained glass on restaurant door   **5.** Panelled corridor   **6.** Kitchen positioned at one end of restaurant car

MAHARAJA RESTAURANT

Royal blue-coloured drapes adorn the elegant, mahogony-led decor of the Maharani dining carriage. The seating is arranged in groups of four. Both restaurants serve different varieties of cuisine, although there is an emphasis on Rajasthani dishes.

7. Name plaque above the door   **8.** Air vent in central ceiling panel   **9.** Wall light with painted glass shade   **10.** Gold-embroidered *zari* work on velvet drape   **11.** Restaurant carriage decorated with mahogany panelling

ROYAL SPA

The Palace on Wheels boasts a car dedicated to spa services. It is the most recent addition to the luxury experience. Although still majestic, the decor of the treatment rooms is toned down to encourage maximum customer relaxation. The fully equipped spa offers massages, treatments, and various revitalizing solutions.

12. Corridor in the Royal Spa **13.** Double-bed massage suite **14.** Reclining chair and sink **15.** Pedicure bowl with rose petals

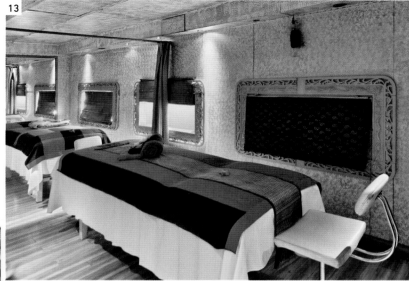

GENERATOR CAR AND GUARD'S COMPARTMENT

The guard's compartment and generator car are located away from the palatial setting of the passenger carriages. The generator provides electricity to power the lights, appliances, kitchen, and bar equipment. In the guard's cabin, a close eye is kept on gauge and meter readings to ensure the train runs smoothly and that passengers have a comfortable trip.

16. Power control panel in the generator car **17.** Guard's compartment **18.** Handbrake **19.** Temperature control panel **20.** Vent control **21.** Air brake

The fine dining restaurant in the Maharajas' Express recreates a luxurious royal experience. Named Mayur Mahal, after India's national bird, the peacock, it is ornately decorated, with a golden statue of a peacock adorning its entrance. The menu comprises flavourful dishes from cuisines around the world and guests are served with gold-plated cutlery.

TRAINS OF TODAY

As the country inched towards a new millennium, it was faced with the challenge of catering to the changing requirements of its people. The need for an efficient, cheap, and comfortable way to travel along long routes and to remote areas became more than evident. Indian Railways introduced many new categories of trains in the first decade of the 21st century to make its services accessible to people with different economic backgrounds.

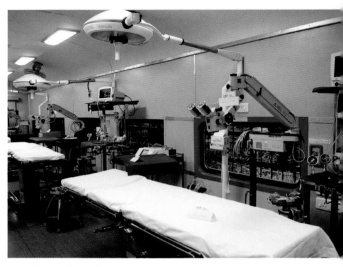

HOSPITAL ON WHEELS

The Lifeline Express, also called the Jeevan Rekha Express, is a hospital tra providing medical care to people living in remote rural areas. Launched in 1991 in collaboration with a Mumbai-based non-governmental organization (NGO) Impact India Foundation, the train travels across the country to state such as Rajasthan in the north-west, Maharashtra in the west, and Tripura a Assam in the north-east. The train is styled like a hospital, with operation theatres, pharmacies, patient wards, as well as dental and mammography units. Over the years, it has provided medical support to millions of people

POINT-TO-POINT

Introduced in 2009, the Duronto Express is a long-distance, non-stop train service running between major cities in the country. It derives its name from the Bengali word *duronto*, meaning "without a stop". One of the fastest train services in India with a maximum speed of 130 km/h, the first train in this category ran between Sealdah, Kolkata, and New Delhi in September 2009. These trains have both air-conditioned (AC) and non-AC sleeper coaches. The coaches are characterized by bright yellow- and green-coloured abstract designs.

WITHIN THE STATES

The Rajya Rani Express connects state capitals to other important cities in the states. Launched in 2011, the first one ran between Mysore and Bengaluru in July. Other routes include Lucknow–Meerut, Mumbai–Manmad, Bengaluru–Pune, and Patna–Saharsa. These trains run on a daily basis, with the exception of the Bankura–Howrah Express and Jharsuguda–Bhubaneswar Express, both of which run triweekly. While most of these have chair cars, some offer sleeping accommodation.

CAPITAL CONNECTION

The Sampark Kranti literally meaning "connectivity revolution", provides connectivity between the national capital, Delhi, and other cities. The Express train is effectively a more affordable version of the famous Rajdhani Express. Initially a non-stop service, stoppages were added later. With a maximum speed of 110 km/h and fewer stops, it has drastically reduced the travel time. It also offers value-added services, such as a public address system and dedicated staff. The first train ran between Delhi's Hazrat Nizamuddin and Bengaluru's Yeshwanthpur in February 2004.

FOR THE PEOPLE

The Garib Rath Express was started by the Indian Railways in 2006 with an aim to provide passengers with affordable, long-distance, air-conditioned train service. The first train from this category ran between Saharsa in northern Bihar to Amritsar in Punjab in October 2006. The speed matches Rajdhani and Duronto Express. The Garib Raths have chair cars for seating and three-tier coaches, with more accommodation than in regular AC coaches. The Kapurthala Coach Factory provided the coaches for this service.

FLOOR ON FLOOR

Similar to double-decker buses, the Double Decker Express has two floors of accommodation and can thus cater to far more passengers than other trains. The first double-decker train ran between Howrah in West Bengal and Dhanbad in Jharkhand in 2011. These air-conditioned trains usually run on shorter routes, such as Jaipur–New Delhi, Mumbai–Ahmedabad, and Chennai–Bengaluru. One of the fast train services in Indian Railways, these are given high priority on the network.

FAST AND FURIOUS

The Tejas Express was introduced as the first semi-high speed train service in India. Though capable of running at 180 km/h, its operational speed is restricted to a maximum of 130 km/h. The first train ran between Mumbai and Goa in May 2017. This fully air-conditioned train service has modern facilities, such as LED TVs, bio-vacuum toilets, and Wi-Fi connections. The Lucknow–New Delhi Tejas Express is the first train to be operated independently by the IRCTC, followed by a second one between Mumbai and Ahmedabad.

VANDE BHARAT EXPRESS

In 2018, India took another leap towards railway advancement with the production of its first semi-high speed train set. Code-named Train 18, later renamed the Vande Bharat Express, it was manufactured by the Integral Coach Factory (ICF) in Chennai under the Government's "Make in India" programme. The first one, bound for Varanasi in Uttar Pradesh, was flagged off from New Delhi in February 2019. In the same year in October, a second train ran between New Delhi and Katra in Jammu and Kashmir.

This engineless train can gain speed up to 160 km/h, reducing the journey time considerably. Moreover, it is equipped with modern facilities, such as onboard Wi-Fi, touch-free bio-vacuum toilets, and a climate control system that automatically adjusts the temperature. The trains also have soothing LED lighting, GPS-based information systems, automatic doors, dual-mode lighting, improved insulation, a talk-back facility for the driver, and a pantry attached to each coach.

The train, one of the fastest to have ever run on Indian tracks, has 16 air-conditioned coaches. It also has two centre executive class compartments with rotating seats to match the direction of the train.

A major breakthrough was its production cost, which was far lower than the cost at which it would have been if imported. It will revolutionize the way Indians travel in the years to come.

Each of the 16 coaches of the Vande Bharat Express have 78 spacious, comfortable seats, with inbuilt entertainment facilities.

This world-class, white-nosed train, was built by Indian engineers from the Integral Coach Factory (ICF) in 18 months. The Vande Bharat Express was manufactured keeping in mind industry standard specifications with zero compromise on safety parameters.

ICONIC TRAIN JOURNEYS

Train journeys in India are experiential. The geography of the country is so varied, encompassing mountains, rivers, forests, and deserts, that while undertaking train journeys, travellers are bound to get immersed in mesmerizing views of lush green vegetation, breathtaking waterfalls, or spectacular ocean waters. Train journeys can encapsulate the entire idea of India itself.

Dudhsagar Falls

◀ **THROUGH THE WATER**

Goa Express, *Vasco da Gama, Goa–New Delhi*

When it rains, the waters over the four-tiered waterfall known as the Dudhsagar Falls in Goa turn into a sea of milk. Hold your breath for the Goa Express that crawls its way, almost nonchalantly, over a moss-covered bridge, and past the white foam tumbling over the rocks from a height of 310 m. This section of the track is called the Braganza Ghat, 26-km-long, connecting Goa with the southern state of Karnataka on a ruling gradient of 1 in 37, passing through several tunnels. This is the highlight of the route that passes through the Konkan zone and connects Goa, a state along the western coast of India, with New Delhi, the capital of the country. While one can see the waterfalls and travel by train anytime during the year, it is best to experience it in the monsoon (June–August) as the Sahyadri Hills turn an emerald green and a train journey through this section is a sight to behold.

Darjeeling Himalayan Railway

▲ INTO THE CLOUDS

Darjeeling Himalayan Railway,
New Jalpaiguri–Darjeeling,
West Bengal

Travel to Darjeeling under the shadow of the mighty Kanchenjunga, the third highest mountain in the world and marvel at the sheer ingenuity of railway engineering while travelling on the Darjeeling Himalayan Railway (see pp.86–87), a UNESCO World Heritage Site. A must for train enthusiasts, it is perfect for those seeking to explore the breathtaking Himalayas, technically challenging reversing stations, and stomach-churning loops, one of which takes the train right up to the very edge of the mountain. A quick fix lies in the special two-hour "joyrides" in trains pulled by steam locomotives that can take the traveller from Darjeeling to Ghum, the highest railway station in the country, and back. Though the real experience belongs to the seven-hour journey of 88 km that begins at New Jalpaiguri in Siliguri. Leave the hustle of city life along the way to travel through the ever-changing landscape along the Hill Cart Road, from the very edge of the forests where the trees almost scrape the train, past the tortuous Agony Point and up the mountain, to Darjeeling.

▶ AROUND THE LAKE

Konark Express,
Bhubaneswar–Brahmapur

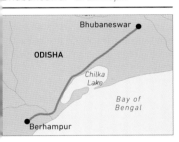

offering stunning views of the lagoon, the never-ending expanse of water, some with the fields in the foreground, and bamboo boundaries marking the fishing areas. Certain trains run right along the lake, so keep an eye out for the moment when the track curves to catch a glimpse of the locomotive as it turns.

Chilika Lake, Odisha

Asia's largest saltwater lagoon, the Chilika Lake is spread across 1,100 sq km and is situated in the eastern state of Odisha. A favourite with birdwatchers, it is one of the largest breeding grounds for flamingoes. Dotted with small islands, salt pans, and fisheries, the spectacular lake is equally impressive from a train window. Fast trains take 15 minutes to pass the lake,

Nilgiri Mountain Railways

▲ DESERT TRAIN

Delhi–Jaisalmer Express,
Jodhpur–Jaisalmer

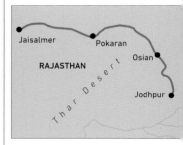

There are several trains that make their way to Jaisalmer in the desert state of Rajasthan. However, the Delhi–Jaisalmer Express is the best way to savour the actual breadth of the state. An overnight journey from the capital, the actual desert experience begins as the train pulls into Jodhpur. Watch the early morning sun over the blue city and the dunes emerge past the ancient town of Osian, an oasis and an important pilgrimage centre. The barren Pokhran, the famous nuclear test site, is another stop before the final destination, Jaisalmer, a city in the heart of the massive Thar desert. The never-ending, arid landscape adds its own charm to the journey, which offers a glimpse into the colourful towns and villages that the train passes through.

▲ THROUGH THE BLUE MOUNTAINS

Nilgiri Mountain Railway,
Mettupalayam–Udhagamandalam

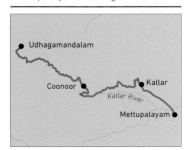

Rolling, green hills, tiny stations with quaint names, and innumerable bridges and tunnels, all form a part of an unforgettable, one-of-a-kind train journey through the Nilgiri Mountains of southern India. The journey begins at the foothills in Mettupalayam in Coimbatore, where the Nilgiri Mountain Railway (see pp.92–93), the star of many Indian films, begins its service. The metre-gauge rack railway winds its way through forests, past waterfalls and tea estates on its 46-km-journey to Ooty or Ootamaund (officially known as Udagamandalam), climbing from 326 m to 2,203 m. It has one of the steepest gradients in the country, which is why, at the rack section, the train almost seems to crawl, making its way up at 13 km/h. This, however, makes it the perfect speed to take in the surroundings, admire the ingenuity of the railway engineers, and look around in awe at the craggy hills, deep tunnels, and steep bridges.

▶ SNOWY PARADISE

74614, *Banihal–Baramulla*

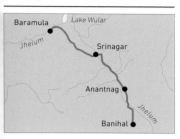

Don't go by the train's rather prosaic name. The journey from Banihal to the ancient town of Baramulla in the Vale of Kashmir is far more poetic. The landscape changes dramatically through the course of the journey, which begins at Banihal and crosses the Pir Panjal range, separating Jammu from the Kashmir Valley. The DEMU (Diesel–electric Multiple Unit) makes its way past the Jammu hills through the Pir Panjal railway tunnel, which at over 11 km is the longest in India. A little over nine minutes later, it emerges into the Kashmir Valley, with its rolling hills, Chir pines, and snow-clad mountains. En route, the train travels 110 km in two and-a half hours through Anantnag, Srinagar, Kashmir's capital, and finally Baramulla on the banks of the Jhelum River. It is best to make the trip during winter when the region is snowbound or after the monsoon in August to experience the breathtaking landscape in its glory.

Banihal–Baramulla

The 13–Arch bridge

▲ ROYAL TRAIN

Chennai Egmore–Kollam Junction Express, *Sengottai–Punalur*

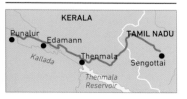

For over a century, the small town of Sengottai was a part of an important rail link, which connected the Madras Presidency with Kollam, the capital of the Travancore kingdom and now in Kerala. Passing through the foothills of the Western Ghats, the line connected the south-western coast with the south-eastern side. It was crucial for the trade and transportation of spices and cashew. The train became popular with the royal families as well. The Sengottai–Punalur section, however, became popular for its scenic beauty. The section closed in 2010 while the line was converted from metre to broad gauge, reopening in 2018. Travel by the Chennai–Kollam line, considered a reincarnation of the original royal line inaugurated in 1904, to take in the lush Ghats and admire the iconic 102-m 13 Kannara or 13-Arch Bridge that curves to connect two hills. Along the way, as the train enters the Aryankavu Tunnel, try to spot a conch engraved into the pillars, a symbol of the Travancore dynasty.

▶ THE KONKAN EXPERIENCE

Mandovi Express,
Mumbai–Madgaon

This journey is the perfect way to experience the Konkan Railway in all its glory. The monsoon is the best time to travel, accompanied by moody, overcast skies and surrounded by the lush green of the Western Ghats as the train, twists, turns, and curves its way towards the coast. This is also the time to see the waterfalls as they are full to the brim during the rains. Among these is the Ranpat Waterfall near Ratnagiri in Maharashtra. The train also crosses over the vertigo-inducing Panval Nadi viaduct in Ratnagiri, once India's tallest bridge. The landscape from the train window constantly changes, passing over swift rivers, through paddy fields, coconut trees, and little stations, giving but a hint of life along the Konkan coast.

Konkan Railways train

Pamban Bridge

◀ AT SEA

Sethu Express, *Mandapam–Pamban–Rameswaram*

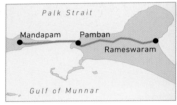

Visualize a train, tentatively making its way across a bridge, bordered as it is by the deceptive calm of a blue-green sea. This is the highlight of a train ride in Tamil Nadu, from the small town of Mandapam to Rameswaram, considered one of the holiest places for Hindus. The line crosses the iconic Pamban Bridge (see pp.98–99), the first of its kind in India, when it opened in 1915. It was briefly closed for repair work in December 2018. Breathe in the salty air of the Indian Ocean that almost seems to envelop the bridge. One could take the Boat Mail as well which at one point went up to the abandoned town of Dhanushkodi on Pamban Island, to watch the early morning sun over the ocean as the train crosses over the bridge to enter Rameswaram.

Along the river

▲ INTO THE HEART OF THE NORTH-EAST

Kanchenjunga Express,
Silchar–Lumding

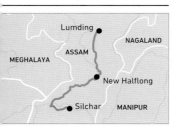

Curved bridges, tracks, and almost never-ending tunnels, valleys, plantations, hills, and rivers are all packed into this 210-km journey into the north-eastern state of Assam. Known as the "pahad" or mountain line, the curvy tracks allow travellers to see the train twist and turn as it chugs through the mountains or peer over the edge at the rivers below. The new broad-gauge line is as impressive as the old metre-gauge one, even though its construction proved as challenging as the first line in the 1880s. A key stop is New Haflong, which serves the state's only hill station, Halflong at nearly 700 m before ending its journey at Lumding, one of the oldest stations in the region.

TOUCH OF THE SOUTH

Island Express,
Kanyakumari, Tamil Nadu – Thiruvananthapuram, Kerala

No one really knows why this train is called the Island Express, for it does not cross an island at any point in its journey from Kanyakumari, on the southernmost tip of the country to Thiruvananthapuram, in Kerala, God's own country. It is not an official name either, but is entrenched in public memory. It is possible that this happened sometime in the 1960s, when the train began its journey from Willingdon Island, an artificial island in Kerala. Travel by the train as it makes its slow, meandering journey past quaint stations, palm trees, tiny temples and, as the train crosses into Kerala, churches that dot the landscape. This is the best way to experience the heart of southern India.

GLOSSARY

ADHESION
Frictional grip between the wheels of a locomotive and the rail of a track, which is affected by axle weight.

AIR BRAKE
Braking system that uses compressed air as its operating medium. While applying the brake, compressed air is released into a cylinder, pushing a piston and spring that pushes the brake block against the wheel.

ALTERNATING CURRENT (AC)
Electric current that reverses its direction of flow rapidly at regular intervals. *See also* Direct current (DC).

AQUEDUCT
Bridge built on arches with stone channels to supply water. Aqueducts source water from distant waterbodies and carry it across difficult landscapes.

AXLE
Rod that connects a pair of wheels.

BOILER
Part of the steam engine where steam is produced and circulated. The boiler must be filled with water almost to the brim. This water is generally heated to produce steam, which builds a high pressure.

BRAKE
Brakes help to slow down or halt a locomotive. They are activated by either air, steam, or a vacuum. *See also* Air brake, Vacuum brake.

BRAKE VAN
Usually, located at the end of a train, brake vans are a railway carriage or vehicle from which brakes can be applied by the train's guard.

BRANCH LINE
Secondary rail line that branches off of a main line, usually to serve local stations.

BALLAST
The bed of stone or gravel on which a railway track is laid.

BO-BO
A common axle configuration that describes a locomotive that has two groups of twin-set powered axles.

CHIMNEY
Opening in the top of the smokebox through which exhaust gases and steam escape. Also called a smokestack or stack.

CO-CO
A common axle configuration that describes a diesel or electric locomotive that has two triple-sets of powered axles.

COMPOUND LOCOMOTIVE
Steam locomotive that uses two sets of cylinders, where the second one is powered by exhaust steam from the first.

CONNECTING ROD
A connecting rod links the piston rods to the crankpins of the drive wheels in a steam engine.

CONTAINER
Standardized metal freight box that can be packed with goods, sealed, and then transported by specially adapted trains. Containers are intermodal, ensuring door-to-door transportation.

COUPLING
The mechanism for connecting rolling stock. Methods are standardized across a single line to allow any rolling stock to be coupled together. *See also* Rolling stock.

CAB
Control room of a locomotive, housing the engine crew.

CAR, CARRIAGE, COACH
Various terms that describe a passenger-carrying vehicle.

CLASS
Group of locomotives built as per a common design. It can also refer to the level of comfort and services provided on a particular train, for instance, first class and second class.

CRIMINAL TRIBES
A discriminatory term that was first used during the British rule under the Criminal Tribes Act. The tribes listed under the Act were classified as "habitual criminals". They were denotified in 1952.

CYLINDER
Enclosed chamber in which a piston moves to produce power that is transmitted to the wheels. On a steam locomotive, the piston is moved by the force of high pressure steam acting against it.

DIESEL-ELECTRIC
Any locomotive, multiple unit, or car that utilizes the diesel-electric system. In a diesel-electric, mechanical power generated by combustion is then converted into an electric charge in a generator or alternator, and this electricity is used to power motors that drive the axles.

DIRECT CURRENT (DC)
An electric current that flows in a constant direction. *See also* Alternating current (AC).

ELEVATED RAILWAY
Railway built on raised platforms.

EMBANKMENT
Raised pathway across a depression in the landscape that enables a rail track to maintain a shallow gradient.

ENGINE
Power source of a locomotive. It can be driven by steam, electricity, or diesel.

EXPRESS TRAIN
A train that stops only at certain stations on its route in order to reach its final destination faster. An express train need not be a particularly fast train, although it is expected to run faster than the ordinary passengers on the same route.

SUPERFAST TRAIN
A train that averages a speed of above 55 km/h from its origin to its destination.

FIREBOX
Section at the rear of a steam locomotive boiler that houses the fire that heats the water in the boiler. Fuel is fed into the firebox from the cab, and the generated heat is fed through the boiler by the fire tubes.

FIVE-YEAR PLAN
An economic programme with objectives spread over five years adopted by the Government of India. The Government prepares a document that has a plan for all its income and expenditure for the next five years. The 12th Five Year Plan (2012–17) was the last in India.

FREIGHT
Load of materials or products carried on trains. The term is also used to describe trains transporting finished goods and raw materials.

GAUGE
Distance between the inside running edges of the rails of a track.

GENERATOR
An electromechanical device that converts mechanical energy to electrical energy in the form of direct current (DC).

GRADIENT
The slope of a track. It is expressed in ratio form in terms of the height covered per unit of horizontal distance.

INJECTOR
Device that feeds water into the boiler of a steam locomotive against the pressure of steam in that boiler.

LIGHT RAIL
Form of rail that typically operates within urban environments or in low density non-urban areas.

LOCOMOTIVE
A wheeled vehicle used for pulling trains. Steam and diesel locomotives generate their own power, while electric locomotives collect electricity from an external source.

LOOP
A railway formation where tracks cross over themselves as they ascend a mountain.

MAIL TRAINS
Earmarked for carrying mail in addition to passengers, mail trains have special mail vans attached. Historically, these were accorded higher priority and ran with high speed to enable quick delivery of mail.

MAIN LINE
An important rail line, often running between major towns or cities.

MONORAIL
Railway system based on a single rail.

MULTIPLE UNIT (MU)
A term used in diesel and electric traction that refers to the semi-permanent coupling of several powered and unpowered vehicles to form a single train.

PASSENGER TRAIN
A train with cars intended to transport people. These trains travel between stations at which passengers may embark or disembark.

RACK RAILWAY
A railway with an additional toothed rack-rail. A train or locomotive running on the railway is equipped with a cog that has lines with the teeth on the rail, enabling it to climb slopes that would not be possible for a normal train.

REVERSER
Mechanism with a wheel or lever that controls the forward and reverse motion of a steam locomotive.

ROLLING STOCK
A collection of vehicles that is run by the railways, such as locomotives, carriages, and wagons.

ROUTE KILOMETRE
Distance between two points on the railways irrespective of the number of lines connecting them.

RUNNING BOARD
Footway around a locomotive's engine compartment or boiler.

RUNNING GEAR
Parts that are involved in the movement of an engine, including wheels, axles, axleboxes, bearings, and springs.

SADDLE TANK
Tank locomotive that has the water tank mounted on top of its boiler.

SAFETY VALVES
Relief valves in a steam locomotive boiler. These are set to lift automatically, to allow steam to escape in case the boiler pressure exceeds the set limit.

SALOON
Luxurious rail carriages that were typically used by high-ranking people and royalty for travel. They often had a lounge, and private accommodations.

SIGNAL
Mechanical or electronic fixed unit with an arm or a light that indicates whether a train should stop, go, or use caution.

SLEEPER
Coach or train with beds for passengers on overnight or long-distance journeys. The term also refers to the lateral item that keeps two rails apart at a fixed distance. Sleepers were earlier made of wood, but were later followed by tie-rod sleepers, steel trough sleepers and finally by concrete sleepers on the Indian Railways. Today, all main lines of the Indian Railways use concrete sleepers.

SMOKEBOX
Leading section of a steam locomotive boiler assembly that houses the main steam pipes to the cylinders, the blastpipe, the stack, and the ends of the firetubes. Ash drawn through the firetubes collects here.

STEAM LOCOMOTION
Steam locomotion is founded on the principle that when water is heated above its boiling point, it turns to steam and its volume becomes 1,700 times greater. When this expansion takes place within a sealed vessel such as a boiler, the pressure of the steam becomes a source of energy.

SWITCH
Trackwork mechanism at the point where two tracks diverge, allowing a train to move from one track to another.

TANK LOCOMOTIVE
A steam engine that carries its fuel and water on its own chassis rather than on a separate tender. Water is held in side tanks or in saddle tanks that carry the boiler. *See also* Tender.

TENDER
A vehicle attached to a steam engine that carries fuel and water.

TRACK
Rails, ballast, and fastenings that supply a runway for the wheels of a train.

TRACTION
A force that relies on friction between a wheel and a rail to generate motion.

TRAIN
A form of transport that either has passenger, freight, or both vehicles put together, travelling as one unit along a rail line. Trains are either self-propelled or hauled by a locomotive.

VACUUM BRAKE
Braking system that is held off by a partial vacuum and applied when air is let into the system. This was earlier used in the place of air brakes.

VALVE
Found in steam locomotives, valves coordinate the movement of steam in and out of cylinders. In diesel engines, valves control the fuel intake and expulsion of exhaust gases.

VALVE GEAR
Linkages that connect valves of a steam locomotive and keep in control movement of the valves.

VIADUCT
A long bridge supported by a series of arches. It carries a road or railway across a valley or low-lying land.

WAGON
Type of a rail vehicle that carries freight.

WHEEL ARRANGEMENT
A method of classifying locomotives by the distribution of different types of wheels. For steam locomotives, the Whyte notation is a common system according to which the leading wheels, driving wheels, and trailing wheels, are denoted by a numeral each. Diesel and electric locomotives and powered cars are categorized by the number of powered and unpowered axles they have.

WHEELSET
Assembly that consists of two wheels attached to an axle on a rail vehicle.

YARD
A separate area with multiple tracks and sidings (a short railway track beside the main tracks) for storage, maintenance, and loading and unloading of rolling stock.

ZIGZAG, REVERSING STATION
Method of railway track construction on steep inclines. The train goes up the track in a zigzag fashion.

INDEX

SELECTED BIBLIOGRAPHY

150 Years of Locomotive Works, Jamalpur (1862–2012).

Agarwal, Avinash Kumar, Atul Dhar, Anirudh Gautam, and Ashok Pandey, eds. *Locomotives and Rail Road Transportation: Technology, Challenges and Prospects.* Singapore: Springer, 2017.

Aitken, Bill. *Exploring Indian Railways.* Delhi: Oxford University Press, 1994.

Aiyar, Swarna. "'August Anarchy': The Partition Massacres in Punjab, 1947." South Asia, Vol XVIII, *Special Issue* (1995): 13–36.

Aklekar, Rajendra B. *A Short History of Indian Railways.* New Delhi: Rupa Publications, 2019.

Aklekar, Rajendra B. *Halt Station India: The Dramatic Tale of the Nation's First Rail Lines.* New Delhi: Rupa Publications India, 2014.

Aklekar, Rajendra B. *India's Railway Man: A Biography of E. Sreedharan.* New Delhi: Rupa, 2017.

Ambler, HR. "An Indian "Might-Have-Been"." *The Railway Magazine,* February 1969.

Anand, YP. *Mahatma Gandhi & the Railways.* Ahmedabad: Navajivan Publishing House, 2002.

Anderson, Valerie ER. *The Eurasian problem in nineteenth century India.* PhD Thesis, SOAS (School of Oriental and African Studies), 2011.

Arnold, David. *The New Cambridge History of India: Science, Technology and Medicine in Colonial India.* New York: Cambridge University Press. 2000.

Arora, AK, and BS Misra. *Nehru and Indian Railways.* New Delhi:

Government of India, Ministry of Railways (Railway Board), 1989.

Awasthi, Aruna, and Mohan Menon. *On a Trailblazer's Run... Shaping Indian Railway Managers.* Vadodara: National Academy of Indian Railways, 2019.

Awasthi, Aruna. *History and Development of Railways in India.* New Delhi: Deep & Deep Publications, 1994.

Bayley, Victor. *Permanent Way Through the Khyber.* London: Jarrolds Publishers (London), 1939.

Bear, Laura. *Lines of the Nation: Indian Railway Workers, Bureaucracy, and the Intimate Historical Self.* New York: Columbia University Press, 2007.

Bell, Horace. *Railway Policy in India.* London: Rivington, Percival & Co, 1894.

Berridge, PSA. *Couplings to the Khyber: The Story of the North

Western Railway. Newton Abbot: David & Charles, 1969.

Bhandari, RR. *Exotic Indian Mountain Railways.* New Delhi: Ministry of Railways, 1984.

Bhandari, RR. *Indian Railways: Glorious 150 Years.* New Delhi: Publications Division, Ministry of Information and Broadcasting, Government of India, 2006.

Bhandari, RR. *Kalka-Simla and Kangra Valley Railways.* New Delhi: Northern Railway, 1983.

Bhandari, RR. *Kalka Simla Railway.* New Delhi: National Rail Museum, 2002.

Bhandari, RR. *Nilgiri Railway.* New Delhi: National Rail Museum, 2002.

Bhandari, RR. *Southern Railway: A Saga of 150 Glorious Years, 1852–2003.* Chennai: Southern Railway.

Bhargava, MBL. *India's Services in the War*. Lucknow: MBL Bhargava, 1919.

Bhattacharjea, Ajit. *Countdown to Partition: The Final Days*. New Delhi: Harper Collins, 1997.

Bon Voyage (National Rail Museum Guide). Published by National Rail Museum, New Delhi.

Bose, Saibal, and Subhasis Ganguly. *The Revival of the Beyer-Garratt*. Kolkata: South Eastern Railway, November 2006.

Browning, Oscar. *Impressions of Indian Travel*. London: Hodder and Stoughton, 1903.

Building the Great Himalayan Railway: Udhampur-Srinagar-Baramulla Rail Link (USBRL). CMYK Printech, and USBRL Project, 2018.

Campion, David A. "Railway Policing and Security in Colonial India, c.1860–1930." In *Our Indian Railway: Themes in India's Railway History*, edited by Roopa Srinivasan, Manish Tiwari, and Sandeep Silas, 121–153. New Delhi: Foundation Books, 2006.

Carter, Lionel, ed. *Partition Observed: British Official Reports from South Asia*, 2 Volumes. New Delhi: Manohar, 2011.

Chakrabarty, Dipesh. "The Colonial Context of the Bengal Renaissance: A Note on Early Railway–Thinking in Bengal." In *Our Indian Railway: Themes in India's Railway History*, edited by Roopa Srinivasan, Manish Tiwari, and Sandeep Silas, 2–21. New Delhi: Foundation Books, 2006.

Chandra, Bipin, Mridula Mukherjee et al. *India Since Independence*. Gurgaon: Penguin Random House, 2008.

Chandra, Bipin, Mridula Mukherjee et al. *India's Struggle for Independence*. Gurgaon: Penguin Random House, 2016.

Chandra, Bipin. "Economic Nationalism and the Railway Debate, circa 1880–1905." In *Our Indian Railway: Themes in India's Railway History*, edited by Roopa Srinivasan, Manish Tiwari, and Sandeep Silas, 77–119. New Delhi: Foundation Books, 2006.

Chandra, Satish, and MM. Agarwal. *Railway Engineering*. New Delhi: Oxford University Press, 2007.

Chatterjee, Arup K. *The Purveyors of Destiny: A Cultural Biography of the Indian Railways*. New Delhi: Bloomsbury Publishing India, 2017.

Clarke, Hyde. *Colonization, Defence, and Railways in Our Indian Empire*. London: John Weale, 1857.

Daly, FC. *Manual of Criminal Classes Operating in Bengal*. Calcutta: The Bengal Secretariat Press, 1916.

Darvill, Simon. "India's First Railways." IRFCA, December 2011. https://www.irfca.org/docs/history/india-first-railways.html#ftn1

Darvill, Simon. "The Patiala State Monorail Tramway – A State Reappraisal." IRFCA, 2012. https://www.irfca.org/articles/patiala-monorail-reappraisal.html

Datta, Antar. *Refugees and Borders in South Asia: The Great Exodus of 1971*. New York: Routledge, 2013.

Datta, VN. "The Punjab Boundary Commission Award (12 August, 1947)." *Proceedings of the Indian History Congress*, Vol 59 (1998): 850–862.

Davidson, Edward. *The Railways of India: With an Account of Their Rise, Progress, and Construction*. London: E & FN Spon, 1868.

Debroy, Bibek, Sanjay Chadha, and Vidya Krishnamurthi. *Indian Railways: The Weaving of a National Tapestry*. Gurgaon: Penguin Random House, 2017.

Debroy, Bibek. *The Railway Chronicles*. New Delhi: Synergy Books India, 2019.

Deefholts, Margaret. *Haunting India*. New Jersey: Calcutta Tiljallah Relief, 2003.

Derbyshire, Ian. "The Building of India's Railways: The Application of Western Technology in the Colonial Periphery 1850–1920." In *Railways in Modern India*, edited by Ian J Kerr, 268–303. New Delhi: Oxford University Press, 2001.

Dutta, Arup Kumar. *Indian Railways, the Final Frontier: Genesis and Growth of the North-East Frontier Railway*. Guwahati: Northeast Frontier Railway, 2002.

Dutta, Joydeep. "The Romance of Steam." In *Steaming On: 20 Years of ISRS (Selected Writings from the ISRS Journals)*, 167–171.

Eleventh Five-Year Plan (2007–2012), Planning Commission, Government of India.

French, Patrick. *Liberty or Death: India's Journey to Independence and Division*. London: Flamingo, 1998.

Ganachari, Aravind. "First World War: Purchasing Indian Loyalties: Imperial Policy of Recruitment and "Reward"." *Economic and Political Weekly*, Vol 40, No 8, 19–25 February (2005): 779–788.

Gandhi, MK. *Hind Swaraj or Indian Home Rule*. Ahmedabad: Navajivan Publishing House.

Ghosh, Sitansu Sekhar. *Railways in India—A Legend: Origin & Development (1830–1980)*. Kolkata, Jogemaya Prokashani, 2006.

Gupta, Amit Kumar. "Defying Death: Nationalist Revolutionism in India, 1897–1938." *Social Scientist*, Vol 25, No 9/10, September–October (1997): 3–27.

Gupta, Arvind. "Indian Contribution to the First World War." *Journal of Defence Studies*, Vol 8, No 3, July–September (2014): 121–133.

Gupta, Manmathnath. *They Lived Dangerously: Reminiscences of a Revolutionary*. Delhi: People's Publishing House, 1969.

Hasan, Mushirul. "Memories of a Fragmented Nation: Rewriting the Histories of India's Partition." *Economic and Political Weekly*, Vol 33, No 41, 10–16 October (1998): 2662–2668.

Headrick, Daniel R. *The Tentacles of Progress: Technology Transfer in the Age of Imperialism, 1850–1940*. New York: Oxford University Press, 1988.

Hookm, Jo. *The Koochpurwanaypore Swadeshi Railway*. Calcutta: Thacker, Spink & Co.

Hurd, John, and Ian J Kerr. *Indian's Railway History: A Research Handbook*. Leiden: Brill, 2012.

Hurd, John. "Railways." In *Railways in Modern India*, edited by Ian J Kerr, 147–172. New Delhi: Oxford University Press, 2001.

Hutheesing, Krishna Nehru. *With No Regrets: An Autobiography*. Bombay: Padma Publications, 1946.

Indian Mutiny: Brief Narrative of the Defence of the Arrah Garrison (written by one of the besieged party). London: W Thacker & Co, 1858.

Indian Railways Fan Club (IRFCA). https://www.irfca.org/

Jhingron, AK. *Western Railway: Heritage, Traditions and Legend*. Mumbai: Western Railway, 2009.

Kennedy, Michael. *The Criminal Classes in India*. Delhi: Mittal Publications, 1985.

Kerr, Ian J. *Building the Railways of the Raj: 1850–1900*. Delhi: Oxford University Press, 1995.

Kerr, Ian J. *Engines of Change: The Railroads That Made India*. Westport: Praeger, 2007.

Kerr, Ian J. "Representation and Representations of the Railways of Colonial and Post-Colonial South Asia." *Modern Asian Studies*, Vol 37, No 2, May (2003): 287–326.

Khanna, ML. "Waging War!" In *Steaming On: 20 Years of ISRS (Selected Writings from the ISRS Journals)*, 43–45.

Khosla, GS. *Railway Management in India*. Bombay: Thacker & Co, 1972.

Kipling, Rudyard. *Kim*. New York: Doubleday & Company, 1901.

Kitchlew, RN. *Gauge Policy of Indian Railways*. Allahabad: R.N. Kitchlew, 1933.

Lawrence, John T. "The Railway System of Northern India." *The Railway Magazine*, November 1898.

Lehmann, Fritz. "Empire and Industry: Locomotive Building Industries in Canada and India, 1850–1939." *Proceedings of the Indian History Congress*, Vol 40 (1979): 985–996.

Lindley, Mark. *J.C. Kumarappa: Mahatma Gandhi's Economist*. Mumbai: Popular Prakashan, 2007.

Macgeorge, GW. *Ways and Works in India: Being an Account of the Public Works in that Country from the Earliest Times up to the Present Day*. Westminster: Archibald Constable and Company, 1894.

Manto, Saadat Hasan. "Toba Tek Singh." Translated by Tahira Naqvi. *Manoa*, Vol 19, No 1 (2007): 14–19.

Marx, Karl. "The Future Results of the British Rule in India." In *Railways in Modern India*, edited by Ian J Kerr, 62–67. New Delhi: Oxford University Press, 2001.

Mathur, Vinoo N. *Bridges, Buildings & Black Beauties of Northern Railway: Glimpses of the Rich Heritage of India's Premier Railway*. New Delhi: Institute of Rail Transport, 2008.

Mcgirk, Tim. "The last gasp for India's age of steam: Drivers mourn locomotives that united a nation." *Independent*, 19 December 1993.

Menon, Visalakshi, and Sucheta Mahajan. "Indian Nationalism and

Railways." In *Our Indian Railway: Themes in India's Railway History*, edited by Roopa Srinivasan, Manish Tiwari, and Sandeep Silas, 155–171. New Delhi: Foundation Books, 2006.

Millions on the Move: The Aftermath of Partition. Delhi: Publications Division, Ministry of Information & Broadcasting, Government of India.

Mitchell, John W. *The Wheels of Ind*. London: Thornton Butterworth Ltd, 1934.

Morris, Jan, and Simon Winchester. *Stones of Empire: The Buildings of the Raj*. Oxford: Oxford University Press, 1983.

Mughal, Owais. "The Chappar Rift." IRFCA, October 2009. https://www.irfca.org/articles/chappar-rift.html

Naidu, Rai Bahadur M Pauparao. *The History of Railway Thieves in India: With Illustrations & Hints on Detection*. Haryana: Vintage Books, 1996.

Naidu, V Parankusam. *Our Railways*. Chennai: Santhi Publishers, 2010.

Narayan, RK. *My Days: A Memoir*. New York: Viking Press, 1974.

Nilakant, V, and S Ramnarayan. *Changing Tracks: Reinventing the Spirit of Indian Railways*. Noida: Collins Business, 2009.

Nilgiri Railway (India) No 944 bis, UNESCO World Heritage Site.

Nock, OS. *Railways of Asia and the Far East* (Volume 5 in *Railways of the World*). New Delhi: Allied Publishers, 1980.

O'Dwyer, Sir Michael. *India as I Knew It, 1885–1925*. London: Constable & Company, 1925.

Pandey, Amitabh. *When It Clicks: Field Notes from India's E-Commerce Revolution*. New Delhi: Pan Macmillan, 2019.

Pinto, Jerry. "Railways' Filmy Chakkar." In *India Junction: A Window to the Nation*, edited by Seema Sharma, 91–101. New Delhi: Rupa Publications India, 2014.

Ponnuswamy, S. *Bridge Engineering*. New Delhi: Tata McGraw-Hill Publishing Company, 2008.

Prasad, Ritika. *Tracks of Change: Railways and Everyday Life in Colonial India*. Delhi: Cambridge University Press, 2015.

Railway budget speeches, Government of India.

Rajaraman, V. "History of Computing in India, 1955–2010." Bangalore: Supercomputer Education and Research Centre (Indian Institute of Science), 2012.

Ramani, KV. "Impact of Computerisation on Indian Railways." IIMA Working Papers, No 924, March 1991.

Rao, BV Rama. "Computers on the Indian Railways." *Economic and Political Weekly*, Vol 8, No 47, November 24 (1973): 117–119.

Rao, MA. *Indian Railways*. New Delhi: National Book Trust, 1999.

Report of the Committee appointed by the Secretary of State for India to enquire into the administration and working of Indian Railways. London: His Majesty's Stationery Office, 1921.

Report of the Railway Police Committee, Simla, 1921.

Russell, William Howard. *The Prince of Wales' Tour: A Diary in India; with Some Account of the Visits of His Royal Highness to the courts of Greece, Egypt, Spain, and Portugal*. London: S Low, Marston, Searle & Rivington, 1877.

Sahni, JN. *Indian Railways: One Hundred Years, 1853 to 1953*. New Delhi: Government of India, Ministry of Railways (Railway Board), 1953.

Sanyal, Nalinaksha. *Development of Indian Railways*. Calcutta: University of Calcutta, 1930.

Sarkar, Sumit. *Modern India, 1885–1947*. Noida: Pearson India Education Services, 2017.

Satow, Michael, and Ray Desmond. *Railways of the Raj*. London: Scolar Press, 1980.

Simla Agreement, 2 July 1972.

Singh, JL, ed. *More Miles... More Smiles*. New Delhi: Government of India, Ministry of Railways, 2014.

Singh, Karnail. *A Complete Story of the Assam Rail Link Project with Technical Papers on Important Works*. New Delhi: Government of India, Ministry of Railways, 1951.

Singh, Surender. *Territorial Army: History of India's Part-Time Soldiers*. New Delhi: Ocean Books, 2013.

Singh, Vijaya. *Level Crossing: Railway Journeys in Hindi Cinema*. Hyderabad: Orient BlackSwan, 2017.

Sonwalker, Prasun. "UK scraps 'raj' era Indian railway laws." *Hindustan Times*, 7 November 2013.

Srinivasan, Roopa. "Introduction." In *Our Indian Railway: Themes in India's Railway History*, edited by Roopa Srinivasan, Manish Tiwari, and Sandeep Silas, 2–21. New Delhi: Foundation Books, 2006.

Steaming On: 20 Years of ISRS (Selected Writings from the ISRS Journals)

Swanberg, JW. "Streamlined Steam." *Railroad History*, No 186, Spring 2002: 102–111.

Symphony of Progress: The Saga of Eastern Railway, 1854–2003. Kolkata: Eastern Railway, 2003.

Tayler, William. *Thirty-eight Years in India: From Juganath to the Himalaya Mountains*. London: WH Allen & Co, 1881.

The Imperial Gazetteer of India, Vol VI, Argaon to Bardwan, 1908.

The Rail Enthusiast, Vol 2, No 3, November 2017.

The Rail Enthusiast, Vol 3, No 1, January 2018.

The Rail Enthusiast, Vol 3, No 2, May 2018.

The Rail Enthusiast, Vol 3, No 3, October 2018.

The Rail Enthusiast, Vol 4, No 1, January 2019.

The Railway Magazine, June 1917.

The Train Book: The Definitive Visual History. London: Dorling Kindersley, 2014.

Third Report, Indian Engineering Heritage (Railways), Indian National Academy of Engineering, June 2012.

Thorner, Daniel. "The Pattern of Railway Development in India." In *Railways in Modern India*, edited by Ian J Kerr, 80–96. New Delhi: Oxford University Press, 2001.

Timins, DT. "A Trip On the Darjeeling-Himalayan Railway." *The Railway Magazine*, Vol I, July to December 1897.

Tully, Sir Mark. "The Great Indian Railways." In *India Junction: A Window to the Nation*, edited by Seema Sharma, 17–36. New Delhi: Rupa Publications India, 2014.

Twain, Mark. *Following the Equator: A Journey Around the World*. Connecticut: The American Publishing Company, 1897,

Vaidyanathan, KR. *150 Glorious Years of Indian Railways*. Mumbai: English Edition Publishers and Distributors (India), 2003.

Varady, Robert G. "Modern Agents of Change." In *Railways in Modern India*, edited by Ian J Kerr, 257–261. New Delhi: Oxford University Press, 2001.

Venkatraman, S. *Indian Railways: The Beginning Upto 1900: How Britishers Made Railways in India (Rare Historical Vignettes 1800–1900)*.

Vir, RK. *History of Electric Traction*. New Delhi: Institution of Railway Electric Engineers, 2010.

Westwood, JN. *Railways of India*. Newton Abbot: David & Charles, 1974.

Wheels of Change, South Central Railway. South Central Railway and *The Times of India*.

Whitman, Walt. "To a Locomotive in Winter." 1876

Wright, Gillian. "Railways: A 160-Year Heritage." In *India Junction: A Window to the Nation*, edited by Seema Sharma, 103–127. New Delhi: Rupa Publications India, 2014.

"Assam Rail Link." *Economic & Political Weekly*, Vol 5, Issue No 16, 18 Apr 1953.

"Mountain Railways of India." World Heritage List, UNESCO

"Rowland Macdonald Stephenson." 1896 Institution of Civil Engineers: Obituaries, Grace's Guide to British Industrial History. https://gracesguide.co.uk/Rowland_Macdonald_Stephenson

PUBLISHER'S NOTE

Dorling Kindersley would like to thank the following people for their assistance in the preparation of this book:

Bibek Debroy, Chairman, Economic Advisory Council to the Prime Minister, for his invaluable support and introducing us to the fascinating and inspiring world of the railways in India. **Subrata Nath,** former Executive Director (Heritage), Indian Railways, and presently Additional Director General at National Museum, New Delhi, for his support and guidance while we conceptualized and executed the book. **Vinita Srivastava**, Executive Director (Heritage), Indian Railways, for her support in accessing the archives at the National Rail Museum, which have been crucial to the making of this book.

Dedicated Freight Corridor Corporation of India Limited, CONCOR, and IRCTC for their support. Rajnish Kumar, Director, Ministry of Human Resource Development, Department of School Education & Literacy and former Director, Vigilance (Mechanical), Railway Board; Vinoo N Mathur, former Member (Traffic), Railway Board; Vijay Kumar Dutt, IRSEE and ex Additional Member Railway Board; Mahesh Mangal, IRSSE and retired General Manager, CORE, and SP Mahi, Executive Director, Establishment (Reservation), Railway Board for guidance on content. Amit Saurastri, former Director, National Rail Museum; Udai Singh, Assistant Director, National Rail Museum; and Shubhabrata Chattopadhyay and other staff members at the National Rail Museum for their invaluable guidance and access to the museum archives. Usha Sehgal, Section Officer, Railway Board Library, and the Nehru Memorial Museum and Library for access to their material on the Indian Railways. Sanjay Gupta, Chairman and Managing Director, Konkan Railway Corporation Ltd; Girish Karandhikar, DGM PR, Konkan Railway Corporation Ltd; Nikhil Kumar Chakraborty, CPRO, Eastern Railway; Sanjoy Ghosh, CPRO, South Eastern Railway; and Bidhan Chandra, PRO, South Eastern Railway for sharing the photographs from their respective regions.

Priyanka Kharbanda for assistance with content planning, Priyal Mote for illustrations, and Suresh Kumar for cartography.

CONSULTANTS

SANJOY MOOKERJEE

After working in the Indian Railways for over 37 years, Sanjoy Mookerjee laid down office as the Financial Commissioner & Member (Finance) in 2016. Passionate about railway heritage, he has been instrumental in many conservation projects and has also been involved in policy formulation for railway heritage. The articles – "Financing the railways" (pp.30–31), "Economic Experiments" (pp.66–67), and "The Modified Guarantee System" (pp.68–69) – have been written by him.

MANOJ PANDE

A postgraduate from Delhi School of Economics (DSE), Manoj Pande has also studied business administration and law. He joined the Indian Railways in 1983. Over the years, he has written several articles on the railways. Edited versions of two of his articles – "When Bombay Met Calcutta" (pp.60–61) and "Nizam's State Railway" (pp.74–75) – appear in this volume. He retired in 2019 as Member (Staff) of Indian Railways.

JL SINGH

An engineer by qualification and a railway man by profession, JL Singh has worked with the Indian Railways for 25 years. He was also associated with the Rail India Technical and Economic Service (RITES) for 12 years. Instrumental in setting up the Rail Enthusiasts' Society, he currently serves as its Secretary. He is also the editor of the Society's quarterly magazine *The Rail Enthusiast*.

CONTRIBUTORS

RAMARAO ANNAVARAPU

Born in Guntur, Andhra Pradesh, and educated in Nagpur, Maharashtra, Ramarao Annavarapu has worked in different capacities with the Indian Railways. He retired as Chief Operations Manager, Eastern Railway, in 1991. He has published three collections of short stories and two books on railway history. The article on Mughalsarai (pp.102–03) in this volume is written by him.

WARREN MILLER

A retired electrical engineer, with a passion for railways and history, Warren Miller lives in Sydney with his wife. He has travelled widely on the railways of Australia, Europe, Southern Africa, and India. Over the years, he has written several articles on rail travel. An edited version of his article "Rail Timetables: Timetables from the Past" (pp.176–77), previously published in *The Rail Enthusiast*, features in this volume.

PK MISHRA

An officer of Indian Railway Service of the Mechanical Engineers cadre, Prashant Mishra has worked in the Indian Railways for more than 30 years. As Divisional Railway Manager of Asansol and Malda, he has restored more than 50 heritage buildings, including the Durand Institute. An edited version of his article "All Aboard: The First Train Journey to Raneegunge" (pp.40–41) appears in this volume.

GK MOHANTY

With over 30 years experience in freight operations of the steel sector, coal fields, iron ore fields, and CONCOR, GK Mohanty has authored two books - *Freight Legacy of BNR* (2013) and *Bengal Nagpur Railway - A Legacy* (2019). He was also the former Chief Operations Manager of the South Eastern Railway. The article "The Freight Story" (pp.256–57) has been written by him.

JK SAHA

Since joining the railway service in 1984, JK Saha has worked as a power and diesel officer, production engineer in workshops, production units, and open line carriage and wagon maintenance depots. He has also worked with the chief cinister of West Bengal and the railway minister in various capacities. Currently, he works as the Principle Chief Engineer of the South Eastern Railways. The articles "Beyer-Garratt" (pp.158–59) and "Iron Strength" (pp.200–01) in this book are written by him.

ACKNOWLEDGMENTS

The publisher would like to thank Tamanna Bhasin and Naorem Anuja for their text contribution to the following pages:

Tamanna Bhasin: 44–45, 52–53, 76–77, 96–97, 100–01, 108–09, 118–19, 120–21, 156–57, 218–19

Naorem Anuja: 20–21, 34–35, 36–37, 64–65, 106–07, 124–25, 130–31, 136–37, 140–41, 144–45, 152–53, 154–55, 172–73, 178–79, 188–89, 190–91, 196–97, 206–07, 212–13, 222–23, 228–29, 232–33, 240–41, 246–47

Every effort has been made to acknowledge those individuals, organizations, and corporations that have helped with this book and to trace copyright holders. DK apologizes in advance if any omission has occurred. If an omission does come to light, DK will be pleased to insert the appropriate acknowledgment in the subsequent editions of the book.

The publisher would like to thank the following for their kind permission to reproduce their photographs:

(Key: a-above; b-below/bottom; c-centre; f-far; l-left; r-right; t-top)

1 Dorling Kindersley: Surya Sankash (cb). 2 CPRO Konkan Railway. 4 Getty Images: Rajpipla / Atherton Archives (br). 5 Getty Images: Hulton Archive / Stringer (bl); Jane Sweeney / Alloy (br). 6 CPRO Konkan Railway: (bl). Dreamstime.com: Paul Prescott (br). 7 Alamy Stock Photo: Tuul and Bruno Morandi (br). Getty Images: Pradeep Gaur / Mint (bl). 8-9 CPRO WESTERN RAILWAY: (b). 10 Getty Images: Science & Society Picture Library. 11 Alamy Stock Photo: Artokoloro Quint Lox Limited (br). Library of Congress, Washington, D.C.: Clyde O. DeLand (t). 12 Alamy Stock Photo: Granger Historical Picture Archive (tr). Getty Images: John Stevenson / Asian Art & Archaeology, Inc. / CORBIS (bl). 13 Getty Images: De Agostini / Biblioteca Ambrosiana (b). 14 Getty Images: Rail Photo / Construction Photography / Avalon (t). 15 Dorling Kindersley: Ribble Steam Railway / Science Museum Group (tr). Getty Images: Sankei Archive (b). 16-17 Getty Images: Visual China Group (b). 18-19 Dorling Kindersley: Priyal Mote. 20 Alamy Stock Photo: Chronicle (bc). Getty Images: Science & Society Picture Library. 20-21 Wellcome Collection http://creativecommons.org/licenses/by/4.0/: (bc). 21 Alamy Stock Photo: Universal Images Group North America LLC (br). Getty Images: The Print Collector / Hulton Archive (bc). 22 Dreamstime.com: Amanda Lewis (tr). The illustrated London news: Page 284 (bl). 23 Wellcome Collection http://creativecommons.org/licenses/by/4.0/: (br). 24 Getty Images: Historica Graphica Collection / Heritage Images (cla). 24-25 Getty Images: Universal History Archive / Universal Images Group (b). 26 Dorling Kindersley: Priyal Mote (b). General Sir Arthur Cotton, R. E., K. C. S. I.. by Hope, Elizabeth, Lady; Digby, William, 1849-1904: (cra). 27 General Sir Arthur Cotton, R. E., K. C. S. I.. by Hope, Elizabeth, Lady; Digby, William, 1849-1904: Pg. 122 (t). 28 CPRO Eastern Railway: (bl). Science & Society Picture Library: National Railway Museum (tr). 29 Alamy Stock Photo: Dinodia Photos (b). 30-31 Getty Images: The Print Collector / Hulton Archive (b). 30 National Rail Museum, New Delhi: (tr). 31 Getty Images: Universal History Archive / Universal Images Group (tr). 32 National Rail Museum, New Delhi. 33 Alamy Stock Photo: 19th era 2 (tr). CPRO Eastern Railway: (br). 34-35 National Rail Museum, New Delhi. 35 Getty Images: Raj K Raj / Hindustan Times (br). 36-37 Jayasankar Madhavadas- RAILPICTURES(https://www.railpictures.net/jayrailfotographia/) TRAINSPO(https://trainspo.com/jmadhavadas). 38 Alamy Stock Photo: Chronicle (b). 39 National Rail Museum, New Delhi: (br). Wellcome Collection http://creativecommons.org/licenses/by/4.0/: (tc). 40 CPRO Eastern Railway. 41 Alamy Stock Photo: Antiqua Print Gallery (tr). 42 Getty Images: CORBIS / Historical (tr). 42-43 Alamy Stock Photo: Art Collection 2 (b). 43 National Rail Museum, New Delhi: (tr). 44 Alamy Stock Photo: Dinodia Photos (cl). 45 Alamy Stock Photo: Dinodia Photos (b). National Rail Museum, New Delhi: (tc). 46-47 Getty Images: Hulton-Deutsch Collection / CORBIS. 48 Getty Images: SSPL (cl). 48-49 Getty Images: DEA / Biblioteca Ambrosiana / Contributor (t). 50 Getty Images: Hulton Archive / Stringer. 51 Alamy Stock Photo: Universal Images Group North America LLC (br, tr). 52-53 DeGolyer Library, Southern Methodist University: (b). 52 National Rail Museum, New Delhi: (cla). 53 Alamy Stock Photo: PSF Collection (tl). 54 CPRO Eastern Railway: (bl). 54-55 National Rail Museum, New Delhi: Subrata Nath / Google arts and culture, at g.co / IndianRailways. 56-57 Alamy Stock Photo: Dinodia Photos. 58-59 Alamy Stock Photo: Richard Sowersby. 59 Alamy Stock Photo: David Gee 1 (br). 60 Rail Enthusiast Society Archives: Vinoo Mathur / Google arts and culture, at g.co / IndianRailways. 61 Getty Images: The Print Collector / Hulton Archive (tr). Alon Siton/Historical Railway Images: (b). 62-63 Dorling Kindersley: Priyal Mote. 64 Getty Images: Popperfoto / Contributor (bc). Alon Siton/Historical Railway Images: (bl). 64-65 National Rail Museum, New Delhi: (bc). 65 Getty Images: DEA / A. Dagli Orti (br). National Rail Museum, New Delhi: (bc). 66 Getty Images: DEA / Biblioteca Ambrosiana / Contributor (b). 67 National Rail Museum, New Delhi: (tr/All logos). 68 National Rail Museum, New Delhi: (cl). 68-69 CPRO WESTERN RAILWAY: (b). Alon Siton/Historical Railway Images: (tc). 70 Alamy Stock Photo: Lordprice Collection (tr). 70-71 Alon Siton/Historical Railway Images: (b). 72 Alamy Stock Photo: Historic Collection (bc). National Rail Museum, New Delhi: (tr). Alon Siton/Historical Railway Images: (cla). 73 Getty Images: Rajpipla / Atherton Archives (t). 74-75 National Rail Museum, New Delhi. 76-77 Dorling Kindersley: Surya Sankash (t). Joe Wallace: 76 Dorling Kindersley: Surya Sankash (c). National Rail Museum, New Delhi: (clb). 77 Dorling Kindersley: Tanvi Sahu (crb). National Rail Museum, New Delhi: (bc); Google Arts & Culture, at g.co / IndianRailways (cl). 78-79 Dorling Kindersley: Surya Sankash. 80-81 Dorling Kindersley: Surya Sankash. 82 Alamy Stock Photo: Pump Park Vintage Photography. 83 Library of Congress, Washington, D.C.: Jackson, William Henry, 1843-1942. World's Transportation Commission photograph collection (tr). 84-85 Alamy Stock Photo: Dinodia Photos. Getty Images: Himanshu Khagta / Moment Open (b). 86 Alamy Stock Photo: Sabyasachi Ghosh. 87 Dorling Kindersley: Christopher Pillitz (c, crb). 88-89 Getty Images: Jane Sweeney / Alloy. 90-91 National Rail Museum, New Delhi. 90 National Rail Museum, New Delhi: (b). 92-93 National Rail Museum, New Delhi. 93 Raj Singh Dhaiya, Guard Mail Express, HQ Kalka Ambala Division. Northern Railway: (br). 94 Alamy Stock Photo: UtCon Collection (bl). National Rail Museum, New Delhi: (tr). 95 Alamy Stock Photo: David O'Shea. 96-97 Alon Siton/Historical Railway Images: (b). 98 National Rail Museum, New Delhi: (b). 98-99 Heritage Directorate Indian Railways: Google Arts & Culture, at g.co / IndianRailways. 100-101 Getty Images: commoner28th / Moment (c). 101 National Rail Museum, New Delhi: (br). 102-103 National Rail Museum, New Delhi. 104 Dorling Kindersley: Tanvi Sahu (tr). Alon Siton/Historical Railway Images: (c). 105 Alamy Stock Photo: Ian Thomas (bl). Getty Images: Indranil Bhoumik / Mint / Hindustan Times (tr). 106-107 National Rail Museum, New Delhi. 107 National Rail Museum, New Delhi: Google Arts & Culture, at g.co / IndianRailways (b). 108-109 Dorling Kindersley: Surya Sankash (c). 108 Dorling Kindersley: Surya Sankash (clb). National Rail Museum, New Delhi: Abhishek Sethi / Google Arts & Culture, at g.co / IndianRailways (cl). Mick Pope (www.irfca.org): (br). 109 Dorling Kindersley: Surya Sankash (clb, cr, cra). Joe Wallace: (br). 110-111 National Rail Museum, New Delhi: Google Arts & Culture, at g.co / IndianRailways. 111 National Rail Museum, New Delhi: Google Arts & Culture, at g.co / IndianRailways (br). 112 Alamy Stock Photo: The Picture Art Collection (tr). National Rail Museum, New Delhi: (bl). 113 THE INDIAN RAILWAYS ACT, 1890: Railway Board Library / Usha Sehgal, Section Officer (tr). The railway and canal traffic acts, 1854, 1873, 1888, and 1894, and other statutes; with the general rules of the Railway and canal commission: (tc). Report On The Administration And Working Of Indian Railways: Railway Board Library / Usha Sehgal, Section Officer (tr/Administration Report). 114 Bridgeman Images: Look and Learn / Illustrated Papers Collection (c). 115 Getty Images: Science & Society Picture Library (crb). Alon Siton/Historical Railway Images: (bc). 116-117 CPRO South Eastern Railway. 118-119 Alamy Stock Photo: UtCon Collection (br). National Rail Museum, New Delhi: Google Arts & Culture, at g.co / IndianRailways (tc). 118 National Rail Museum, New Delhi: (cl). 119 Getty Images: Science & Society Picture Library (cra). 120 Dreamstime.com: Aliaksandr Mazurkevich (bl). 120-121 Alamy Stock Photo: Tuul and Bruno Morandi (t). 122 Getty Images: PA Images. 124 Getty Images: DEA / A. Dagli Orti (tr); Dinodia Photos (cb). 125 ©Imperial War Museum: Ariel Varges (Q_24739) (t). 126 University of Pennsylvania: Rare Book Collection / Kislak Center for Special Collections, Rare Books and Manuscripts (t). 127 University of Pennsylvania: Rare Book Collection / Kislak Center for Special Collections, Rare Books and

Manuscripts (b). **128-129 Dorling Kindersley:** Priyal Mote. **130 Getty Images:** Dinodia Photos (bl). **Alon Siton/ Historical Railway Images:** (bc). **130-131 Alon Siton/ Historical Railway Images:** (bc). **131 Alamy Stock Photo:** Dinodia Photos (br). **Getty Images:** Keystone / Hulton Archive (bl). **132 Library of Congress, Washington, D.C.:** (bl). **132-133 Alamy Stock Photo:** colaimages (tc). **133 Library of Congress, Washington, D.C.:** George Grantham Bain Collection (br). **134-135 Getty Images:** Science & Society Picture Library. **134 Getty Images:** Hulton Archive (bl). **137 Alamy Stock Photo:** Chronicle. **138 Alamy Stock Photo:** Tuul and Bruno Morandi. **139 Dreamstime.com:** Matthew Ragen (bc). **140-141 Getty Images:** Science & Society Picture Library. **140** Ashish Kuvelkar (www.irfca. org): (bl). **142 Getty Images:** Universal History Archive / UIG. **143 Getty Images:** Hulton Archive (bl). **144 Alamy Stock Photo:** Dinodia Photos. **145 Alamy Stock Photo:** Dinodia Photos (tc). **146-147 Alamy Stock Photo:** Dinodia Photos. **148 Library of Congress, Washington, D.C.:** George Grantham Bain Collection (cla). **148-149 Nehru Memorial Museum & Library:** (c). **149 Alamy Stock Photo:** The Picture Art Collection (tr). **CPRO Eastern Railway:** (br). **Nehru Memorial Museum & Library:** (bl). **150 Nehru Memorial Museum & Library. 151 Dorling Kindersley:** Priyal Mote (bc). **Dreamstime.com:** W.scott Mcgill (tr). **152-153 Getty Images:** Print Collector / Hulton Archive. **154 National Rail Museum, New Delhi:** (bl). **155 CPRO South Eastern Railway:** (t). **Getty Images:** AFP Photo / Indranil Mukherjee (br). **156-157 Dorling Kindersley:** Surya Sankash (c). **156 Dorling Kindersley:** Surya Sankash (br, tr). **157 Dorling Kindersley:** Surya Sankash (tc, crb). **National Rail Museum, New Delhi:** (tl). **Joe Wallace:** (cr, clb). **158-159 Alamy Stock Photo:** Chronicle. **160 CPRO WESTERN RAILWAY:** (b). **Dreamstime.com:** Cagkan Sayin (tr). **161 CPRO Eastern Railway:** (tr). **Dreamstime.com:** Selvam Raghupathy (b). **162 National Rail Museum, New Delhi:** (bl). **163 Getty Images:** Science & Society Picture Library (b). **164 The Criminal Classes In India, 1907. 165 Manual Of Criminal Classes Operating In Bengal, 1916:** (tr). **166-167 Getty Images:** Science & Society Picture Library. **168 Bridgeman Images:** Look and Learn. **169 Alon Siton/Historical Railway Images:** (tc, tc/ opening ceremony, br). **170-171 Dorling Kindersley:** Priyal Mote. **172 Alamy Stock Photo:** Eye-Stock (bl). **Getty Images:** William Vandivert / The LIFE Picture Collection (bc). **172-173 Getty Images:** Bettmann (bc). **173 Getty Images:** Margaret Bourke-White / The LIFE Picture Collection (bc). **Alon Siton/Historical Railway Images:** (br). **174 ©Imperial War Museum:** IND_517. **175 Getty Images:** Keystone (br). **National Rail Museum, New Delhi:** (tl). **176** Warren Miller. **177 Warren Miller:** (tr, crb). **178-179 ©Imperial War Museum:** Indian Army official photographer (K_9874). (b). **180 Getty Images:** Keystone Features / Hulton Archive (br). **National Rail Museum, New Delhi:** (tr). **181 Alamy Stock Photo:** dpa picture alliance. **182 Getty Images:** Bettmann. **183 Getty Images:** Margaret Bourke-White / The LIFE Picture Collection (tr). **184-185 Getty Images:** Bettmann. **186-187 Alon Siton/Historical Railway Images:** (bc). **186 Alamy Stock Photo:** Historic Collection (br). **187 iStockphoto.com:** Aroybarman (b). **188-189 Alamy Stock Photo:** Jyoti Kapoor / Pacific Press. **190 Getty Images:** DEA / G. DAGLI ORTI (r). **Penguin Random House:** Cover illustration by Ramya Mohan / Design by Ahlawat Gunjan (l). **191 Alamy Stock Photo:**

Artokoloro Quint Lox Limited (tc). **The Kipling Society:** kiplingsociety.co.uk: (br). **Penguin Random House:** Cover illustration by Shruti Mahajan / Design by Ahlawat Gunjan (cra). **192-193 iStockphoto.com:** Aroybarman. **194-195 Dorling Kindersley:** Priyal Mote. **196-197 Alamy Stock Photo:** Mark Hicken (bc). **196 CPRO Eastern Railway:** (br). **Photo Division, PIB, Ministry of Information and Broadcasting:** (bl). **197 Getty Images:** AFP (bl); Vipin Kumar / Hindustan Times (br). **198-199 CPRO WESTERN RAILWAY:** (b). **199 Getty Images:** Keystone / Hulton Archive (tr). **200** Dr Ashok Kolluru. **201 CPRO South Eastern Railway:** (tr, b). **202 Getty Images:** pilesasmiles / iStock Unreleased (l). **203 Alamy Stock Photo:** travelib india (b). **204 Alamy Stock Photo:** Mark Hicken (tr). **Getty Images:** Satish Bate / Hindustan Times (b). **205 Alamy Stock Photo:** Dinodia Photos (cr). **206-207 CPRO Eastern Railway. 207 Alamy Stock Photo:** AY Images (bc). **208-209 Dorling Kindersley:** Rewari Steam Loco Shed (All images). **210-211 Dorling Kindersley:** Rewari Steam Loco Shed (All images). **212** Ashutosh Gowariker Productions. **213 Images Courtesy of S.M.M Ausaja Pvt. Archive:** Sagar Movietone (bc). **Rewari Steam Loco shed:** Abhishek Sethi / Google Arts & Culture, at g.co / IndianRailways (tc). **Ashim Samanta / Shakti Films:** (crb). **214-215 Images Courtesy of S.M.M Ausaja Pvt. Archive:** Pandro S. Berman. **216 Alamy Stock Photo:** John Frost Newspapers (tr). **Heritage Directorate Indian Railways:** Google Arts & Culture, at g.co / IndianRailways (b). **217 Getty Images:** Vipin Kumar / Hindustan Times (tr). **218-219 Dreamstime.com:** Sivaprasad Rao Mallampali. **220 Getty Images:** Mono Mitra / Keystone / Hulton Archive (b). **221 Alamy Stock Photo:** dbimages (tl). **Samir Malhotra:** (br). **222-223 Jayasankar Madhavadas- RAILPICTURES(https://www.railpictures. net/jayrailfotographia/) TRAINSPO(https://trainspo.com/ jmadhavadas). 224-225 Dreamstime.com:** LakshmiPrasad Lucky. **224 Image Courtesy, Dedicated Freight Corridor Corporation of India:** (bl). **225 CONCOR:** (b). **226-227 Dorling Kindersley:** Priyal Mote. **228 Dreamstime.com:** Johnnydevil (br). **Getty Images:** Rail Photo / Construction Photography / Avalon (bl). **228-229 CPRO Konkan Railway:** (bc). **229 Dreamstime.com:** Amlan Mathur (bl). **Getty Images:** Raj K Raj / Hindustan Times (br). **230 Alamy Stock Photo:** Rapp Halour (b). **CPRO Eastern Railway:** (tr). **231 CPRO Konkan Railway:** (ca). **232-233** Mohitkumar Tandel aka Tandel Baba. **232 ©Sachin Buddhisagar:** (bl). **234 CPRO Eastern Railway:** (bc). **Dreamstime.com:** Joe Ravi (c). **Getty Images:** Shreyas Kulkarni / 500px (clb). **234-235 Alamy Stock Photo:** Bhaswaran Bhattacharya (c). **Rajesh Tukdeo:** (tc). **235 Jayasankar Madhavadas- RAILPICTURES(https://www. railpictures.net/jayrailfotographia/) TRAINSPO(https:// trainspo.com/jmadhavadas):** (crb). **Samit Roychoudhury (www.irfca.org):** (tr). **236 Getty Images:** Manan Vatsyayana / AFP. **237 Getty Images:** Rail Photo / Construction Photography / Avalon (br). **238 Getty Images:** Pradeep Gaur / Mint (b). **238-239 Rewari Steam Loco shed:** Abhishek Sethi / Google Arts & Culture, at g.co / IndianRailways (tc). **239 Alamy Stock Photo:** Dinodia Photos (br). **240 Getty Images:** Science & Society Picture Library (bl). **240-241 Shutterstock:** Azhar khan. **240 Alamy Stock Photo:** Ivan Vdovin (cr). **Heritage Directorate Indian Railways:** Google Arts & Culture, at g.co / IndianRailways (tr, cl, br). **Raj Singh Dhaiya, Guard Mail Express, HQ Kalka Ambala Division. Northern Railway:** (tl,

clb). **243 Alamy Stock Photo:** Ivan Vdovin (cl). **Heritage Directorate Indian Railways:** Google Arts & Culture, at g.co / IndianRailways (tr, cra, br, clb). **Rail Enthusiast Society Archives:** JL Singh / Google Arts & Culture, at g.co / IndianRailways (bl). **Raj Singh Dhaiya, Guard Mail Express, HQ Kalka Ambala Division. Northern Railway:** (tl, crb, cb). **244 Getty Images:** Narinder Nanu / AFP. **245 Dreamstime. com:** Chris Burton (br). **Getty Images:** Robert Nickelsberg (tl). **Heritage Directorate Indian Railways:** Google Arts & Culture, at g.co / IndianRailways (br). **246 Getty Images:** Central Press / Hulton Archive (b). **247 Dreamstime.com:** Chris Burton (br). **Getty Images:** Junji Kurokawa / AFP (tc). **248 CPRO Konkan Railway:** (bl). **248-249 CPRO Konkan Railway:** (t). **249 Photo Division, PIB, Ministry of Information and Broadcasting:** (bl). **250 IRCTC. 251 Heritage Directorate Indian Railways:** Google Arts & Culture, at g.co / IndianRailways (bl). **IRCTC:** (tr). **Raj Singh Dhaiya, Guard Mail Express, HQ Kalka Ambala Division. Northern Railway:** (br). **252-253 Dorling Kindersley:** Priyal Mote (c). **254-255 Getty Images:** Chandan Khanna / AFP (c). **255 Getty Images:** Longkiri Ingti / Moment (br). **256 CPRO South Eastern Railway:** (tr). **256-257 Getty Images:** Dhiraj Singh / Bloomberg (b). **258-259 Image Courtesy, Dedicated Freight Corridor Corporation of India. 260 Alamy Stock Photo:** Rana Sajid Hussain / Pacific Press Agency (t). **261 Dreamstime.com:** Vinod Kumar M (tr). **Getty Images:** Strdel / AFP (br). **262-263 Getty Images:** Waseem Andrabi / Hindustan Times. **263 Dreamstime.com:** Indiatraveler (cr). **264-265 Rail Enthusiast Society Archives. 265 Rail Enthusiast Society Archives:** (br). **266-267 Getty Images:** Puneet Vikram Singh, Nature and Concept photographer / Moment Open. **268-269 Getty Images:** Arun Sankar / **AFP. 270-271 IRCTC:** (bc, cb). **270 Alamy Stock Photo:** Deccan Odyssey train (br). **Dorling Kindersley:** Safdarjung Railway Station (bl). **IRCTC:** (t). **271 Getty Images:** Dibyangshu Sarkar / AFP (tr). **IRCTC:** (cra, bc). **272-273 Dorling Kindersley:** Safdarjung Railway Station (All images). **274-275 Dorling Kindersley:** Safdarjung Railway Station (All Images). **276-277 Dorling Kindersley:** Safdarjung Railway Station (All Images). **278-279 IRCTC. 280 CPRO Eastern Railway:** (bl). **Getty Images:** Manan Vatsyayana / AFP (tr). **Anirudh Jolly:** (br). **281 CPRO Konkan Railway:** (br). **Getty Images:** Bhaswaran Bhattacharya / IndiaPictures / Universal Images Group (bl); Qamar Sibtain / The India Today Group (tl). **Jayasankar Madhavadas- RAILPICTURES(https:// www.railpictures.net/jayrailfotographia/) TRAINSPO(https://trainspo.com/jmadhavadas):** (tr). **282-283 Getty Images:** Gurpreet Singh / Hindustan Times. **282 Getty Images:** Burhaan Kinu / Hindustan Times (bl). **284 Dreamstime.com:** Pavel Sipachev. **285 Alamy Stock Photo:** Design Pics Inc (c). **Getty Images:** Copyright Soumya Bandyopadhyay Photography (b). **286 Alamy Stock Photo:** Luciano Mortula (tr). **Getty Images:** © Naufal MQ / Moment Open (tl). **287 Getty Images:** Waseem Andrabi / Hindustan Times (tr). **Sriskandh Subramanian (www.irfca.org):** (cb). **288 CPRO Konkan Railway:** (tr). **Getty Images:** Wenkit M / EyeEm (bl). **289 Shutterstock:** Saurov Nandy (t). **301 SANJOY MOOKERJEE:** (cl). **MANOJ PANDE:** (clb). **JL SINGH:** (bl). **302 Ravi Anupindi:** (tl). **Warren Miller:** (cla). **PK MISHRA:** (cl). **GK MOHANTY:** (clb). **JK SAHA:** (bl)

All other images © Dorling Kindersley
For further information see: www.dkimages.com